Android Programming for Beginners
Third Edition

Build in-depth, full-featured Android apps starting
from zero programming experience

John Horton

BIRMINGHAM—MUMBAI

Android Programming for Beginners – Third Edition

Associate Group Product Manager: Pavan Ramchandani

Publishing Product Manager: Rohit Rajkumar

Senior Editor: Keagan Carneiro

Content Development Editor: Divya Vijayan

Technical Editor: Shubham Sharma

Copy Editor: Safis Editing

Project Coordinator: Manthan Patel

Proofreader: Safis Editing

Indexer: Rekha Nair

Production Designer: Jyoti Chauhan

First published: December 2015

Second edition: October 2018

Third edition: April 2021

Production reference: 1080421

Published by Packt Publishing Ltd.

Livery Place

35 Livery Street

Birmingham

B3 2PB, UK.

ISBN 978-1-80056-343-8

www.packt.com

Contributors

About the author

John Horton is a programming and gaming enthusiast based in the UK. He has a passion for writing apps, games, books, and blog articles. He is the founder of Game Code School.

About the reviewers

Brandon Kitt is a 24-year-old mobile app developer and enthusiast. He has worked on all kinds of projects, ranging from Java, Kotlin, Flutter, and a list of other non-mobile-specific applications, and is passionate about modern development and set on simplifying and accelerating all development processes.

Brandon believes architecture, simplicity, and innovation are the building blocks of all great apps and the core foundation they are laid on.

Through self-learning and an eye for clean, readable, and maintainable code, Brandon has furthered his education, exploring new technologies and toolkits that are released exceptionally quickly in the mobile development industry, to take full advantage of those changes in the process of making modern, attractive apps.

Brandon's always available for partnership and collaboration whenever and wherever possible. You can reach Brandon on LinkedIn, Facebook, or on hotmail at brandon.kitt.

Mohammed Fathy is a creative software engineer. He does what is possible with code in order to make life more efficient for people. He has been in the software engineering business for over 10 years, building new and innovative solutions for top companies in many countries. He works with Java and Kotlin to build Android apps.

Table of Contents

3

Exploring Android Studio and the Project Structure

4

Getting Started with Layouts and Material Design

5

Beautiful Layouts with CardView and ScrollView

6

The Android Lifecycle

7

Java Variables, Operators, and Expressions

8

Java Decisions and Loops

9

Learning Java Methods

10
Object-Oriented Programming

11
More Object-Oriented Programming

12

The Stack, the Heap, and the Garbage Collector

13

Anonymous Classes – Bringing Android Widgets to Life

14

Android Dialog Windows

15

Arrays, Maps, and Random Numbers

16

Adapters and Recyclers

17

Data Persistence and Sharing

18

Localization

19

Animations and Interpolations

22

Particle Systems and Handling Screen Touches

23

Supporting Different Versions of Android, Sound Effects, and Spinner Widget

24

Design Patterns, Multiple Layouts, and Fragments

25

Building a Simple Image Gallery App

26

Advanced UI with Navigation Drawer and Fragment

27

Android Databases

Preface

Are you trying to start a career in programming, but haven't found the right way in? Do you have a great idea for an app, but don't know how to make it a reality? If so, then this book is for you!

This updated third edition of *Android Programming for Beginners* will be your companion for creating Android applications from scratch. We will introduce you to all the fundamental concepts of programming in an Android context, from the basics of Java to working with the Android API. All examples use the up-to-date API classes and are created from within Android Studio, the official Android development environment that helps supercharge your application development process.

Following this crash course, we'll dive deeper into Android programming and you'll learn how to create applications with a professional-standard UI through fragments and store your user's data with SQLite. In addition, you'll see how to make your apps multilingual, draw to the screen with a finger, and work with graphics, sound, and animations, too.

By the end of this book, you'll be ready to start building your own custom applications in Android and Java.

Who this book is for

This book is for you if you are completely new to Java, Android, or programming, and want to make Android applications. This book will also act as a refresher for those of you who already have experience of using Java on Android to enable you to advance your knowledge and make rapid progress through the early projects.

What this book covers

Chapter 1, Beginning Android and Java, will see you not waste any time in getting started with developing Android apps. We will look at what is so great about Android, what exactly Android and Java are, how they work and complement each other, and what that means to us as future developers. Moving quickly on, we will set up the required software so that we can build and deploy a simple first app.

Chapter 2, First Contact: Java, XML, and the UI Designer, explains how, at this stage, we have a working Android development environment and we have built and deployed our first app. We need to explore this autogenerated code so that we can begin to understand Android and then learn how to build on this useful template

Chapter 3, Exploring Android Studio and the Project Structure, explains how to create and run two more Android projects. The purpose of these exercises is to explore in more depth Android Studio and the structure of Android projects. Along with understanding the composition of our projects, it will also be beneficial to make sure we get the most from the emulator.

Chapter 4, Getting Started with Layouts and Material Design, covers the building of three more layouts—still quite simple, yet a step up from what we have done so far. Before we get hands-on, we will have a quick introduction to the concept of Material Design. We will also cover the different types of layout called LinearLayout, ConstraintLayout, and TableLayout. We will also write some Java code to switch between our different layouts within a single app/project. This is the first major app that links together multiple topics in one neat parcel.

Chapter 5, Beautiful Layouts with CardView and ScrollView, is the final chapter on layouts before we spend some time focusing on Java and object-oriented programming. We will formalize our learning on some of the different attributes we have already encountered, and we will also introduce two more cool layouts: ScrollView and CardView. To conclude this chapter, we will run a CardView project on a tablet emulator.

Chapter 6, The Android Lifecycle, will see us become familiar with the lifecycle of an Android app. The lifecycle is the way that all Android apps interact with the Android OS. We will see the phases of the lifecycle that an app goes through, from creation to destruction, and how this helps us know where to put our Java code, depending on what we are trying to achieve.

Chapter 7, Java Variables, Operators, and Expressions, covers the core fundamentals of Java: the code that goes into the classes and the methods that we create, along with the data that the code acts upon. In this chapter, we will focus on the data. We will dive into learning how to write our very own Java code. By the end of the chapter, you will be comfortable writing Java code that creates and uses data within Android.

Chapter 8, Java Decisions and Loops, explains how we can take a course of action dependent upon the value of a variable. We will look at making decisions in Java with `if`, `else`, and `switch`. We will also look at loops in Java with `while`, `do - while`, `for`, and `break`.

Chapter 9, Learning Java Methods, takes a closer look at methods, because although we know that you can call them to make them execute their code, there is more to them than we have discussed hitherto.

Chapter 10, Object-Oriented Programming, explains how in Java, classes are fundamental to just about everything. We will begin to understand why the software engineers at Sun Microsystems back in the early 1990s made Java the way they did. We have already talked about reusing other people's code, specifically the Android API, but in this chapter, we will really get to grips with how this works and learn about object-oriented programming and how to use it.

Chapter 11, More Object-Oriented Programming, is the second part of our whirlwind tour (theoretical and practical) into OOP. We have already briefly discussed the concepts of encapsulation, inheritance, and polymorphism, but in this chapter, we will get to see them in action in some demo apps. While the working examples will show these concepts in their simplest forms, it will still be a significant stepping stone toward taking control of our XML layouts via our Java code.

Chapter 12, The Stack, the Heap, and the Garbage Collector, reveals the missing link between Java and our XML layouts, leaving us with the power to add all kinds of widgets to our apps, as we have done before, but this time we will be able to control them through our Java code. In this chapter, we will get to take control of some fairly simple UI elements, such as Button and TextView. To enable us to understand what is happening, we need to find out a bit more about the memory in an Android device and two areas of it—the Stack and the Heap.

Chapter 13, Anonymous Classes – Bringing Android Widgets to Life, explains how, now that we have a good overview of both the layout and coding of an Android app, as well as our newly acquired insight into object-oriented programming and how we can manipulate the UI from our Java code, we are ready to experiment with more widgets from the palette alongside anonymous classes. In this chapter, we will diversify a lot by going back to the Android Studio palette and looking around at half a dozen widgets that we have either not seen at all or have not used fully yet. Once we have done so, we will put them all into a layout and practice manipulating them with Java code.

Chapter 14, Android Dialog Windows, covers how to present the user with a pop-up dialog window. We can then put all that we know into the first phase of our first major app, Note to self. We will also then learn about new Android and Java features in this chapter and the four following (up to chapter 18), and then use our newly acquired knowledge to enhance the Note to self app each time. In each chapter, we will also build a selection of smaller apps that are separate from this main app.

Chapter 15, Arrays, Maps, and Random Numbers, talks about Java arrays, which allow us to manipulate a potentially huge amount of data in an organized and efficient manner. We will also use a close Java relation to arrays, the ArrayList, and see the differences between them. Once we are comfortable handling substantial amounts of data, we will see what the Android API has in order to help us easily connect our new-found data handling skills to the UI without breaking sweat.

Chapter 16, Adapters and Recyclers, first covers the theory of adapters and lists. We will learn how to extend RecyclerAdapter in Java code and add a RecyclerView, which acts as a list to our UI, and then, through the apparent magic of the Android API, bind them together so that RecyclerView displays the contents of RecyclerAdapter and allows the user to scroll through the contents.

Chapter 17, Data Persistence and Sharing, examines a couple of different ways to save data to the Android device's permanent storage. Also, for the first time, we will add a second activity to our app. It often makes sense when implementing a separate "screen", such as a settings screen in our app, to do so in a new activity. We will see how to add an activity and navigate the user between them.

Chapter 18, Localization, explains how to add additional languages. We will see how adding text the correct way via String resources benefits us when it comes to adding multiple languages.

Chapter 19, Animations and Interpolations, covers how we can use the Animation class to make our UI a little less static and a bit more interesting. As we have come to expect, the Android API will allow us to do some quite advanced things with relatively straightforward code, and the Animation class is no different.

Chapter 20, Drawing Graphics, is devoted to the Android Canvas class and a number of related classes, such as Paint, Color, and Bitmap. These classes combined bring great power when it comes to drawing to the screen. If we want to make a drawing app, draw graphs, or perhaps a game, we need to take control of every pixel that the Android device has to offer.

Chapter 21, Threads and Starting the Live Drawing App, gets started on the next app. This app will be a kid's style drawing app where the user can draw on the screen with their finger. This drawing app will be slightly different, however. The lines that the user draws will comprise particle systems that explode into thousands of pieces. We will call the project *Live Drawing*.

Chapter 22, Particle Systems and Handling Screen Touches, explains how to create the entities that will exist and evolve in this real-time system as if they have a mind of their own and form the appearance of the drawings that the user can achieve. We will also see how the user draws these entities by learning how to respond to interaction with the screen. This is different to interacting with a widget in a UI layout.

Chapter 23, Supporting Different Versions of Android, Sound Effects, and Spinner Widget, explains how we can detect and handle different versions of Android. We will then be able to study the SoundPool class and the different ways we use it, depending on the Android version the app is running on. At this point, we can then put everything we have learned into producing a cool sound demo app that will also introduce us to a new UI widget – the Spinner.

Chapter 24, Design Patterns, Multiple Layouts, and Fragments, is more about your future apps than anything in the book so far. We will look at a few aspects of Java and Android that you can use as a framework or template for making ever more exciting and complex apps at the same time as keeping the code manageable. Furthermore, I will suggest areas of further study that there is simply not enough room to even scratch the surface of in this book.

Chapter 25, Building a Simple Image Gallery App, explains how to create an app using paging and swiping with images as you might find in a photo gallery app. Also, using the RecyclerView widget, we will selectively load just the data required for the current page and perhaps the data for the previous and next pages.

Chapter 26, Advanced UI with Navigation Drawer and Fragment, covers what is (arguably) the most advanced UI. NavigationView can be created simply by choosing it as a template when you create a new project. We will then examine the autogenerated code and learn how to interact with it. Then, we will use all we know about Fragment to populate each of the "drawers" with different behaviors and views.

Chapter 27, Android Databases, explains how, if we are going to make apps that offer our users significant features, then almost certainly we are going to need a way to manage, store, and filter significant amounts of data. JSON and SharedPreferences classes have their place but, at some point, we need to move on to using real databases for real-world solutions. Android uses the SQLite database management system and, as you would expect, there is an API to make it as easy as possible.

Chapter 28, A Quick Chat Before You Go, brings our journey to an end. This chapter is simply includes a few ideas and pointers that you might like to look at before rushing off and making your own apps.

To get the most out of this book

To succeed with this book, you don't need any experience whatsoever. If you are confident with your operating system of choice (Windows, macOS, or Linux), you can learn to make Android apps while learning the Java programming language. Learning to develop professional quality apps is a journey that anybody can embark upon and stay on for as long as they want.

If you do have previous programming (Java or any other language), Android, or other development experience, then you will make faster progress with the earlier chapters.

If you are using the digital version of this book, we advise you to type the code yourself or access the code via the GitHub repository (link available in the next section). Doing so will help you avoid any potential errors related to the copying and pasting of code.

Download the example code files

You can download the example code files for this book from GitHub at `https://github.com/PacktPublishing/Android-Programming-for-Beginners-Third-Edition`. In case there's an update to the code, it will be updated on the existing GitHub repository.

We also have other code bundles from our rich catalog of books and videos available at `https://github.com/PacktPublishing/`. Check them out!

Download the color images

We also provide a PDF file that has color images of the screenshots/diagrams used in this book. You can download it here: `https://static.packt-cdn.com/downloads/9781800563438_ColorImages.pdf`.

Conventions used

There are a number of text conventions used throughout this book.

`Code in text`: Indicates code words in text, database table names, folder names, filenames, file extensions, pathnames, dummy URLs, user input, and Twitter handles. Here is an example: "Th last member variable is a `LayoutInflater` instance, which will be used to inflate each of the instances of `pager_item.xml`."

A block of code is set as follows:

```
@Override
public int getCount() {

    return images.length;
}
```

When we wish to draw your attention to a particular part of a code block, the relevant lines or items are set in bold:

```
import androidx.appcompat.app.AppCompatActivity;
import androidx.viewpager.widget.PagerAdapter;
import androidx.viewpager.widget.ViewPager;
```

Any command-line input or output is written as follows:

```
$ mkdir css
$ cd css
```

Bold: Indicates a new term, an important word, or words that you see on screen. For example, words in menus or dialog boxes appear in the text like this. Here is an example: "Select **System info** from the **Administration** panel."

> **Tips or important notes**
> Appear like this.

Get in touch

Feedback from our readers is always welcome.

General feedback: If you have questions about any aspect of this book, mention the book title in the subject of your message and email us at customercare@packtpub.com.

Errata: Although we have taken every care to ensure the accuracy of our content, mistakes do happen. If you have found a mistake in this book, we would be grateful if you would report this to us. Please visit www.packtpub.com/support/errata, selecting your book, clicking on the Errata Submission Form link, and entering the details.

Piracy: If you come across any illegal copies of our works in any form on the internet, we would be grateful if you would provide us with the location address or website name. Please contact us at copyright@packt.com with a link to the material.

If you are interested in becoming an author: If there is a topic that you have expertise in, and you are interested in either writing or contributing to a book, please visit authors.packtpub.com.

Reviews

Please leave a review. Once you have read and used this book, why not leave a review on the site that you purchased it from? Potential readers can then see and use your unbiased opinion to make purchase decisions, we at Packt can understand what you think about our products, and our authors can see your feedback on their book. Thank you!

For more information about Packt, please visit packt.com.

1
Beginning Android and Java

Welcome to *Android Programming for Beginners Third Edition*. In this first chapter, we won't waste any time getting started with developing Android apps. We will look at what is so great about Android, what exactly Android and Java are, how they work and complement each other, and what that means to us as future developers. Moving quickly on, we will set up the required software so we can build and deploy a simple first app.

> **Note**
> It is my aim to keep this book up to date. Please check the following web page for any discussion and tips on any changes to Android Studio since the book was first printed: `http://gamecodeschool.com/books/android-programming-for-beginners-3rd-edition#android-studio-updates`.

By the end of this chapter, we will have done the following:

- Discovered what is new in this third edition

- Learned how Java and Android work together

- Set up our development environment – Android Studio – which takes care of all the components involved in building the Android apps that we will learn about next

- Learned about the **Java Development Kit (JDK)** and the Android **Application Programming Interface (API)** and how we use them through Android Studio

- Built our very first Android app

- Deployed the app on an Android emulator

- Run our app on an Android emulator and a real device

That's a lot to get through, so let's get started.

Technical requirements

The following are the official technical requirements for Android development with Android Studio and its related tools. However, these are the absolute bare minimum. Please see the *Setting up Android Studio* section for further details.

The requirements for Windows are as follows:

- Microsoft® Windows® 7/8/10 (64-bit)

- 4 GB RAM as a minimum; 8 GB RAM recommended

- 2 GB of available disk space as a minimum; 4 GB recommended (500 MB for the **Integrated Development Environment (IDE)** + 1.5 GB for the Android **Software Development Kit (SDK)** and emulator system image)

- 1,280 x 800 minimum screen resolution

The requirements for Mac are as follows:

- Mac® OS X® 10.10 (Yosemite) or higher, up to 10.14 (macOS Mojave)

- 4 GB RAM as a minimum; 8 GB RAM recommended

- 2 GB of available disk space as a minimum; 4 GB recommended (500 MB for the IDE + 1.5 GB for the Android SDK and emulator system image)

- 1,280 x 800 minimum screen resolution

The requirements for Linux are as follows:

- GNOME or KDE desktop

- Tested on gLinux based on Debian

- 64-bit distribution capable of running 32-bit applications

- GNU C Library (glibc) 2.19 or later

- 4 GB RAM as a minimum; 8 GB RAM recommended

- 2 GB of available disk space as a minimum; 4 GB recommended (500 MB for the IDE + 1.5 GB for the Android SDK and emulator system image)

- 1,280 x 800 minimum screen resolution

You can find the code files present in this chapter on GitHub at `https://github.com/PacktPublishing/Android-Programming-for-Beginners-Third-Edition/tree/main/chapter%2001`.

What's new in the third edition?

The second edition saw huge amounts of additional topics compared to the first edition. Unfortunately, there are only so many pages that can fit in a paperback book. Therefore, this edition focuses on improving the way that the Java, Android, and app development concepts are taught. We have rethought the way that topics are explained and made it more visual than before. In addition, I have managed to squeeze in about a dozen new mini topics. These are either Java fundamentals such as variable types not covered in earlier editions, new Android Studio features such as the profiler, or classic programming concepts such as method recursion and the live debugging of our code. Hopefully, this third edition will therefore make your Android and Java journeys smoother and more complete.

Why Java and Android?

When Android first arrived in 2008, it was a bit drab compared to the much more stylish iOS on the Apple iPhone/iPad. But quite quickly, through diverse handset offerings that struck a chord with both the practical price-conscious as well as the fashion-conscious and tech-savvy, the Android user numbers exploded.

For many, myself included, developing for Android is the most rewarding pastime and business bar none.

Quickly putting together a prototype of an idea, refining it, and then deciding to run with it and wire it up into a fully fledged app is such an exciting and rewarding process. Any programming can be fun, and I have been programming all my life, but creating for Android is somehow extraordinarily rewarding.

Defining exactly why this is the case is quite difficult. Perhaps it is the fact that the platform is free and open source. You can distribute your apps without needing the permission of a big, controlling corporation – nobody can stop you. At the same time, you have well-established, corporate-controlled mass markets such as Amazon Appstore and Google Play.

More likely, the reason why developing for Android gives such a good feeling is the nature of the devices themselves. They are deeply personal. You can develop apps that interact with people's lives – educate, entertain, tell a story, and so on – and it is there in their pockets ready to go, in the home, in the workplace, or on holiday.

You can certainly build something bigger for the desktop. But knowing that thousands (or millions) of people are carrying your work in their pockets and sharing it with friends gives more than just a buzz.

In fact, developing for Android is considered highly skillful and the most successful developers are hugely admired, even revered.

If all this fluffy and spiritual stuff doesn't mean anything to you, then that's fine too; developing for Android can make you a living or even make you wealthy. With the continued growth of device ownership, the ongoing increase in CPU and GPU power, and the non-stop evolution of the Android operating system itself, the need for professional app developers is only going to grow.

In short, the best Android developers – and, more importantly, the Android developers with the best ideas and most determination – are in greater demand than ever. Nobody knows who these future Android app developers are and they might not even have written their first line of Java yet.

So, why isn't everybody an Android developer? Obviously, not everybody will share my enthusiasm for the thrill of creating software that can help people make their lives better, but I am guessing that because you are reading this, you might!

The beginner's first stumbling block

Unfortunately, for those that do share my enthusiasm, there is a kind of glass wall on the path of progress that frustrates many aspiring Android developers.

Android uses Java to make apps. Every Android book, even those aimed at so-called beginners, assumes readers have at least an intermediate level of Java knowledge, and most need an advanced level. So, good-to-excellent Java knowledge *was* a prerequisite for learning Android.

Unfortunately, learning Java in a completely different context to Android can sometimes be a little dull and much of what you learn is not directly transferable to the world of Android anyway. You can see why beginners to Android and Java are often put off from starting.

But it doesn't need to be like this. In this book, I have carefully placed all the Java topics you would learn in a thick and weighty Java-only beginner's tome and reworked them into four multi-chapter apps and more than a dozen quick mini-apps, starting from a simple memo app and then progressing to a cool drawing app, a database app, and a playable game (available online).

If you want to become a professional Android developer or just want to have more fun when learning Java and Android, this book will help.

How Java and Android work together

Before we start our Android quest, we need to understand how Android and Java work together. Android is a complex system, but you do not need to understand it in depth to be able to make amazing apps.

After we write a program in Java for Android, we click a button and our code is transformed into another form, the form that is understood by Android. This other form is called **bytecode** and the transformation process is called **compiling**.

Then, when the user installs our application, the bytecode is translated by another process known as the **Android Runtime (ART)** into machine code. This is the fastest possible execution format. So, if you have ever heard people saying that you shouldn't use Java because it is slow, then you know they are mistaken. Java is fast for the programmer to program and is then, upon installation, changed to machine code that is fast for the device. What could be better?

Not only does ART enable super-fast execution of our apps, but it also lowers battery use. Furthermore, the ART system doesn't just create the machine code and then sit back and relax; it provides hooks into our application that enhance memory management while the application is running. This makes our app run more efficiently and, as we will see in *Chapter 12, The Stack, the Heap, and the Garbage Collector*, easier to write by handling critical aspects of memory management.

The ART itself is a software system written in another language that runs on a specially adapted version of the Linux operating system. So, what the user sees of Android is itself just an app running on yet another operating system.

Android is a collection of sub-systems. The typical Android user doesn't see the Linux operating system or know anything of the presence of ART but they are both there making things tick.

The purpose of the Linux part of the system is to hide the complexity and diversity of the hardware and software that Android runs on, but at the same time exposing all its useful features. This exposing of features works in two ways:

- First, the system itself must have access to the hardware, which it does.

- Second, this access must be programmer-friendly and easy to use – and this is because of the Android **API**.

Let's continue by talking more about the Android API.

> **Note**
>
> This book is about learning Java and building Android apps from scratch, so I won't go any deeper than I have into how Android works. If, however, you want to know more, then the Wikipedia page is a good reference: `https://en.wikipedia.org/wiki/Android_(operating_system)`.

Understanding the Android API

The Android API is code that makes it easy to do exceptional things. A simple analogy could be drawn with a machine, perhaps a car. When you press on the accelerator, a whole bunch of things happen under the hood. We don't need to understand combustion or fuel pumps because some smart engineer has made an **interface** for us – in this case, a mechanical interface: the accelerator pedal.

For example, the following line of Java code probably looks a little intimidating at this stage in the book, but it serves as a good example of how the Android API helps us:

```
locationManager.getLastKnownLocation(LocationManager.GPS_
PROVIDER)
```

Once you learn that this single line of code searches for available satellites in space, and then communicates with them in their orbits around the Earth, then retrieves your precise latitude and longitude on the surface of the planet, it becomes easy to begin to glimpse the power and depth of the Android API in conjunction with the compiled bytecode and ART.

For sure, that code does look a little challenging – even mind-boggling at this stage of the book – but imagine trying to talk to a satellite some other way!

The Android API has a whole bunch of Java code that has already been written for us to use as we like.

> **Note**
>
> There are many different estimates of the number of lines of code that have gone into Android. Some estimates are as low as 1 million, while some are as high as 20 million. What might seem surprising is that despite this vast amount of code, Android is known in programming circles for being "lightweight."

The question we must ask and the one this book tries to answer is as follows:

How do we use all this code to do cool stuff? Or to frame the question to fit the earlier analogy, how do we find and manipulate the pedals, steering wheel, and sunroof of the Android API?

The answer to this question is the Java programming language and the fact that Java was designed to help programmers handle complexity. Let's talk a bit about Java and **Object-Oriented Programming (OOP)**.

Java is object-oriented

Java is a programming language that has been around a lot longer than Android. It is an **object-oriented** language. This means it uses the concept of reusable programming objects. If this sounds like technical jargon, another analogy will help. Java enables us and others (such as the Android development team) to write Java code that can be structured based on real-world things, and here is the important part: it can be **reused**.

So, using the car analogy, we could ask the question: if a manufacturer makes more than one car in a day, do they redesign every part for each and every car?

The answer, of course, is no. They get highly skilled engineers to develop exactly the right components, honed, refined, and improved over years. Then, that same component is reused again and again as well as being occasionally improved.

If you are going to be fussy about my analogy, then you can point out that each of the car's components still has to be built from the raw materials using real-life engineers or robots and so on.

This is true. What software engineers do when they write their code is build a blueprint for an object. We then create an object from their blueprint using Java code and once we have that object, we can configure it, use it, combine it with other objects, and more besides.

Furthermore, as well as this, we can design blueprints ourselves and make objects from them as well. The compiler then transforms (manufactures) our bespoke creation into bytecode. Hey, presto! We have an Android app.

In Java, a blueprint is called a **class**. When a class is transformed into a real working "thing," we call it an **object** or an **instance** of the class.

> **Objects concisely**
>
> We could go on making analogies all day long. All we care about at this point, however, is the following.
>
> Java is a language that allows us to write code once that can then be used repeatedly. This is very useful because it saves us time and allows us to use other people's code to perform tasks we might otherwise not have the time or knowledge to write ourselves. Most of the time, we do not even need to see this code or even know how it works! One last analogy: we just need to know how to use the code just as we need to learn how to drive a car.

So, some smart software engineer up at Android HQ writes a desperately complex Java program that can talk to satellites. They then consider how they can make this code useful to all the Android programmers who want to make amazing apps that use the user's location to do cool things. One of the things they will do is make features such as getting the device's location in the world a simple one-line task.

So, the one line of code we saw previously sets in action many more lines of code that we don't see and don't need to see. This is an example of using somebody else's code to make our code infinitely simpler.

> **Note**
>
> If the fact that you don't have to see all the code is a disappointment to you, then I understand how you feel. Some of us, when we learn about something, want to learn every intricate detail. If you are like this, then be reassured that the best place to start learning how the Android API works internally is to use it as the API programmers intended. Throughout the book, I will regularly point out further learning opportunities where you can find out about the inner workings of the Android API. Also, we will be writing classes that are themselves reusable, kind of like our own API, except that our classes will focus on what we want our app to do.

Welcome to the world of **object-oriented programming – OOP**. I will constantly refer to OOP in every chapter and there is the big reveal of how it works in *Chapter 10, Object-Oriented Programming*.

Run that by me again – what exactly is Android?

To get things done on Android, we write Java code of our own, which also uses the Java code of the Android API. This is then compiled into bytecode and translated by ART when installed by the user into machine code, which in turn has connections to an underlying operating system called Linux, which handles the complex and extremely diverse range of hardware that are the different Android devices.

The manufacturers of the Android devices and the individual hardware components obviously know this too and they write advanced software called **drivers**, which ensure that their hardware (CPU, GPU, GPS receivers, memory chips, hardware interfaces, and so on) can run on the underlying Linux operating system.

The bytecode (along with some other resources) is placed in a bundle of files called an **Android Application Package** (**APK**) and this is what ART needs to run to prepare our app for the user.

> **Note**
>
> It is not necessary to remember the details of the steps that our code goes through when it interacts with the hardware. It is enough just to understand that our Java code goes through some automated processes to become the apps that we will publish to the Google Play Store.

The next question is "where exactly does all this Java coding and compiling into bytecode along with APK packaging take place?". Let's look at the development environment we will be using.

Android Studio

A **development environment** is a term that refers to having everything you need to develop, set up, and be ready to go in one place. We need two things to get started:

- We talked a fair bit about compiling our Java code, as well as other people's Java code, into bytecode that in turn will be converted into executable machine code on the user's Android device. To use Java code, we need some free software called the **JDK**. The JDK includes even more of other people's code, which is separate from the Android API.

- There is an entire range of tools needed to develop for Android, and we also need the Android API, of course. This whole suite of requirements is collectively known as the Android **SDK**. Fortunately, downloading and installing a single application will give us these things all bundled together. The application is called **Android Studio**.

Android Studio is an **IDE** that will take care of all the complexities of compiling our code and linking with the JDK and the Android API. Once we have installed Android Studio, we can do everything we need inside this single application and put to the back of our minds many of the complexities we have been discussing.

> **Tip**
>
> Over time, these complexities will become second nature. It is not necessary to master them to make further progress.

So, we had better get hands-on with Android Studio.

Setting up Android Studio

Setting up Android Studio is quite straightforward if a little lengthy. Grab some refreshments and get started with the following steps. This tutorial will install Android Studio to the D drive. I chose the D drive because it is a big install, around 12 GB once we have everything downloaded, and the D drive on many PCs is typically larger and has more free space than the C drive. Should you wish to install on the C drive (or any other drive), then these instructions should be easy to adjust:

1. Visit `https://developer.android.com/studio` and click the **Download Android Studio** button. This will begin the download of the latest stable version for Windows. You will need to accept the terms and conditions to commence the download.

2. While you are waiting for the download to complete, create a new folder on the root of your D drive called `Android`. Inside the `Android` folder, create another new folder called `Android Studio`. Navigate back to the `Android` folder and create another new folder named `Projects`. This is where we will keep all the project files we will create throughout the book. Create another new folder called `Sdk`, which is where we will ask the installer program to install the Android SDK. You should now have a `D:\Android` folder that looks like this:

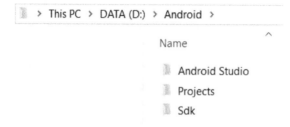

Figure 1.1 – D:\Android folder

3. Once the download is complete, find the downloaded file. It will be called `android-studio-ide.....` Double-left-click the file to run it.

4. You will be asked to grant the installer program administrative privileges, then you can left-click **Next** to begin the installation. On the **Choose Components** screen, make sure that both the **Android Studio** and **Android Virtual Device** options are checked, and then left-click the **Next** button:

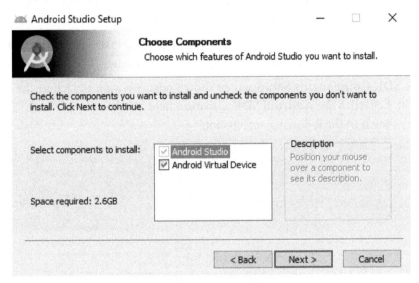

Figure 1.2 – Choose Components screen

5. On the **Configuration Settings** window, left-click the **Browse** button and navigate to `D:\Android\Android Studio`, and then left-click the **OK** button:

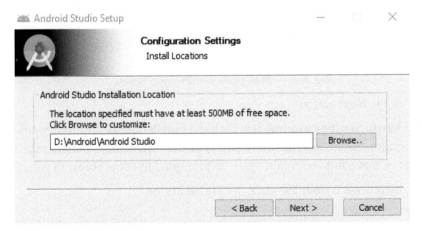

Figure 1.3 – Configuration Settings window

6. Left-click the **Next** button shown in the preceding screenshot. On the **Choose Start Menu Folder** window, left-click **Install** to accept the default option. The first part of the installation will now proceed.

7. Once you get the **Installation Complete** message, left-click the **Next** button. You can then left-click the **Finish** button.

    Android Studio should start automatically. If it doesn't, you can find and start the Android Studio app from your Windows start menu.

8. You will be prompted that you have a missing SDK (unless this is not the first time you have used Android Studio). Left-click **Next** to continue.

9. On the **SDK Components Setup** screen shown next, we want to change the install location. Left-click the **Android SDK Location** field and browse to D:\Android\ Sdk, as shown in the following screenshot:

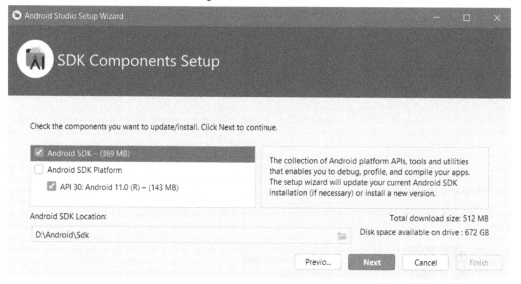

Figure 1.4 – SDK Components Setup screen

10. Left-click the **Next** button.

11. On the **Verify Settings** window, left-click the **Finish** button. Android Studio will now download some more files and complete the installation. It could take a few minutes or more and you might again be prompted to allow access to your PC.

12. When the process is over, left-click the **Finish** button.

You will be greeted with the Android Studio welcome screen, shown next:

Figure 1.5 – Android Studio welcome screen

If you are carrying straight on with the next section, then leave this screen up. If you want, you can close it down and run Android Studio from the Windows start menu, just like any other app, when you are ready to proceed.

Let's talk about all the different things that an Android app comprises.

What makes an Android app?

We already know that we will write Java code that will itself use other people's Java code and will be compiled into bytecode that is converted into machine code on our users' Android devices. In addition to this, we will also be adding and editing other files that are included in the final APK as well. These files are known as **Android resources**.

Android resources

Our app will include resources such as images, sound, and **User Interface** (**UI**) layouts, which are kept in separate files from the Java code. We will slowly introduce ourselves to them over the course of the book.

It will also include files that have the textual content of our app. It is the convention to refer to the text in our app through separate files because it makes them easy to change and easy to create apps that work for different languages and geographical regions.

Furthermore, the actual UI layout of our apps, despite the option to implement them with a visual designer, is actually read from text-based files by Android.

Android (or any computer), of course, cannot read and recognize text in the same way that a human can. Therefore, we must present our resources in a highly organized and predefined manner. To do so, we will use **eXtensible Markup Language (XML)**. XML is a huge topic but fortunately, its whole purpose is to be both human- and machine-readable. We do not need to learn this language; we just need to note (and then conform to) a few rules. Furthermore, most of the time that we interact with XML, we do so through a neat visual editor provided by Android Studio. We can tell when we are dealing with an XML resource because the filename will end with the extension `.xml`.

You do not need to memorize this as we will constantly be returning to this concept throughout the book.

The structure of Android's Java code

In addition to these resources, it is worth noting that Java as used in Android has a structure to its code. There are many millions of lines of code that we can take advantage of. This code will obviously need to be organized in a way that makes it easy to find and refer to. It is organized into **packages** that are specific to Android.

Packages

Whenever we create a new Android app, we will choose a unique name known as a **package**. We will see how we do this in the *Building our first Android app* section. Packages are often separated into **sub-packages**, so they can be grouped together with other similar packages. We can simply think of this as folders and sub-folders, which is almost exactly what it is.

We can think of all the packages that the Android API makes available to us as code from a code library. Some common Android packages we will use include the following:

- `android.graphics`
- `android.database`
- `android.view.animation`

As you can see, they are arranged and named to make what is in them as obvious as possible.

> **Note**
>
> If you want to get an idea of the sheer depth and breadth of the Android API, then look at the Android package index: `https://developer.android.com/reference/packages`.

Classes

Earlier, we learned that the reusable code blueprints that we can transform into objects are called **classes**. Classes are contained in these packages. We will see in our very first app how we can easily **import** other people's packages along with specific classes from those packages for use in our projects. A class will almost always be contained in its own file with the same name as the class and it will also have the `.java` file extension.

Methods

In Java (and therefore Android), we further break up our classes into sections that perform the different actions of our class. We call these action-oriented sections **methods**. It is most often the methods of the class that we will use to access the functionality provided within all those millions of lines of code.

We do not need to read the code. We just need to know which class has what we need, which package it is in, and which methods from within the class give us precisely the result we are after.

The next diagram shows a representation of the Android API. The structure of the code we will be writing will be similar to the way this example is structured, although we will usually have just one package per app.

Of course, because of the object-oriented nature of Java, we will only be using selected parts from this API. Notice also that each class has its own distinct data. Typically, if you want access to the data in a class, you need to have an object of that class:

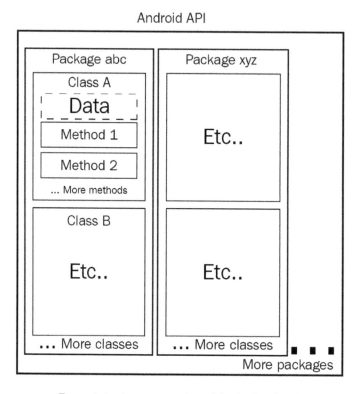

Figure 1.6 – A representation of the Android API

You do not need to memorize this as we will constantly be returning to this concept throughout the book.

By the end of this chapter, we will have imported multiple packages, as well as dozens of classes from them, and we will have used many of their methods as well. By the end of *Chapter 2, First Contact: Java, XML, and the UI Designer*, we will have even written our very own methods. Now we can get started with the first app.

Building our first Android app

In programming, it is tradition for the first app of a new student to use whatever language/operating system they are using to say hello to the world. We will quickly build an app that does just that and in *Chapter 2, First Contact: Java, XML, and the UI Designer*, we will go beyond that and add some buttons that respond to the user when they are pressed.

> **Note**
>
> The complete code as it stands at the end of this chapter is in the download
> bundle in the `Chapter 1` folder for your reference. You can't simply copy
> and paste this code, however! You still need to go through the project creation
> phase explained in this chapter (and at the beginning of all the projects) as
> Android Studio does lots of work behind the scenes. Once you become familiar
> with these steps and understand which code is typed by you the programmer
> and which code/files are generated by Android Studio, you will then be
> able to save time and typing by copy and pasting the files I supply in the
> download bundle.

Follow these steps to start the project:

1. Run Android Studio in the same way you run any other app. On Windows 10, for
    example, the launch icon appears in the start menu.

> **Tip**
>
> If you are prompted with **Import Studio settings from…**, choose **Do not
> import settings**.

2. You will be greeted with the Android Studio welcome screen, as shown in the
    following screenshot. Locate the start a new Android Studio project option and
    left-click it:

Figure 1.7 – Android Studio welcome screen

3. The window that follows is **Select a Project Template**.

    These are some useful project templates that Android Studio can generate for you depending on the type of app you are going to develop. We will use the **Basic Activity** option. Android Studio will auto-generate a small amount of code and a selection of resources to get our project started. We will discuss the code and the resources in detail in the next chapter.

4. Select **Basic Activity**. Here is a picture of the **Select a Project Template** window with the **Basic Activity** option selected:

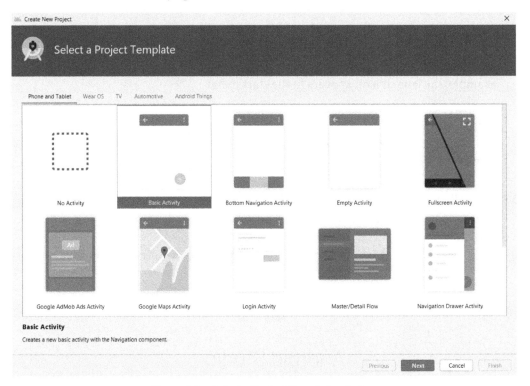

Figure 1.8 – Select a Project Template window

5. Make sure **Basic Activity** is selected as it is in the preceding screenshot, and then click **Next**.

6. After this, Android Studio will bring up the **Configure Your Project** window. This is where we will do the following:

a. Name the new project.

b. Choose where on our computer the project files should go.

c. Provide a package name to distinguish our project from any others in case we should ever decide to publish the app on the Play Store.

d. Select the programming language we will use.

The name of our project is going to be `Hello World` and the location for the files will be your `Projects` folder that we created in the *Setting up Android Studio* section.

The package name can be almost anything you like. If you have a website, you could use the format `com.yourdomainname`. If not, feel free to use my domain name, `com.gamecodeschool.helloworld`, or something that you just make up yourself. It is only important when you come to publish.

To be clear, in case you can't see the details in the following screenshot clearly, here are the values I used. Remember that yours might vary depending upon your choices for package name and project location:

Option	Value entered
Name	Hello World
Package name	com.gamecodeschool.helloworld
Save location	D:\Android\Projects\HelloWorld
Language	Java
Minimum SDK	Leave this and any other options at their defaults

> **Tip**
>
> Note that the application name has a space between `Hello` and `World` but the project location does not and will not work if it does.

7. The next screenshot shows the **Configure Your Project** screen once you have entered all the information:

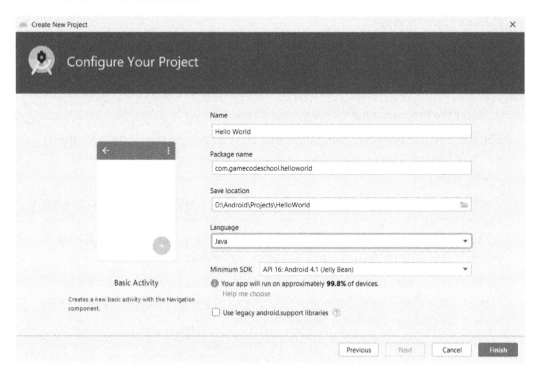

Figure 1.9 – Configure Your Project screen

8. In the previous screenshot, you can see that Android Studio has auto-generated a package name based on the information entered. Mine is **com.gamecodeschool. helloworld**. Yours might be the same or not; it doesn't matter.

> **Note**
>
> You can write Android apps in a few different languages, including C++ and Kotlin. There are various advantages and disadvantages to each compared to using Java. Learning Java will be a great introduction to other languages and Java is also an official language of Android. Most top apps and games on the Play Store are currently written in Java.

You can also see the **Minimum SDK** option. Leave this at the default but note that the default might be different for you at the time of writing.

> **Note**
>
> We already know that the Android SDK is the collection of packages of code that we will be using to develop our apps. Like any good SDK, the Android SDK is regularly updated and each time it gets a significant update, the version number is increased. Simply put, the higher the version number, the newer the features you get to use; the lower the version number, the more devices our app will work on. For now, Android Jelly Bean will give us lots of great features and near-100% compatibility with the Android devices currently in use. If at the time of reading Android Studio is suggesting a newer API and Android version, then go with that.
>
> If you are reading this some years in the future, then the **Minimum SDK** option will probably default to something different but the code in this book will still work.

9. Click the **Finish** button and we will run the app to see what we have achieved.

> **Note**
>
> The first time you create a new project, Android Studio will initiate another download. Android Studio will set up the Gradle build system that it uses to manage project configuration and deployment. This will only happen for the first project. No knowledge of Gradle is required for the book but if you are curious, a simple web search will reveal more.

Let's look at our app in action.

Deploying the app so far

Before we explore any of the code and learn our first bit of Java, you might be surprised to learn that we can already run our project. It will just be a fairly featureless app but as we will be running the app as often as possible to check our progress, let's see how to do that now. You have three options:

- Run the app on the emulator on your PC (part of Android Studio) in debug mode.
- Run the app on a real Android device in USB debugging mode.
- Export the app as a full Android project that can be uploaded to the Play Store.

The first option (debug mode) is the easiest to set up because we did it as part of setting up Android Studio. If you have a powerful PC, you will hardly notice the difference between the emulator and a real device. However, screen touches are emulated by mouse clicks and proper testing of the user's experience is not possible in some of the later apps we will create, such as the drawing app. Furthermore, you might just prefer to test out your creations on a real device occasionally – I know I do.

The second option, using a real device, has a couple more steps but once set up is as good as option 1 and the screen touches are for real.

The final option takes about 5 minutes (at least) to prepare, and then you need to manually put the created package onto a real device and install it every time you make a change to the code.

Probably the best way is to use the emulator to quickly test and debug minor increments in your code, and then fairly regularly use USB debugging mode on a real device to make sure things are still as expected. Only occasionally will you want to export an actual deployable package.

For these reasons, we will now go through how to run the app using the emulator and USB debugging on a real device.

Running and debugging the app on an Android emulator

Follow these simple steps to run the app on the default Android emulator:

1. From the Android Studio menu bar, select **Tools | AVD Manager**. **AVD** stands for **Android Virtual Device** (an emulator). You will see the following window:

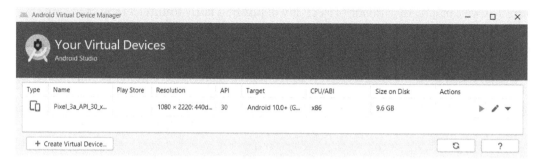

Figure 1.10 – AVD Manager

Notice there is an emulator on the list. In my case, it is **Pixel_3a_API_30_x....** If you are following this sometime in the future, it may be a different emulator that was installed by default. It won't matter.

> **Important Note**
>
> The emulator should have been installed by the steps we have performed previously. I noticed while testing with one pre-release version that it wasn't installed by default. In the event that there is no emulator listed on the **Your Virtual Devices** screen, select **Tools | AVD Manager | Create Virtual Device... | Next| R Download | Accept | Next** and a default emulator will be downloaded and installed. When the installation is done, click **Finish** followed by **Next** and finally **Finish** again. Now you can refer to the previous step to run the emulator.

2. Click the green play icon (to the right) shown in the next screenshot and wait as the emulator boots up:

Figure 1.11 – Play icon

3. Now you can click the play icon on the Android Studio quick launch bar as shown in the next screenshot, and if prompted, choose **Pixel_3a_API_30_x...** (or whatever your emulator is called) and the app will launch on the emulator:

Figure 1.12 – Play icon on the Android Studio quick launch bar

You're done. Here is what the app looks like so far in the emulator. Remember that you might (probably do) have a different emulator – that's fine:

Figure 1.13 – What the app looks like so far

Clearly, we have more work to do before we move to Silicon Valley and look for financial backing, but it is a good start. The message on the screen is **Hello first fragment**. A **fragment** is a building block of many Android apps and we will explore them further throughout the book. If you click on the **Next** button, you will see a new empty layout, and if you then click on the **Previous** button, you will see the **Hello first fragment** screen again. Not bad considering we haven't written any code yet.

We need to test and debug our apps often throughout development to check for any errors, crashes, or anything else unintended.

> **Note**
>
> We will see how we get errors and other feedback for debugging from our apps in the next chapter.

It is also important to make sure it looks good and runs correctly on every device type/ size that you want to target. Obviously, we do not own one of each of the many thousands of Android devices. This is where emulators come in.

Emulators, however, are sometimes a bit slow and cumbersome, although they have improved a lot recently. If you want to get a genuine feel for the experience your users will get, then you can't beat deploying to a real device. So, we will want to use both real devices and emulators while developing our apps.

> **Tip**
>
> If you are planning on using the emulator again soon, then leave it running to avoid having to wait for it to start again.

If you want to try out your app on a tablet, you're going to need a different emulator.

> **Creating a new emulator**
>
> If you want to create an emulator for a different Android device, this is simple. From the main menu, select **Tools | AVD Manager**. In the AVD Manager window, left-click **Create Virtual Device**. Now, left-click on the type of device you want to create, **TV**, **Phone**, **Wear OS**, or **Tablet**. Now, simply left-click **Next** and follow the instructions to create your new AVD. Next time you run your app, the new AVD will appear as an option to run the app on. We will create a new tablet emulator step by step in the next chapter.

Now we can look at how to get our app onto a real device.

Running the app on a real device

The first thing to do is to visit your device manufacturer's website and obtain and install any drivers that are needed for your device and operating system.

> **Note**
>
> Most newer devices won't need a driver. So, you may want to just try the following steps first.

The next few steps will set up the Android device for debugging. Note that different manufacturers structure the menu options slightly differently from others. But the following sequence is probably very close, if not exactly the same, for enabling debugging on most devices:

1. Tap the **Settings** menu option or the **Settings** app on your phone/tablet.

2. This next step will vary slightly for different versions of Android. The **Developer options** menu is hidden away so as not to trouble regular users. You must perform a slightly odd task to unlock the menu option. Tap the **About device** or **About Phone** option. Find the **Build Number** option and repeatedly tap it until you get a message informing you that **You are now a developer!**.

> **Note**
>
> Some manufacturers have different and obscure methods for achieving this step. If this step doesn't work, do a web search for your device and "unlocking developer options."

3. Go back to the **Settings** menu.

4. Tap **Developer options**.

5. Tap the checkbox for **USB Debugging**.

6. Connect your Android device to the USB port of your computer.

7. Click anywhere on Android Studio to get Android Studio to detect that your device has been connected. You should now find an **Allow USB debugging?** prompt on your device; hit **Allow**.

8. Click the play icon from the Android Studio toolbar, as shown in the next screenshot:

Figure 1.14 – Play icon from the Android Studio toolbar

9. When prompted, click **OK** to run the app on your chosen device.

We are now ready to learn some Java and add our own Java code to the Hello World project, which we will cover in the next chapter.

Frequently asked questions

1. So, is Android not really an operating system, just a virtual machine, and are all the phones and tablets really Linux machines?

   No, all the different sub-systems of an Android device, which include Linux, the ART, and the libraries and drivers, are together what make up the Android operating system.

2. I still don't understand all these technical terms, such as ART, object-oriented, APK, and so on. Should I re-read this chapter?

   No, that isn't necessary as we just needed to introduce this jargon and we will be revisiting it all as well as clarifying it as the book progresses. If you understand the following, you are ready to proceed to *Chapter 2, First Contact: Java, XML, and the UI Designer*:

   We will be writing Java code and creating other resources in Android Point Studio, which, with the help of the JDK, will turn this code and resources into real Android apps.

Summary

So far, we have set up our Android development environment, created a new Android app, and deployed our app to both an emulator and a real device. If you still have unanswered questions (and you probably have more than you did at the start of the chapter), don't worry because as we dig deeper into the world of Android and Java, things will become clearer.

As the chapters progress, you will build a very rounded understanding of how everything fits together, and then success will just be a matter of practice and digging even deeper into the Android API.

In the next chapter, we will edit the UI using the visual designer and raw XML code, as well as writing our first Java methods and getting to use some of the methods provided for us by the Android API.

2
First Contact: Java, XML, and the UI Designer

At this stage, we have a working Android development environment and we have built and deployed our first app. It is obvious, however, that the auto-generated code from Android Studio is not going to make the next top-selling app on Google Play. We need to explore this auto-generated code so we can begin to understand Android and then learn how to build upon this useful template. With this aim in mind, in this chapter, we will do the following:

- See how to get technical feedback from our apps
- Examine the Java code and UI XML code from our first app
- Get our first taste of using the Android Studio **User Interface** (**UI**) designer
- Learn some core Java fundamentals and how they relate to Android
- Write our first Java code

First, let's see how to get feedback from our apps.

Technical requirements

You can find the code for this chapter on GitHub at `https://github.com/PacktPublishing/Android-Programming-for-Beginners-Third-Edition/tree/main/chapter%2002`.

Examining the logcat output

In the previous chapter, we mentioned that our app was running in debug mode on the emulator or real device, so we can monitor it and get feedback when things go wrong. So, where is all this feedback then?

You might have noticed a whole load of scrolling text at the bottom of the Android Studio window. If not, click on the **Logcat** tab, as shown by the highlighted area labeled **1** in the next figure:

> **Note**
>
> The emulator must be running, or a real device must be attached in debugging mode, for you to see the following window. Furthermore, if you restarted Android Studio for some reason and have not executed the app since restarting, then the **Logcat** window will be empty. Refer to the first chapter to get the app running on an emulator or a real device.

Figure 2.1 – The Logcat tab

You can drag the window to make it taller, just like you can in most other Windows applications if you want to see more.

This window is called **logcat** or is sometimes referred to as the **console**. It is our app's way of telling us what is going on underneath what the user sees. If the app crashes or has errors, the reason or clues to the reason will appear here. If we need to output debugging information, we can do so here as well.

> **Note**
>
> The app we are building should not have any problems at this stage, but in the future, if you just cannot work out why your app is crashing, copying and pasting a bit of text from logcat into Google will often reveal the reason.

Filtering the logcat output

You might have noticed that most if not all of the contents of logcat is almost unintelligible. That's OK. For now, we are only interested in errors, which will be highlighted in red, and the debugging information, about which we will learn next. So that we see less of the unneeded text in our logcat window, we can turn on some filters to make things clearer.

In the previous figure, I highlighted two more areas, as **2** and **3**. Area **2** is a drop-down list that controls the first filter. Left-click it now and change it from **Verbose** to **Info**. We have cut down the text output significantly. We will see how this is useful when we have made some changes to our app and redeployed it. We will do this after we have explored the code and the assets that make up our project. Also, double-check in the area that is labeled **3** that says **Show only the selected application**. If it doesn't, left-click on it and change it to **Show only the selected application** now.

Now we can look at what Android Studio automatically generated for us and then we can set about changing and adding to the code to personalize it beyond what we got from the project creation phase.

Exploring the project Java and the main layout XML

We are going to look at the resource files that have the code that defines our simple UI layout and the file that has our Java code. At this stage, we will not try to understand it all, as we need to learn some more basics before it makes sense to do so. What we will see, however, is the basic contents and structure of both files, so we can reconcile their contents with what we already know about Android resources and Java.

Examining the MainActivity.java file

Let's look at the Java code first. If, for some reason, this isn't currently visible, you can see this code by left-clicking on the **MainActivity.java** tab, as shown in the next figure:

Figure 2.2 – MainActivity.java tab

As we are not looking at the intricate details of the code, an annotated screenshot is more useful than reproducing the actual code in text form. Regularly refer to the next figure while reading on in this section:

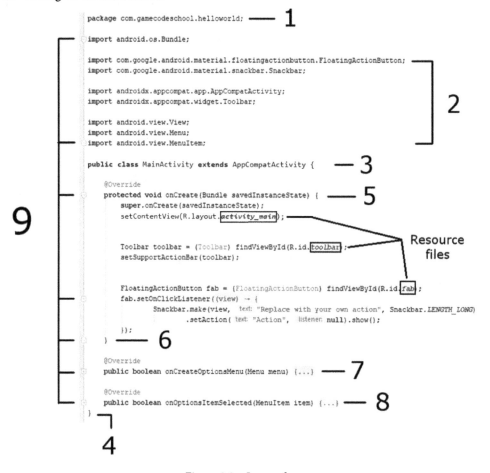

Figure 2.3 – Java code

The first thing to note is that I have added a few empty lines among the code to space things out a little bit and present a clearer image.

Code folding (hiding) in Android Studio

Now look at the left-hand side of the figure where multiple parts are labeled **9**. This points to all the little + and - buttons in the editor, which can collapse and expand parts of the code. I have indeed collapsed some parts of the code, and other parts I have left visible. So, what you can see on your screen is slightly different to what you will see if you look at the figure. In Android Studio, play with the + and – buttons for a while to practice hiding and unhiding sections of the code. You might want to get your screen to look like the figure, but this is not a requirement to continue. The technical term for hiding code like this is **folding**.

The package declaration

Part **1** is called the **package declaration** and, as you can see, it is the package name we chose when we created the project preceded by the word `package`. Every Java file will have a package declaration at the top.

Importing classes

Part **2** is eight lines of code that all begin with the word `import`. After the word `import`, we can see there are various dot-separated words. The last word of each line is the name of the class that line imports into our project and all the earlier words in each line are the packages and sub-packages that contain these classes.

For example, this next line imports the `AppCompatActivity` class from the `androidx.appcompat.app` package and sub-packages:

```
import androidx.appcompat.app.AppCompatActivity;
```

> **Note**
> The semicolon at the end of the lines shows the compiler that it is the end of that line of code.

This means that in this file we will have access to these classes. In fact, it is these classes that the auto-generated code uses to make the simple app that we saw in action in the previous chapter.

We will not discuss all these classes in this chapter. It is just the concept that we can do this importing that is significant right now. Note that we can add extra classes from any package at any time and we will when we improve upon our app shortly.

The class

Part **3** of our code is called the **class declaration**. Here is that line in full; I have highlighted one part of it:

```
public class MainActivity extends AppCompatActivity {
```

The class declaration is the start of a class. Notice the highlighted part, MainActivity. This is the name Android Studio gave the class when we created the project and it is also the same as the MainActivity.java filename as we would expect having discussed Java classes previously.

The class and the file can be renamed, but since this is the key/main activity of our app, MainActivity seems appropriate. The extends keyword means that our class called MainActivity will be of the type AppCompatActivity.

We can, and will, use some classes without this extends part. We use extends here because we want to use all the code that went into the AppCompatActivity class, as well as adding our own code to it as well. So, we **extend** it. All this and more will become clear in *Chapter 10, Object-Oriented Programming.*

Finally, for part **3**, look at the opening curly brace at the end of the line: {. Now look at the bottom of the figure at part **4** of our code. This closing curly brace } denotes the end of the class. Everything in between the opening and closing curly braces, { . . . }, is part of the MainActivity class.

Methods inside the class

Now look at part **5** of the code. Here is that line of code in full with the key part for our discussion highlighted:

```
protected void onCreate(Bundle savedInstanceState) {
```

This is a method **signature**. The highlighted part, onCreate, is the method **name**. We make a method execute its code by using its name. We say we are **calling** a method when we do this.

Although we will not concern ourselves now with the details of the parts of the code on either side of the method name, you might have noticed Bundle, one of the classes we imported at part **2** of our code. If we removed that related import line, Android Studio would not know what Bundle was and it would be unusable and indicated with a red underline as an error.

Our code would then not compile and run. Notice the very last thing in the preceding line of code is an opening curly brace, {. This denotes the start of the code contained within the onCreate method. Now jump to part **6** of our code and you will see a closing curly brace, }. You might have guessed that this is the end of the method. Everything in between the opening and closing curly braces of the onCreate method is the code that executes when the method is called.

We do not need to go into what this code does yet, but as an overview, it sets up the appearance/layout of the app by referring to a resource file that was auto-generated by Android Studio when we created the project. I have highlighted the resource files with an outline in the previous figure.

Parts **7** and **8** are also methods that I have collapsed to make the image and this discussion more straightforward. Their names are onCreateOptionsMenu and onOptionsItemSelected.

We know enough about our Java code to make some progress. We will see this code again and change it later in this chapter.

Summary of the Java code so far

It is true that contained within the code we have just had an overview of, there is some complex syntax. However, what we are doing is building up just enough knowledge about this code, so we can work with it to begin to make fast progress in learning Java and Android without having to learn hundreds of pages of Java theory first. By the end of the book, all the code will make sense, but to make quick progress now, we just need to accept that some of the details will remain a mystery for a little while longer.

Examining the app layout file

Now we will look at just one of the many .xml files. There are several different layout files and we will meet them all throughout the course of the book, but let's start with the most recognizable one, which decides most of the appearance of our app.

In the project explorer window, left-click on the **res** folder and then left-click on the **layout** folder. Now double left-click on the fragment_first.xml file. The XML code contents of the file is now displayed in the main window of Android Studio.

We can ignore the **res generated** folder.

We will explore this XML code soon but first find and left-click the **Design** button (shown next) to switch to the design view:

Figure 2.4 – To open design view

Now we can see the design view that shows us what the XML code will cause to be displayed when the app is run in the emulator:

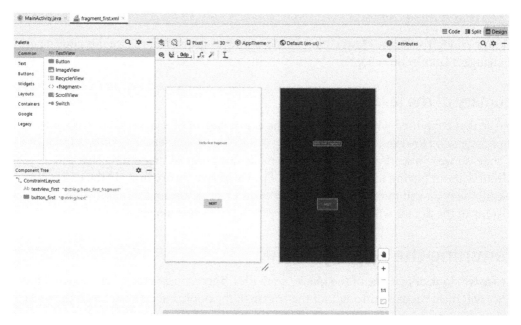

Figure 2.5 – App display

The preceding figure should look familiar because it shows the layout of our first app that we ran at the end of the previous chapter – the one with the **Hello first fragment** text and the **Next** button. If you look in the `fragment_second.xml` file from the same folder as `fragment_first.xml`, you will see the second layout we saw in the previous chapter, the one that had the **Previous** button on it. In fact, there are even more layout-related files than we might first expect, but we will get to discussing them in this chapter and the next.

Most of the work that we do throughout the book when we design apps will be done in this design view. It is important, however, to know what is going on behind the scenes.

The design view is a graphical representation of the XML code contained in the fragment_first.xml file. Click on the **Code** tab (near the **Design** tab in the previous figure) to see the XML code which forms the layout. I have annotated a screenshot of the XML text, so we can discuss it next:

```
<?xml version="1.0" encoding="utf-8"?>
<androidx.constraintlayout.widget.ConstraintLayout xmlns:android="http://schemas.android.com/apk/res/android"    1
    xmlns:app="http://schemas.android.com/apk/res-auto"
    xmlns:tools="http://schemas.android.com/tools"
    android:layout_width="match_parent"
    android:layout_height="match_parent"
    tools:context=".FirstFragment">    ── 1b

    <TextView    ── 3
        android:id="@+id/textview_first"
        android:layout_width="wrap_content"
        android:layout_height="wrap_content"
        android:text="Hello first fragment"
        app:layout_constraintBottom_toTopOf="@id/button_first"
        app:layout_constraintEnd_toEndOf="parent"
        app:layout_constraintStart_toStartOf="parent"
        app:layout_constraintTop_toTopOf="parent" />    ── 4

    <Button    ── 5
        android:id="@+id/button_first"
        android:layout_width="wrap_content"
        android:layout_height="wrap_content"
        android:text="Next"
        app:layout_constraintBottom_toBottomOf="parent"
        app:layout_constraintEnd_toEndOf="parent"
        app:layout_constraintStart_toStartOf="parent"
        app:layout_constraintTop_toBottomOf="@id/textview_first" />    ── 6
</androidx.constraintlayout.widget.ConstraintLayout>    ── 2
```

Figure 2.6 – Screenshot of the XML text

The first thing to note is that this file does not represent the entire layout. It does however represent most of the surface area and the entire **Hello first fragment** message and the **Next** button. Also, on the left-hand side, we can see the now-familiar + and – icons so we can fold and unfold sections of the code.

UI layout elements

If we first look at the part of the code labeled **1**, we can see that the very first thing is ... ConstraintLayout. . . . Now, ConstraintLayout is a UI element that is used to wrap other parts of the UI.

When we add a new element to a UI in Android, we always start a line with a < followed by the element's name.

The code that follows that rather long and cumbersome-looking line defines the **attributes** this element will have. This can include dozens of different things depending upon the type of UI element it is. Here, among a bit of other XML, we can see things such as layout_width and layout_height. All these attributes define how the ConstraintLayout element will appear on the user's screen. The attributes for the ConstraintLayout element end at the first > labeled **1b**.

If we look at the bottom of our XML screenshot, we will see some code labeled **2**. This code, </...ConstraintLayout>, marks the end of the ConstraintLayout element. Anything in between the closing > of the element's attributes and </... ConstraintLayout>, which defines its end, is considered a child of the element. So, we can see that our ConstraintLayout has/contains two child elements. Let's look at those children now.

UI text elements

Using what we just learned, we can say that the UI element that starts at position **3** in the screenshot is called a **TextView**. Just like its parent, it starts with a < and its name: <TextView. . . . If we look further into our TextView element, we can see it has several attributes. It has a text attribute that is set to "Hello first fragment". This of course is the exact text that our app shows to the user. It also has layout_width and layout_height attributes that are both set to "wrap_content". This tells TextView it can take up as much space as the content it has needs. As we will see throughout the book, there are many more attributes available for this and other UI elements. The final attribute in TextView is id, and we will see how we and Android use the id attribute in the next section when we improve this first app.

Notice that the code at **4** in our XML screenshot is />. This marks the end of the TextView element. This is slightly different to how the end of the ConstraintLayout element was written. When an element in XML has no children, we can just end it like this: />. When the element has children and its end comes further on in the code from where its attributes are defined, it is much clearer to end the element by repeating its name like this: </...ConstraintLayout>.

> **Note**
>
> You might be wondering why the element name for TextView is clear and concise (simply TextView) yet the full name for the ConstraintView is preceded by complicated apparent clutter (androidx. constraintlayout.widget.ConstraintLayout). This ConstraintLayout element is a special layout that is used to ensure our app's compatibility with older versions of Android. As we will see in a minute when we add buttons to the app, most elements have simple and concise names.

UI Button elements

Now we should be able to quickly identify that the code that starts at **5** in the screenshot is a **Button** element. Just like its parent, it starts with a < and its name: <Button.... If we look further into our Button, we can see it has several attributes. It has a text attribute that is set to "Next". This of course is the exact text displayed on the button the user can click. It also has layout_width and layout_height attributes that are both set to "wrap_content". This, as with the TextView element, causes the onscreen button to take up as much space as the content it has needs. The final attribute in Button is id, and for buttons this is often a vital attribute, even more so than for some other parts of the UI. As the id attribute can distinguish this button from other buttons, we can program different functionality for different buttons based on the value held in the id attribute. We will see this principle in action soon.

Notice that the code at **6** in our XML screenshot is / >. As we have come to know, this marks the end of the Button element.

We will edit and add to this XML code in the next section and learn more about the attributes.

> **Note**
>
> The elements of a layout are often referred to as **widgets**.

Adding buttons to the main layout file

Here we will add a couple of button widgets to the screen and we will then see a fast way to make them actually do something. We will add a button in two different ways, firstly using the visual designer and secondly by adding to and editing the XML code directly.

Adding a button via the visual designer

To get started with adding our first button, `fragment_first.xml`, open it in the editor and switch back to the design view by clicking the **Design** tab (shown next):

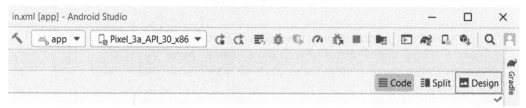

Figure 2.7 – Design tab

Notice to the left-hand side of the layout we have a window that is called the **Palette** and is shown next:

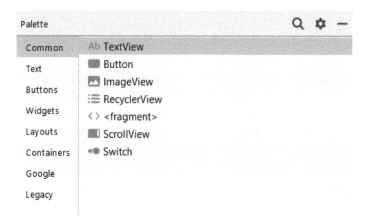

Figure 2.8 – Palette window

The palette is divided into two parts. The left-hand list has the categories of UI elements and allows you to select a category, and then the right-hand side shows you all the available UI elements from the currently selected category.

Make sure that the **Common** category is selected as shown in the previous figure. Now, left-click and hold on the **Button** widget and then drag it onto the layout somewhere near the top center.

It doesn't matter if it is not exact. It is good to practice getting it right, however. So, if you are not happy with the position of your button, then you can left-click it to select it on the layout and then tap the *Delete* key on the keyboard to get rid of it. Now you can repeat the previous step until you have a new neatly placed button that you are happy with, as here:

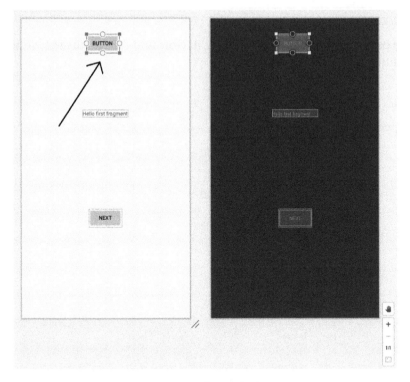

Figure 2.9 – Updating the layout

At this point, we could run the app on the emulator or on a real device and the button would be there – kind of. If we clicked it, there would even be a simple animation to represent the button being pressed and released. Feel free to try this now if you like. If you do, you will notice that the button isn't positioned as you expect it to be:

Figure 2.10 – Button not positioned correctly

Don't concern yourself with this apparent anomaly for now; we will look into this over the next few sections.

Next, we are going to edit the attributes of our button in the **Attributes** window.

Editing the button's attributes

Make sure the button is selected by left-clicking it. Now find the **Attributes** window to the right of the editing window as shown next:

Figure 2.11 – Attributes window

In the previous figure, you can see that we have access to a wide selection of attributes from the currently selected UI element. To reveal more of the attributes, we click the different categories of attributes and scroll through them using the scrollbar to the right. If they are not open already by default, left-click on the **Common Attributes** and **All Attributes** sections' arrows to reveal their options.

Now you can see the full details of the button and we can set about editing it. It might seem surprising the substantial number of attributes that something as simple as a button has. This is a sign of the versatility and power that the Android API provides for UI manipulation.

As you can see, there is a large array of different attributes that we can edit right here in the UI designer. In *Chapter 13, Anonymous Classes – Bringing Android Widgets to Life*, we will also edit and manipulate these attributes using our Java code.

For now, we will edit just one attribute. Scroll the **Attributes** window until you see the **onClick** attribute in the **Common Attributes** section and then left-click it to select it for editing, as shown here:

Figure 2.12 – Common Attributes section

> **Note**
> If you ever have trouble finding an attribute, you can always find it in the
> **All Attributes** section, where attributes are arranged in alphabetical order.
> Therefore, the **onClick** attribute can also be found about two-thirds of the way
> down the lengthy list of the **All Attributes** section.

Type `topClick` in the **onClick** attribute's edit box and press *Enter* on the keyboard. Be sure to use the same case, including the slightly counterintuitive lowercase `t` and uppercase C.

The **Attributes** window will look like this when you are done:

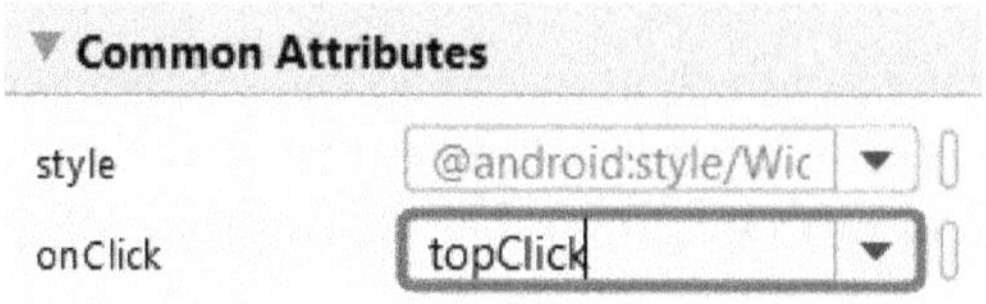

▼ **Common Attributes**

style	@android:style/Wic ▼ ▯
onClick	topClick ▼ ▯

Figure 2.13 – onClick option

What we have done here is named the Java method in our code that we want to call when this button is clicked by the user. The name is arbitrary but as this button is in the top part of the screen, the name seems meaningful and easy to remember. The odd casing that we used is a convention that will help us keep our code clear and easy to read. We will see the benefits of this as our code gets longer and more complicated.

Of course, the `topClick` method doesn't exist yet. Android Studio is very helpful, but there are some things we need to do ourselves. We will write this method using Java code after we have added another button to our UI. You could run the app at this point and it would still work. But if you click the button, it will crash, and you will get an error because the method does not exist. Android Studio is forewarning us of this impending crash by outlining the **onClick** attribute in red, as shown in the previous figure. If you hover the mouse cursor over this red outline, you will see the details of the problem: **Corresponding method handler... Not found**.

Examining the XML code for the new button

Before we add our final button for this project. Click the **Code** tab to switch back to seeing the XML code that makes our UI.

Notice that there is a new block of code among the XML that we examined earlier. Here is an image of the new block of code:

```
<Button
    android:id="@+id/button"
    android:layout_width="wrap_content"
    android:layout_height="wrap_content"
    android:onClick="topClick"
    android:text="Button"
    tools:layout_editor_absoluteX="147dp"
    tools:layout_editor_absoluteY="30dp" />
```

Figure 2.14 – New block of code among the XML

Also, notice the following details, which should correspond to what we know about XML and Android UI elements:

- The new code starts with the text `<Button` and ends with `/>`.
- The code has a range of attributes that define the button, including `layoutWidth` and `layoutHeight`.
- The code includes the `onClick` attribute that we just added with a value of `"topClick"`.
- The `topClick` value of the `onClick` attribute is underlined in red, showing the missing method error.
- The start and end of the code representing the button are enclosed within the `ConstraintLayout` element.

As in the design view, you can hover the mouse cursor over the red-underlined `topClick` code to reveal the details of the problem: **Corresponding method handler... Not found**.

> **Note**
>
> During the writing of this book, Android Studio updated the way it shows errors in XML. Currently, it highlights the error in red, not underlining in red as shown in the figures and descriptions. The underlining is clearer in black and white print so they have been left as they are.

We can see that the issue is that Android Studio expects a method called `topClick` to be implemented within our Java code. We will do this as soon as we have added that second button.

Adding a button by editing the XML code

Just for variety and to prove that we can, we will now add another button using only XML code, not the UI designer. Most of the time, we will use the UI designer, but this quick exercise should cement in your mind the relationship between the UI designer and the underlying XML code.

We will achieve this by copying and pasting the code for the existing button. We will then make some minor edits to the pasted code.

Left-click just before the button code that starts `<Button`. Notice that the beginning and end of the code now have a slight highlight:

```
<Button
    android:id="@+id/button"
    android:layout_width="wrap_content"
    android:layout_height="wrap_content"
    android:onClick="topClick"
    android:text="Button"
    tools:layout_editor_absoluteX="147dp"
    tools:layout_editor_absoluteY="30dp" />
```

Figure 2.15 – Button code

This has identified the part of the code we want to copy. Now left-click and drag to select all the button code, including the highlighted start and end, as shown in this next figure:

```
<Button
    android:id="@+id/button"
    android:layout_width="wrap_content"
    android:layout_height="wrap_content"
    android:onClick="topClick"
    android:text="Button"
    tools:layout_editor_absoluteX="147dp"
    tools:layout_editor_absoluteY="30dp" />
```

Figure 2.16 – Select all the button code

Press the *Ctrl + C* keyboard combination to copy the highlighted text. Place the keyboard cursor below the existing button code and tap the *Enter* key a few times to leave some spare empty lines.

Press the *Ctrl + V* keyboard combination to paste the button code. At this point, we have two buttons. There are a couple of problems, however:

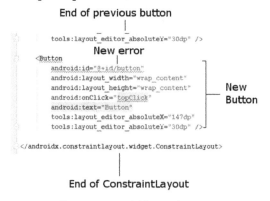

Figure 2.17 – Additional error

We have an additional error in both blocks of code that represent our buttons. The `id` attribute (in both blocks) is underlined in red. The reason for this error is that both buttons have an `id` attribute that is the same. The `id` attribute is supposed to distinguish a UI element from all other UI elements. Let's fix that.

Giving the buttons unique id attributes

We could solve the problem by calling the second button, `button2`, but it would be more meaningful to change them both. Edit the code in the first button to give it an ID of `buttonTop`. To do so, find the following line of code (in the first button):

```
android:id="@+id/button"
```

Change it to this:

```
android:id="@+id/buttonTop"
```

> **Note**
>
> Notice the lowercase b in `button` and the uppercase T in `Top`.

Now identify this line of code in the second button:

```
android:id="@+id/button"
```

Change it to this:

```
android:id="@+id/buttonBottom"
```

The errors on the `id` attribute lines are gone. At this point, you might think we can move on to solve our missing method problem.

However, if you run the app and take a quick glance at it, you will see we only appear to have one button. Not only that but (as alluded to previously) the buttons are not in the place we expected them to be either:

Figure 2.18 – Single button

The reason for this is we haven't explicitly positioned them, so they have defaulted to the top left. The position we see on the **Design** tab is just a design-time position. Let's change that now.

Positioning the two buttons in the layout

The reason we can only see one button is that both buttons are in the same position. The second button is exactly covering the first button. And even in the **Design** tab (feel free to have a look), the buttons are still sat on top of each other, although they are in the middle of the screen.

> **Note**
>
> You might be wondering why the UI layout tool was designed in this apparently counterintuitive way. The reason is flexibility. As we will see in the next two chapters, not only is it possible to position UI elements differently at design time to when the app is running but there is also a whole bunch of different layout schemes that the app designer (that's you) can choose from to suit their plans. This flexibility results in a little awkwardness while learning about Android but great design power once you have got past the awkwardness. Don't worry: we will move a step at a time until you have this thing beaten.

We will make Android Studio solve the problem for us automatically by first adding to our code and then using the UI designer. First, let's get the design-time layout right. In the code for the second button, find this line of code:

```
tools:layout_editor_absoluteY="30dp" />
```

Edit it to be the same as this:

```
tools:layout_editor_absoluteY="100dp" />
```

This subtle change will move the second button down a little, but only for design time. If you look in the **Design** tab, the button is positioned neatly underneath the first button, but if you run the app on the emulator, they are both still in the top-left corner and on top of one another.

> **Note**
>
> It is possible, even likely, that the exact dp measurements in your layout will be slightly different to those shown in the book. As long as the second button's `layout_editor_absoluteY` attribute is about 70dp greater than the first, then all will be neat and tidy. Feel free to play with this attribute on both buttons while switching between the **Code** and **Design** tabs until the buttons are positioned to your liking.

When you are satisfied with the position of the buttons, switch to the **Design** tab and find the **Infer constraints** button, shown next:

Figure 2.19 – Infer constraints button

Click the **Infer constraints** button. Android Studio will edit the XML. Let's take a brief look at what has happened behind the scenes. From the end of both of the buttons, the following lines of code were removed.

If the constraints aren't being applied, hit the **Clear All Constraints** button, which is to the left of **Infer constraints**; sometimes Android Studio can get confused and needs to reset the existing constraints before inferring the rest:

```
tools:layout_editor_absoluteX="147dp"
tools:layout_editor_absoluteY="30dp" />
```

These two lines of code were what positioned the buttons horizontally (...absoluteX) and vertically (...absoluteY).

Android Studio also added four lines of code to the first button and three to the second. Here is the code added near the start of the first button:

```
android:layout_marginTop="30dp"
```

This code causes the button to have a margin of 30 at the top. But at the top relative to what exactly? Look at these three lines of code that were added at the end of the first button:

```
app:layout_constraintEnd_toEndOf="parent"
app:layout_constraintStart_toStartOf="parent"
app:layout_constraintTop_toTopOf="parent" />
```

Notice the new attributes of `layout_constraintEnd_toEndOf`, `layout_constraintStart_toStartOf`, and `layout_constraintTop_toTopOf`. The value assigned to each of these attributes is `"parent"`. This causes the first button to be positioned relative to the *parent* UI element. The parent is the containing layout: the `ConstraintLayout` element.

Now look at the three lines of code added to the second (bottom) button.

Near the start of the code, we see this:

```
android:layout_marginTop="22dp"
```

And at the end of the code for the second button, we see these two extra lines:

```
app:layout_constraintStart_toStartOf="@+id/buttonTop"
app:layout_constraintTop_toBottomOf="@+id/buttonTop" />
```

This means that the second button is positioned with a margin of 22 relative to the `buttonTop` widget.

> **Note**
>
> The `dp` code is a unit of measurement/distance and will be discussed in more depth in *Chapter 5, Beautiful Layouts with CardView and ScrollView*. The precise values for the `dp` measurement will likely vary slightly on your layout.

Now run the app and you will see we have two distinct buttons. One has an `id` attribute of `buttonTop` and it is above the other button, with an `id` attribute of `buttonBottom`:

Figure 2.20 – Two button options

Clearly, there is more to layouts than I have alluded to so far, but you have had your first glance at one of the options we have to design the UI of our apps. We will be taking a closer look at the ConstraintLayout layout element as well as exploring more layout options in *Chapter 4, Getting Started with Layouts and Material Design*.

We want to make one more change in our XML code.

Making the buttons call different methods

Switch back to the **Code** tab and identify this next line of code in the second (buttonBottom) button:

```
android:onClick="topClick"
```

Edit the code to this:

```
android:onClick="bottomClick"
```

Now we have two buttons, one above the other. The top one has an id attribute of buttonTop and an onClick attribute with a value of topClick. The other has an id attribute of buttonBottom and an onClick attribute with a value of bottomClick.

These last XML code changes now mean we need to code two methods (topClick and bottomClick) in our Java code.

> **Note**
> It is OK for two buttons to call the same method when they are clicked; it is not a syntax error. However, most buttons do have distinct purposes, so this exercise will be more meaningful if our buttons do different things.

We will do that soon, but before we do, let's learn a little bit more about Java comments and look at some Java code we can write to send messages. We will learn to send messages to the user to keep them informed and to ourselves for debugging purposes.

Leaving comments in our Java code

In programming, it is always a clever idea to write notes, known as code comments, and sprinkle them liberally throughout your code. This is to remind us what we were thinking at the time we wrote the code. To do this, you simply append a double forward slash and then type your comment, as follows:

```
// This is a comment and it could be useful
```

In addition, we can use comments to *comment out* a line of code. Suppose we have a line of code that we temporarily want to disable. We can do so by adding the two forward slashes, like this:

```
// The code below used to send a message
// Log.i("info","our message here");
// But now it doesn't do anything
// And I am getting ahead of where I should be
```

> **Note**
>
> Using comments to comment out code should only be a temporary measure. Once you have found the correct code to use, commented-out code should be deleted to keep the code file clean and organized.

Let's look at two separate ways to send messages in Android, and then we can write some methods that will send messages when our new UI buttons are pressed.

Coding messages to the user and the developer

In the introduction to this chapter and in the previous chapter, we talked a bit about using other people's code, specifically via the classes and their methods, of the Android API. We saw that we could do some quite complex things with insignificant amounts of code (such as talk to satellites).

To get us started, we are going to use two different classes from the Android API that allow us to output messages. The first class, Log, allows us to output messages to the Logcat window. The second class, Toast, is not a tasty breakfast treat, but it will produce a toast-shaped pop-up message for our app's user to see.

Here is the code we need to write to send a message to the Logcat window:

```
Log.i("info","our message here");
```

Exactly why this works will become clearer in *Chapter 10, Object-Oriented Programming*, but for now, we just need to know that whatever we put between the two sets of quote marks will be output to the Logcat window. We will see where to write this type of code shortly.

Here is the code we need to write to send a message to the user's screen:

```
Toast.makeText(this, "our message",
Toast.LENGTH_SHORT).show();
```

This is a very convoluted-looking line of code, and exactly how it works, again, will not become clear until *Chapter 10, Object-Oriented Programming*. The important thing here is that whatever we put between the quote marks will appear in a pop-up message to our users.

Let's put some code, much like we have just seen, into our app for real.

Writing our first Java code

So, we now know the code that will output to Logcat or the user's screen. But *where* do we write the code? To answer this question, we need to understand that the onCreate method in MainActivity.java executes as the app is preparing to be shown to the user. So, if we put our code at the end of this method, it will execute just as the user sees the app. Sounds good.

> **Note**
>
> We know that to execute the code in a method, we need to call it. We have wired our buttons up to call a couple of methods: topClick and bottomClick. Soon we will write these methods. But who or what is calling onCreate!? The answer to this mystery is that the Android operating system itself calls onCreate. It does so when the user clicks the app icon to run the app. In *Chapter 6, The Android Lifecycle*, we will look deeper at this phenomenon, and it will be clear exactly what code executes and when. You don't need to completely comprehend this now. I just wanted to give you an overview of what was going on.

Let's quickly try this out. Switch to the MainActivity.java tab in Android Studio.

We know that the onCreate method is called just before the app starts. Let's copy and paste some code into the onCreate method of our app and see what happens when we run it.

Adding message code to the onCreate method

Find the closing curly brace } of the onCreate method and add the highlighted code shown next. In the code, I haven't shown the complete contents of the onCreate method but have used ... to indicate some lines of code not being shown. The important thing is to place the new code (shown in full) right at the end but before that closing curly brace, }:

```
@Override
protected void onCreate(Bundle savedInstanceState) {

    ...

    ...

    ...

// Your code goes here
    Toast.makeText(this, "Can you see me?",
                    Toast.LENGTH_SHORT).show();

    Log.i("info", "Done creating the app");
}
```

Notice that the two instances of the word Toast and the word Log are highlighted in red in Android Studio. They are errors. We know that Toast and Log are classes and that classes are containers for code.

The problem is that Android Studio doesn't know about them until we tell it about them. We must add an import for each class. Fortunately, this is semi-automatic.

Left-click on the red Toast code in the onCreate method. Now hold the *Alt* key and then tap *Enter*. When prompted, choose **Import class**. Now repeat this process for Log. Android Studio adds the import directives at the top of the code with our other imports and the errors are gone.

> **Note**
>
> *Alt + Enter* is just one of many useful keyboard shortcuts. The following link is to a keyboard shortcut reference for Android Studio. More specifically, it is for the IntelliJ Idea IDE, upon which Android Studio is based. Look at and bookmark this web page; it will be invaluable over the course of this book: http://www.jetbrains.com/idea/docs/IntelliJIDEA_ReferenceCard.pdf.

Scroll to the top of `MainActivity.java` and look at the added `import` directives. Here they are for your convenience:

```
import android.util.Log;
import android.widget.Toast;
```

Run the app in the usual way and look at the output in the **Logcat** window.

Examining the output

The next figure shows a screenshot of the output in the **Logcat** window:

```
com.gamecodeschool.helloworld W/hool.helloworl: Accessing hidden
com.gamecodeschool.helloworld W/hool.helloworl: Accessing hidden
com.gamecodeschool.helloworld I/info: Done creating the app
com.gamecodeschool.helloworld I/ConfigStore: android::hardware::
com.gamecodeschool.helloworld I/ConfigStore: android::hardware::
```

Figure 2.21 – Output in the Logcat window

Look at the **Logcat** window, you can see our message **Done creating the app** was output, although it is mixed up among other system messages that we are currently not interested in. If you watch the emulator when the app first starts, you will also see the neat pop-up message that the user will see:

Figure 2.22 – Pop-up message

It is possible that you might be wondering why the messages were output at the time they were. The answer is that the `onCreate` method is called just *before* the app starts to respond to the user. It is for this reason, it's common practice among Android developers to put code in this method to get their apps set up and ready for the user.

Now we will go a step further and write our own methods that will be called by our two buttons in the UI. We will place similar `Log` and `Toast` messages inside these new methods.

Writing our own Java methods

Let's get straight on with writing our first Java methods with some more Log and Toast messages inside them.

> **Note**
>
> Now would be a good time, if you haven't already, to get the download bundle that contains all the code files. You can view the completed code for each chapter. For example, the completed code for this chapter can be found in the Chapter 2 folder. I have further subdivided the Chapter 2 folder into java and res folders (for Java and resource files). In chapters with more than one project, I will divide the folders further to include the project name. You should view these files in a text editor. My favorite is Notepad++, a free download from https://notepad-plus-plus.org/download/. The code viewed in a text editor is easier to read than from the book directly, especially the paperback version, and even more so where the lines of code are long. The text editor is also a great way to select sections of the code to copy and paste into Android Studio. You could open the code in Android Studio, but then you'd risk mixing up my code with the auto-generated code of Android Studio.

Identify the closing curly brace, }, of the MainActivity class.

> **Note**
>
> You are looking for the end of the entire class, not the end of the onCreate method as in the previous section. Take your time to identify the new code and where it goes among the existing code.

Inside that curly brace, enter the following code that is highlighted.

```
@Override
protected void onCreate(Bundle savedInstanceState) {
    ...
    ...
    ...
    ...
}


    ...

    ...
```

```
...

public void topClick(View v){
            Toast.makeText(this, "Top button clicked",
                        Toast.LENGTH_SHORT).show();

            Log.i("info","The user clicked the top
                button");
}

public void bottomClick(View v){
            Toast.makeText(this, "Bottom button clicked",
                        Toast.LENGTH_SHORT).show();

            Log.i("info","The user clicked the bottom
                button");
}

} // This is the end of the class
```

Notice that the two instances of the word View might be red, indicating an error. Simply use the *Alt + Enter* keyboard combination to import the View class and remove the errors.

> **Note**
>
> The reason I said there "might" be an error is because it depends on how you entered the code. If you copied and pasted the code, then Android Studio may automatically add the View class import code. If you typed the new code, then the error will appear, and you will need to use the *Alt + Enter* key solution. This is just a quirk of Android Studio.

Deploy the app to a real device or emulator in the usual way and start tapping the buttons so we can observe the output.

Examining the output

At last, our app does something we told it to do when we told it to do it. We can see that the method names we defined in the button `onClick` attribute are indeed called when the buttons are clicked, and the appropriate messages are added to the **Logcat** window and the appropriate `Toast` messages are shown to the user.

Admittedly, we still don't understand why or how the `Toast` and `Log` classes really work, neither do we fully comprehend the `public void` and `(View v)` parts of our method's syntax (or much of the rest of the auto-generated code). This will become clearer as we progress. As said previously, in *Chapter 10, Object-Oriented Programming*, we will take a deep dive into the world of classes, and in *Chapter 9, Learning Java Methods*, we will master the rest of the syntax associated with methods.

Check the **Logcat** window output. You can see that a log entry was made from the `onCreate` method just as before, as well as from the two methods that we wrote ourselves, each time you clicked one of the buttons. In the following figure, you can see I clicked each button three times:

```
com.gamecodeschool.helloworld I/info: The user clicked the top button
com.gamecodeschool.helloworld I/info: The user clicked the top button
com.gamecodeschool.helloworld I/info: The user clicked the top button
com.gamecodeschool.helloworld I/info: The user clicked the bottom button
com.gamecodeschool.helloworld I/info: The user clicked the bottom button
com.gamecodeschool.helloworld I/info: The user clicked the bottom button
```

Figure 2.23 – Logcat window output

As you are now familiar with where to find the **Logcat** window, in future I will present **Logcat** output as trimmed text as follows, as it is easier to read:

```
The user clicked the top button
The user clicked the top button
The user clicked the top button
The user clicked the bottom button
The user clicked the bottom button
The user clicked the bottom button
```

And in the next figure, you can see that the top button has been clicked and the `topClick` method was called, triggering the pop-up `Toast` message highlighted here:

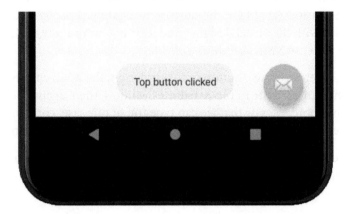

Figure 2.24 – Pop-up Toast message

Throughout this book, we will regularly output to the **Logcat** window, so we can see what is going on behind the UI of our apps. Toast messages are more for notifying the user that something has occurred. This might be a download that has completed, a new email that has arrived, or some other occurrence that the user might want to be informed about.

Frequently asked questions

1. Can you remind me what methods are?

    Methods are containers for our code that can be executed (called) from other parts of our code. Methods are contained within a class.

2. Like the first, I found this chapter tough going. Do I need to reread it?

    No; if you managed to build the app, you have made enough progress to handle the next chapter. All the blanks in your knowledge will be steadily filled in and replaced with glorious moments of realization as the book progresses.

Summary

We have achieved a lot in this chapter. It is true that much of the XML code is still generally incomprehensible. That's OK, because in the next two chapters we will be really getting to grips with the visual designer and learning more about XML, although ultimately our aim is to use XML as little as possible.

We have seen how, when we drag a button onto our design, the XML code is generated for us. Also, if we change an attribute in the **Attributes** window, then, again, the XML code is edited for us. Furthermore, we saw that we can type (or, in our case, copy and paste) XML code directly in the **Code** tab to create new buttons on our UI or edit existing ones.

We have seen as well as written our first Java, including comments that help us document our code, and we have even added our own methods to output debugging messages to the Logcat window and pop-up Toast messages to the user.

In the next chapter, we will take a full guided tour of Android Studio to see exactly where different things get done at the same time as understanding how our project's assets, such as files and folders, are structured and how we can manage them. This will prepare us to go for a more in-depth look at UI design in *Chapter 4, Getting Started with Layouts and Material Design,* and *Chapter 5, Beautiful Layouts with CardView and ScrollView,* when we will build some significant real-world layouts for our apps.

3
Exploring Android Studio and the Project Structure

In this chapter, we will create and run two more Android projects. The purpose of these exercises is to explore more deeply Android Studio and the structure of Android projects.

When we build our apps ready for deployment, the code and the resource files need to be packed away in an **Android Package** (**APK**) file—just right. Therefore, all the layout files (and other resources that we will soon discover) need to be in their correct structures.

Fortunately, Android Studio handles this for us when we create a project from a template. However, we still need to know how to find and amend these files, how to add our own (and sometimes remove) files created by Android Studio, and how the resource files are interlinked, sometimes with each other and sometimes with the Java code (autogenerated and our own).

Along with understanding the composition of our projects, it will also be beneficial to make sure we get the most from the emulator.

> **Note**
>
> Emulators are particularly useful when you want to make sure that your app will work on hardware that you don't own. Also, learning about some of the latest features (as we will in this book) often requires the latest handset, and an emulator is a cost-effective way of following along with all the mini-apps without buying the latest phone.

In this chapter, we will look at the following topics:

- Exploring the file and folder structure of the **Empty Activity** project template
- Exploring the file and folder structure of the **Basic Activity** project template
- Seeing the difference between the **Empty Activity** and **Basic Activity** templates
- Exploring the Android emulator

This chapter will leave us in a good position to build and deploy multiple different **user interface** (**UI**) designs in the next chapter.

Technical requirements

You can find the code present in this chapter on GitHub at `https://github.com/ PacktPublishing/Android-Programming-for-Beginners-Third-Edition/tree/main/chapter%2003`.

Project Explorer and project anatomy

When we create a new Android project, we most often do so using a project template, just as we did in *Chapter 1, Beginning Android and Java*. The template we use determines the exact selection and contents of files that Android Studio will generate. While there are big similarities across all projects that are worth noting, seeing the differences can also help. Let's build two template projects and examine the files, their contents, and how they are all linked together through the code (**Extensible Markup Language** (**XML**) and Java). We begin by creating an **Empty Activity** project.

Exploring the file and folder structure of the Empty Activity project template

The simplest project type with an autogenerated UI is the **Empty Activity** project template. The UI is almost empty, but it is there ready to be added to. When we create a project even with an empty UI, Android Studio also autogenerates the Java code to display the UI. Therefore, when we add it to the empty UI, it is ready to be displayed.

Let's create an **Empty Activity** project. This is almost the same process as in *Chapter 1, Beginning Android and Java*, with one slight difference that I will point out.

If you have the project from *Chapter 2, First Contact: Java, XML, and the UI Designer,* open, select **File | New | New Project…**. Alternatively, if you are on the Android Studio welcome screen, select **Start a new Android Studio project**. Then, proceed as follows:

1. On the **Select a Project Template** window, select **Empty Activity**. This is the bit that is different from what we did in *Chapter 1, Beginning Android and Java*.

2. In the **Configure your project** screen, change the **Name** field to Empty Activity App.

3. The rest of the settings can be left at their defaults, so just click **Finish**.

Android Studio will generate all the code and the other project resources. Now, we can see what has been generated and relate it to what we already know about what to expect in the **Project Explorer** window.

If the emulator is not already running, launch it by selecting **Tools | AVD Manager**, and then start your emulator in the **Your Virtual Devices** window. Run the app on the emulator by clicking the play button in the quick launch bar, as we have done a few times already for our previous project.

Look at the app and notice how it is a little bit different from that of the first project. It is—well—empty: no menu at the top; no floating button at the bottom. It does, however, still have some text that says **Hello World!**, as can be seen in the following screenshot:

Figure 3.1 – Hello world!

Now that we have a brand-new **Empty Activity** project, let's explore the files and folders that Android Studio has generated for us.

Exploring an Empty Activity project

Now, it is time to go on a deep dive into the files and folders of our app. This will save us lots of time and head-scratching later in the book. Please note, however, that there is no need to memorize where all these files go, and there is even less need to understand the code within the files. In fact, parts of the XML will remain a mystery even at the end of the book, but this will not stop you designing, coding, and releasing amazing apps.

In the following screenshot, look at the Project Explorer window as it is just after the project is created:

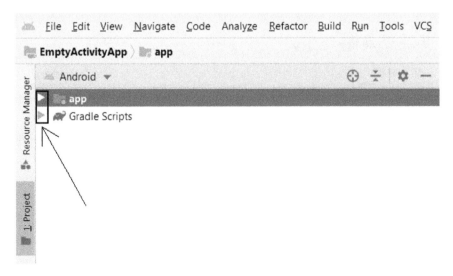

Figure 3.2 – Project Explorer window

Notice the two arrows indicated in the previous screenshot? These, as you can probably guess, allow us to expand the app and Gradle Scripts folders. It is possible that your folders are already expanded. Why not try out the arrows, and expand and collapse them a few times?

> **Note**
>
> We do not need to explore the Gradle Scripts folder in the context of this book. Gradle is a significant part of Android Studio, but its role is to hide from the user the quite complicated processes that Android Studio performs— things such as adding resource files, and compiling and building projects. Therefore, we don't need to dig into this any further. If, however, you decide to take Android to the next level, then getting a good understanding of Gradle and its relationship with Android Studio is time well invested.

We will explore in detail the app folder. Click the arrow next to the app folder to expand its contents, and we will begin exploring. The first level of contents is shown in the following screenshot:

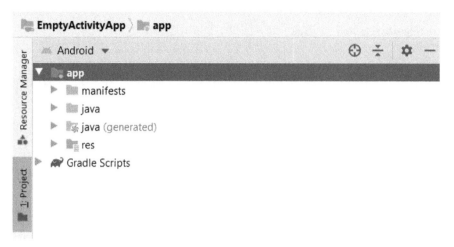

Figure 3.3 – Exploring the app folder

We have revealed four more folders: manifests, java, java (generated), and res. Let's look at all four, starting at the top.

> **Note**
> The style guidelines that Packt uses for its books suggest **this font** for text that appears on the user's screen and this font for filenames and folder names. As the files and folders that we are discussing are both files and folders, as well as appearing on the screen, I have opted for using just the latter font for consistency and because it is more compact, and I will use this option whenever the choice is ambiguous throughout the book.

The manifests folder

The manifests folder has just one file inside it. Expand the manifests folder and double-click the AndroidManifest.xml file. Notice that the file has been opened in the editor window, and a tab has been added so that we can easily switch back between this and other files. The next screenshot shows the new tab that has been added, as well as the XML code contained in the AndroidManifest.xml file within the manifests folder:

```
    activity_main.xml ×    © MainActivity.java ×    AndroidManifest.xml ×
1        <?xml version="1.0" encoding="utf-8"?>
2      <manifest xmlns:android="http://schemas.android.com/apk/res/android"
3          package="com.gamecodeschool.emptyactivityapp">
4
5          <application
6              android:allowBackup="true"
7              android:icon="@mipmap/ic_launcher"
8              android:label="@string/app_name"
9              android:roundIcon="@mipmap/ic_launcher_round"
10             android:supportsRtl="true"
11             android:theme="@style/AppTheme">
12             <activity android:name=".MainActivity">
13                 <intent-filter>
14                     <action android:name="android.intent.action.MAIN" />
15
16                     <category android:name="android.intent.category.LAUNCHER" />
17                 </intent-filter>
18             </activity>
19         </application>
20
21     </manifest>
```

Figure 3.4 – New tab added

We don't need to understand everything in this file, but it is worth pointing out that we will make occasional amendments here—for example, when we need to ask the user for permission to access features of their device. We will also edit this file when we want to make a fullscreen app for immersivity, such as the drawing app that starts in *Chapter 21, Threads and Starting the Live Drawing App*.

Notice that the structure of the file is similar to the structure of the layout file we saw in the previous chapter—for instance, there are clearly denoted sections that start with <section name and end with </section name>. Real examples of this are <application and </application>, as well as <activity and </activity>.

Indeed, the entire file contents, apart from the first line, are wrapped in <manifest and </manifest>.

Just as if we were entering the brackets of a calculation into a calculator, these opening and closing parts must match or the file will cause an error in our project. Android Studio indents (places tabs) in front of the lines to make the sections and their depth in this structure clearer.

A couple of specific parts of this code are worth noting, so I will point out some of the lines.

The line shown next tells Android that the icon we want to show the user in their app drawer/home screen to launch the app is contained in the `mipmap` folder and is called `ic_launcher`:

```
android:icon="@mipmap/ic_launcher"
```

We will verify this for ourselves as we continue our exploration.

The next line has two aspects worth discussing. First, it denotes the name that we gave our app; and second, that name is contained as a **String** with a label of `app_name`, as illustrated here:

```
android:label="@string/app_name"
```

> **Note**
>
> In programming, including with Java and XML, a String is any alphanumeric value. We will learn loads more about Strings throughout the book, starting in *Chapter 7, Java Variables, Operators, and Expressions*. We can therefore guess that the alphanumeric value of the label of `app_name` is `Empty Activity App` because that is what we called the app when we created it.

This might sound slightly odd, but we will see this file soon (and its label), and in later projects, we will add more labels and values to it. We will also come to understand the reasons why we add text to our apps in what might at this stage seem quite a convoluted manner.

We could discuss every line in the `AndroidManifest.xml` file but we don't need to. Let's look at just two more, as they are related to each other. The line shown next indicates the name of our Activity, which Android Studio chose when we created the project. I have highlighted the Activity name here, just to make it stand out:

```
<activity android:name=".MainActivity">
```

And this next line, which appears within the `<activity` and `</activity>` tags, denotes that it is an attribute of `activity` and shows that this Activity is the one that should run when the app is started. It is LAUNCHER:

```
<category android:name="android.intent.category.LAUNCHER" />
```

This implies that our apps can have more than one Activity. Very often, if you have an app with multiple screens—such as a home screen, a settings screen, and so on—they are built from multiple `Activity` class **instances**.

A note about `Activity` and `activity`. In XML, as with the `AndroidManifest` file, `activity` is in lowercase, but in Java the `Activity` class has an uppercase A. This is just convention and is nothing to be concerned about. As we have just seen, `activity` in XML has a `name` attribute with a value that refers to an instance of a Java `Activity`.

Let's dig into the `java` folder. I wonder what we will find in there.

The java folder

I apologize for the slightly sarcastic comment. We will, of course, find all the Java code. To begin with, this consists of just one file, but as our projects grow we will add more. Expand the `java` folder and you will find three more folders, as shown in the following screenshot:

Figure 3.5 – Expand the java folder

Throughout this book, we will only need one of these three folders—the top one. The names of these folders are composed of the package name (chosen when we created the app) and the app name, in all lowercase and with no spaces (also chosen when we created the app).

> **Note**
>
> The reason there is more than one folder with the same name is for advanced reasons to do with automated testing, which is beyond the scope of this book. Therefore, you can safely ignore folders that end with (androidTest) and (test).

The only folder we are interested in during the course of this book is the top one, which for this app (on my screen) is com.gamecodeschool.emptyactivityapp. Depending upon your chosen package name and the name of the app we are currently working on, the folder name will change, but it will always be the top one that we need to access and add—or edit—the contents of.

Expand the com.gamecodeschool.emptyactivityapp (or whatever yours is called) folder now to view its contents. In the next screenshot, you can see that the folder has just one file:

Figure 3.6 – com.gamecodeschool.emptyactivityapp folder

This file is MainActivity.java, although the file extension isn't shown in the project window even though it is in the tabs above the editor window. In fact, all the files in the java/packagename.appname folder will have a .java extension. If you double-click the MainActivity.java file, it will open in the editor window, although we could have just clicked the MainActivity.java tab above the editor window. As we add more Java files, knowing where they are kept will be useful.

Examine the `MainActivity.java` file, and you will see it is a simplified version of the Java file we worked with in the first project. It is the same except that there are fewer methods and less autogenerated code in the `onCreate` method. The methods are missing because the UI is simpler and therefore they are not needed, and Android Studio didn't generate them.

For reference, look at the contents of the `MainActivity.java` file in this next screenshot. I have outlined one line from the code:

```
package com.gamecodeschool.emptyactivityapp;

import ...

public class MainActivity extends AppCompatActivity {

    @Override
    protected void onCreate(Bundle savedInstanceState) {
        super.onCreate(savedInstanceState);
        setContentView(R.layout.activity_main);
    }
}
```

Figure 3.7 – MainActivity.java file

It still has the `onCreate` method that executes when the app is run by the user, but there is much less code in it and `onCreate` is the only method. Look at the last line of code in the `onCreate` method—we will discuss this before moving on to explore the `res` folder. Here is the line of code under discussion:

```
setContentView(R.layout.activity_main);
```

The code is calling a method named `setContentView` and it is passing some data into the `setContentView` method, for the code in the `setContentView` method to make use of. The data being passed to `setContentView` is `R.layout.activity_main`.

For now, I will just mention that the `setContentView` method is provided by the Android **application programming interface** (**API**), and it is the method that prepares and displays the UI to the user. So, what exactly is `R.layout.activity_main`?

We will find out by exploring the `res` folder, but a quick mention of the `Java` (`generated`) folder so that we don't trouble ourselves with it as we progress. The first thing to note is that the folder is autogenerated the first time the app is run on the emulator or a real device, so if you haven't run the app, you won't see it.

The Java (generated) folder

This folder contains code generated by Android Studio and we do not need to concern ourselves with what goes in it. Even advanced users who might need it generally only use it for reference.

Let's get on to the `res` folder and that `R.layout.activity_main` code.

The res folder

The `res` folder is where all the resources go. Left-click to expand the `res` folder, and we will examine what's inside. Here is a screenshot of the top level of folders inside this folder:

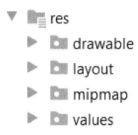

Figure 3.8 – res folder

Let's begin at the top of the list, with the `drawable` folder.

The res/drawable folder

The name gives things away a little bit, but the `drawable` folder holds much more than just graphics. As we progress through the book, we will indeed add graphics to this folder. However, now, it holds just two files.

These files are `ic_launcher_foreground` and `ic_launcher_background`. We will not examine either file because we will never need to alter them, but I will just mention what they are.

If you open the files, you will see they are quite long and technical. They include what appear to be lists of coordinates, colors, and more besides. They are what is known as a **graphical mask**, used by Android to adapt/mask other graphics—specifically, in this case, the launcher icon of the app. The files give instructions to Android on how to adapt the app launcher icon.

This system is made available so that different device manufacturers can create their own masks to suit their own Android devices. The masks, which are in the drawable folder by default (ic_launcher_foreground and ic_launcher_background), are default adaptive masks that add visually pleasing shadows and depth to the launcher icon.

> **Note**
> If the concept of adaptive icons is interesting to you, then you can see a full and very visual explanation at this link to the *Android Developers* website, at https://developer.android.com/guide/practices/ ui_guidelines/icon_design_adaptive. You do not need to see this page to continue.

We know enough about the drawable folder for now, so let's move on to the layout folder.

The res/layout folder

The res folder is where all the resources for your app go, such as icons, layouts (XML files), sounds, and strings. Let's take a closer look.

Expand the layout folder and you will see a layout file named activity_main.xml, and if you open it to view its contents, you will see it is much like the one we edited in the previous chapter. There is less in it this time because we generated an **Empty Activity** project. It is not entirely empty as it still holds a ConstraintLayout element, wrapping a TextView widget that says Hello World!.

Be sure to look at the contents, but this is not the most interesting thing here. Look closely at the name of the file (without the XML file extension): activity_main.

Now, think back to the Java code in the MainActivity.java file. Here is the line of code that we said sets up the UI. I have highlighted a portion of the code:

```
setContentView(R.layout.activity_main);
```

The R.layout.activity_main code is indeed a reference to the activity_main file within the res/layout file. This is the connection between our Java code and our XML layout/design.

> **Note**
>
> There is a difference from the first project other than the contents of `activity_main.xml`—in the `layout` folder of the first project, there were multiple additional files. Later in this chapter, we will build another project using the same template we used in the first chapter (**Basic Activity**) to understand why.

Before that, let's explore the final two folders and all their sub-folders, starting with the next in the list: `mipmap`.

The res/mipmap folder

The `mipmap` folder is straightforward—well, fairly. Expand the folder to see its contents, as illustrated in the following screenshot:

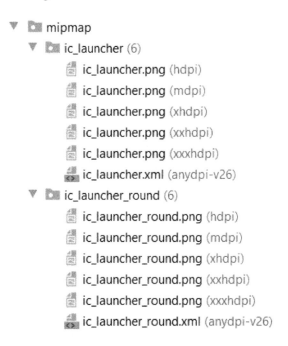

Figure 3.9 – mipmap folder

Here, we can see two sub-folders: `ic_launcher` and `ic_launcher_round`. The contents of `ic_launcher` are graphics for the regular launcher icon we see in the app drawer/home screen of the device, and `ic_launcher_round` contains graphics for devices that use round icons. Double-click on one of the `.png` files from each folder to have a look. I have Photoshopped one of each side by side in this next screenshot to aid our discussion:

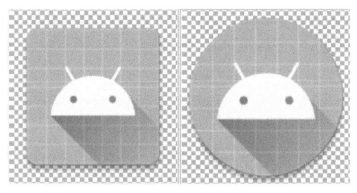

Figure 3.10 – Launcher icons

You are probably also wondering why there are five ic_launcher….png files in each folder. The reason for this is it is good practice to provide icons suitably scaled for different screen sizes and resolutions. By providing an image with the hdpi, mdpi, xhdpi, xxhdpi, and xxxhdpi qualifications, this allows different Android devices to choose an icon that will look best for the user.

> **Note**
>
> The letters dpi stand for **dots per inch**, and the h, m, xh, xxh, and xxxh prefixes stand for high, medium, extra high, extra extra high, and so on. These are known as **qualifiers**, and we will see as we progress that Android has lots of qualifiers that help us build our apps to suit the wide range of different Android devices.

The final conundrum of the mipmap folder is that there is also an XML file in each of the two sub-folders. Open one of them up and you will see that they refer to the ic_launcher_foreground and ic_launcher_background files that we looked at in the drawable folder. This tells the Android device where to get details of the adaptive icons. These files are not required but they make the icons look better, as well as adding flexibility to their appearance.

We have one more folder and all its files, and then we will understand the structure of an Android app well.

The res/values folder

Open the res/values folder to reveal three files that we will talk about briefly in turn. All these files interlink/refer to each other and/or other files that we have seen already.

For the sake of completeness, here is a screenshot of the three files in the `res/values` folder:

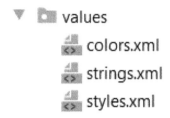

Figure 3.11 – res/values folder

> **Note**
> There is also a `themes` folder inside the `values` folder, but we do not need to explore this in the context of this book.

The key to understanding is not in memorizing the connections, and certainly not trying to memorize or even understand the code in the files, but rather to get an appreciation of the interlinked nature of all the files and code we have seen so far.

Let's glance inside the files one at a time.

The colors.xml file

We'll look next at the contents of the `colors.xml` file, as follows:

```xml
<?xml version="1.0" encoding="utf-8"?>
<resources>
    <color name="colorPrimary">#6200EE</color>
    <color name="colorPrimaryDark">#3700B3</color>
    <color name="colorAccent">#03DAC5</color>
</resources>
```

Notice that the starting and closing tags take the usual pattern we have come to expect from XML files. There is an opening `<resources>` tag and a closing `</resources>` tag. As children of resources, there are three pairs of `<color>` ... `</color>` tags.

Within each `color` tag is a `name` attribute and curious-looking code, consisting of numbers and letters. The `name` attribute is the name of a color. We will see in another of the files that follow that various names are referred to.

The code is what defines an actual color itself. Therefore, when the name is referred to, the color defined by the related code is what is produced on the screen. We will see where these names are referred to in a moment.

> **Note**
>
> The code is called **hexadecimal** code because in each position of the code, the values 0 through 9 and a through f can be used, giving 16 possible values. If you want to find out more and play around with hex colors, visit `http://www.color-hex.com/color-wheel/`. If you are intrigued about number bases such as hexadecimal (base 16), binary (base 2), and others, then look at the following article that explains them and talks about why humans typically use base 10: `https://betterexplained.com/articles/numbers-and-bases/`. You do not need to explore these articles to proceed with the book.

The strings.xml file

Most modern apps are made for as wide an audience as possible. Furthermore, if an app is of a significant size or complexity, then roles in a software company are often divided up into many different teams—for example, the person writing the Java code for an Android app very possibly had little to do with designing the layout of the UI.

By separating the content of the app from the programming of the app it is easier to make changes at any time, and it is also possible to create content for multiple different spoken languages without altering the Java code for each.

Look at the content of the `strings.xml` file, reproduced next:

```
<resources>
    <string name="app_name">Empty Activity App</string>
</resources>
```

We can see that within the now-familiar `<resources>`...`</resources>` tags, we have a `<string>`...`</string>` tag. Within the `string` tag, there is an attribute called `name` with an `app_name` value, and then a further value of `Empty Activity App`.

Let's look at one more line from the `AndroidManifest.xml` file we explored earlier in the *The manifests folder* section. The line in question follows next, but refer to the file itself in Android Studio if you want to see the line in its full context:

```
android:label="@string/app_name"
```

The `android:label` attribute is being assigned a value of `@string/app_name`. In Android, `@string` refers to all the strings in the `strings.xml` file. In this specific app, the `string` attribute with the `app_name` label has an `Empty Activity App` value.

Therefore, the line of code in the `AndroidManifest.xml` file shown previously has the following effect on the screen when the app is running:

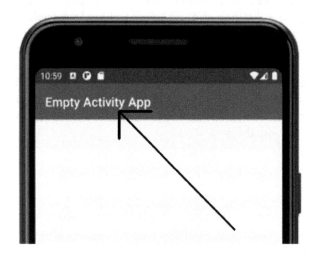

Figure 3.12 – AndroidManifest.xml file effect

Although at first this system might seem convoluted, in practice it separates design and content from the coding, which is very efficient to do. If the designers of an app want to change its name, they simply edit the `strings.xml` file, with no need to interact with the Java programmers; and if all text in an app is provided as a string resource, then all of it can be easily altered and adapted as the project proceeds.

Android takes this flexibility further by allowing developers to use different files for string resources for each language/locale. This means that a developer can cater to a planet full of happy users with exactly the same Java code. A Java programmer just needs to refer to the `name` attribute of a string resource instead of **hardcoding** the text itself into the Java, and then other departments can design the text content and handle tasks such as language translation. We will make an app multilingual in *Chapter 18, Localization*.

> **Note**
>
> It is possible to hardcode the actual text directly into the Java code instead of using string resources, and from time to time we will do so for the sake of easily showing some Java without getting bogged down with editing or adding to the `strings.xml` file. We did this in the previous chapter when we made toast messages and output text to the console.

The Android system allows designers to choose a selection of colors, text, images, sound, and other resources as well, and easily produce a variation of their app for different regions of the world.

For example, in Western culture, green can represent themes such as nature and correctness; and in many Middle Eastern countries, green represents fertility and is the color associated with Islam. While you might just about get away with distributing green in both these regions, your app will be perceived very differently.

If you then roll your app out into Indonesia, green is culturally despised among many (although not all) Indonesians. Next, you launch in China, and green has potential negative connotations to do with unfaithful spouses. It is a minefield that a typical Java programmer will never learn to navigate—and fortunately, because of the way we can divide up responsibilities in Android Studio, they don't need to learn about this.

Colors—and, therefore, styles and themes—is a very specialized topic. While we won't be exploring any more deeply than that quick foray into green, hopefully you see the benefit of a system that separates responsibility for programming, layout, color, and textual content.

It is also worth mentioning that it is entirely possible to produce a fantastic app that is enjoyed by thousands—or even millions—of users without catering individually to every region. However, even if we are not going to employ teams of designers, translators, and cultural experts, we still must work within this system that was designed to enable them, and that is why we are going into such depth.

At this stage, we have a good grasp of what goes into an Android project and how the different aspects link together. Let's build one more app, not to go into it in the same detail but to see the differences that different app templates make to the underlying files that Android Studio generates.

Exploring the file and folder structure of the Basic Activity project template

The next-simplest project type with an autogenerated UI is a **Basic Activity** project. This is the same type of project that we created in *Chapter 1, Beginning Android and Java*. Feel free to open that project up now, but it is just as quick to generate a new one, and we can then also examine it without any of our alterations and additions clouding the discussions.

Proceed as follows:

1. Run Android Studio and left-click the **Start a new Android Studio project** option.

2. The window that follows is the **Select a Project Template** window. Select **Basic Activity** and click **Next**.

3. In the **Configure Your Project** window, set up the project as follows:

Option	Value entered
Name:	Basic Activity App
Package name:	`com.gamecodeschool.` `basicactivityapp`
Save location:	`D:\Android\Projects\` `BasicActivityApp`
Language:	Java
Minimum SDK:	Leave this and any other options at their default settings

4. Click the **Finish** button, and we will run the app to see what we have achieved.

Now, we can dig into the files. We won't look at everything in the same detail that we did for the **Empty Activity** project; instead, we will just look at the interconnectedness of the files and make a few comparisons.

Exploring a Basic Activity project

Let's look at the Java code first in the `MainActivity.java` tab in the code editor. As already stated, a **Basic Activity** project has more to it than an **Empty Activity** project.

> **Note**
> You can open as many instances of Android Studio as you like. If you want to compare projects side by side, select **File | Open** then choose the project, and when prompted select **New Window** to open the project, without closing any projects that are already open.

The first thing to note is that there is some extra code in the `onCreate` method.

The MainActivity.java file

I mentioned very briefly back in *Chapter 2, First Contact: Java, XML, and the UI Designer,* these interconnections in the Java code and the XML code. Let's look through the resource files and point out the XML files that this Java code points to.

Here is the Java code shown next. I have slightly reformatted it to make it more readable in a book:

```
Toolbar toolbar = (Toolbar) findViewById(R.id.toolbar);
setSupportActionBar(toolbar);


FloatingActionButton fab = findViewById(R.id.fab);
fab.setOnClickListener(new View.OnClickListener() {
    @Override
    public void onClick(View view) {
        Snackbar.make(view, "Replace with your own
            action", Snackbar.LENGTH_LONG)
                        .setAction("Action", null).show();
    }
});
```

To understand this code fully will take quite a few more chapters, but to point out where this code uses files in the resources will only take a moment and will then leave us even more aware of the components that make up our projects.

The code refers to two resources. The first is a `Toolbar` resource and is referred to via `R.id.toolbar`. The second is a `FloatingActionBar` resource and refers to the XML files we will see soon via `R.id.fab`.

If we open the `res/layout` folder and the `java` folder in the project window, we can see that things look different from how they did in the **Empty Activity** project, as illustrated in the following screenshot:

Figure 3.13 – res/layout folder and java folder

There are now three Java files that were autogenerated, and four XML layout files that were autogenerated.

Remember that this app has two screens—a first screen with a **Hello first fragment** message and a **Next** button; and a second screen, which simply had a **Previous** button.

What is happening is that Android Studio is not only providing separate layout files for the appearance of each screen, but it is also providing separate Java files for the code that controls each screen. If you take what I just said at face value, you would, therefore, expect two layout files and two Java files, but we have more.

As we already know, when the app is run by the user, the `onCreate` method of the `MainActivity.java` file is executed. This sets up the app, including the layout. The layout is in `activity_main.xml` but this file no longer controls the layout of the two main screens. It has elements that are consistent between both screens and delegates the layout to `content_main.xml`. The `content_main.xml` file then defines an area of the screen that it occupies and delegates the details that will appear in this area to yet another file, the `nav_graph.xml` file in the `res/navigation` folder. This `nav_graph.xml` file then determines which layout to use (`fragment_first.xml` or `fragment_second.xml`) and which corresponding Java file will control the layout (`FirstFragment.java` or `SecondFragment.java`).

At this stage, the apparent convolution might be overwhelming. It is my guess that this is one of the things could make learning Android development without any previous development experience so challenging. But the good news is this:

- We don't need to remember and understand the details of all this interconnectedness.

- We can build loads of apps without using any of it.

- As we progress through the book and work with the different pieces of this puzzle, we will become familiar with them a piece at a time.

Take a look at this next figure, which shows how the **Basic Activity** template app works:

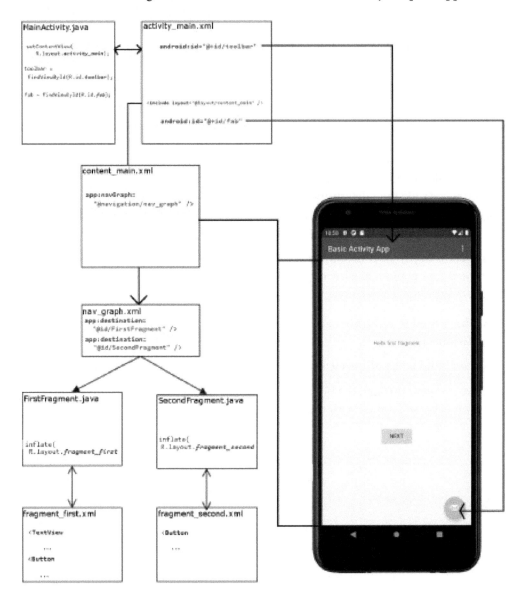

Figure 3.14 – Basic Activity template

If the apparent complexity seems frustrating, then understanding why it is done like this might help. We have already talked about separating layouts from programming and further separating out text and graphics, to allow different teams to work on different aspects of an app. Well, now, we can further separate out not just navigation between different screens of our app—say, the main menu screen, the settings screen, and some other screen—but as the layouts and programming associated with each of these screens are separate, they too can be worked on simultaneously by separate teams. More on this as we progress through the chapters.

We will look into coding separate fragment layouts and separate Java code that controls each of them, as well as learning more about why we want to do it like this, from *Chapter 24, Design Patterns, Multiple Layouts, and Fragments,* onward, and we will be digging deeper into interconnected layout files such as `activity_main.xml` and `content_main.xml` in the next chapter.

For now, let's look a little deeper at how the `MainActivity.java` file code links up with the `activity_main.xml` layout. We will see that although the `activity_main.xml` file is responsible for placing the toolbar and the floating action button, the `MainActivity.java` file is responsible for controlling what happens when the user interacts with them.

The activity_main.xml file

For now, open up the `activity_main.xml` file, and you will see that there are some elements to represent both `toolbar` and `fab`. The Java code referring to these elements is setting up the toolbar and the floating action bar ready for use. The XML code, as we have come to expect, describes what they look like.

Here is the XML code for the toolbar:

```
<androidx.appcompat.widget.Toolbar
    android:id="@+id/toolbar"
    android:layout_width="match_parent"
    android:layout_height="?attr/actionBarSize"
    android:background="?attr/colorPrimary"
    app:popupTheme="@style/AppTheme.PopupOverlay" />
```

Notice that it refers to a toolbar, a color, and a style, as well as some other aspects.

For clarity, this is the toolbar in the actual working app:

Figure 3.15 – Toolbar of the app

Here is the XML code for the floating action button. I have slightly reformatted the first line of the code onto two lines so that it displays better in the printed version of this book:

```
<com.google.android.material.floatingactionbutton.
FloatingActionButton

    android:id="@+id/fab"
    android:layout_width="wrap_content"
    android:layout_height="wrap_content"
    android:layout_gravity="bottom|end"
    android:layout_margin="@dimen/fab_margin"
    app:srcCompat="@android:drawable/ic_dialog_email" />
```

Notice it has an id value of fab. It is through this id value that we gain access to the floating action button in our Java code—specifically, this line in MainActivity.java:

```
FloatingActionButton fab = findViewById(R.id.fab);
```

After this line of code executes, the fab object in our Java code can now directly control the floating action button and all its attributes. In *Chapter 13, Anonymous Classes – Bringing Android Widgets to Life*, we will learn how to do this in detail.

Here is the floating action button in the actual app:

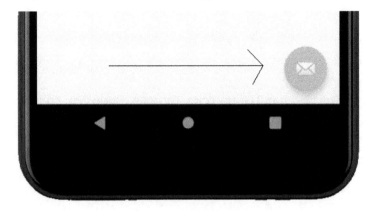

Figure 3.16 – Floating action button

I haven't explained the code in detail, as there is no point at this stage. Just start to make a mental note of the interconnections, outlined here:

- XML files can refer to other XML files.

- Java can refer to XML files (and, as we will see soon, other Java files).

- And now, we have seen that in Java we can grab control of a specific part of the UI in an XML file via its id attribute.

We have seen enough from this file, so let's move on and dip into the remaining files.

The extra methods in MainActivity.java

So, what do the methods do and when are they called, and by whom? The next difference is this extra method (again, slightly reformatted for presentation):

```java
@Override
public boolean onCreateOptionsMenu(Menu menu) {
    // Inflate the menu; this adds items to the
    // action bar if it is present.
    getMenuInflater().inflate(R.menu.menu_main, menu);
    return true;
}
```

This code prepares (inflates) the menu that is defined in the menu_main.xml file, and just as with the onCreate method, the onCreateOptionsMenu method is an overridden method and is called by the operating system directly.

Then, there is yet another method, shown next:

```
@Override
public boolean onOptionsItemSelected(MenuItem item) {
    // Handle action bar item clicks here. The action bar
       will
    // automatically handle clicks on the Home/Up button, so
       long
    // as you specify a parent activity in
       AndroidManifest.xml.
    int id = item.getItemId();


    //noinspection SimplifiableIfStatement
    if (id == R.id.action_settings) {
        return true;
    }


    return super.onOptionsItemSelected(item);
}
```

This method is overridden as well, and it too is called directly by the operating system. It handles what happens when an item (option) from the menu is selected by a user. At the moment, it handles just one option—the settings option—and currently, it takes no action, as can be seen here:

```
The code if (id == R.id.action_settings) {
```

This determines whether any options from the **Settings** menu were clicked, and if they were, the `return true` code executes, and control is returned to whatever part of the app was executing before it was interrupted by a user clicking the **Settings** menu option.

We know nearly enough for now. Don't worry about memorizing all these connections. We will be coming back to each connection, investigating more deeply, and cementing our understanding of each.

Now, we can take a closer look at the Android emulator.

Exploring the Android emulator

As we progress, it helps to be familiar with exactly how to use the Android emulator. If you haven't used the latest version of Android, some of the ways even simple tasks are executed (such as viewing all the apps) can be different from how your current device works. In addition, we want to know how to use the extra controls that come with all emulators.

Emulator control panel

You probably noticed the mini control panel that appears beside the emulator when you run it. Let's go through some of the most useful controls. Look at this screenshot of the emulator control panel. I have annotated it to aid discussion of it:

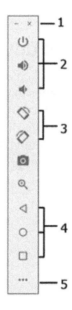

Figure 3.17 – Emulator control panel

I will just mention the more obvious controls as follows, and go into a bit more depth when necessary:

1. These are the window controls. Minimize or close the emulator window.

2. From top to bottom, power off the emulator, simulating powering off the actual device. The next two icons raise and lower the volume.

3. These two buttons allow you to rotate the emulator left and right. This means you can test what your app looks like in all orientations, as well as how it handles orientation changes while the app is running. The icons immediately below these take a screenshot and zoom in, respectively.

4. These icons simulate the back button and home button, and viewing running apps. Have a play with these buttons as we will need to use them from time to time, including in *Chapter 6, The Android Lifecycle*.

5. Press this button to launch the **Advanced Settings** menu, where you can interact with things such as sensors, the **Global Positioning System** (**GPS**), the battery, the fingerprint reader, and more. Have a play around with some of these settings if you are curious.

Let's have a play with the emulator itself.

Using the emulator as a real device

The emulator can emulate every feature of a real phone, so it would be possible to write a whole book on using it. If you want to write apps that your users love, then understanding a whole range of Android devices is well worth taking the time to do. I just want to point out a few of the most basic features here, because without these basic interactions it will be hard to follow along with the book. Furthermore, if you have an older Android device, then some essential basics (such as accessing the app drawer) have changed and you might be left a little baffled.

Accessing the app drawer

Hold the mouse cursor on the bottom of the home screen and drag upward to access the app drawer (all the apps). The following screenshot shows this action halfway through:

Figure 3.18 – Drag upwards to access app drawer

Now, you can run any app installed on the emulator. Note that when you run one of your apps through Android Studio, it remains installed on the emulator and is therefore runnable from the app drawer. However, every change you make to the app in Android Studio will require you to run/install the app again by clicking the play button on the Android Studio quick launch bar—as we have been doing.

Viewing active apps and switching between apps

To view active apps, you can use the emulator control panel, the square labeled as number **4** on the screenshot of the emulator control panel (*Figure 3.17*). To access the same option using the phone screen (as you would have to do on a real device), swipe up, just as when accessing the app drawer, but do so only for about one quarter the length of the screen. This process is illustrated in the following screenshot:

Figure 3.19 – Swipe up

You can now swipe left and right through recent apps, swipe an app up to close it, or tap the back button to return to what you were doing before you viewed this option. Do try this out as we will use these basic features quite often.

Summary

Remember that the goal of this chapter was familiarization with the system/structure of Android/an Android project? Android projects are a sometimes-complex interweaving of Java and a multitude of resource files. Resource files can contain XML to describe our layouts, textual content, styles, and colors, as well as images. Resources can be produced to target different languages and regions of the world. Other resource types that we will see and use throughout the book include themes and sound effects.

It is not important to remember all the different ways in which different resource files and Java files are interconnected. It is only important to realize that they are, and be able to examine files of various types and realize when they are dependent on code in another file. Whenever we create connections from our Java code to the XML code, I will always point out details of the connection again.

We do not need to learn XML as well as Java, but we will become a little bit familiar with it. Java will be the focus of this book but our Java will frequently refer to the XML code, so understanding and having seen some examples of the interconnections will stand you in good stead to make faster progress.

We have also explored the emulator to get the most out of it when testing our apps.

In the next chapter, we will build two custom layouts using two different Android layout schemes. We will also write some Java code so that we can switch between them with the tap of a button.

4
Getting Started with Layouts and Material Design

We have already seen the Android Studio **user interface** (**UI**) designer, as well as Java, in action. In this hands-on chapter, we will build three more layouts—still quite simple, yet a step up from what we have done so far.

Before we get to the hands-on part, we will have a quick introduction to the concept of **Material Design**.

We will see another type of layout called `LinearLayout`, and step through using it to create a usable UI. We will take things a step further using `ConstraintLayout`, both with understanding constraints and with designing more complex and precise UI designs. Finally, we will meet `TableLayout`, for laying out data in an easily readable table.

We will also write some Java code to switch between different layouts within our app/project. This is the first major app that links together multiple topics into one neat parcel. The app is called **Exploring Layouts**.

In this chapter, we will look at the following topics:

- Finding out about Material Design

- Exploring Android UI design

- Introducing layouts

- Building a `LinearLayout` and learning when it is best to use this type of layout

- Building another, slightly more advanced `ConstraintLayout` and finding out a bit more about using constraints

- Building a `TableLayout` and filling it with data to display

- Linking everything together in one app called **Exploring Layouts**

First on the list is Material Design.

Technical requirements

You can find the code present in this chapter on GitHub at `https://github.com/PacktPublishing/Android-Programming-for-Beginners-Third-Edition/tree/main/chapter%2004`.

Finding out about Material Design

You might have heard of Material Design, but what exactly is it? The objective of Material Design is quite simple—to create beautiful UIs. It is also, however, about making these UIs consistent across Android devices. Material Design is not a new idea; it is taken straight from the design principles used in pen-and-paper design, such as having visually pleasing embellishments through shadows and depth.

Material Design uses the concept of layers of materials, which you can think of in the same way you would think of layers in a photo-editing app. Consistency is achieved with a set of principles, rules, and guidelines. It must be stressed that Material Design is entirely optional, but it also must be stressed that Material Design works—and if you are not following it, there is a good chance your design will be less appreciated by the user. The user has after all become used to a certain type of UI, and that UI was most likely created using Material Design principles.

Material Design is a sensible standard to strive for, but while we are learning the details of it, we mustn't let that hold us back from learning how to get started with Android.

This book will focus on getting things done, while occasionally pointing out when Material Design has influenced the design, how it has influenced the design, and further resources for those who want to look at Material Design in more depth.

Exploring Android UI design

We will see with Android UI design that so much of what we learn is context-sensitive. The way that a given widget's *x* attribute will influence its appearance might depend on a widget's *y* attribute or even on an attribute on another widget. It isn't easy to learn this verbatim. It is best to expect to gradually get better and faster results with practice.

For example, if you play with the designer by dragging and dropping widgets onto the design, the **Extensible Markup Language** (**XML**) code that is generated will vary quite considerably, depending upon which layout type you are using. We will see this as we go ahead throughout this chapter.

This is because different layout types use different means to decide the position of their children—for example, the LinearLayout we will explore next works very differently from the ConstraintLayout that was added by default to our project in *Chapter 1, Beginning Android and Java*.

This information might initially seem to be a problem, or even a bad idea, and it certainly is a little awkward at first. What we will grow to learn, however, is that this clear abundance of layout options and their individual quirks is a good thing because they give us almost unlimited design potential. There are very few layouts you can imagine that are not possible to achieve.

This almost unlimited potential comes with a bit of complexity, however. The best way to start to get to grips with this is to build some working examples of several types. In this chapter, we will see three types of layouts, outlined as follows:

- LinearLayout
- ConstraintLayout
- TableLayout

We will see how to make things easier using the distinctive features of the visual designer, and we will also pay some attention to the XML that is autogenerated, to make our understanding more rounded.

Introducing layouts

We have already seen ConstraintLayout in *Chapter 1, Beginning Android and Java*, but there are more layouts than this. Layouts are the building blocks that group together the other UI elements. Layouts can also contain other layouts.

Let's look at some commonly used layouts in Android, because knowing the different layouts and their pros and cons will make us more aware of what can be achieved and will therefore expand our horizons in terms of what is possible.

We have already seen that once we have designed a layout, we can put it into action with the setContentView method in our Java code.

Let's build three designs with different layout types, and then put setContentView to work and switch between them.

Creating and exploring a layout project

One of the toughest things in Android is not just finding out *how to do something* but finding out *how to do something in a particular context*. That is why throughout this book, as well as showing you how to do some neat stuff, we will link lots of topics together into apps that span multiple topics and, often, chapters. The **Exploring Layouts** project is the first app of this type. We will learn how to build multiple types of layout while linking them all together in one handy app.

Let's get started, as follows:

1. Create a new project in Android Studio. If you already have a project open, select **File | New Project**. When prompted, choose **Open in same window** as we do not need to refer to our previous project.

    > **Important note**
    >
    > If you are on the start screen of Android Studio, you can create a new project simply by clicking the **Create new project** option.

2. Make sure to select the **Empty Activity** project template, as we will build most of the UI from scratch. Click the **Next** button.

3. Enter Exploring Layouts for the application name and then click the **Finish** button.

Look at the `MainActivity.java` file. Here is the code, excluding the `import...` statements:

```java
public class MainActivity extends AppCompatActivity {

    @Override
    protected void onCreate(Bundle savedInstanceState) {
        super.onCreate(savedInstanceState);

        setContentView(R.layout.activity_main);
    }
}
```

Locate the call to the `setContentView` method and delete the entire line. The line is shown highlighted in the previous code snippet.

This is just what we want because now, we can build our very own layouts, explore the underlying XML, and write our own Java code to display these layouts. If you run the app now, you will just get a blank screen with a title; not even a Hello World! message.

The first type of layout we will explore is the `LinearLayout` type.

Building a layout with LinearLayout

`LinearLayout` is probably the simplest layout that Android offers. As the name hints at, all the UI items within it are laid out linearly. You have just two choices: vertical and horizontal. By adding the following line of code (or editing via the **Attribute** window) you can configure a `LinearLayout` to lay things out vertically:

```
android:orientation="vertical"
```

You can then (as you could probably have guessed) change `"vertical"` to `"horizontal"` to lay things out horizontally.

Before we can do anything with `LinearLayout`, we need to add one to a layout file; and as we are building three layouts in this project, we also need a new layout file.

Adding a LinearLayout layout type to a project

In the project window, expand the `res` folder. Now, right-click the `layout` folder and select **New**. Notice there is an option for **Layout resource file**, as shown in the following screenshot:

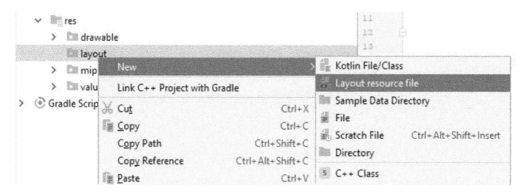

Figure 4.1 – Adding LinearLayout to project

Select **Layout resource file** and you will see the **New Resource File** dialog window. In the **Root element:** field, enter `LinearLayout`, as illustrated in the following screenshot:

Figure 4.2 – Creating new resource file

In the **File name:** field, enter main_menu. The name is arbitrary, but this layout is going to be our main menu that is used to select the other layouts, so the name seems appropriate.

Click the **OK** button, and Android Studio will generate a new LinearLayout in an XML file called main_menu and place it in the layout folder, ready for us to build our new main menu UI. The new file is automatically opened in the editor, ready for us to get designing.

Preparing your workspace

Click the **Design** tab to switch to design view if you are not already in this view. Adjust the windows by dragging and resizing their borders (as you can in most windowed apps) to make the palette, design, and attributes as clear as possible but no bigger than necessary. The following screenshot shows the approximate window proportions I chose to make designing our UI and exploring the XML as clear as possible. The detail in the screenshot is not important:

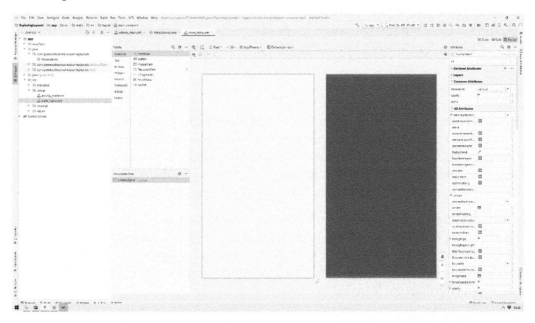

Figure 4.3 – Preparing workspace

> **Important note**
>
> I have made the project, palette, and attribute windows as narrow as possible yet without obscuring any content. I have also closed the Build/logcat window at the bottom of the screen, the result being that I have a nice clear canvas on which to build the UI.

Examining the generated XML

Click on the **Code** tab, and we will have a look at the current state of the XML code that forms our design at this stage. Here is the code so that we can talk about it (I have reformatted it slightly to make it appear more clearly on the page):

```xml
<?xml version="1.0" encoding="utf-8"?>
<LinearLayout
xmlns:android="http://schemas.android.com/apk/res/android"

android:orientation="vertical"
android:layout_width="match_parent"
    android:layout_height="match_parent">

</LinearLayout>
```

We have the usual starting and closing tags and, as we could have predicted, they are called `<LinearLayout` and `</LinearLayout>`. There is no child element yet, but there are three attributes. We know they are attributes and not children of the `LinearLayout` because they appear before the first closing `>`. The three attributes that define this `LinearLayout` have been highlighted in the previous code for clarity.

The first attribute is `android:orientation`, or—more succinctly—we will just refer to the attributes without the `android:` part. The `orientation` attribute has a value of `vertical`. This means that when we start to add items to this layout, it will arrange them vertically from top to bottom. We could change the `vertical` value to `horizontal`, and it would lay things out from left to right.

The next two attributes are `layout_width` and `layout_height`. These determine the size of the `LinearLayout`. The value given to both attributes is `match_parent`. The parent of a layout is the entire available space. By matching the parent horizontally and vertically, the layout will fill the entire space available.

Adding a TextView to the UI

Switch back to the **Design** tab, and we will add some elements to the UI.

First, find the TextView widget in the palette. This can be found in both the **Common** and **Text** categories. Left-click and drag the TextView onto the UI, and notice that it sits neatly at the top of the LinearLayout.

Look at the XML on the **Code** tab and confirm that it is a child of the LinearLayout and that it is indented by one tab to make this clear. Here is the code for the TextView widget, without the surrounding code for the LinearLayout:

```
<TextView
    android:id="@+id/textView"
    android:layout_width="match_parent"
    android:layout_height="wrap_content"
    android:text="TextView" />
```

Notice it has four attributes: an id attribute, in case we need to refer to it from another UI element or from our Java code; a layout_width attribute set to match_parent, which means the TextView stretches across the whole width of the LinearLayout; and a layout_height attribute set to wrap_content, which means the TextView is precisely tall enough to contain the text within it. Finally, for now, it has a text element, which determines the actual text it will display, and this is currently set to just "TextView".

Switch back to the **Design** tab, and we will make some changes.

We want this text to be the heading text of this screen, which is the menu screen. In the **Attributes** window, click the **search** icon and type text into the search box, as shown in the following screenshot. Find the text attribute and change its value to Menu:

Figure 4.4 – Adding TextView to UI

Tip

You can find any attribute by searching or just by scrolling through the options. When you have found the attribute you want to edit, left-click it to select it and then press the *Enter* key on the keyboard to make it editable.

Next, find the textSize attribute using your preferred search technique, and set textSize to 50sp. When you have entered this new value, the text size will increase.

Important note

The sp value stands for **scalable pixels**. This means that when the user changes the font-size settings on their Android device, the font will dynamically rescale itself.

Now, search for the gravity attribute and expand the options by clicking the little arrow indicated in the following screenshot:

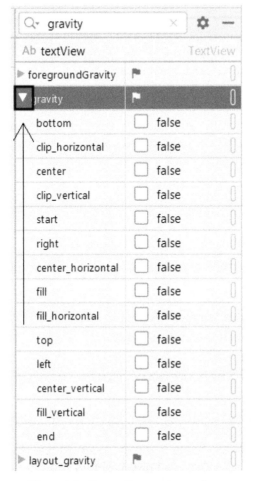

Figure 4.5 – Expanding gravity attribute

Add center_horizontal to the gravity by setting that value to **true**, as illustrated in the following screenshot:

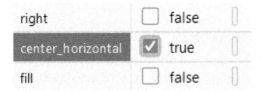

Figure 4.6 – Adding center_horizontal to gravity by setting the value to true

The gravity attribute refers to the gravity within the TextView itself, and our change has the effect of moving the actual text inside the TextView to the center.

> **Important note**
>
> The gravity attribute is different from the layout_gravity attribute. The layout_gravity attribute sets the gravity within the layout—in this case, the parent LinearLayout. We will use layout_gravity later in this project.

At this point, we have changed the text of the TextView widget, increased its size, and centered it horizontally. The UI designer should now look like this:

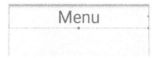

Figure 4.7 – Adjusting textView on the UI

A quick glance at the **Code** tab to see the XML would reveal the following code:

```
<TextView
    android:id="@+id/textView"
    android:layout_width="match_parent"
    android:layout_height="wrap_content"
    android:gravity="center_horizontal"
    android:text="Menu"
    android:textSize="50sp" />
```

You can see the new attributes as follows: gravity, which is set to center_horizontal; text, which has been changed to Menu; and textSize, which is set to 50sp.

If you run the app, you might not see what you expected. This is because we haven't called the setContentView method in our Java code to load the UI. You will still see the blank UI. We will fix this once we have made a bit more progress with our design.

Adding a multiline TextView to the UI

Switch back to the **Design** tab and find **Multiline Text** from the **Text** category of the palette, and drag it onto the design just below the TextView widget we added a moment ago.

Using your preferred search technique, set the `text` attribute to the following: `Select a layout type to view an example. The onClick attribute of each button will call a method which executes setContentView to load the new layout.`

Now, your layout will look like this:

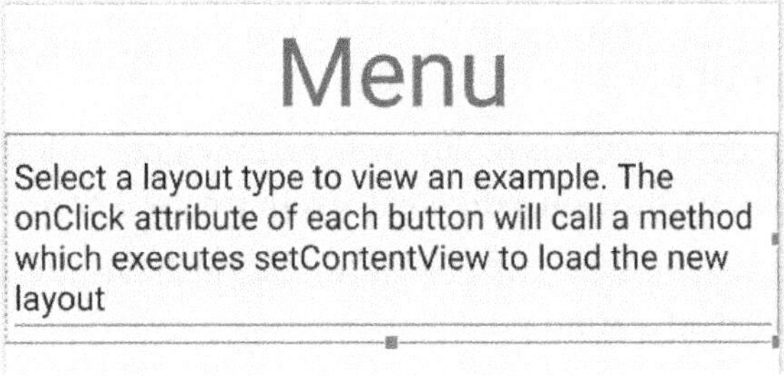

Menu

Select a layout type to view an example. The
onClick attribute of each button will call a method
which executes setContentView to load the new
layout

Figure 4.8 – Multiline textView added to UI

Your XML will be updated with another child in the `LinearLayout` (after the `TextView`) that looks like this (I have slightly reformatted it for presenting it on the page):

```
<EditText
    android:id="@+id/editTextTextMultiLine"
    android:layout_width="match_parent"
    android:layout_height="wrap_content"
    android:ems="10"
    android:gravity="start|top"
    android:inputType="textMultiLine"
    android:text="Select a layout type to view an example.
        The onClick attribute of each button will call a
        method which executes setContentView to load the
        new layout" />
```

You can see the details of the UI item. A look at the XML reveals we have an `inputType` attribute, indicating that this text is editable. There is also another attribute that we haven't seen before, and that is `ems`. The `ems` attribute controls how many characters can be entered per line, and the value of 10 was chosen automatically by Android Studio. However, another attribute, `layout_width="match_parent"`, overrides this value because it causes the element to expand to fit its parent— that is, the whole width of the screen.

When you run the app in the next section, you will see the text is indeed editable, although for the purposes of this demo app it serves no practical purpose.

Wiring up the UI with the Java code (Part 1)

To achieve an interactive app, we will do the following three things:

1. We will call the setContentView method from the onCreate method to show the progress of our UI when we run the app.

2. We will write two more methods of our own, and each one will call the setContentView method on a different layout (that we have yet to design).

3. Then, later in this chapter when we design two more UI layouts, we will be able to load them at the click of a button.

As we will be building a ConstraintLayout and a TableLayout, we will call our new methods loadConstraintLayout and loadTableLayout, respectively.

Let's do that now, and then we can see how we can add some buttons that call these methods.

Switch to the MainActivity.java file, then inside the onCreate method add the following highlighted code:

```java
@Override
protected void onCreate(Bundle savedInstanceState) {
    super.onCreate(savedInstanceState);

    setContentView(R.layout.main_menu);
}
```

The code uses the setContentView method to load the UI we are currently working on. You can now run the app to see the following result:

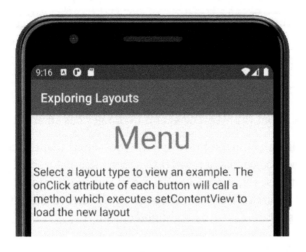

Figure 4.9 –Exploring Layouts menu

Add these two new methods inside the `MainActivity` class after the `onCreate` method, as follows:

```
public void loadConstraintLayout(View v){
    setContentView(R.layout.activity_main);
}


public void loadTableLayout(View v){
    setContentView(R.layout.my_table_layout);
}
```

There is one error with the first method and two errors with the second. The first error we can fix by adding an `import` statement so that Android Studio is aware of the `View` class. Left-click the word `View` to select the error. Hold down the *Alt* key and then tap the *Enter* key. You will see the following messages pop up:

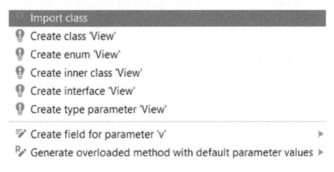

Figure 4.10 – Selecting Import class to eliminate the error

Choose **Import class**. The error is gone. If you scroll to the top of the code, you will see that a new line of code has been added by that shortcut we just performed. Here is the new code:

```
import android.view.View;
```

Android Studio knows about the `View` class and no longer has an error.

The second method still has an error, however. The problem is that the code calls the `setContentView` method to load a new UI (`R.layout.my_table_layout`). As this UI layout does not exist yet, it produces an error. You can comment out this call to remove the error until we create the file and design the UI layout later in this chapter. Add the comment forward slashes (`//`), as highlighted next:

```
public void loadConstraintLayout(View v){
    setContentView(R.layout.activity_main);
}

public void loadTableLayout(View v){
    // setContentView(R.layout.my_table_layout);
}
```

The reason why the `loadConstraintLayout` method does not have an error is because that method loads the `activity_main.xml` layout, which was created by Android Studio when we generated the project.

Now, we want to add some buttons we can click to call our new methods and load the new layouts we will be building. But adding a couple of buttons with some text on is too easy—we have done that before. What we want to do is line up some text with a button to the right of it. The problem is our `LinearLayout` has the `orientation` attribute set to `vertical` and, as we have seen, all the new parts we add to the layout will be lined up vertically.

Adding layouts within layouts

The solution to laying out some elements with a different orientation from others is to nest layouts within layouts. Here is how to do it.

From the **Layouts** category of the palette, drag a **LinearLayout (Horizontal)** onto our design, placing it just below the **Multiline Text**. Notice in the following screenshot that there is a blue border occupying all the space below the **Multiline Text**:

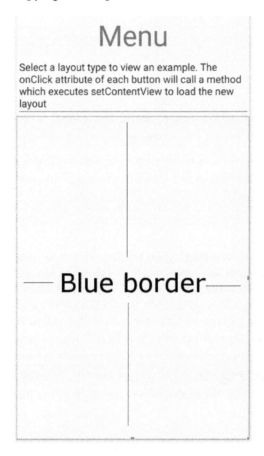

Figure 4.11 – Dragging a LinearLayout (Horizontal) from the Layouts category onto our design and placing it just below the Multiline Text

This indicates that our new **LinearLayout (Horizontal)** is filling the space. Keep this blue border area in mind, as this is where we will put the next item on our UI.

Now, go back to the **Text** category of the palette and drag a `TextView` widget onto the new `LinearLayout` we just added. Notice in the following screenshot how the `TextView` widget sits snuggly in the top left-hand corner of the new `LinearLayout`:

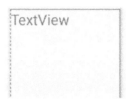

Figure 4.12 – Dragging a TextView widget from the Text category of the palette onto the new LinearLayout

This at first seems no different from what happened with the previous vertical `LinearLayout`, which was part of our UI from the start. But watch what happens when we add our next piece of the UI.

> **Important note**
> The term used to refer to adding layouts within layouts is **nesting**. The Android term applied to any item that appears on the UI (buttons, text, and so on) is **view**, and anything that contains views is a **view group**. As the terms *view* and *view group* do not always make their meanings clear in certain contexts, I will usually refer to parts of the UI either specifically (such as `TextView`, `Button`, `LinearLayout`) or more broadly (UI element, item, or widget).

From the **Button** category, drag a `Button` widget onto the right-hand side of the previous `TextView` widget. Notice that the button sits to the right of the text, as shown here:

Figure 4.13 – Dragging a Button widget from the Button category onto the right-hand side of the previous TextView widget

Next, select the `LinearLayout` (the horizontal one) by clicking on an empty part of it. Find the `layout_height` attribute and set it to `wrap_content`. Notice that the `LinearLayout` is now taking up only as much space as it needs, and there is space below where we can add more widgets. This is shown in the following screenshot:

Figure 4.14 – Selecting the LinearLayout (the horizontal one) by clicking on an empty part

Let's configure the `text` attribute of the `TextView` widget and the `Button` widget before we add the next part of the UI. Change the `text` attribute of the `Button` widget to LOAD. Change the text attribute of our new `TextView` widget to Load `ConstraintLayout`.

This screenshot shows what the layout should look like currently:

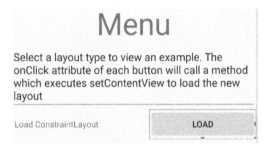

Figure 4.15 – Configuring the text attribute of the TextView widget and the Button widget

---

Tip

Did that work? Yes? Excellent. You are now familiar with editing attributes of Android views. No? Left-click the item you want to edit (in this case, the `TextView` widget), search using the search icon, or scroll to find the attribute you want to edit in the **Attributes** window (in this case, the `text` attribute), select the attribute, and press *Enter* to edit it. I can now give more succinct instructions on how to build future UI projects, and this makes your journey to becoming an Android Ninja much quicker.

Now, we can repeat ourselves and add another TextView widget and Button widget within another **LinearLayout (Horizontal)**, just below the one we have just finished. To do so, follow these steps in order:

1. Add another **LinearLayout (Horizontal)** just below the previous one.

2. Add a **TextView** to the new LinearLayout.

3. Change the text attribute of the TextView to Load TableLayout.

4. Add a Button widget on the right-hand side of the TextView widget.

5. Change the text attribute of the Button widget to LOAD.

6. Resize the LinearLayout by changing the layout_height attribute to wrap_ content.

7. Just for fun and for the sake of exploring the palette a bit more, find the **Widgets** category of the palette and drag a RatingBar widget onto the design, just below the final LinearLayout.

Now, your UI should look like this:

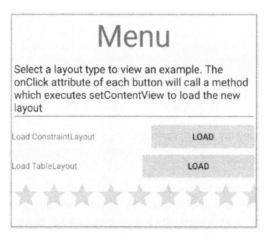

Figure 4.16 – Another TextView widget and Button widget added within another LinearLayout (Horizontal)

Let's add some visual finishing touches to the layout.

Making the layout look pretty

In this section, we will explore some more attributes that control the finer details of our UI. You have probably noticed the UI looks a bit squashed in some places and wonky and unsymmetrical in others. As we progress through the book, we will continually add to our repertoire to improve our layouts, but these short steps will introduce and take care of some of the basics.

Before you get started with the next steps, consider the following tip.

> **Tip**
>
> When you are configuring the attributes of widgets, you can select multiple widgets at a time—for example, in *Step 3* in the instructions that follow, you could left-click to select the first TextView widget and then *Shift* and left-click to select the second TextView widget. You could then alter attributes for both simultaneously. This tip will also work for *Step 4* with the Button widgets. It will even work when the widgets are different types, provided you are only editing attributes that all the selected widgets have. So, in *Step 5* that follows, you can simultaneously select and edit the padding attribute on both TextView and both Button widgets.

Follow these instructions:

1. Select the Multiline Text widget, and find then expand the padding attribute. Set the padding option to 15sp. This has made a neat area of space around the outside of the text.

2. To make a nice space below the Multiline Text widget, find and expand the Layout_Margin attribute and set bottom to 50sp.

3. On both button-aligned TextView widgets, set the textSize attribute to 20sp; layout_gravity to center_vertical; the layout_width attribute to match_parent; and layout_weight to .7.

4. On both buttons, set the weight to .3. Notice how both buttons now take up exactly .3 of the width and the text takes up .7 of the LinearLayout, making the whole appearance more pleasing.

5. On both TextView widgets and both Button widgets, select padding then padding, and set the value to 10dp.

6. On the RatingBar widget, find the Layout_Margin attribute, then set left and right to 15sp.

7.   Still with the `RatingBar` widget and the `Layout_Margin` attribute, change top to `75sp`.

You can now run the app and see our first full layout in all its glory, as illustrated here:

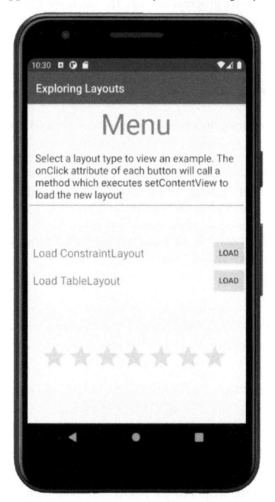

Figure 4.17 – The improved layout

Notice that you can play with the `RatingBar` widget, although the rating won't persist when the app is turned off.

Unfortunately, the buttons in our app don't do anything yet. Let's fix that now.

Wiring up the UI with Java code (Part 2)

To enable the user to interact with our buttons, follow the next two steps to make the buttons in the layout call our methods:

1. Select the button next to the `Load ConstraintLayout` text. Find the `onClick` attribute and set it to `loadConstraintLayout`.

2. Select the button next to the `Load TableLayout` text. Find the `onClick` attribute and set it to `loadTableLayout`.

Now, the buttons will call the methods, but the code inside the `loadTableLayout` method is commented out to avoid errors. Feel free to run the app and check that you can switch to the `ConstraintLayout` by clicking the `loadConstraintLayout` button. But all the `ConstraintLayout` currently has is a **Hello World!** message.

We can now move on to building this `ConstraintLayout`.

Building a precise UI with ConstraintLayout

Open the `ConstraintLayout` that was autogenerated when we created the project. It is probably open already in a tab at the top of the editor. If not, it will be in the `res/layout` folder. The filename is `activity_main.xml`.

Inspect the XML in the **Code** tab and note that it is empty, apart from a `TextView` that says `Hello World`. Switch back to the `Design` tab, left-click the `TextView` to select it, and tap the *Delete* key to get rid of it.

Now, we can build ourselves a simple yet intricate UI. The `ConstraintLayout` is most useful when you want to position parts of your UI very precisely and/or relative to the other parts and not just in a linear fashion.

Adding a CalendarView

To get started, look in the **Widgets** category of the palette and find the `CalendarView`. Drag and drop the `CalendarView` near the top and horizontally central. As you drag the `CalendarView` around, notice that it jumps/snaps to some locations.

Also, notice the subtle visual cues that show when the view is aligned. I have highlighted the horizontally central visual cue in the following screenshot:

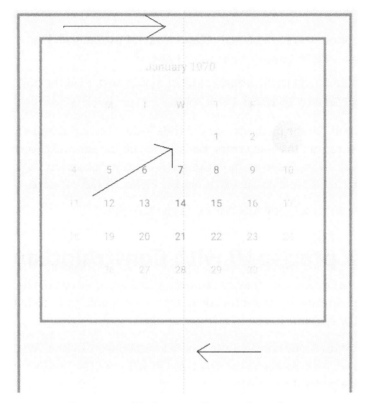

Figure 4.18 – The horizontally central visual cue

Let go when it is horizontally central, as it is in the preceding screenshot. Now, we will resize it.

Resizing a view in a ConstraintLayout

Left-click and hold one of the corner squares that are revealed when you let go of the CalendarView, and drag inward to decrease the size of the CalendarView, as illustrated in the following screenshot:

Figure 4.19 – Resizing a view in the ConstaintLayout

Reduce the size by about half and leave the CalendarView near the top and horizontally central. You might need to reposition the widget a little after you have resized it. The result should look like this:

Figure 4.20 – Repositioning the widget

You do not need to place the `CalendarView` in exactly the same place, as the purpose of the exercise is to get familiar with the visual cues that inform you where you have placed it, not to create a replica of my layout.

Using the Component Tree window

Now, look at the **Component Tree** window, the window to the left of the visual designer and below the palette. A component tree is a way of visualizing the layout of the XML but without all the details.

If you don't see this, look for a tab at the bottom of the **Palette** tab that says Component Tree vertically. Click on this to open up the **Component Tree** tab.

In the next screenshot, we can see that the `CalendarView` is indented to the right of the `ConstraintLayout` and is therefore a child. In the next UI we build, we will see that we sometimes need to take advantage of the **Component Tree** to build the UI.

For now, I just want you to see there is a warning sign by our `CalendarView`. I have highlighted it here:

Figure 4.21 – Warning sign by our CalendarView

The error says **This view is not constrained. It only has designtime positions, so it will jump to (0,0) at runtime unless you add the constraints**. Remember when we first added buttons to the screen in *Chapter 2, First Contact: Java, XML, and the UI Designer*, they simply moved off to the top-left corner?

> **Tip**
> Run the app now and click on the `Load ConstraintLayout` button if you want to be reminded of this problem.

Now, we could fix this by clicking the **Infer constraints** button that we used in *Chapter 2, First Contact: Java, XML, and the UI Designer*. Here it is again as a reminder:

Figure 4.22 – Fixing error by clicking the Infer constraints button

But learning to add constraints manually is worthwhile because it offers us more options and flexibility. Also, as your layouts get more complex, there is always an item or two that doesn't behave as you want it to, and fixing it manually is nearly always necessary.

Adding constraints manually

Make sure the `CalendarView` is selected, and notice the four small circles on the top, bottom, left, and right, as illustrated in the following screenshot:

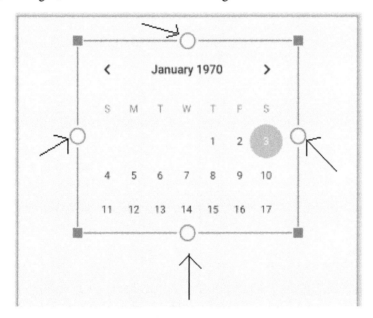

Figure 4.23 – The four constraint handles

These are the **constraint handles**. We can click and drag them to anchor them with other parts of the UI or the sides of the screen. By anchoring the `CalendarView` with the four edges of the screen, we can lock it into position when the app is run.

One at a time, click and drag the top handle to the top of the design, the right handle to the right of the design, the bottom handle to the bottom, and the left handle to the left. Notice how the `CalendarView` is jumping around as we're applying these constraints? That's because the designer is applying the constraints as soon as we put them in, so we can see exactly how it will look at runtime.

Notice that the `CalendarView` is now constrained in the center. Left-click and drag the `CalendarView` back to the upper part of the screen, somewhere like the position shown in the following screenshot. Use the visual cues (also shown in the next screenshot) to make sure the `CalendarView` is horizontally central:

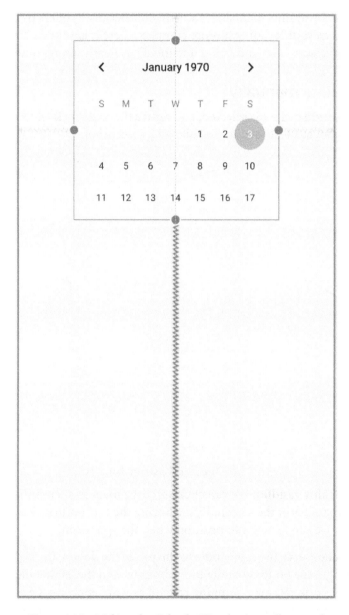

Figure 4.24 – Making the CalendarView horizontally central

At this stage, you could run the app and the `CalendarView` would be positioned as just pictured in the preceding screenshot.

Let's add a couple more items to the UI and see how to constrain them.

Adding and constraining more UI elements

Drag an `ImageView` from the **Widgets** category of the palette and position it below and to the left of the `CalendarView`. When you place the `ImageView`, a pop-up window will prompt you to choose an image. You can choose any image you like, but for the purposes of seeing another Android Studio feature in action, choose the image from the top of the list, **Avatar**, in the **Sample data** section. Click **OK** to add the image to the layout. We will see in the forthcoming *Making the text clickable section* the effect of adding an image from the **Sample data** section has on our project.

Constrain the left-hand side of the `ImageView` and the bottom of the `ImageView` to the left and bottom of the UI respectively. Here is the position you should be in now:

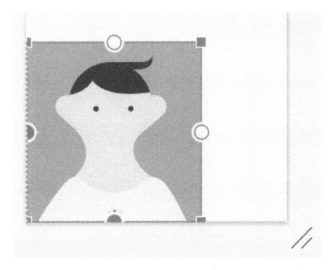

Figure 4.25 – Constraining the left-hand-side and the bottom of the ImageView respectively to the left and bottom of the UI

The `ImageView` is constrained in the bottom-left corner. Now, grab the top constraint handle on the `ImageView` and drag it to the bottom constraint handle of the `CalendarView`. This is now the current situation:

Figure 4.26 – Edited UI

The `ImageView` is only constrained horizontally on one side and so is pinned/ constrained to the left. It is constrained vertically and equally between the `CalendarView` and the bottom of the UI.

Next, add a `TextView` to the right of the `ImageView`. Constrain the right of the `TextView` to the right of the UI and constrain the left of the `TextView` to the right of the `ImageView`. Then, constrain the top of the `TextView` to the top of the `ImageView` and constrain the bottom of the `TextView` to the bottom of the UI. Now, you will be left with something resembling this:

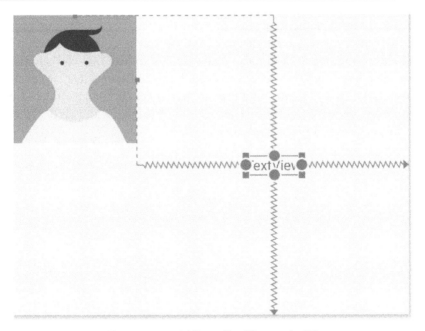

Figure 4.27 – Adding a TextView to the UI

> **Important note**
>
> All the warnings in the **Component Tree** window about unconstrained items are gone. There are warnings about hardcoded strings because we are adding text directly to the layout instead of the `strings.xml` file, and a warning about missing the `contentDescription` attribute. The `contentDescription` attribute should be used to add a textual description so that visually impaired users can get a spoken description of images in the app. For the sake of making fast progress with the `ConstraintLayout`, we will ignore these two warnings. We will look at adding String resources more correctly in *Chapter 18, Localization*, and you can read about accessibility features in Android Studio on the *Android Developers* website, at `https://developer.android.com/studio/intro/accessibility`.

You can move the three UI elements around and line them up neatly, just how you want them. Notice that when you move the `ImageView`, the `TextView` moves with it because the `TextView` is constrained to the `ImageView`. But also notice that you can move the `TextView` independently and, wherever you drop it, this represents its new constrained position relative to the `ImageView`. Whatever an item is constrained to, its position will always be relative to that item. And as we have seen, the horizontal and vertical constraints are distinct from each other. I positioned mine like this:

Figure 4.28 – Positioning the TextView

> **Tip**
>
> ConstraintLayout could be considered the default layout type, and while it is more complex than the other layouts it is the most powerful, as well as the one that runs the best on our user's device. It is worth spending time looking at some more tutorials about ConstraintLayout. Especially look on *YouTube*, as video is a great way to learn about tweaking ConstraintLayout. We will return to ConstraintLayout throughout the book, and you do not need to know any more than we have covered already to be able to move on.

Making the text clickable

We are nearly done with our ConstraintLayout. We just want to wire up a link back to the main menu screen. This is a good opportunity to demonstrate that TextView (and most other UI items) are also clickable. In fact, clickable text is probably more common in modern Android apps than conventional-looking buttons.

Change the text attribute of the TextView widget to Back to the menu. Now, find the onClick attribute and enter loadMenuLayout.

Now, add the following method to the MainActivity.java file just after the loadTableLayout method, as highlighted next:

```
public void loadTableLayout(View v){
    //setContentView(R.layout.my_table_layout);
}


public void loadMenuLayout(View v){
    setContentView(R.layout.main_menu);
}
```

Now, whenever the user clicks the **Back to the menu** text, the loadMenuLayout method will be called and the setContentView method will load the layout in main_menu.xml.

You can run the app and click back and forth between the main menu (LinearLayout) and the CalendarView widget (ConstraintLayout), but have you noticed that the image in the following screenshot seems to be missing?

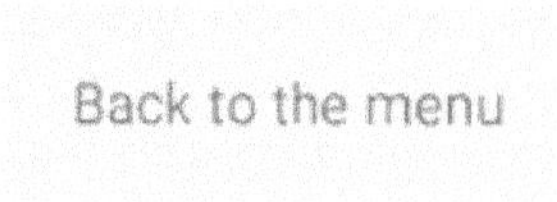

Back to the menu

Figure 4.29 – Image missing from the UI

The TextView widget is neatly positioned as if the ImageView widget were there, but as we can see from the preceding screenshot, the avatar icon that is visible in Android Studio is absent. The reason for this is because we chose the image from the **sample data** category. Android Studio allows us to use sample data so that we can get on with the job of laying out our apps before the images are available. This is useful because it is quite common that images will need to be produced/sourced throughout the development life cycle of an app.

To solve this missing image problem, we can simply find the srcCompat attribute in the Attributes window, left-click it, and choose any image that is not from the **Sample data** category. I chose sym_def_app_icon, which is the cool Android icon shown next:

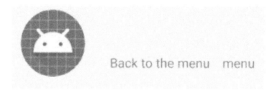

Figure 4.30 – Adding an icon from the srcCompat attribute

Let's build the final layout for this chapter.

Laying out data with TableLayout

Now, we will build a layout that resembles a spreadsheet. It will have neatly aligned cells with titles and data. In a real-world app, you would most likely use real live data from the user. As we are just practicing with different layouts, we will not go to this extent.

Follow these steps:

1. In the project window, expand the res folder. Now, right-click the layout folder and select **New**. Notice that there is an option for **Layout resource file**.

2. Select **Layout resource file**, and you will see the **New Resource File** dialog window.

3. In the **File name:** field, enter my_table_layout. This is the same name we used in the call to setContentView within the loadTableLayout method.

4. Notice in the **Root element:** field that it has selected by default ...**ConstraintLayout** as the option. Delete ...ConstraintLayout and type TableLayout.

5. Click the **OK** button, and Android Studio will generate a new TableLayout in an XML file called my_table_layout and place it in the layout folder, ready for us to build our new table-based UI. Android Studio will also open the UI designer (if it isn't already open) with the palette on the left and the **Attributes** window on the right.

6. You can now uncomment the loadTableLayout method in the MainActivity.java file, as follows:

```
void loadTableLayout(View v){
    setContentView(R.layout.my_table_layout);
}
```

You can now switch to the screen with the new TableLayout widget when you run the app, although at the moment it is blank and there is no way of switching back to the main menu screen; therefore, you will have to quit the app.

Adding a TableRow element to TableLayout

Drag a TableRow element from the Layouts category on to the UI design. Notice that the appearance of this new TableRow element is virtually imperceptible, so much so that it is not worth putting a screenshot of it in the book. There is just a thin blue line at the top of the UI. This is because the TableRow element has collapsed itself around its contents, which are currently empty.

It is possible to drag and drop our chosen UI elements onto this thin blue line, but it is also a little awkward, even counterintuitive. Furthermore, once we have multiple TableRow elements next to each other, it gets even harder. The solution lies in the **Component Tree** window, which we introduced briefly when building the ConstraintLayout.

Using the Component Tree for when the visual designer won't do

Look at the **Component Tree** and notice you can see the `TableRow` as a child of the `TableLayout`. We can drag our new UI widgets directly onto the `TableRow` in the **Component Tree**. Drag three `TextView` widgets onto the `TableRow` in the **Component Tree**, and that should leave you with the following layout. I have Photoshopped the next screenshot to show you the **Component Tree** and the regular UI designer at the same time:

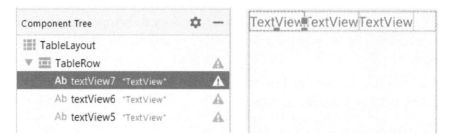

Figure 4.31 – Dragging three TextView widgets onto the TableRow element in the Component Tree

Now, add another two `TableRow` widgets (from the **Layouts** category). You can add them via the **Component Tree** window or the main UI designer.

> **Tip**
>
> You need to drop the widgets on the far left of the window, otherwise the new `TableRow` will become a child of the previous `TableRow`. This would leave the whole table in a bit of a muddle. If you accidentally add a `TableRow` as a child of the previous `TableRow`, you can either select it then tap the *Delete* key, use the *Ctrl + z* keyboard combination to undo it, or drag the mispositioned `TableRow` to the left (in the **Component Tree**) to make it a direct child of the `Table` (instead of `TableRow`).

Now, add three TextView widgets to each of the new TableRow elements. This will be most easily achieved by adding them via the **Component Tree** window. Check your layout to make sure it is like this:

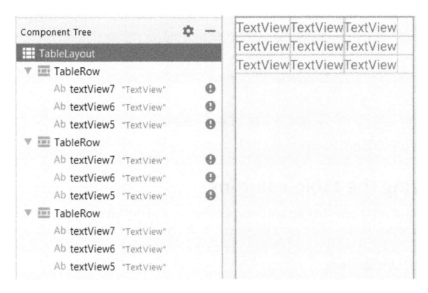

Figure 4.32 – Adding three TextView widgets to each of the new TableRow elements

Let's make the table look more like a genuine table of data you might get in an app by changing some attributes.

On the TableLayout, set the layout_width and layout_height attributes to wrap_content. This gets rid of extra cells

Change all the outer (along the top and down the left-hand side) TextView widgets to black by editing the textColor attribute. You can achieve this by selecting the first TextView, searching for its color attribute, and then starting to type black into the color attribute values field. You will then be able to select @android:color/black from a drop-down list. Do this for each of the outer TextView widgets.

> **Tip**
> Remember you can select multiple widgets at the same time by holding the *Shift* key and left-clicking each required widget in turn.

Find the padding category for all the TextView widgets, and change the padding attribute to 10sp.

This next screenshot shows what the table looks like in Android Studio at this stage:

TextView	TextView	TextView
TextView	TextView	TextView
TextView	TextView	TextView

Figure 4.33 – The table in Android Studio

Let's add some finishing touches to the table.

Organizing the table columns

It might seem at this point that we are done, but we need to organize the data better. Our table, as with many tables, will have a blank cell in the top left to divide the column and row titles. To achieve this, we need to number all the cells. For this, we need to edit the layout_column attribute.

> **Tip**
> Cell numbers are numbered from 0 from the left.

Start by deleting the top-left TextView. Notice the TextView from the right has moved into the top-left position.

Next, in the new top-left TextView, edit the layout_column attribute to be 1 (this assigns it to the second cell because the first cell is 0, and we want to leave the first one empty), and for the next cell along, edit the layout_column attribute to be 2.

The result should look like this:

Figure 4.34 – Table column organized

For the next two rows of cells, edit their `layout_column` attributes from 0 to 2 from left to right.

If you want clarification on the precise code for this row after editing, here is a snippet, and remember to look in the download bundle in the Chapter 4 folder to see the whole file in context.

Important note

In the code snippet that follows, I have also added some values to the `text` attributes throughout.

```
<TableRow
    android:layout_width="wrap_content"
    android:layout_height="wrap_content">
    <TextView
        android:id="@+id/textView2"
        android:layout_width="wrap_content"
        android:layout_height="wrap_content"
        android:layout_column="1"
        android:padding="10sp"
        android:text="India"
        android:textColor="@android:color/black" />
    <TextView
        android:id="@+id/textView1"
        android:layout_width="wrap_content"
        android:layout_height="wrap_content"
        android:layout_column="2"
        android:padding="10sp"
        android:text="England"
        android:textColor="@android:color/black" />
</TableRow>
```

Try to complete this exercise, however, using the **Attributes** window if possible.

Linking back to the main menu

Finally, for this layout, we will add a button that links back to the menu, as follows:

1. Add another `TableRow` via the **Component Tree**.

2. Drag a button onto the new `TableRow`.

3. Edit its `layout_column` attribute to `1` so that it is in the middle of the row.

4. Edit its `text` attribute to `Menu` and edit its `onClick` attribute to match our already existing `loadMenuLayout` method.

You can now run the app and switch back and forth between the different layouts.

If you want to, you can add some meaningful titles and data to the table by editing all the `text` attributes of the `TextView`, as I have done in the following screenshot, which shows the `TableLayout` running in the emulator:

Figure 4.35 – Adding some significant titles and data to the table by editing all the text attributes of the
TextView

> **Note**
> The author admits that the preceding data might be considered overly optimistic.

As a final thought, think about an app that presents tables of data. Chances are that data will be added to the table dynamically, not by the developer at design time as we have just done, but more likely by the user or from a database on the web. In *Chapter 16, Adapters and Recyclers*, we will see how to dynamically add data to different types of layout using adapters; and in *Chapter 27, Android Databases*, we will also see how to create and use databases in our apps.

Summary

We have covered many topics in just a few dozen pages. We have not only built three different types of layout—including `LinearLayout` with nested layouts, `ConstraintLayout` with manually configured constraints, and `TableLayout` (albeit with fake data) —but we have also wired all the layouts together with clickable buttons and text that trigger our Java code to switch between all these different layouts.

In the next chapter, we will stick with the topic of layouts. We will review many attributes we have seen, and we will build our most aesthetically pleasing layout so far by incorporating multiple `CardView` layouts, complete with depth and shadow into a smooth-scrolling `ScrollView` layout.

5
Beautiful Layouts with CardView and ScrollView

This is the last chapter on layouts before we spend some time focusing more on Java and object-oriented programming. We will formalize our learning of some of the different attributes we have already met, and we will also introduce two more cool layouts: `ScrollView` and `CardView`. To finish the chapter off, we will run the `CardView` project on a tablet emulator.

In this chapter, we will cover the following:

- A quick summary of UI attributes
- Build our neatest layout so far using `ScrollView` and `CardView`
- Create and use a tablet emulator

Let's start by recapping some attributes.

Technical requirements

You can find the code files present in this chapter on GitHub at `https://github.com/PacktPublishing/Android-Programming-for-Beginners-Third-Edition/tree/main/chapter%2005`.

Attributes quick summary

In the last few chapters, we used and discussed quite a few different attributes. I thought it would be worth a quick summary and further investigation of a few of the more common attributes.

Sizing using dp

As we know, there are thousands of different Android devices. To try and have a system of measurement that works across different devices, Android uses **density-independent pixels**, or **dp**, as a unit of measurement. The way this works is by first calculating the density of the pixels on the device an app is running on.

> **Important Note**
> We can calculate density by dividing the horizontal resolution by the horizontal size in inches of the screen. This is all done on the fly, on the device on which our app is running.

All we must do is use `dp` in conjunction with a number when setting the size of the various attributes of our widgets. Using density-independent measurements, we can design layouts that scale to create a uniform appearance on as many different screens as possible.

So, does that mean problem solved then? We just use `dp` everywhere and our layouts will work everywhere? Unfortunately, density independence is only part of the solution. We will see more of how we can make our apps look great on a range of different screens throughout the rest of the book.

As an example, we can affect the height and width of a widget by adding the following code to its attributes:

```
. . .
android:height="50dp"
android:width="150dp"
. . .
```

Alternatively, we can use the attributes window and add them through the comfort of the appropriate edit boxes.

We can also use the same dp units to set other attributes, such as margin and padding. We will look more closely at margin and padding in a minute.

Sizing fonts using sp

Another device-dependent unit of measurement used for sizing Android fonts is **scalable pixels**, or **sp**. The sp unit of measurement is used for fonts and is pixel density-dependent in the exact same way that dp is.

The extra calculation that an Android device will use when deciding how big your font will be, based on the value of sp you use, is the user's own font size settings. So, if you test your app on devices and emulators with normal-sized fonts, then a user who has a sight impairment (or just likes big fonts) and has the font setting on large will see something different from what you saw during testing.

If you want to try playing around with your Android device's font size settings, you can do so on the emulator or a real device by selecting **Settings** | **Display** | **Advanced** | **Font size** and try adjusting the slider highlighted in the following screenshot:

Figure 5.1 – Sizing fonts using sp

We can set the size of fonts using sp in any widget that has text. This includes Button, TextView, and all the UI elements under the **Text** category in the palette as well as some others. We do so by setting the textSize property like so:

```
android:textSize="50sp"
```

As usual, we can also use the attributes window to achieve the same thing.

Determining size with wrap or match

We can also decide how the size of UI elements, and many other UI elements, behave in relation to the containing/parent element. We can do so by setting the layoutWidth and layoutHeight attributes to either wrap_content or match_parent.

For example, say we set the attributes of a lone button on a layout to the following:

```
. . .
android:layout_width="match_parent"
android:layout_height="match_parent"
. . . .
```

Then, the button will expand in both height and width to **match** the **parent**. We can see that the button in the next screenshot fills the entire screen:

> **Important Note**
> I added the button on a new layout to the project from the previous chapter.

Figure 5.2 – The button expanded in both height and width to match the parent

More common for a button is `wrap_content`, as shown next:

```
. . . .
android:layout_width="wrap_content"
android:layout_height="wrap_content"
. . . .
```

This causes the button to be as big as it needs to **wrap** its **content** (width and height in dp and text in sp).

Using padding and margin

If you have ever done any web design, then you will be very familiar with the next two attributes. **Padding** is the space from the edge of the widget to the start of the content in the widget. **Margin** is the space outside of the widget that is left between other widgets – including the margins of other widgets, should they have any. Here is a visual representation:

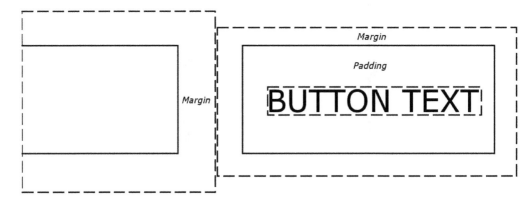

Figure 5.3 – Padding and margin used

We can set the padding and margin in a straightforward way, equally for all sides, like this:

```
. . .
android:layout_margin="43dp"
android:padding="10dp"
. . .
```

Look at the slight difference in naming convention for the margin and padding. The padding is just called `padding` but the margin is referred to as `layout_margin`. This reflects the fact that the padding only affects the UI element itself, but the margin can affect other widgets in the layout.

Alternatively, we can specify different top, bottom, left, and right margins and paddings, like this:

```
android:layout_marginTop="43dp"
android:layout_marginBottom="43dp"
android:paddingLeft="5dp"
android:paddingRight="5dp"
```

Specifying margin and padding values for a widget is optional and a value of 0 will be assumed if nothing is specified. We can also choose to specify some of the different sides' margins and paddings but not others, as in the earlier example.

It is probably becoming obvious that the way we design our layouts is extremely flexible, but also that it is going to take some practice to achieve precise results with this many options. We can even specify negative margin values to create overlapping widgets.

Let's look at a few more attributes, and then we will go ahead and play around with a stylish layout – `CardView`.

Using the layout_weight property

Weight refers to a relative amount compared to other UI elements. So, for `layout_weight` to be useful, we need to assign a value to the `layout_weight` property on two or more elements.

We can then assign portions that add up to 100% in total. This is especially useful for dividing up screen space between parts of the UI where we want the relative space they occupy to remain the same regardless of screen size.

Using `layout_weight` in conjunction with `sp` and `dp` units can make for a simple and flexible layout. For example, look at this code:

```
<Button
        android:layout_width="match_parent"
        android:layout_height="0dp"
        android:layout_weight=".1"
        android:text="one tenth" />
```

```
<Button
        android:layout_width="match_parent"
        android:layout_height="0dp"
        android:layout_weight=".2"
        android:text="two tenths" />

<Button
        android:layout_width="match_parent"
        android:layout_height="0dp"
        android:layout_weight=".3"
        android:text="three tenths" />

<Button
        android:layout_width="match_parent"
        android:layout_height="0dp"
        android:layout_weight=".4"
        android:text="four tenths" />
```

Here is what this code will do:

Figure 5.4 – The UI with the layout_weight property in use

Notice that all the `layout_height` attributes are set to 0dp. Effectively, `layout_weight` is replacing the `layout_height` property. The context in which we use `layout_weight` is important or it won't work. Also note that we don't have to use fractions of 1; we can use whole numbers, percentages, or any other number; as long as they are relative to each other, they will probably achieve the effect you are after. Note that `layout_weight` only works in certain contexts.

Using gravity

Gravity can be our friend and can be used in so many ways in our layouts. Just like gravity in the solar system, it affects the position of items by moving them in a given direction, as if they were being acted upon by gravity. The best way to see what gravity can do is to look at some example code and pictures.

Say we set the `gravity` property on a button (or another widget) to `left|center_vertical` like this:

```
android:gravity="left|center_vertical"
```

This will have an effect that looks like this:

Figure 5.5 – Setting the gravity property on a widget

Notice that the contents of the widget (in this case the button's text) are indeed aligned left and centrally vertical.

In addition, a widget can influence its own position within a layout element with the `layout_gravity` element, like this:

```
android:layout_gravity="left"
```

This would set the widget within its layout, as expected, like this:

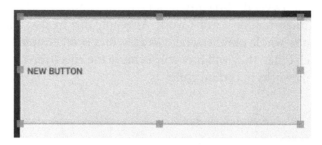

Figure 5.6 – Setting the gravity layout to left

The previous code allows different widgets within the same layout to be affected as if the layout has multiple different gravities.

The contents of all the widgets in a layout can be affected by the `gravity` property of their parent layout by using the same code as a widget:

```
android:gravity="left"
```

There are in fact many more attributes than those we have discussed. Many we won't need in this book and some are quite obscure, and you might never need them in your entire Android career. But others are quite commonly used, such as `background`, `textColor`, `alignment`, `typeface`, `visibility`, and `shadowColor`. Let's explore some more attributes and layouts now.

Building a UI with CardView and ScrollView

Create a new project in the usual way and choose the **Empty Activity** project template. Name the project `CardView Layout`.

We will design our `CardView` masterpiece inside a `ScrollView` layout, which, as the name suggests, allows the user to scroll through the contents of the layout.

Expand the folders in the project explorer window so you can see the `res` folder. Expand the `res` folder to see the `layout` folder.

Right-click the **layout** folder and select **New**. Notice there is an option for **Layout resource file**. Select **Layout resource file** and you will see the **New Resource File** dialog window.

In the **File name** field, enter `main_layout`. The name is arbitrary, but this layout is going to be our main layout, so the name makes that plain.

Notice it is set to **…ConstraintLayout** in the **Root element** field. Change it to ScrollView. This layout type appears to work just like LinearLayout; the difference is that when there is too much content to display onscreen, it will allow the user to scroll through the content by swiping with their finger.

Click the **OK** button and Android Studio will generate a new ScrollView in an XML file called main_layout and place it in the layout folder ready for us to build our CardView-based UI.

Android Studio will open the UI designer ready for action.

Setting the view with Java code

As we have done before, we will now load the main_layout.xml file as the layout for our app by calling the setContentView method in the MainActivity.java file.

Select the **MainActivity.java** tab. In the unlikely event that the tab isn't there by default, you can find it in the project explorer under app/java/your_package_name, where your_package_name is equal to the package name that was auto-generated when you created the project.

Amend the code in the onCreate method to look exactly like this next code. I have highlighted the line that you need to add:

```
@Override
protected void onCreate(Bundle savedInstanceState) {
    super.onCreate(savedInstanceState);

    setContentView(R.layout.main_layout);
}
```

You could now run the app but there is nothing to see except an empty ScrollView.

Adding image resources

We are going to need some images for this project. This is so that we can demonstrate how to add them into the project (this section) and neatly display and format them in a CardView widget (next section).

It doesn't really matter where you get your images from; it is the practical, hands-on experience that is the purpose of this exercise. To avoid copyright and royalty problems, I am going to use some book images from the Packt Publishing website. This also makes it easy for me to provide you with all the resources you need to complete the project and should relieve the bother of you acquiring your own images. Feel free to swap the images in the `Chapter 5/res/drawable` folder.

There are three images: `image_1.png`, `image_2.png`, and `image_3.png`. To add them to the project, follow these steps:

1. Find the picture files using your operating system's file browser.

2. Highlight them all and press *Ctrl + C* to copy them.

3. In the Android Studio project explorer, select the **res/drawable** folder by left-clicking it.

4. Right-click the **drawable** folder and select **Paste**.

5. In the pop-up window that asks **Choose Destination Directory**, click **OK** to accept the default destination, which is the `drawable` folder.

6. Click **OK** again to **Copy Specified Files**.

You should now be able to see your images in the `drawable` folder along with a couple of other files that Android Studio placed there when the project was created, as shown in this next screenshot:

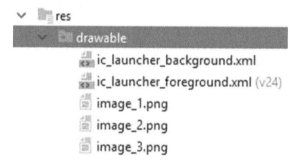

Figure 5.7 – Expanding the drawable folder

Before we move on to the `CardView` widget itself, let's design what we will put inside our cards.

Creating the contents for the cards

The next thing we need to do is create the contents for our cards. It makes sense to separate the content from the layout. What we will do is create three separate layouts, called `card_contents_1`, `card_contents_2`, and `card_contents_3`. They will each contain a `LinearLayout`, which itself will contain an image and some text.

Let's create three more layouts with a `LinearLayout` layout at their root:

1. Right-click the **layout** folder and select **New layout resource file**.

2. Name the file `card_contents_1` and change **…ConstraintLayout** to **LinearLayout** for the root element.

3. Click **OK** to create the new file in the `layout` folder.

4. Repeat *steps 1* through *3* two more times, changing the filename each time to `card_contents_2` and then `card_contents_3`.

Now, select the **card_contents_1.xml** tab and make sure you are in the design view. We will drag and drop some elements to the layout to get the basic structure, and then we will add some `sp`, `dp`, and `gravity` attributes to make them look nice:

1. Drag a `TextView` onto the top of the layout.

2. Drag an `ImageView` onto the layout below the `TextView`.

3. In the **Resources** pop-up window, select **Project | image_1**, then click **OK**.

4. Drag another two `TextView` below the image.

This is what your layout should look like now:

Figure 5.8 – Making the layout look nicer by adding sp, dp, and gravity attributes

Now let's use some Material Design guidelines to make the layout look more appealing:

> **Important Note**
> It is possible that as you proceed through these modifications the UI elements
> on the bottom of the layout might disappear off the bottom of the design view.
> If this happens to you, remember you can always select any UI element from
> the **Component Tree** window underneath the palette.

1. Set the `textSize` attribute for the `TextView` widget at the top to `24sp`.

2. Still working on the `TextView` widget at the top, set the **layout_margin | layout_margin** attribute to `16dp`.

3. Set the `text` attribute to `Learning Java by Building Android Games` (or whatever title suits your image).

4. On the `ImageView` widget, set the `layout_width` and `layout_height` attributes to `wrap_content`.

5. Still working on the `ImageView` widget, set the `layout_gravity` attribute to `center_horizontal`.

6. On the `TextView` widget below `ImageView`, set `textSize` to `16sp`.

7. On the same `TextView` widget, set **layout_margin | layout_margin** to `16dp`.

8. On the same `TextView` widget, set the `text` attribute to `Learn Java and Android from scratch by building 6 playable games` (or something that describes your image).

9. On the bottom `TextView` widget, change the `text` attribute to `BUY NOW`.

10. On the same `TextView` widget, set **layout_margin | layout_margin** to `16dp`.

11. On the same `TextView` widget, set the `textSize` attribute to `24sp`.

12. On the same `TextView` widget, set the `textColor` attribute to `@color/teal_200`.

13. On the `LinearLayout` layout holding all the other elements, set **padding | padding** to `15dp`. Note that it is easiest to select `LinearLayout` from the **Component Tree** window.

At this point, your layout will look very similar to as in the following screenshot:

Figure 5.9 – Enhancing the appeal of the layout using some Material Design guidelines

Now lay out the other two files (`card_contents_2` and `card_contents_3`) with the exact same dimensions and colors. When you get the **Resources** popup to choose an image, use `image_2` and `image_3`, respectively. Also, change all the `text` attributes on the first two `TextView` elements so that the titles and descriptions are unique. The titles and descriptions don't really matter; it is the layout and appearance we are learning about.

> **Note**
>
> Note that all the sizes and colors were derived from the Material Design website here: `https://material.io/design/introduction` and the Android-specific UI guidelines here: `https://developer.android.com/guide/topics/ui/look-and-feel`. These are well worth studying alongside or soon after you complete this book.

Now we can move on to the `CardView` widgets.

Defining dimensions for CardView

Right-click the **values** folder and select **New | Values resource file**. In the **New Resource File** pop-up window, name the file `dimens` (short for dimensions) and click **OK**. Android Studio will create and open a file called `dimens.xml`. We will use this file to create some common values that our `CardView` will use by referring to them.

To achieve this, we will edit the XML directly in the **Code** tab. Edit the `dimens.xml` file to be the same as the following code:

```xml
<?xml version="1.0" encoding="utf-8"?>
<resources>
    <dimen name="card_corner_radius">16dp</dimen>
    <dimen name="card_margin">10dp</dimen>
</resources>
```

Be sure to make it exactly the same because a small omission could cause an error and prevent the project from working.

We have defined two resources, the first called `card_corner_radius` with a value of `16dp` and the second called `card_margin` with a value of `10dp`.

We will refer to these resources from the `main_layout` file and use them to consistently configure our three `CardView` elements.

Adding CardView to our layout

Switch to the **main_layout.xml** tab and make sure you are in the design view. You probably recall that we are now working with a ScrollView that will scroll the contents of our app, rather like how a web browser scrolls the contents of a web page that doesn't fit on one screen.

ScrollView has a limitation – it can only have one direct child layout. We want it to contain three CardView widgets.

To overcome this problem, drag a LinearLayout layout from the Layouts category of the palette. Be sure to pick **LinearLayout (vertical)**, as represented by this icon in the palette:

Figure 5.10 – The LinearLayout (vertical) icon

We will add our three CardView inside the LinearLayout, and then the whole thing will scroll nice and smoothly without any errors.

The CardView widget can be found in the **Containers** category of the palette, so switch to that and locate CardView.

Drag a CardView onto the LinearLayout on the design and you might or might not get a pop-up message in Android Studio. This is the message:

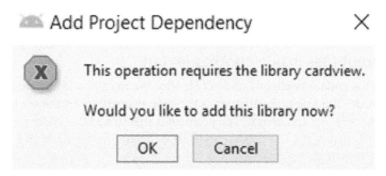

Figure 5.11 – The popup asking for permission to add CardView

If you do get this message, click the **OK** button. Android Studio will do some work behind the scenes and will add the necessary parts to the project. Android Studio has added some more classes to the project, specifically, classes that provide CardView features to older versions of Android that wouldn't otherwise have them.

You should now have a CardView on the design. Until there are some contents in it, the CardView is only easily visible in the **Component Tree** window.

Select the `CardView` via **Component Tree** and configure the following attributes:

1. Set `layout_width` to `wrap_content`.

2. Set `layout_gravity` to `center`.

3. Set **layout_margin | layout_margin** to `@dimen/card_margin` to use the value for a margin that we defined in the `dimens.xml` file.

4. Set the `cardCornerRadius` attribute to `@dimen/card_corner_radius` to use the value for a radius that we defined in the `dimens.xml` file.

5. Set `cardElevation` to `2dp`.

Now switch to the **Code** tab and you will find you have something like this next code:

```
<androidx.cardview.widget.CardView
    android:layout_width="wrap_content"
    android:layout_height="match_parent"
    android:layout_gravity="center"
    android:layout_margin="@dimen/card_margin"
    app:cardCornerRadius="@dimen/card_corner_radius"
    app:cardElevation="2dp" />
```

The previous code listing only shows the code for `CardView`.

The problem at the moment is that our `CardView` is empty. Let's fix that by adding the contents of `card_contents_1.xml`. Here is how to do it.

Including layout files inside another layout

We need to edit the code very slightly and here is why. We need to add an `include` element to the code. The `include` element is the code that will insert the contents from the `card_contents_1.xml` layout. The problem is that to add this code, we need to slightly alter the format of the `CardView` XML. The current format starts and concludes `CardView` with one single tag, like this:

```
<androidx.cardview.widget.CardView
...
.../>
```

We need to change the format to a separate opening and closing tag like this (don't change anything just yet):

```
<androidx.cardview.widget.CardView

    ...

    ...

</androidx.cardview.widget.CardView>
```

This change in format will enable us to add the include... code and our first CardView widget will be complete. With this in mind, edit the code of the CardView to be exactly the same as the following code. I have highlighted the two new lines of code but note that the forward slash that was after the cardElevation attribute has also been removed:

```
<androidx.cardview.widget.CardView
    android:layout_width="wrap_content"
    android:layout_height="match_parent"
    android:layout_gravity="center"
    android:layout_margin="@dimen/card_margin"
    app:cardCornerRadius="@dimen/card_corner_radius"
    app:cardElevation="2dp" >


        <include layout="@layout/card_contents_1" />


</androidx.cardview.widget.CardView>
```

You can now view the `main_layout` file in the visual designer and see the layout inside the `CardView` element. The visual designer does not reveal the real aesthetics of `CardView`, however. We will see all the `CardView` widgets together scrolling nicely in the completed app shortly. Here is a screenshot of the screen in the emulator showing where we are up to so far:

Figure 5.12 – The layout inside the CardView element

Add two more `CardView` widgets to the layout and configure them the same as the first with one exception. On the second `CardView`, set `cardElevation` to `22dp` and on the third `CardView`, set `cardElevation` to `42dp`. Change the `include` code to reference `card_contents_2` and `card_contents_3`, respectively.

> **Tip**
>
> You could do this very quickly by copy and pasting the `CardView` XML and simply amending the elevation and the `include` code as mentioned in the previous paragraph.

This is what the `CardView`-related code inside the `LinearLayout` code will look like when you are done:

```xml
<androidx.cardview.widget.CardView
    android:layout_width="wrap_content"
    android:layout_height="match_parent"
    android:layout_gravity="center"
    android:layout_margin="@dimen/card_margin"
    app:cardCornerRadius="@dimen/card_corner_radius"
    app:cardElevation="2dp" >
    <include layout="@layout/card_contents_1" />
</androidx.cardview.widget.CardView>
<androidx.cardview.widget.CardView
    android:layout_width="wrap_content"
    android:layout_height="match_parent"
    android:layout_gravity="center"
    android:layout_margin="@dimen/card_margin"
    app:cardCornerRadius="@dimen/card_corner_radius"
    app:cardElevation="22dp" >
    <include layout="@layout/card_contents_2" />
</androidx.cardview.widget.CardView>
<androidx.cardview.widget.CardView
    android:layout_width="wrap_content"
    android:layout_height="match_parent"
    android:layout_gravity="center"
    android:layout_margin="@dimen/card_margin"
    app:cardCornerRadius="@dimen/card_corner_radius"
    app:cardElevation="42dp" >

    <include layout="@layout/card_contents_3" />
</androidx.cardview.widget.CardView>
```

Now we can run the app and see our three beautiful, elevated `CardView` widgets in action. In this next screenshot, I have captured it so that you can see the effect the elevation setting has on creating a very pleasing depth with shadow effect:

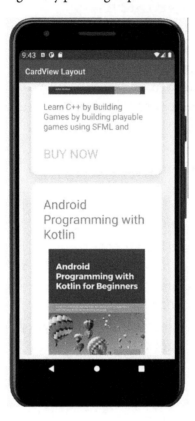

Figure 5.13 – A pleasing depth with shadow effect

Important Note

The screenshot will likely be slightly unclear in the black and white printed version of this book. Be sure to build and run the app for yourself to see this cool effect.

Let's explore our latest app on a tablet emulator.

Creating a tablet emulator

We will often want to test our apps on multiple different devices. Fortunately, Android Studio makes it easy to create as many different emulators as we like. Follow these next steps to make a tablet emulator.

Select **Tools | AVD Manager** and then click the **Create Virtual Device...** button on the **Your Virtual Devices** window. You will see the **Select Hardware** window pictured next:

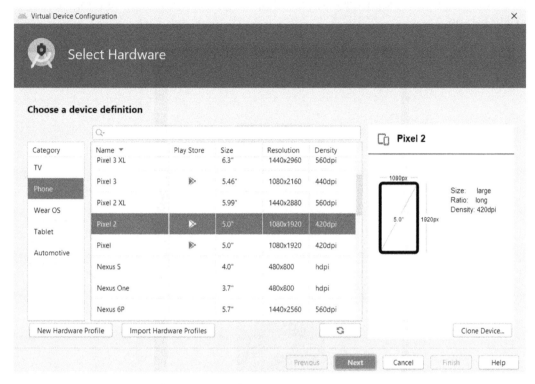

Figure 5.14 – The Select Hardware window

Select the **Tablet** option from the **Category** list, and then highlight the **Pixel C** tablet from the choice of available tablets.

> **Tip**
>
> If you are reading this sometime in the future, the Pixel C option might have been updated. The choice of tablet is less important than practicing this process of creating a tablet emulator and then testing our apps.

Click the **Next** button. On the **System Image** window that follows, just click **Next** because this will select the default system image. It is possible that choosing your own image will cause the emulator not to work properly.

Finally, on the **Android Virtual Device** screen, you can leave all the default options. Feel free to change the **AVD Name** option for your emulator or the **Startup Orientation** (portrait or landscape) option if you want to. Click the **Finish** button when you are ready.

Shut down the phone emulator if you have it running. Now, whenever you run one of your apps from Android Studio, you will be given the option to choose Pixel C (or whatever tablet you created). Here is a screenshot of my Pixel C emulator running the CardView app:

Figure 5.15 – Pixel C emulator running the CardView app

Not too bad, but there is quite a large amount of wasted space and it looks a bit odd. Let's try it in landscape mode. If you try running the app with the tablet in landscape mode, the results are worse. What we can learn from this is that we are going to have to design our layouts for different-sized screens and different orientations. Sometimes they will be clever designs that scale to suit different sizes or orientations, but often they will be completely different designs in separate layout files.

Frequently asked question

1. Do I need to master all this stuff about Material Design?

    No, not unless you want to be a professional designer. If you just want to make your own apps and sell them or give them away on the Play Store, then knowing just the basics is good enough.

Summary

In this chapter, we built aesthetically pleasing `CardView` layouts and put them in a `ScrollView` so the user can swipe through the contents of the layout a bit like browsing a web page. To finish the chapter off, we launched a tablet emulator and saw that we are going to need to get smart with how we design our layouts if we want to cater to different device sizes and orientations. In *Chapter 24, Design Patterns, Multiple Layouts, and Fragments*, we will begin to take our layouts to the next level and learn how to cope with such a diverse array of devices using fragments.

Before we do, however, it will serve us well to learn more Java and how we can use it to control our UI and interact with the user. That will be the focus of the next seven chapters.

Of course, the elephant in the room at this point is that despite learning a lot about layouts, project structure, the connection between Java and XML, and much more besides, our UIs, no matter how pretty, don't actually do anything! We need to seriously upgrade our Java skills while also learning more about how to apply them in an Android context. In the next chapter, we will do exactly that. We will see how to add Java code that executes at exactly the moment we need it to by working with the **Android Activity life cycle**.

6
The Android Lifecycle

In this chapter, we will get familiar with the lifecycle of an Android app. At first, this might sound a bit strange, that a computer program has a lifecycle, but it will make sense soon.

The lifecycle is the way that all Android apps interact with the Android OS. Just like the lifecycle of humans interacts with the world around them, we have no choice but to interact with it and must be prepared to handle different events without notice if we want our apps to survive.

We will see the phases of the lifecycle that an app goes through from creation to destruction and how this helps us know where to put our Java code, depending on what we are trying to achieve.

In brief, in this chapter we will look at the following:

- The life and times of an Android app
- What is method overriding
- The phases of the Android lifecycle
- What exactly we need to know and do to code our apps

- A lifecycle demonstration mini app.

- A quick look at code structure ready to get Java coding in the next chapter

Let's start learning about the Android lifecycle.

Technical requirements

You can find the code files present in this chapter on GitHub at `https://github.com/PacktPublishing/Android-Programming-for-Beginners-Third-Edition/tree/main/chapter%2006`.

The life and times of an Android app

We have talked a bit about the structure of our code; we know that we can write classes, and within those classes we have methods, and the methods contain our code, which gets things done. We also know that when we want the code within a method to run (be executed), we call that method by using its name.

Also, in *Chapter 2, First Contact: Java, XML, and the UI Designer*, we learned that Android itself calls the `onCreate` method just before the app is ready to start. We saw this when we output to the logcat and used the `Toast` class to send a pop-up message to the user.

What we will look at in this chapter is what happens throughout the lifecycle of every app we write – when it starts and ends as well as a few stages in between as well. And what we will see is that Android interacts with our app on numerous occasions, each time it is run.

How Android interacts with our apps

It does so by calling methods that are contained within the `Activity` class. Even if the method is not visible within our Java code, it is still being called by Android at the appropriate time. If this doesn't seem to make any sense, then read on.

Did you ever wonder why the `onCreate` method had a strange-looking line of code just before it?

```
@Override
```

What is going on here is that we are saying to Android, when you call `onCreate`, please use our overridden version because we have some things to do at that time.

Furthermore, you might remember the odd-looking first line of code in the onCreate method:

```
super.onCreate(savedInstanceState)
```

This is telling Android to call the original/official version of onCreate before proceeding with our overridden version. This is not just a quirk of Android – **method overriding** is built into Java.

There are also many other methods that we can optionally override, and they allow us to add our code at appropriate times within the lifecycle of our Android app. Just as onCreate is called just before the app is shown to the user, there are more methods that are called at other times. We haven't seen them yet, we haven't overridden them yet, but they are there, they are called, and their code executes.

The reason we need to care about the methods of **our** app that Android calls whenever it wants is they control the very life and death of our code. For instance, what if our app allows the user to type an important reminder. Then, halfway through typing the reminder their phone rings, our app disappears, and the data (the reminder) is gone.

It is vital and thankfully quite straightforward that we learn when, why, and which methods Android will call as part of the lifecycle of our app. We can then know where we need to override methods to add our own code and where to add the real functionality (code) that defines our app.

Let's examine the Android lifecycle, then we can move on to the ins and outs of Java and we will know exactly where to put the code that we write.

A simplified explanation of the Android lifecycle

If you have ever used an Android device, you have probably noticed it works quite differently from many other operating systems. For example, you could be using an app – say you're checking what people are doing on Facebook. Then, you get an email notification and you tap the notification to read it. Midway through reading the email, you might get a Twitter notification and because you're waiting on important news from someone you follow, you interrupt your email reading and change apps to Twitter with a touch.

After reading the tweet, you fancy a game of Angry Birds but midway through the first fling, you suddenly remember that Facebook post. So, you quit Angry Birds and tap the Facebook icon.

Then you resume Facebook, probably at the exact same point you left it. You could have resumed reading the email, decided to reply to the tweet, or started an entirely new app.

All this backwards and forwards takes quite a lot of management on the part of the operating system, independently of the individual apps themselves.

The difference between, say, a Windows PC and Android in the context we have just discussed is this: with Android, although the user decides which app they are using, the OS decides when to close down (destroy) an application and **our user's data** (like the hypothetical note) along with it. We just need to consider this when coding our apps. Just because we might write code to do some cool thing with our user's input, it doesn't mean that Android will let the code execute.

The lifecycle phases demystified

The Android system has multiple distinct phases that any given app can be in. Depending upon the phase, the Android system decides how the app is viewed by the user – or whether it is viewed at all.

Android has these phases so it can decide which app is in current use and so that it can then give the right amount of resources, such as memory and processing power.

In addition, as the user interacts with the device, for example, by touching the screen, Android must give the details of that interaction to the correct app. For instance, a drag-and-release movement in Angry Birds means taking a shot, but in a messaging app, it might mean delete a text message.

We have already raised the issue of when the user quits our app to answer a phone call; will they lose their progress/data/important note?

Android has a system that, when simplified a little for the purposes of explanation, means that every app on an Android device is in one of the following phases:

- Being created
- Starting
- Resuming
- Running
- Pausing
- Stopping
- Being destroyed

The list of phases will hopefully appear logical. As an example, the user presses the Facebook app icon and the app is **created**. Then it is **started**. All straightforward so far, but next on the list is **resuming**.

It is not as illogical as it might first appear if, for a moment, we can just accept that the app resumes after it starts and then all will become clear as we continue.

After **resuming,** the app is **running**. This is when the Facebook app has control of the screen and the greater share of system memory and processing power and is receiving the details of the user's input.

Now, what about our example when we switched from the Facebook app to the email app?

As we tap to go to read our email, the Facebook app will have entered the **paused** phase, followed by the **stopping** phase, and the email app will enter the **being created** phase, followed by **resuming**, then **running**.

If we decide to revisit Facebook, as in the scenario earlier, the Facebook app will probably skip being created and go straight to **resume** and then be **running** again, most likely exactly in the place we left it.

Note that at any time, Android can decide to **stop** then **destroy** an app. In which case, when we run the app again, it will need to be **created** at the first phase all over again.

So, had the Facebook app been inactive long enough, or perhaps Angry Birds had needed so many system resources that Android had **destroyed** the Facebook app, then our experience of finding the exact post we were previously reading might have been different.

If all this phase stuff is starting to get confusing, then you will be pleased to know that the only reasons to mention it are the following:

- You know it exists
- We occasionally need to interact with it
- We will take things step by step when we do

Now we know about the lifecycle phases, let's learn about how we can handle them.

How we handle the lifecycle phases

When we are programming an app, how do we interact with this complexity? The good news is that the Android code that was autogenerated when we created our first project does most of it for us.

As we have discussed, we just don't see the methods that handle this interaction, but we do have the opportunity to **override** them and add our own code to that phase if we need to.

This means we can get on with learning Java and making Android apps until we come to one of the occasional instances where we need to do something in one of the phases.

> **Important note**
>
> If our app has more than one activity, they will each have their own lifecycle. This doesn't have to complicate things and overall it will make things easier for us.

Coming up is a quick explanation of the methods provided by Android, for our convenience, to manage the lifecycle phases. To clarify our discussion of lifecycle methods, they are listed next to their corresponding phases that we have been discussing. However, as you will see, the method names make it clear on their own where they fit in.

There is also a brief explanation or suggestion for when we might use a given method and thereby interact during a specific phase. We will meet most of these methods as we progress through the book. We have of course already seen `onCreate`:

- `onCreate`: This method is executed when the activity is being **created**. Here, we get everything ready for the app, including the UI (such as calling `setContentView`), graphics, and sound.

- `onStart`: This method is executed when the app is in the **starting** phase.

- `onResume`: This method runs after `onStart` but can also be entered (most logically) after our activity is resumed after being previously paused. We might reload previously saved user data (such as an important note) from when the app was interrupted, perhaps by a phone call or the user running another app.

- `onPause`: This occurs when our app is **pausing**. Here, we might save unsaved data (such as the note) that could be reloaded in `onResume`. Activities always transition into a paused state when another UI element is displayed on top of the current activity (for example, a pop-up dialog) or when the activity is about to be stopped (for example, when the user navigates to a different activity).

- `onStop`: This relates to the **stopping** phase. This is where we might undo everything we did in `onCreate`, such as releasing system resources or writing information to a database. If we reach here, we are probably going to get destroyed sometime soon.

- onDestroy: This is when our activity is finally being **destroyed**. There is no turning back from this phase. It's our last chance to dismantle our app in an orderly manner. If we reach here, we will be going through the lifecycle phases from the beginning next time.

This diagram shows the likely flows of execution between the methods:

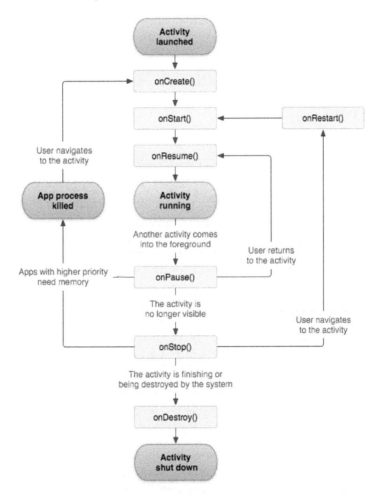

Figure 6.1 – Flow of execution

All the method descriptions and their related phases should appear straightforward. The only real question is what about the running phase? As we will see when we write our code in the other methods/phases, the onCreate, onStart, and onResume methods will prepare the app, which then persists, forming the running phase. Then the onPause, onStop, and onDestroy methods will occur afterward.

Now we can look at these lifecycle methods in action with a mini app. We will do so by overriding them all and adding a `Log` message and a `Toast` message to each. This will visually prove the phases our app passes through.

Lifecycle demo app

In this section, we will do a quick experiment that will help familiarize ourselves with the lifecycle methods our app uses as well as giving us a chance to play around with a bit more Java code.

Follow these steps to start a new project and then we can add some code:

1. Start a new project.

2. Choose the **Basic Activity** template.

3. Call the project **Lifecycle Demo**. Of course, the code is in the download bundle in the `Chapter 6` folder should you wish to refer to it or copy and paste it.

4. Wait for Android Studio to generate the project files and then open the `MainActivity.java` file in the code editor.

You have created a new project with all the default settings. We will only need the `MainActivity.java` file for this demonstration and will not be building a UI.

Coding the lifecycle demo app

In the `MainActivity.java` file, find the onCreate method and add these two lines of code just before the closing curly } brace, which marks the end of the `onCreate` method:

```
Toast.makeText(this, "In onCreate", Toast.LENGTH_SHORT).show();
Log.i("info", "In onCreate");
```

The entire `onCreate` method should now look like this next code, where the highlighted code is the two lines we just added and the ... is where we have skipped some lines of autogenerated code to make the book more readable. For the full code listing, check the `MainActivity.java` file in the download bundle. Here is the code:

```
@Override
protected void onCreate(Bundle savedInstanceState) {
    super.onCreate(savedInstanceState);
    setContentView(R.layout.activity_main);
```

```
            Toast.makeText(this, "In onCreate",
            Toast.LENGTH_SHORT).show();

        Log.i("info", "In onCreate");
}
```

> **Tip**
>
> Remember you will need to use the *Alt + Enter* keyboard combination twice to
> import the classes needed for `Toast` and `Log`.

After the closing curly brace, }, of the `onCreate` method, leave one clear line and add
the following five lifecycle methods and their contained code. Also note that it doesn't
matter in what order we add our overridden methods. Android will call them in the
correct order regardless of the order in which we type them:

```
@Override
public void onStart() {
    // First call the "official" version of this method
    super.onStart();

    Toast.makeText(this, "In onStart",
        Toast.LENGTH_SHORT).show();

    Log.i("info", "In onStart");
}

@Override
public void onResume() {
    // First call the "official" version of this method
    super.onResume();

    Toast.makeText(this, "In onResume",
        Toast.LENGTH_SHORT).show();
```

```
        Log.i("info", "In onResume");
}


@Override
public void onPause() {
    // First call the "official" version of this method
    super.onPause();

    Toast.makeText(this, "In onPause",
        Toast.LENGTH_SHORT).show();

    Log.i("info", "In onPause");
}


@Override
public void onStop() {
    // First call the "official" version of this method
    super.onStop();

    Toast.makeText(this, "In onStop",
        Toast.LENGTH_SHORT).show();

    Log.i("info", "In onStop");
}


@Override
public void onDestroy() {
    // First call the "official" version of this method
    super.onDestroy();

    Toast.makeText(this, "In onDestroy",
        Toast.LENGTH_SHORT).show();

    Log.i("info", "In onDestroy");
}
```

First, let's talk about the code itself. Notice that the method names all correspond to the lifecycle methods and phases we discussed earlier in this chapter. Notice that all the method declarations are preceded by the `@Override` line of code. Also see that the first line of code inside each method is `super.on....`

What exactly is going on here is the following:

- Android calls our methods at the various times we have already discussed.
- The `@Override` keyword shows that these methods replace/override the original version of the method that is provided as part of the Android API. Note that we don't see these overridden methods but they are there, and if we didn't override them these original versions would be called by Android instead of ours.

The `super.on...`, which is the first line of code within each of the overridden methods, then calls these original versions. So, we don't simply override these original methods in order to add our own code – we also call them, and their code is executed too.

> **Tip**
>
> For the curious, the keyword `super` is for super-class. We will explore method overriding and super classes in several chapters as we progress.

Finally, the code that you added will make each of the methods output one `Toast` message and one `Log` message. However, the messages that are output vary, as can be seen by the text in between the double quote marks `" "`. The messages that are output will make it clear which method produced them.

Running the lifecycle demo app

Now that we have looked at the code, we can play with our app and learn about the lifecycle from what happens:

1. Run the app on either a device or an emulator.
2. Watch the screen of the emulator and you will see the following appear one after the other as `Toast` messages on the screen: **In onCreate**, **In onStart**, and **In onResume.**

3. Notice the following messages in the logcat window. If there are too many messages, remember you can filter them by setting the **Log level** drop-down to **Info**.

    ```
    info:in onCreate
    info:in onStart
    info:in onResume
    ```

4. Now tap the back button on the emulator or the device. Notice you get the following three `Toast` messages in exactly this order: **In onPause**, **In onStop**, and **In onDestroy**. Verify that we have matching output in the logcat window.

5. Next, run a different app – perhaps the *Hello Android* app from *Chapter 1, Beginning Android and Java,* (but any app will do) – by tapping its icon on the emulator/device screen.

6. Now try the following: open the task manager on the emulator.

7. See *Chapter 3, Exploring Android Studio and the Project Structure,* and the *Using the emulator as a real device* section for how to do this on the emulator if you are unsure.

8. You should now see all the recently run apps on the device.

9. Tap the **Lifecycle Demo** app and notice that the usual three starting messages are shown. This is because our app was previously destroyed.

10. Now, however, tap the **task manager** button again and switch to the **Hello Android** app. Notice that this time, only the **In onPause** and **In onStop** messages are shown. Verify that we have matching output in the logcat. The app has *not* been destroyed.

11. Now, again using the **task manager** button, switch to the **Lifecycle Demonstration** app. You will see that only the **In onStart** and **In onResume** messages are shown, indicating that `onCreate` was not required to get the app running again. This is as expected because the app was not previously destroyed, merely stopped.

Next, let's talk about what we saw when we ran the app.

Examining the lifecycle demo app output

When we started the lifecycle demo app for the first time, we saw that the `onCreate`, `onStart`, and `onResume` methods were called. Then, when we closed the app using the **back** button, the `onPause`, `onStop`, and `onDestroy` methods were called.

Furthermore, we know from our code that the original versions of all these methods are also called because we are calling them ourselves with the super.on... code, which is the first thing we do in each of our overridden methods.

The quirk in our app's behavior came when we used the task manager to switch between apps – when switching away from the lifecycle demo, it was not destroyed and, subsequently, when switching back, it was not necessary to run onCreate.

> **Where's my Toast?**
>
> The opening three and closing three Toast messages are queued and the methods have already completed by the time they are shown. You can verify this by running the experiments again and will see that all three starting/closing log messages are output before even the second Toast message is shown. However, the Toast messages do reinforce our knowledge about the order, if not the timing.

It is entirely possible (but not that likely) that you got slightly different results when you followed the preceding steps. What we know for sure is that when our apps are run on thousands of different devices by millions of different users who have different preferences for interacting with their devices, Android will call the lifecycle methods at times we cannot easily predict.

For example, what happens when the user exits the app by pressing the home button? When we open two apps one after the other and then use the back button to switch to the earlier app, will that destroy or just stop the app? What happens when the user has a dozen apps in their task manager and the operating system needs to destroy some apps that were previously only stopped; will our app be one of the "victims"?

You can, of course, test out all the preceding scenarios on the emulator. But the results will only be true for the one time you test it. It is not guaranteed that the same behavior will be shown every time and certainly not on every different Android device.

At last some good news! The solution to all this complexity is to follow a few simple rules:

- Set up your app ready to run in the onCreate method.
- Load your user's data in the onResume method.
- Save your user's data in the onPause method.
- Tidy up your app and make it a good Android citizen in the onDestroy method.
- Watch out throughout the book for a couple of occasions when we might like to use onStart and onStop.

If we do what we mentioned above (we will see how over the course of the book), we can just stop worrying about all this lifecycle stuff and let Android handle it! There are a few more methods we can override as well. So, let's look at them.

Some other overridden methods

You may have noticed that there are two other autogenerated methods in the code of all our projects using the Basic Activity template. They are `onCreateOptionsMenu` and `onOptionsItemSelected`. Most Android apps have a pop-up menu so Android Studio generates one by default; including the basic code to make it work.

You can see the XML that describes the menu in `res/menu/menu_main.xml` from the project explorer. The key line of XML code is this:

```
<item
        android:id="@+id/action_settings"
        android:orderInCategory="100"
        android:title="@string/action_settings"
        app:showAsAction="never" />
```

This describes a menu **item** with the text **Settings**. If you run any of the apps built with the Basic Activity template we have created so far, you will see the button as shown next:

Figure 6.2 – Settings button

If you tap the button, you will see it in action as shown next:

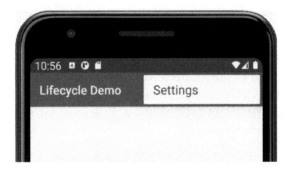

Figure 6.3 – Settings option

So, how do the onCreateOptionsMenu and onOptionsItemSelected methods produce these results?

The onCreateOptionsMenu method loads the menu from the menu_main.xml file with this line of code:

```
getMenuInflater().inflate(R.menu.menu_main, menu);
```

It is called by the default version of the onCreate method, which is why we don't see it happen.

> **Tip**
> We will use the pop-up menu in *Chapter 17, Data Persistence and Sharing,* to switch between different screens of our app.

The onOptionsItemSelected method is called when the user taps the menu button. This method handles what will happen when an item is selected. Now nothing happens – it just returns true.

Feel free to add Toast and Log messages to these methods to test out the order and timing I have just described. I just thought it was a good time to quickly introduce these two methods because they have been lurking around in our code without an introduction and I didn't want them to feel left out.

Now we have seen how the Android lifecycle works and been introduced to a whole bunch of methods we can override to interact with the lifecycle, we had better learn the fundamentals of Java so that we can write some code to go in these methods as well as our own methods.

The structure of Java code – revisited

We have already seen that each time we create a new Android project, we also create a new Java **package** as a kind of container for the code we write.

We have also learned about and played around with **classes**. We have imported and taken direct advantage of classes from the Android API such as `Log` and `Toast`. We have also used the `AppCompatActivity` class, but in a different manner to `Log` and `Toast`. You might remember the first line of code in all our projects so far, after the `import` statements, used the `extends` keyword:

```
public class MainActivity extends AppCompatActivity {
```

When we extend a class as opposed to just importing it, we are making it our own. In fact, if you take another look at the line of code, you can see that we are making a new class with a new name, `MainActivity`. but basing it on the `AppCompatActivity` class from the Android API.

> **Important note**
>
> The `AppCompatActivity` class is a slightly modified version of the `Activity` class. It gives extra features for older versions of Android that would otherwise not be present. Everything we have discussed regarding `Activity` is equally true for `AppCompatActivity`. We will see some more variations in the `Activity` class as we progress. It is entirely possible that you have a different class in place of `AppCompatActivity`, dependent upon changes that have taken place since this was written. Updates of Android Studio will sometimes change the default `Activity` class that it uses when it creates a new project. If the name ends in `...Activity`, it doesn't matter because everything we have discussed and will discuss is equally true. I will just refer to this class simply as `Activity`.

In summary:

- We can import classes to use them.
- We can extend classes to use them.
- We will eventually make our own classes.

> **The crucial point here is this:**
>
> Classes, in their various forms, are the foundations of every single line of code in Java. Everything in Java is or is part of a class.

Our own classes and those written by others are the building blocks of our code and the methods within the classes wrap the functional code – the code that does the work.

We can write methods within the classes that we extend; as we did with `topClick` and `bottomClick` in *Chapter 2, First Contact: Java, XML, and the UI Designer*. Furthermore, we overrode methods that are already part of classes written by others – such as `onCreate` and `onPause` and so on.

The only code, however, that we put in these methods was a few calls using `Toast` and `Log`. We aren't going to code the next killer app with just that. But now we can take some more steps.

Introducing fragments and the lifecycle

You probably remember from *Chapter 2, First Contact: Java, XML, and the UI Designer,* that the Java code in the Basic Activity template is not just contained in the `MainActivity.java` file. There are also the `FirstFragment.java` and `SecondFragment.java` files. These files, we learned, contain the code that controls what happens when the user navigates between the two screens of the Basic Activity template app. The code inside these two files is different in structure from the `MainActivity.java` file. Here is a quick peek at `FirstFragment.java`:

```java
public class FirstFragment extends Fragment {

    @Override
    public View onCreateView(
            LayoutInflater inflater, ViewGroup container,
            Bundle savedInstanceState
    )
    {
        ...
    }

    ...
}
```

I have omitted much of the code from this file because it is unnecessary for the purpose of this introductory discussion. A **Fragment** is also a class just as an **Activity** is a class. A `Fragment` can, and in this app does, represent a screen from the app. The `Fragment` classes of this app and other apps that contain them are controlled by the `Activity` class(es). We will look closely at the `Fragment` class in *Chapter 24, Design Patterns, Multiple Layouts, and Fragments*. The thing to notice here is that the `Fragment` class has an `onCreateView` method.

When our app uses one or more instances of the `Fragment` class, they will also be a part of the Android lifecycle and the `Fragment` class has its own set of lifecycle methods, of which `onCreateView` is one.

Exactly how the OS lifecycle, the `Activity` class, and the `Fragment` class interact with each other will be explained in *Chapter 24, Design Patterns, Multiple Layouts, and Fragments*. It is just worth knowing for now that they are all interconnected.

Summary

We have learned about the Android lifecycle and how the operating system calls set methods at set times.

We have also seen that it is not only us that can call our code. The operating system can also call the code contained within the methods we have overridden. By adding the appropriate code into the various overridden lifecycle methods, we can be sure that the right code will be executed at the right time.

What we need to do now is learn how to write some more Java code. In the next chapter, we'll start to focus on Java, and because we have such a good grounding already on Android, we will have no problem practicing and using everything we learn.

7
Java Variables, Operators, and Expressions

In this chapter and the next, we are going to learn and practice the core fundamentals of Java data and how to manipulate that data. In this chapter, we will focus on creating and understanding the data itself, and in the next chapter, we will see how to manipulate and respond to it.

We will also quickly recap on what we learned in the earlier chapters about Java, and then dive into learning how to write our very own Java code. The principles we are about to learn are not limited to Java but are applicable to other programming languages as well.

By the end of the chapter, you will be comfortable writing Java code that creates and uses data within Android. This chapter takes you through the following topics:

- Understanding Java syntax and jargon
- Storing and using data with variables
- Using variables

- Changing values in variables with operators
- Trying out expressions

Let's learn some Java.

Technical requirements

You can find the code files present in this chapter on GitHub at `https://github.com/PacktPublishing/Android-Programming-for-Beginners-Third-Edition/tree/main/chapter%2007`.

Java is everywhere

The core Java fundamentals that we are about to learn apply when working within classes that we inherit from (such as `AppCompatActivity`), as well as classes that we write ourselves (as we will start to do in *Chapter 10, Object-Oriented Programming*).

As it is more logical to learn the basics before we write our own classes, we will be using an extended `Activity` class, `AppCompatActivity`, to add some Java code in a mini project. We will use the `Log` and `Toast` classes again to see the results of our coding in the overridden `onCreate` method of the `Activity` class, to trigger the execution of our code.

When however, we move on to *Chapter 10, Object-Oriented Programming* and start to write our own classes, as well as understand more about how classes written by others work, everything we have learned here will apply then too—in fact, all the Java that you learn in this chapter and the next will apply, if you strip it out of the `Activity` class and paste it into another Java environment, such as the following:

- Any of the major desktop operating systems
- Many modern TVs
- Sat nav
- Smart fridges

Java will work there too!

> **Calling all Java gurus**
>
> If you have already done some Java programming and understand the following keywords (`if`, `else`, `while`, `do while`, `switch`, and `for`), you can probably skip to *Chapter 10, Object-Oriented Programming*. Alternatively, you might like to skim over this information as a refresher.

Let's get on with learning how to code in Java.

Understanding Java syntax and jargon

Throughout this book, we will use plain English to discuss some technical things. You will never be asked to read a technical explanation of a Java or Android concept that has not been previously explained in non-technical language.

So far, on a few occasions I have asked that you accept a simplified explanation to offer a fuller explanation at a more appropriate time, as I have done with classes and methods.

Having said that, the Java and Android communities are full of people who speak in technical terms, and to join in and learn from these communities, you need to understand the terms they use. So, the approach this book takes is to learn a concept or appreciate an idea using entirely plain-speaking language, but at the same time introduce the jargon/technical term as part of the learning.

Java syntax is the way we put together the language elements of Java to produce code that works in the Dalvik **virtual machine** (**VM**). The Java syntax is a combination of the words we use and the formation of those words into sentence-like structures that make up our code.

These Java "words" are many in number, but taken in small chunks are certainly easier to learn than any human-spoken language. We call these words **keywords**.

I am confident that if you can read then you can learn Java, because learning Java is much easier. What, then, separates someone who has finished an elementary Java course and an expert programmer?

The exact same things that separate a student of language and a master poet. Expertise in Java comes not in the number of Java keywords we know how to use but in the way we use them. Mastery of the language comes through practice, further study, and using the keywords more skillfully. Many consider programming an art as much as a science, and there is some truth to this.

More code comments

As you become more advanced at writing Java programs, the solutions you use to create your programs will become longer and more complicated. Furthermore, as we will see in later chapters, Java was designed to manage complexity by having us divide up our code into separate classes, very often across multiple files.

Code comments are parts of the Java program that do not have any function in the program execution. A compiler ignores these comments. They serve to help a programmer to document, explain, and clarify their code, to make it more understandable to themselves later or to other programmers who might need to use or change it.

We have already seen a single-line comment. This is reproduced here:

```
// this is a comment explaining what is going on
```

The preceding comment begins with the two // forward-slash characters. The comment ends at the end of the line. So, anything on that line is for humans only, whereas anything on the next line (unless it's another comment) needs to be syntactically correct Java code, as illustrated here:

```
// I can write anything I like here
but this line will cause an error
```

We can use multiple single-line comments, as illustrated here:

```
// Below is an important note
// I am an important note
// We can have as many single line comments like this as we
like
```

Single-line comments are also useful if we want to temporarily disable a line of code. We can put // in front of the code and it will not be included in the program. Remember this code, which tells Android to load our layout?

```
// setContentView(R.layout.activity_main);
```

In the preceding situation, the layout will not be loaded and the app will have a blank screen when run, as the entire line of code is ignored by the compiler.

Important note

We saw this in *Chapter 5, Beautiful Layouts with CardView and ScrollView*, when we temporarily commented out one of our methods.

There is another type of comment in Java, known as a **multiline comment**. A multiline comment is useful for longer comments that span multiple lines and for adding things such as copyright information at the top of a code file. As with a single-line comment, a multiline comment can be used to temporarily disable code—in this case, usually across multiple lines.

Everything in between the leading /* and the ending */ is ignored by the compiler. Here are some examples:

```
/*
    You can tell I am good at this because my
    code has so many helpful comments in it.
*/
```

There is no limit to the number of lines in a multiline comment; which type of comment is best to use will depend upon the situation. In this book, I will always explain every line of code explicitly in the text, but you will often find liberally sprinkled comments within the code itself that add further explanation, insight, or context. So, it's always a good idea to read all the code thoroughly too.

```
/*
    The winning lottery numbers for next Saturday are
    9,7,12,34,29,22
    But you still want to make Android apps?
*/
```

> **Tip**
> All the best Java programmers liberally sprinkle their code with comments!

Storing and using data with variables

We can think of a **variable** as a named storage box. We choose a name, perhaps variableA. These names are like our programmer's window into the memory of the user's Android device.

Variables are values in memory, ready to be used or altered when necessary by using their name.

Computer memory has a highly complex system of addressing, which fortunately we do not need to interact with. Java variables allow us to devise our own convenient names for all the data we need our program to work with. The **Dalvik VM (DVM)** will handle all the technicalities to interact with the operating system, and the operating system will in turn interact with the physical memory.

So, we can think of our Android device's memory as a huge warehouse, just waiting for us to add our variables. When we assign names to our variables, they are stored in the warehouse, ready for when we need them. When we use our variable's name, the device knows exactly what we are referring to. We can then tell it to do things such as this:

- Assign a value to `variableA`

- Add `variableA` to `variableB`

- Test the value of `variableB` and take an action based on the result

- …and more, as we will soon see

In a typical app, we might have a variable named `unreadMessages`, perhaps to hold the number of unread messages a user has. We could add to it when a new message arrives, take away from it when the user reads a message, and show it to the user somewhere in the app layout so that they know how many unread messages they have.

Here are some situations that might arise:

- A user gets three new messages, so add 3 to the value of `unreadMessages`.

- A user logs in to the app, so use `Toast` to display a message along with the value stored in `unreadMessages`.

- A user sees that a bunch of messages are from someone they don't like, and deletes six messages. We could then subtract 6 from `unreadMessages`.

These are arbitrary examples of names for variables, and if you don't use any of the characters or keywords that Java restricts, you can actually call your variables whatever you like.

In practice, however, it is best to adopt a **naming convention** so that your variable names will be consistent. In this book, we will use a loose convention of variable names, starting with a lowercase letter. When there is more than one word in the variable's name, the second word will begin with an uppercase letter. This is called **camel casing**.

Here are some examples of this:

- `unreadMessages`
- `contactName`
- `isFriend`

Before we look at some real Java code with some variables, we need to first look at the types of variables we can create and use.

Types of variables

It is not hard to imagine that even a simple app will have quite a few variables. In the previous section, we introduced the `unreadMessages` variable as a hypothetical example. What if an app has a list of contacts and needs to remember each of their names? We might then need variables for each contact.

And what about when an app needs to know whether a contact is also a friend or just a regular contact? We might need code that tests for friend status and then adds messages from that contact into an appropriate folder so that the user knows if they were messages from a friend or not.

Another common requirement in a computer program, including Android apps, is the true or wrong false.

To cover this and many other types of data you might want to store or manipulate, Java has **types**.

Primitive types

There are many types of variables, and we can even invent our own types as well. But for now, we will look at the most used built-in Java types, and to be fair, they cover just about every situation we are likely to run into for a while. Providing some examples is the best way to explain types.

We have already discussed the hypothetical `unreadMessages` variable. This variable is of course a number, so we have to tell the Java compiler this by giving it an appropriate type.

On the other hand, the hypothetical `contactName` variable will of course hold the characters that make up a contact's name.

The type that holds a regular number is called an **int** type, and the type that holds name-like data is called a **String** type; and if we try to store a contact name in an int type such as unreadMessages, meant for numbers, we will certainly run into trouble, as we can see from the following screenshot:

Figure 7.1 – Storing contact name

As we can see, Java was designed to make it impossible for such errors to make it into a running program.

Here are the main types of variables in Java:

- int: An int type is for storing integers, whole numbers. This type uses 32 pieces (**bits**) of memory and can therefore store values a little in excess of 2 billion, including negative values too.

- long: As the name hints at, long data types can be used when even larger numbers are needed. A long type uses 64 bits of memory, and 2 to the power of 63 is what we can store in this. If you want to see what that looks like, here it is: 9,223,372,036,854,775,807. Perhaps surprisingly, there are uses for long variables, but the point is that if a smaller variable will do, we should use it because our program will use less memory.

> **Important note**
>
> You might be wondering when you might use numbers of this size. The obvious examples would be math or science applications that do complex calculations, but another use might be for timing. When you time how long something takes, the Java Date class uses the number of milliseconds since January 1, 1970. A millisecond is one-thousandth of a second, so there have been quite a few of them since 1970.

- `float`: This is for floating-point numbers—that is, numbers where there is precision beyond the decimal point. As the fractional part of a number takes memory space just as the whole-number part, the range of a number possible in a `float` type is therefore decreased compared to non-floating-point numbers. So, unless our variable will use the extra precision, `float` would not be our data type of choice.

- `double`: When the precision in a `float` type is not enough, we have `double`.

- `boolean`: We will be using plenty of Booleans throughout the book. The `boolean` variable type can be either `true` or `false`; nothing else. Booleans answer questions such as the following:

Is the contact a friend?

Are there any new messages?

Are two examples for a Boolean enough?

- `char`: Store a single alphanumeric character in a `char` type. It's not going to change the world on its own, but could be useful if we put lots of them together.

- `short`: This type is like a space-saving version of `int`. It can be used to store whole numbers with both positive and negative values, and can have mathematical operations performed on it. Where it differs from `int` is that it uses only 16 bits of memory, which is just half the amount of memory compared to `int`. The downside to `short` is that it can only store half the range of values compared to `int`, from -32768 to 32767.

- `byte`: This type is like an even more space-saving version of `short`. It can be used to store whole numbers with both positive and negative values, and can have mathematical operations performed on it. Where it differs from `int` and `short` is that it uses only 8 bits of memory, which is just half the amount of memory compared to `byte`, and quarter the memory of `int`. The downside to `byte` is that it can only store half the range of values compared to `int`, from -32768 to 32767. Saving 8 or even 16 bits in total is unlikely to ever matter; however, if you needed to store millions of whole numbers in a program, then `short` and `byte` are worth considering.

> **Important note**
>
> I have kept this discussion on data types to a practical level that is useful in the context of this book. If you are interested in how a data type's value is stored and why the limits are what they are, then have a look at the *Oracle Java Tutorials* site at `http://docs.oracle.com/javase/tutorial/java/nutsandbolts/datatypes.html`. Note that you do not need any more information than we have already discussed to continue with this book.

As we just learned, each type of data that we might want to store will need a specific amount of memory. For this reason, we must let the Java compiler know the type of the variable before we begin to use it.

The variables described previously are known as **primitive** types. Most primitive types are used throughout different programming languages (as well as keywords), so if you have a good understanding of the types and keywords, then jumping into another language will be far easier than the first time! These types use predefined amounts of memory, and so, using our warehouse storage analogy, fit into predefined sizes of storage box.

As the "primitive" label suggests, they are not as sophisticated as **reference** types.

Reference types

You might have noticed that we didn't cover the `String` variable type we previously used to introduce the concept of variables that hold alphanumeric data, such as a contact's name.

Strings

Strings are one example of a special type of variable, known as a **reference** type. They quite simply refer to a place in memory where storage of the variable begins, but the reference type itself does not define a specific amount of memory. The reason for this is straightforward: it's because we don't always know how much data will need to be stored in it until the program is run.

We can think of Strings and other reference types as continually expanding and contracting storage boxes. So, won't one of these `String` reference types bump into another variable eventually?

As we are thinking about a device's memory as a huge warehouse full of racks of labeled storage boxes, then you can think of a DVM as a super-efficient forklift truck driver that puts the different types of storage boxes in the most appropriate place; and, if it becomes necessary, the DVM will quickly move stuff around in a fraction of a second to avoid collisions. Also, when required, Dalvik, the forklift truck driver, will even vaporize any unneeded storage boxes.

This all happens at the same time as constantly unloading new storage boxes of all types and placing them in the best place for that type of variable. Dalvik keeps reference variables in a different part of the warehouse from primitive variables, and we will learn more details about this in *Chapter 12, The Stack, the Heap, and the Garbage Collector*.

Strings can be used to store any keyboard character, like a `char` type but of almost any length. Anything from a contact's name to an entire book can be stored in a single `String` type. We will be using Strings regularly, including in this chapter.

There are a couple more reference types we will explore as well.

Arrays

Arrays are a way to store lots of variables of the same type, ready for quick and efficient access. We will look at arrays in *Chapter 15, Arrays, Maps, and Random Numbers*.

Think of an array as an aisle in our warehouse, with all variables of a certain type lined up in a precise order. Arrays are reference types, so Dalvik keeps these in the same part of the warehouse as Strings. We might, for example, use an array to store dozens of contacts in.

Classes

Another reference type is the `class` type, which we have already discussed but not explained properly. We will be getting familiar with classes in *Chapter 10, Object-Oriented Programming*.

Now, we know that each type of data that we might want to store will require an amount of memory. Hence, we must let the Java compiler know the type of the variable before we begin to use it. We do this with a variable **declaration**.

Using variables

That's enough theory. Let's see how we would use our variables and types. Remember that each primitive type needs a specific amount of real device memory. This is one of the reasons why the compiler needs to know what type a variable will be.

Variable declaration

We must first **declare** a variable and its type before we try to do anything with it. To declare a variable of type int with the name unreadMessages, we would type the following:

```
int unreadMessages;
```

That's it—simply state the type (in this case, int), then leave a space and type the name you want to use for this variable. Note also that the ; semicolon at the end of the line will tell the compiler that we are done with this line and that what follows, if anything, is not part of the variable declaration.

Similarly, for almost all the other variable types, the declaration would occur in the same way. Here are some examples. The variable names in the examples are arbitrary. This is like reserving a labeled storage box in a warehouse.

Have a look at the following code snippet:

```
long millisecondsElapsed;
float accountBalance;
boolean isFriend;
char contactFirstInitial;
String messageText;
```

Notice I said *almost all the other variable types*. One of the exceptions is variables of the class type. We have already seen some code declaring variables of the class type. Do you remember this code snippet from *Chapter 3, Exploring Android Studio and the Project Structure* in the MainActivity.java file?

```
FloatingActionButton fab...
```

This edited snippet of code is declaring a variable called fab of type FloatingActionButton. But we are off track a little, and will come back to classes in *Chapter 10, Object-Oriented Programming*.

Variable initialization

Initialization is the next step. Here, for each type, we initialize a value to the variable. This is like placing a value inside a storage box in a warehouse.

```
unreadMessages = 10;
millisecondsElapsed = 14381651168411;// 29th July 2016 11:19am
accountBalance = 129.52f;
isFriend = true;
contactFirstInitial = 'C';
messageText = "Hi reader, I just thought I would let you know
that Charles Babbage was an early computing pioneer and he
invented the difference engine. If you want to know more about
him, you can click find look here: www.charlesbabbage.net";
```

Notice that the `char` variable uses `'` single quotes around the initialized value, while the `String` type uses `"` double quotes.

We can also combine the declaration and initialization steps. Here, we declare and initialize the same variables as we have previously, but in one step:

```
int unreadMessages = 10;
long millisecondsElapsed = 14381651168411;//29th July 2016
11:19am
float accountBalance = 129.52f;
boolean isFriend = true;
char contactFirstInitial = 'C';
String messageText = " Hi reader, I just thought I would let
you know that Charles Babbage was an early computing pioneer
and he invented the difference engine. If you want to know more
about him, you can click this link www.charlesbabbage.net";
```

Whether we declare and initialize separately or together is dependent upon the specific situation. The important thing is that we must do both at some point.

```
int a;
// That's me declared and ready to go!
// The line below attempts to output a to the console
Log.i("info", "int a = " + a);
// Oh no I forgot to initialize a!!
```

This would cause the following:

Compiler Error: Variable a might not have been initialized

There is a significant exception to this rule. In certain circumstances, variables can have **default values**. We will see this in *Chapter 10, Object-Oriented Programming*; however, it is good practice to both declare and initialize variables.

Changing values in variables with operators

Of course, in almost any program, we are going to need to "do things" with these variables' values. We manipulate (change) variables with **operators**. Here is a list of perhaps the most common Java operators that allow us to manipulate variables. You do not need to memorize them as we will look at every line of code as and when we use them for the first time. We have already seen the first operator when we initialized our variables, but we will see it again, this time being a bit more adventurous.

The assignment operator

This is the assignment operator: =

It makes the variable to the left of the operator the same as the value to the right—for example, like in this line of code:

```
unreadMessages = newMessages;
```

After the previous line of code has executed, the value stored in `unreadMessages` will be the same as the value stored in `newMessages`.

The addition operator

This is the addition operator: +

It will add together values on either side of the operator and is usually used in conjunction with the assignment operator. For example, it can add together two variables that have numeric values, like in this next line of code:

```
unreadMessages = newMessages + unreadMessages;
```

Once the previous code has executed the combined value of the values held by `newMessages` and `unreadMessages`, this is now stored in `unreadMessages`. As another example of the same thing, look at this line of code:

```
accountBalance = yesterdaysBalance + todaysDeposits;
```

> **Important note**
>
> Notice that it is perfectly acceptable to use the same variable simultaneously on both sides of an operator.

The subtraction operator

This is the subtraction operator: -

It will subtract the value on the right side of the operator from the value on the left. This is usually used in conjunction with the assignment operator, as in this code example:

```
unreadMessages = unreadMessages - 1;
```

Or, as a similar example, it is used in this line of code:

```
accountBalance = accountBalance - withdrawals;
```

After the previous line of code has executed, `accountBalance` will hold its original value minus whatever the value held in `withdrawals` is.

The division operator

This is the division operator: /

It will divide the number on the left by the number on the right. Again, it is usually used in conjunction with the assignment operator. Here is an example line of code:

```
fairShare = numSweets / numChildren;
```

If in the previous line of code `numSweets` held nine sweets and `numChildren` held three sweets, then `fairShare` will now hold the value of three sweets.

The multiplication operator

This is the multiplication operator: *

It will multiply variables and numbers together and, as with many of the other operators, is usually used in conjunction with the assignment operator. For example, look at this line of code:

```
answer = 10 * 10;
```

Alternatively, look at this line of code:

```
biggerAnswer = 10 * 10 * 10;
```

After the previous two lines of code have executed, `answer` holds the value 100 and `biggerAnswer` holds the value 1000.

The increment operator

This is the increment operator: ++

The increment operator is a quick way to add one to something. For example, look at this next line of code, which uses the addition operator:

```
myVariable = myVariable + 1;
```

The previous line of code has the same result as this much more compact code here:

```
myVariable ++;
```

The decrement operator

This is the decrement operator: - -

The decrement operator (as you probably guessed) is a quick way to subtract one from something. For example, look at this next line of code, which uses the subtraction operator:

```
myVariable = myVariable -1;
```

The previous line of code is the same as `myVariable --;`.

> **Important note**
>
> The formal names for these operators are slightly different from those explained previously—for example, the division operator is one of the multiplicative operators. But the names given previously are far more useful for the purpose of learning Java, and if you used the term *division operator* while conversing with someone from the Java community, they would know exactly what you mean.

There are even more operators than this in Java. We will meet some of them in the next chapter, when we learn about making decisions in Java.

> **Important note**
>
> If you are curious about operators, there is a complete list of them on the *Oracle Java Tutorials* website, at `http://docs.oracle.com/javase/tutorial/java/nutsandbolts/operators.html`. All the operators needed to complete the projects in this book will be fully explained in this book. The link is provided for the more curious among us.

Trying out expressions

Let's try using some declarations, assignments, and operators. When we bundle these elements together into some meaningful syntax, we call this an **expression**. Let's write a quick app to try some expressions out. We will then use `Toast` and `Log` to check our results.

Expressing Yourself demo app

Create a new project called `Expressing Yourself`, use the **Basic Activity** project, and leave all the other settings at their defaults. The completed code that we will write in this project can be found in the `Chapter 7/Expressing Yourself` folder of the download bundle.

Switch to the **MainActivity.java** tab in the editor, and we will write some code. In the `onCreate` method, just before the `}` closing curly brace, add this code:

```
int numMessages;
```

Directly below the previous line of code, we will initialize a value to `numMessages`.

Next, add this line of code:

```
numMessages = 10;
```

Immediately after the previous line of code and before the `}` closing curly brace of `onCreate`, add the following code:

```
// Output the value of numMessages
Log.i("numMessages = ", "" + numMessages);


numMessages++;
numMessages = numMessages + 1;
Log.i("numMessages = ", "" + numMessages);
// Now a boolean (just true or false)
```

```
boolean isFriend = true;
Log.i("isFriend = ", "" + isFriend);
// A contact and an important message
String contact = "James Gosling";
String message = "Dear reader, I invented Java.";
// Now let's play with those String variables
Toast.makeText(this, "Message from " + contact, Toast.LENGTH_
SHORT).show();
Toast.makeText(this, "Message is: " + message, Toast.LENGTH_
SHORT).show();
```

> **Important note**
>
> You will need to import the Toast and Log classes, as we have done
> previously.

Run the app, and we can examine the output and then the code. In the logcat window, you
will see the following output:

```
numMessages =: 10
numMessages =: 12
isFriend =: true
```

On the screen, you will see two pop-up Toast messages. The first says **Message from
James Gosling.** The second says **Message is:Dear reader, I invented Java.** This is shown
in the following screenshot:

Figure 7.2 – The second pop-up Toast message

Let's step through the code and make sure that each line is clear before moving on.

First, we declared and initialized an `int` type variable called `numMessages`. We could have done it on one line, but we did it like this:

```
int numMessages;
numMessages = 10;
```

Next, we used `Log` to output a message. Instead of simply typing the message between the `""` double quote marks, this time we used the + operator to add `numMessages` onto the output, and as we saw in the console, the actual value of `numMessages` was output, as follows:

```
// Output the value of numMessages
Log.i("numMessages = ", "" + numMessages);
```

Just to further prove that our `numMessages` variable is as versatile as it should be, we used the ++ operator, which should have increased its value by 1 and then added `numMessages` to itself, using + 1. We then output the new value of `numMessages`, and indeed found its value has increased to 12 from 10, as illustrated in the following code snippet:

```
numMessages ++;
numMessages = numMessages + 1;
Log.i("numMessages = ", "" + numMessages);
```

Next, we created a `boolean`-type variable called `isFriend`, and output that to the console. We saw from the output that `true` was displayed. This variable type will fully prove its usefulness when we look at decision making in the next section. The code is illustrated in the following snippet:

```
// Now a boolean (just true or false)
boolean isFriend = true;
Log.i("isFriend = ", "" + isFriend);
```

After this, we declared and initialized two `String`-type variables, as follows:

```
// A contact and an important message
String contact = "James Gosling";
String message = "Dear reader, I invented Java.";
```

Finally, we output the `String` variables using `Toast`. We used a hardcoded part of the `"Message from "` message, and added the variable part of the message with + `contact`. We used the same technique to form the second `Toast` message as well.

> **Tip**
>
> When we add two Strings together to make a longer `String` type, this is called **concatenation**.

```
// Now let's play with those String variables
Toast.makeText(this, "Message from " + contact, Toast.LENGTH_
SHORT).show();
Toast.makeText(this, "Message is:" + message, Toast.LENGTH_
SHORT).show();
```

Now, we can declare variables, initialize them to a value, change them around a bit, and output them using `Toast` or `Log`.

Summary

At last, we have used some serious Java. We learned about variables, declaration, and initialization. We saw how to use operators to change the value of variables. It's all right if you don't remember everything straight away as we will constantly be using these techniques and keywords throughout the book.

In the next chapter, let's look at how we can make decisions based on the values of these variables and find out how this is useful to us.

8
Java Decisions and Loops

We have just learned about variables and we know how we can change the values that they hold with expressions, but how can we take a course of action dependent upon the value of a variable?

We can certainly add the number of new messages to the number of previously unread messages, but how might we, for example, trigger an action within our app when the user has read all their messages?

The first problem is that we need a way to test the value of a variable and then respond when the value falls within a range of values or is a specific value.

Another problem that is common in all forms of programming is that we need sections of our code to be executed a certain number of times (more than once or sometimes not at all) depending on the value of variables.

To solve the first problem, we will look at making decisions in Java with `if`, `else`, and `switch`. To solve the latter, we will look at loops in Java with `while`, `do while`, `for`, and `break`.

Coming up in this chapter, we will cover the following:

- Making decisions with `if`, `else`, `else if`, and `switch`
- The `switch` demo app
- Java `while` loops and `do while` loops
- Java `for` loops
- Loops demo app

Let's learn some more Java.

Technical requirements

You can find the code files present in this chapter on GitHub at `https://github.com/PacktPublishing/Android-Programming-for-Beginners-Third-Edition/tree/main/chapter%2008`.

Making decisions in Java

Our Java code will constantly be making decisions. For example, we might need to know whether the user has new messages or whether they have a certain number of friends. We need to be able to test our variables to see whether they meet certain conditions and then execute a certain section of code depending upon whether they do or not.

In this section, as our code gets more complicated, it helps to present it in a way that makes it more readable. Let's look at code indenting to make our discussion about decisions easier.

Indenting code for clarity

You have probably noticed that the Java code in our projects is indented. For example, the first line of code inside the `MainActivity` class is indented by one tab. Also, the first line of code is indented inside each method. Here is an annotated screenshot to make this clear and as another quick example:

```
public class MainActivity extends AppCompatActivity {

TAB @Override
  protected void onCreate(Bundle savedInstanceState) {
    TAB super.onCreate(savedInstanceState);
      setContentView(R.layout.activity_main);
      Toolbar toolbar = (Toolbar) findViewById(R.id.toolbar);
      setSupportActionBar(toolbar);

    FloatingActionButton fab = (FloatingActionButton) findViewById(R.id.fab);
    fab.setOnClickListener((view) → {
        Snackbar.make(view, text: "Replace with your own action", Snackbar.LENGTH_LONG)
              .setAction( text: "Action", listener: null).show();
    });
  }
}
```

Figure 8.1 – Indented Java code

Notice also that when the indented block has ended, often with a closing curly brace, },
the } is indented to the same extent as the line of code that began the block.

We do this to make the code more readable. It is not part of the Java syntax, however, and
the code will still compile if we don't do this.

As our code gets more complicated, indenting, along with comments, helps to keep the
meaning and structure of our code clear. I mention this now because when we start to
learn the syntax for making decisions in Java, indenting becomes especially useful and it is
recommended that you indent your code the same way.

Much of this indenting is done for us by Android Studio but not all of it.

Now we know how to present our code more clearly, let's learn about some more
operators, and then we can really get to work with making decisions with Java.

More operators

We can already add (+), take away (-), multiply (*), divide (/), assign (=), increment (++),
and decrement (--) with operators. Let's introduce some more useful operators, and then
we will go straight into actually understanding how to use them in Java.

> **Important Note**
>
> Don't worry about memorizing every operator that follows. Glance over them
> and their explanations and then move quickly on to the next section. There,
> we will put some operators to use and they will become much clearer as we see
> a few examples of what they allow us to do. They are presented here in a list
> so they are more convenient to refer back to when not intermingled with the
> discussion about implementation that follows.

We use operators to create an expression that is either true or false. We wrap that expression in parentheses like this: `(expression goes here)`.

The comparison operator

This is the comparison operator and it tests for equality; it is either true or false: `==`

An expression such as `(10 == 9)`, for example, is false. 10 is obviously not equal to 9. However, an expression such as `(2 + 2 == 4)` is obviously true.

> **Note**
>
> Except in *1984* when 2 + 2 == 5 (`https://en.wikipedia.org/wiki/Nineteen_Eighty-Four`).

The logical NOT operator

This is the logical NOT operator: `!`

It is used to test the negation of an expression. Negation means if the expression is false, then the NOT operator causes the expression to be true. An example will help.

The expression `(!(2 + 2 == 5))` evaluates to true because 2 + 2 *is NOT* 5. But a further example of `(!(2 + 2 = 4))` would be false. This is because 2 + 2 obviously *is* 4.

The NOT equal operator

This is the NOT equal operator and it is another comparison operator: `!=`

The NOT equal operator tests whether something is NOT equal. For example, the expression `(10 != 9)` is true. 10 is not equal to 9. On the other hand, `(10 != 10)` is false because 10 clearly is equal to 10.

The greater than operator

Another comparison operator (and there are a few more as well) is the greater than operator. Here it is: `>`

This operator tests whether something is greater than something else. The expression `(10 > 9)` is true but the expression `(9 > 10)` is false.

The less than operator

You can probably guess that this operator tests for values being less than others. This is what the operator looks like: `<`

The expression `(10 < 9)` is false because 10 is not less than 9, while the expression `(9 < 10)` is true.

The greater than or equal to operator

This operator tests whether one value is greater than or equal to another and if either is true, the result is true. This is what the operator looks like: `>=`

As an example, the expression `(10 >= 9)` is true, the expression `(10 >= 10)` is also true, but the expression `(10 >= 11)` is false because 10 is neither greater than nor equal to 11.

The less than or equal to operator

Like the previous operator, this one tests for two conditions but this time less than or equal to. Look at the operator shown next and then we will see some examples: `<=`

The expression `(10 <= 9)` is false, the expression `(10 <= 10)` is true, and the expression `(10 <= 11)` is also true.

The logical AND operator

This operator is known as logical AND. It tests two or more separate parts of an expression and all parts must be true for the entire expression to be true: `&&`

Logical AND is usually used in conjunction with the other operators to build more complex tests. The expression `((10 > 9) && (10 < 11))` is true because both parts are true. On the other hand, the expression `((10 > 9) && (10 < 9))` is false because only one part of the expression is true, `(10 > 9)`, and the other is false, `(10 < 9)`.

The logical OR operator

This operator is called logical OR and it is just like logical AND except that only one of two or more parts of an expression needs to be true for the expression to be true: `||`

Let's look at the last example we used for logical AND but switch the `&&` for `||`. The expression `((10 > 9) || (10 < 9))` is now true because at least one part of the expression is true.

The modulus operator

This operator is called modulus (`%`). It returns the remainder of two numbers after dividing them. For example, the expression (`16 % 3 > 0`) is true because 16 divided by 3 is 5 remainder 1 and 1 is, of course, greater than 0.

Seeing these operators in a more practical context in this chapter and throughout the rest of the book will help clarify the different uses. Now we know how to form expressions with operators, variables, and values. Next, we can look at a way of structuring and combining expressions to make some deep decisions.

How to use all these operators to test variables

All these operators are virtually useless without a way of properly using them to make real decisions that affect real variables and code.

Now we have all the information we need, we can look at a hypothetical situation, then actually see some code for decision making.

Using the Java if keyword

As we saw, operators serve very little purpose on their own, but it was probably useful to see just part of the wide and varied range available to us. Now, when we look at putting the most common operator, `==`, to use, we can start to see the powerful yet fine control that operators offer us.

Let's make the previous examples less abstract. Meet the Java `if` keyword. We will use `if` and a few conditional operators along with a small story to demonstrate their use. Next follows a made-up military situation that will hopefully be less abstract than the previous examples.

The captain is dying and, knowing that his remaining subordinates are not very experienced, he decides to write a Java program to convey his last orders after he has died. The troops must hold one side of a bridge while awaiting reinforcements – but with a few rules that determine their actions.

The first command the captain wants to make sure his troops understand is this:

If they come over the bridge, shoot them.

So, how do we simulate this situation in Java? We need a Boolean variable, isComingOverBridge. The next bit of code assumes that the isComingOverBridge variable has been declared and initialized to either true or false.

We can then use if like this:

```
if (isComingOverBridge) {

    // Shoot them

}
```

If the isComingOverBridge Boolean is true, the code inside the opening and closing curly braces will execute. If isComingOverBridge is false, the program continues after the if block, without running the code within it.

Else do this instead

The captain also wants to tell his troops what to do if the enemy is not coming over the bridge. In this situation, he wants them to stay where they are and wait.

Now we introduce another Java keyword, else. When we want to explicitly do something when if does not evaluate to true, we can use else.

For example, to tell the troops to stay put if the enemy is not coming over the bridge, we could write this code:

```
if (isComingOverBridge) {

    // Shoot them

}else{

    // Hold position

}
```

The captain then realizes that the problem isn't as simple as he first thought. What if the enemy comes over the bridge but has too many troops? His squad would be overrun and slaughtered.

So, he comes up with this code (we'll use some variables as well this time):

```java
boolean isComingOverBridge;
int enemyTroops;
int friendlyTroops;

// Code that initializes the above variables one way or another

// Now the if
if(isComingOverBridge && friendlyTroops > enemyTroops){

    // shoot them

}else if(isComingOveBridge && friendlyTroops < enemyTroops) {

    // blow the bridge

}else{

    // Hold position

}
```

The preceding code has three possible paths of execution. The first is if the enemy is coming over the bridge and the friendly troops are greater in number:

```java
if(isComingOverBridge && friendlyTroops > enemyTroops)
```

The second is if the enemy troops are coming over the bridge but outnumber the friendly troops:

```java
else if(isComingOveBridge && friendlyTroops < enemyTroops)
```

Then, the third and final possible outcome that will execute if neither of the others is true is captured by the final else without an if condition.

Reader challenge

Can you spot a flaw with the preceding code? One that might leave a bunch of inexperienced troops in complete disarray? The possibility of the enemy troops and friendly troops being exactly equal in number has not been handled explicitly and would therefore be handled by the final else, which is meant for when there are no enemy troops. I guess any self-respecting captain would expect his troops to fight in this situation and he could have changed the first if statement to accommodate this possibility:

```
if(isComingOverBridge && friendlyTroops >=
enemyTroops)
```

Finally, the captain's last concern is that if the enemy comes over the bridge waving the white flag of surrender and is promptly slaughtered, then his men would end up as war criminals. The Java code needed is obvious. Using the wavingWhiteFlag Boolean variable, he writes this test:

```
if (wavingWhiteFlag){

    // Take prisoners

}
```

But where to put this code is less clear. In the end, the captain opts for the following nested solution and changes the test for wavingWhiteFlag to logical NOT, like this:

```
if (!wavingWhiteFlag){

    // not surrendering so check everything else

    if(isComingOverTheBridge && friendlyTroops >=
        enemyTroops){

            // shoot them
    }else if(isComingOverTheBridge && friendlyTroops <
                enemyTroops) {

            // blow the bridge

    }
```

```
}else{

    // this is the else for our first if
    // Take prisoners

{

    // Holding position
```

This demonstrates that we can nest if and else statements inside of one another to create quite deep and detailed decisions.

We could go on making more and more complicated decisions with if and else but what we have seen is more than sufficient as an introduction.

It is probably worth pointing out that very often there is more than one way to arrive at a solution to a problem. The *right* way will usually be the way that solves the problem in the clearest and simplest manner.

Let's look at some other ways to make decisions in Java, and then we can put them all together in an app.

Switching to make decisions

We have seen the vast and virtually limitless possibilities of combining the Java operators with if and else statements. But sometimes a decision in Java can be better made in other ways.

When we are deciding based on a clear list of possibilities that don't involve complex combinations, switch is usually the way to go.

We start a switch decision like this:

```
switch(argument){

}
```

In the previous example, argument could be an expression or a variable. Within the curly braces, { }, we can make decisions based on the argument with case and break elements:

```
case x:
    // code for case x
    break;


case y:
    // code for case y
    break;
```

You can see in the previous example that each case states a possible result and each break denotes the end of that case, as well as the point at which no further case statements should be evaluated.

The first break encountered breaks out of the switch block to proceed with the next line of code after the closing brace, }, of the entire switch block.

We can also use default without a value to run some code in case none of the case statements evaluate to true, like this:

```
default:// Look no value
    // Do something here if no other case statements are
        true
    break;
```

Let's write a quick demo app that uses switch.

The switch demo app

To get started, create a new Android project called Switch Demo, use the **Empty Activity** template, and leave all the other settings at their default. Switch to the MainActivity.java file by left-clicking on the **MainActivity.java** tab above the editor and we can start coding.

Let's pretend we are writing an old-fashioned text adventure game, the kind of game where the player types commands such as "Go East," "Go West," "Take Sword," and so on.

In this case, switch could handle that situation with something such as this example code and we could use default to handle the player typing a command that is not specifically handled.

Enter the following code in the onCreate method just before the closing curly brace, }:

```
// get input from user in a String variable called command
String command = "go east";

switch(command) {

    case "go east":
            Log.i("Player: ", "Moves to the East" );
            break;

    case "go west":
            Log.i("Player: ", "Moves to the West" );
            break;

    case "go north":
            Log.i("Player: ", "Moves to the North" );
            break;

    case "go south":
            Log.i("Player: ", "Moves to the South" );
            break;

    case "take sword":
            Log.i("Player: ", "Takes the silver sword" );
            break;

    // more possible cases

    default:
            Log.i("Message: ", "Sorry I don't speak Elfish" );
```

```
            break;

}
```

Run the app a few times. Each time, change the initialization of command to something new. Notice that when you initialize command to something that is explicitly handled by a case statement, we get the expected output. Otherwise, we get the default **Sorry I don't speak Elfish** message.

If we had a lot of code to execute for case, we could contain it all in a method – perhaps like in this next piece of code, where I have highlighted the new line:

```
    case "go west":
                        goWest();
            break;
```

Of course, we would then need to write the new goWest method. Then, when command is initialized to "go west", the goWest method would be executed, and when goWest completes, execution would return to the break statement, which would cause the code to continue after the switch block.

Of course, one of the things this code seriously lacks is interaction with a UI. We have seen how we can call methods from button clicks but even that isn't enough to make this code worthwhile in a real app. We will see how we solve this problem in *Chapter 12, The Stack, the Heap, and the Garbage Collector.*

The other problem we have is that after the code has been executed, that's it! We need it to continually ask the player for instructions, not just once but over and over. We will look at a solution to this problem next.

Repeating code with loops

Here we will learn how to repeatedly execute portions of our code in a controlled and precise way by looking at several types of **loops** in Java. These include while loops, do while loops, and for loops. We will also learn about the most appropriate situations to use the different types of loops.

It would be completely reasonable to ask what loops have to do with programming. But they are exactly what the name implies. They are a way of repeating the same part of the code more than once – or looping over the same part of code although potentially for a different outcome each time.

This can simply mean doing the same thing until the code being looped over (**iterated**) prompts the loop to end. It could be a predetermined number of iterations as specified by the loop code itself. It might be until a predetermined situation or **condition** is met. Or it could be a combination of more than one of these things. Along with `if`, `else`, and `switch`, loops are part of the Java **control flow statements**.

The code that executes when a condition is true is known as the **conditional code**. All the types of loops we will discuss, with the exception of one (the `do while` loop), can be illustrated by this simple diagram:

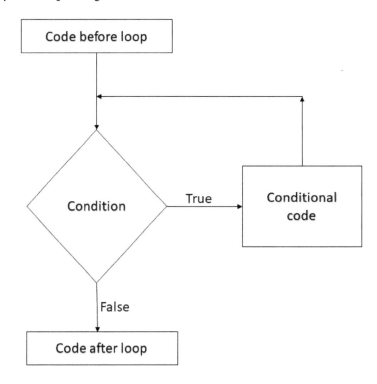

Figure 8.2 – The condition is tested when the loop is reached in the code

This diagram illustrates that when the loop is reached in the code, the condition is tested. If the condition is true, the conditional code is executed. After the conditional code is executed, the condition is tested again. Any time the condition is false, the code continues after the loop. This could mean that the conditional code is never executed.

We will look at all the major types of loops that Java offers us to control our code and we will use some of them to implement a working mini-app to make sure we understand them completely. Let's look at the first and simplest loop type in Java, called the `while` loop.

while loops

Java while loops have the simplest syntax. Think back to the if statements for a moment. We could put virtually any combination of operators and variables in the conditional expression of the if statement. If the expression evaluates to true, then the code in the body of the if block is executed. With the while loop, we also use an expression that can evaluate to true or false. Look at this code:

```
int x = 10;

while(x > 0){
    x--;
    // x decreases by one each pass through the loop
}
```

What happens here is this:

1. Outside of the while loop, an int named x is declared and initialized to 10.
2. Then, the while loop begins. Its condition is x > 0. So, the while loop will execute the code in its body.
3. The code in its body will continue to execute until the condition evaluates to false.

So, the previous code will execute 10 times.

On the first pass, x = 10, on the second pass it equals 9, then 8, and so on. But once x is equal to 0, it is of course no longer greater than 0. At this point, the program will exit the while loop and continue with the first line of code after the while loop.

Just like an if statement, it is possible that the while loop will not execute even once. Look at this example where the code in the while loop will not execute:

```
int x = 10;

while(x > 10){
    // more code here.
    // but it will never run
    // unless x is greater than 10.
}
```

Moreover, there is no limit to the complexity of the conditional expression or the amount of code that can go in the loop body. Here is another example:

```java
int newMessages = 3;
int unreadMessages = 0;


while (newMessages > 0 || unreadMessages > 0) {
    // Display next message
    // etc.
}


// continue here when newMessages and unreadMessages equal 0
```

The preceding `while` loop would continue to execute until both `newMessages` and `unreadMessages` are equal to or less than 0. As the condition uses the logical OR operator, `||`, either one of those conditions being true will cause the `while` loop to continue executing.

It is worth noting that once the body of the loop has been entered, it will always complete even if the expression evaluates to false partway through, as it is not tested again until the code tries to start another pass. Take the following example:

```java
int x = 1;

while (x > 0) {
    x--;
    // x is now 0 so the condition is false
    // But this line still runs
    // and this one
    // and me!
}
```

The preceding loop body will execute exactly once. We can also set a `while` loop that will run forever! This perhaps unsurprisingly is called an infinite loop. Here is an example of an infinite loop:

```
int x = 0;

while(true){
    x++; // I am going to get very big!
}
```

Breaking out of a loop

We might use an infinite loop like this so that we can decide when to exit the loop from a test contained within its body. We would do this by using the `break` keyword when we are ready to leave the loop's body. Here is an example:

```
int x = 0;

while(true){
    x++; //I am going to get very big!
    break; // No, you're not- ha!
    // code doesn't reach here
}
```

You might have been able to guess that we can combine any of the decision-making tools such as `if`, `else`, and `switch` within our `while` loops and all the rest of the loops we will look at in a minute. Take the following example:

```
int x = 0;
int tooBig = 10;

while(true){
    x++; // I am going to get very big!
    if(x == tooBig){
        break;
    } // No, you're not- ha!

    // code reaches here only until x = 10
}
```

It would be simple to go on for many more pages demonstrating the versatility of `while` loops but at some point, we want to get back to doing some real programming. So here is one last concept combined with `while` loops.

The continue keyword

The **continue** keyword acts in a similar way to `break` – up to a point. The `continue` keyword will break out of the loop body but will also check the condition expression afterward so the loop can run again. An example will help:

```java
int x = 0;
int tooBig = 10;
int tooBigToPrint = 5;

while (true) {
    x++; // I am going to get very big!
    if (x == tooBig) {
        break;
    } // No, you're not- ha!

    // code reaches here only until x = 10

    if (x >= tooBigToPrint) {
        // No more printing but keep looping
        continue;
    }
    // code reaches here only until x = 5

    // Print out x

}
```

do while loops

A do `while` loop is very much the same as `while` loops with the exception that a do `while` loop evaluates its expression *after* the body. Look at this modification of the previous figure that represents the flow of a do `while` loop:

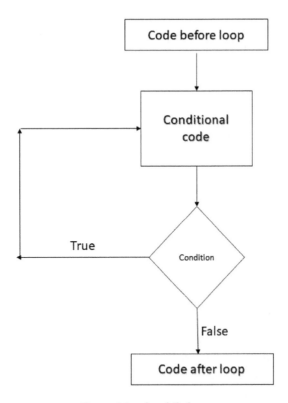

Figure 8.3 – do while loop

This means that a do while loop will always execute the conditional code at least once before checking the loop condition:

```
int x= 1
do{
    x++;
}while(x < 1);
// x now = 2
```

In the previous code, the loop was executed even though the test was false because the test is done after the execution of the loop. The test did, however, prevent the loop body from being executed a second time. This caused x to be incremented once and x now equals 2.

> **Important Note**
> Note that break and continue can also be used in do while loops.

The next type of loop we will cover is the for loop.

for loops

A `for` loop has a slightly more complicated syntax than the `while` or `do while` loops as it takes three parts to initialize. Have a look at the code first, then we will break it apart:

```
for(int i = 0; i < 10;  i++){


    //Something that needs to happen 10 times goes here


}
```

The slightly more complicated form of the `for` loop is clearer when put like this:

```
for(declaration and initialization; condition; change after
each pass through loop).
```

To clarify further, we have the following:

- `declaration and initialization`: We create a new `int` variable, `i`, and initialize it to 0.

- `condition`: Just like the other loops, it refers to the condition that must evaluate to true for the loop to continue.

- `change after each pass through the loop`: In the example, `i++` means that 1 is added/incremented to `i` on each pass. We could also use `i--` to reduce/decrement `i` at each pass:

  ```
  for(int i = 10; i > 0;  i--){
      // countdown
  }
  // blast off i = 0
  ```

  > **Important Note**
  > Note that `break` and `continue` can also be used in `for` loops.

The `for` loop takes control of initialization, condition evaluation, and the modification of the variable.

Loops demo app

To get started, create a new Android project called Loops, use the **Empty Activity** template, and leave all the other settings at their default.

Let's add a few buttons to our UI to make this more fun. Switch to the activity_main. xml file and make sure you are on the **Design** tab, and then follow these steps:

1. Drag a button onto the UI and center it horizontally near the top.
2. In the properties window, change the **text** property to Count Up.
3. In the properties window, change the **onClick** property to countUp.
4. Place a new button just below the previous one and repeat *steps 2* and *3* but this time use Count Down for the **text** property and countDown for the **onClick** property.
5. Place a new button just below the previous one and repeat *steps 2* and *3* but this time use **nested** for the **text** property and the **onClick** property.
6. Click the **Infer Constraints** button to constrain the three buttons in position.

Looks are not important for this demo but run the app and check that the layout looks something like in the following screenshot:

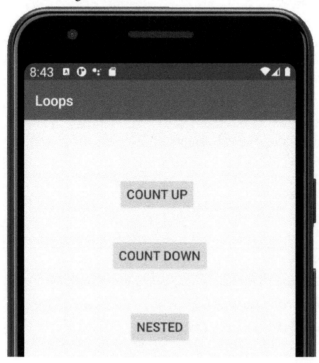

Figure 8.4 – Buttons added to the UI

> **Important Note**
>
> I also deleted the "Hello World!" `TextView` but this is not necessary.

What is important is that we have three buttons labeled **COUNT UP**, **COUNT DOWN**, and **NESTED**, which call methods named **countUp**, **countDown**, and **nested**, respectively.

Switch to the `MainActivity.java` file by left-clicking the **MainActivity.java** tab above the editor and we can start coding our methods.

After the closing curly brace of the `onCreate` method, add the `countUp` method shown next:

```java
public void countUp(View v){
    Log.i("message:","In countUp method");

    int x = 0;

    // Now an apparently infinite while loop
    while(true){

        // Add 1 to x each time
        x++;
        Log.i("x =", "" + x);

        if(x == 3){
            // Get me out of here
            break;
        }
    }
}
```

> **Important Note**
>
> Import the `Log` and `View` classes using your preferred method:
>
> `import android.util.Log;`
>
> `import android.view.View;`

We will be able to call this method we have just written from the appropriately labeled button.

After the closing curly brace of the countUp method, add the countDown method:

```java
public void countDown(View v){
    Log.i("message:","In countDown method");

    int x = 4;
    // Now an apparently infinite while loop
    while(true){

        // Add 1 to x each time
        x--;
        Log.i("x =", "" + x);

        if(x == 1){
            // Get me out of here
            break;
        }
    }
}
```

We will be able to call this method we have just written from the appropriately labeled button.

After the closing curly brace of the countDown method, add the nested method:

```java
public void nested(View v){
    Log.i("message:","In nested method");

    // a nested for loop
    for(int i = 0; i < 3; i ++){

        for(int j = 3; j > 0; j --){

            // Output the values of i and j
            Log.i("i =" + i,"j=" + j);
        }
```

```
        }
    }
```

We will be able to call this method we have just written from the appropriately labeled button.

Now, let's run the app and start tapping buttons. If you tap each of the buttons once from top to bottom, this is the console output you will see:

```
message:: In countUp method
x =: 1
x =: 2
x =: 3
message: : In countDown method
x =: 3
x =: 2
x =: 1
message: : In nested method
i =0: j=3
i =0: j=2
i =0: j=1
i =1: j=3
i =1: j=2
i =1: j=1
i =2: j=3
i =2: j=2
i =2: j=1
```

We can see that the countUp method does exactly that. The int x variable is initialized to 0, an infinite while loop is entered, and x is incremented with the increment ++ operator. Fortunately, on each iteration of the loop, we test for x being equal to 3 with if (x == 3) and break when this is true.

Next, in the countDown method, we do the same in reverse. The int x variable is initialized to 4, an infinite while loop is entered, and x is decremented with the decrement - - operator. This time, on each iteration of the loop, we test for x being equal to 1 with if (x == 1) and break when this is true.

Finally, we nest two `for` loops within each other. We can see from the output that each time i (which is controlled by the outer loop) is incremented, j (which is controlled by the inner loop) is decremented from 3 to 1. Look carefully at this screenshot, which shows where the start and end of each `for` loop is, to help fully understand this:

```
// a nested for loop
for(int i = 0; i < 3; i ++){

    for(int j = 3; j > 0; j --){

        // Output the values of i and j
        Log.i("i =" + i,"j=" + j);

    }

}
```

Figure 8.5 – for loop

You can, of course, keep tapping to observe each button's output for as long as you like. As an experiment, try making the loops longer, perhaps `1000`.

With loops thoroughly learned and tested, let's look at the finer details of methods in the next chapter.

Summary

In this chapter, we learned how to use `if`, `else`, and `switch` to make decisions with expressions and branch our code. We saw and practiced `while`, `for`, and `do while` to repeat parts of our code. Then we put it all together in two quick demo apps.

In the next chapter, we will take a much closer look at Java methods, which is where all our code will go.

9
Learning Java Methods

As we are starting to get comfortable with Java programming, in this chapter we will take a closer look at methods because although we know that you can **call** them to make them execute their code, there is more to them than we have discussed so far.

In this chapter, we will look at the following:

- Method structure
- Method overloading versus overriding
- A method demo mini-app
- How methods affect our variables
- Method recursion

First, let's go through a quick method recap.

Technical requirements

You can find the code files present in this chapter on GitHub at `https://github.com/PacktPublishing/Android-Programming-for-Beginners-Third-Edition/tree/main/chapter%2009`.

Methods revisited

This figure sums up where our understanding of methods is at the moment:

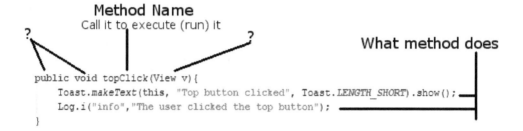

Figure 9.1 – Understanding methods

As we can see in the figure, there are still a couple of question marks around methods. We will totally take the lid off methods and see how they work and what exactly the other parts of the method are doing later in the chapter. In *Chapter 10, Object-Oriented Programming,* and *Chapter 11, More Object-Oriented Programming*, we will clear up the last few parts of the mystery of methods while discussing object-oriented programming.

What exactly are Java methods?

A method is a collection of variables, expressions, and control flow statements bundled together inside an opening and closing curly brace preceded by a **signature**. We have already been using lots of methods, but we just haven't looked very closely at them yet.

Let's start with the method structure.

Method structure

The first part of a method that we write is called the signature. Here is a hypothetical method signature:

```
public boolean addContact(boolean isFriend, string name)
```

If we add an opening and closing pair of curly braces, { }, with some code that the method performs, then we have a complete method – a **definition**. Here is another made up yet syntactically correct method:

```
private void setCoordinates(int x, int y){
    // code to set coordinates goes here
}
```

As we have seen, we could then use our new method from another part of our code like this:

```
// I like it here
```

```
setCoordinates(4,6);// now I am going off to setCoordinates
method
```

```
// Phew, I'm back again - code continues here
```

At the point where we call the setCoordinates method, our program's execution would branch to the code contained within that method. The method would execute all the statements inside it, step by step, until it reaches the end, and then return control to the code that called it, or sooner if it hits a return statement. Then, the code would continue running from the first line after the method call.

Here is another example of a method complete with the code to make the method return to the code that called it:

```
int addAToB(int a, int b){
    int answer = a + b;
    return answer;
}
```

The call to use the preceding method could look like this:

```
int myAnswer = addAToB(2, 4);
```

Clearly, we don't need to write methods to add two `int` variables together, but the example helps us see a little more into the workings of methods. First, we pass in the values 2 and 4. In the method signature, the value 2 is assigned to `int  a` and the value 4 is assigned to `int  b`.

Within the method body, the variables a and b are added together and used to initialize the new variable, `int  answer`. The line `return  answer` returns the value stored in `answer` to the calling code, causing `myAnswer` to be initialized with the value 6.

Notice that each of the method signatures in the preceding examples varies a little. The reason for this is the Java method signature is quite flexible, allowing us to build exactly the methods we need.

Exactly how the method signature defines how the method must be called and how the method must return a value deserves further discussion.

Let's give each part of the signature a name so we can break it up into pieces and learn about the parts.

The following bolded text is a method signature with its parts labeled up ready for discussion. Also, have a look at the table that follows the bolded text to further clarify which part of the signature is which. This will make the rest of our discussion on methods straightforward:

modifier | return-type | name of method (parameters)

Part of signature	Examples
modifier	`public`, `private`, `protected`, `package-private` (without modifier specified).
return-type	`Int`; you can also use any of the Java primitive types (such as `boolean`, `float`, `long`, and so on) or any predefined reference types (such as `String` and class types).
name of method	`addContact`, `setCoordinates`, `addAToB`.
parameters	`(boolean isFriend, String name)`, `(int x, int y)`, `(int a, int b)`.

Modifier

In our earlier examples, we only used a modifier in a couple of examples, partly because the method doesn't have to use a modifier. The modifier is a way of specifying what code can use (call) your method, by using modifiers such as `public` and `private`.

Variables can have modifiers too, as follows:

```
// Most code can see me
public int a;
```

```
// Code in other classes can't see me
private String secret = "Shhh! I am private";
```

Modifiers (for methods and variables) are an essential Java topic, but they are best dealt with when we are discussing the other vital Java topic we have skirted around a few times already – classes. We will do so in the next chapter.

Return type

Next in the table is the return type. Like a modifier, a return type is optional. So, let's look at it a bit closer. We have seen that our methods do anything we can code in Java. But what if we need the results from what a method has done? The simplest example of a return type we have seen so far is as follows:

```
int addAToB(int a, int b){
    int answer = a + b;
    return answer;
}
```

Here, the return type in the signature is highlighted. The return type is an `int`. The addAToB method sends back (returns) to the code that called it a value that will fit in an `int` variable.

The return type can be any Java type we have seen so far. However, the method does not have to return a value at all. When the method does not return a value, the signature must use the `void` keyword as the return type. When the `void` keyword is used, the method body must not try to return a value as this will cause a compiler error. It can, however, use the `return` keyword without a value.

Here are some combinations of the return type and use of the `return` keyword that are valid:

```java
void doSomething(){
    // our code


    // I'm done going back to calling code here
    // no return is necessary
}
```

Another combination is as follows:

```java
void doSomethingElse(){
    // our code


    // I can do this as long as I don't try and add a value
    return;
}
```

The following code is yet another combination:

```java
void doYetAnotherThing(){
    // some code
    if(someCondition){


        // if someCondition is true returning to calling
        code
        // before the end of the method body
        return;
    }


    // More code that might or might not get executed


    return;
    /*
        As I'm at the bottom of the method body
        and the return type is void, I'm
        really not necessary but I suppose I make it
```

```
            clear that the method is over.
    */
}


String joinTogether(String firstName, String lastName){
    return firstName + lastName;
}
```

We could call each of the preceding methods in turn like this:

```
// OK time to call some methods


doSomething();
doSomethingElse();
doYetAnotherThing();
String fullName = joinTogether("Alan ","Turing")


// fullName now = Alan Turing
// continue with code from here
```

The preceding code would execute all the code in each method in turn.

Name of the method

Next in the table is the name of the method. When we design our own methods, the method name is arbitrary. But it is the convention to use verbs that clearly explain what the method will do. Also, use the convention of the first letter of the first word of the name being lowercase and the first letter of any later words being uppercase. This is called camel case, as we learned while learning about variable names. Consider this next example:

```
void XGHHY78802c(){
    // code here
}
```

The preceding method is perfectly legitimate and will work; however, let's look at three much clearer examples that use these conventions:

```java
void doSomeVerySpecificTask(){
    // code here
}


void getMyFriendsList(){
    // code here
}


void startNewMessage(){
    // code here
}
```

This is much clearer as the names make it obvious what the methods will do.

Let's have a look at the parameters in methods.

Parameters

The final topic in the table is **parameters**. We know that a method can return a result to the calling code. But what if we need to share some data values *from* the calling code *with* the method?

Parameters allow us to send values into the called method. We have already seen an example with parameters when we looked at return types. We will look at the same example but a little more closely at the parameters:

```java
int addAToB(int a, int b){
    int answer = a + b;
    return answer;
}
```

Here, the parameters are highlighted. Parameters are contained in parentheses, `(parameters go here)`, immediately after the method name.

Notice that in the first line of the method body, we use a + b as if they are already declared and initialized variables. That is because they are. The parameters of the method signature are their declaration and the code that calls the method initializes them, as highlighted in the next line of code:

```
int returnedAnswer = addAToB(10,5);
```

Also, as we have partly seen in earlier examples, we don't have to just use int in our parameters. We can use any Java type, including types we design ourselves.

What is more, we can mix and match types as well. We can also use as many parameters as is necessary to solve our problem. An example might help:

```
void addToAddressBook(char firstInitial,
String lastName,
String city,
int age){

    /*
            all the parameters are now living, breathing,
            declared and initialized variables.

            The code to add details to address book goes here.
    */
}
```

The preceding example would have four declared and initialized variables that are ready to use.

Now we will look at the method body – what goes inside the method.

The body

In our previous examples, we have been pseudo-coding our method bodies with comments such as the following:

```
// code here
```

The following has also been used:

```
// some code
```

The `addToAddressBook` method has also been used:

```
/*

            all the parameters are now living, breathing,

            declared and initialized variables.


            The code to add details to address book goes

            here.

    */
```

But we know exactly what to do in the body already. Any Java syntax we have learned about so far will work in the body of a method. In fact, if we think back, all the code we have written in this book so far *has* been in a method.

The best thing we can do next is to write a few methods that do something in the body.

Using method demo apps

Here we will quickly build two apps to explore methods a bit further. First, we will explore the fundamentals with the `Real World Methods` app, and then we will glimpse a new topic, **method overloading**, with the `Exploring Method Overloading` app.

As usual, you can open the ready-typed code files in the usual way. The next two examples of methods can be found in the download bundle in the `chapter 9` folder and the `Real World Methods` and `Exploring Method Overloading` sub-folders.

Real-world methods

First, let's make ourselves some simple working methods complete with return type parameters and fully functioning bodies.

To get started, create a new Android project called `Real World Methods`, use the **Empty Activity** template, and leave all the other settings at their default. Switch to the `MainActivity.java` file by left-clicking the **MainActivity.java** tab above the editor and we can start coding.

First, add these three methods to the `MainActivity` class. Add them just after the closing curly brace, }, of the `onCreate` method:

```
String joinThese(String a, String b, String c){
    return a + b + c;
}
```

```
float getAreaCircle(float radius){
    return 3.141f * radius * radius;
}


void changeA(int a){
    a++;
}
```

The first method we added is called joinThese. It will return a String value and needs three String variables passed into it. In the method body, there is only one line of code. The return a + b + c code will concatenate the three strings that are passed into it and return the joined strings as the result.

The next method, named getAreaCircle, takes a float variable as an argument and then returns a float variable too. The body of the method simply uses the formula for the area of a circle, incorporating the passed-in radius, and then returns the answer to the calling code. The odd-looking f on the end of 3.141 is to let the compiler know that the number is of the float type. Any floating-point number is assumed to be of the double type unless it has the trailing f.

The third and final method is the simplest of all the methods. Notice that it doesn't return anything; it has a void return type. We have included this method to make clear an important point that we want to remember about methods. But let's see it in action before we talk about it.

Now, in the onCreate method, after the call to the setContentView method, add this code, which calls our three new methods and then outputs some text to the logcat window:

```
String joinedString = joinThese("Methods ", "are ", "cool ");
Log.i("joinedString = ","" + joinedString);


float area  = getAreaCircle(5f);
Log.i("area = ","" + area);


int a = 0;
changeA(a);
Log.i("a = ","" + a);
```

Run the app and see the output in the logcat window, which is provided here for your convenience:

```
joinedString =:  Methods are cool
area =:  78.525
a =:  0
```

In the logcat output, the first thing we can see is the value of the `joinedString` string. As expected, it is the concatenation of the three words we passed into the `joinThese` method.

Next, we can see that `getAreaCircle` has indeed calculated and returned the area of a circle based on the length of the radius passed in.

The fact that the a variable still holds the value 0 even after it has been passed into the `changeA` method deserves a separate discussion.

Discovering variable scope

The final line of output is most interesting: a=: 0. In the `onCreate` method, we declared and initialized `int a` to 0, and then we called the `changeA` method. In the body of `changeA`, we incremented a with the code a++. Yet, back in the `onCreate` method, we see that when we use the `Log.i` method to print the value of a to the logcat window, it is still **0**.

So, when we passed in a to the `changeA` method, we were actually passing the *value stored in a* not the *actual variable a*. This is referred to as passing by value in Java.

> **Tip**
> When we declare a variable in a method, it can only be *seen* in that method. When we declare a variable in another method, even if it has the exact same name, it is *not* the same variable. A variable only has **scope** within the method it was declared.

With all primitive variables, this is how passing them to methods works. With reference variables, it works slightly differently and we will see how in the next chapter.

> **Important Note**
>
> I have talked about this scope concept with a number of people new to Java. To some, it seems blindingly obvious, even natural. To others, however, it is a cause of constant confusion. Should you fall into the latter category, don't worry, because we will talk a bit more about this later in this chapter, and in future chapters, we will go into greater depth with exploring scope and make sure it is no longer an issue.

Let's look at another practical example of methods and learn something new at the same time.

Exploring method overloading

As we are beginning to realize, methods are quite deep as a topic. But hopefully, by taking them a step at a time, we will see that they are not daunting in any way. We will also be returning to methods in the next chapter. For now, let's create a new project to explore the topic of **method overloading**.

Create a new **Empty Activity** template project called `Exploring Method Overloading`, then we will get on with writing three methods, but with a slight twist.

As we will soon see, we can create more than one method with the same name provided that the parameters are different. The code in this project is simple. It is how it works that might appear slightly curious until we analyze it after.

In the first method, we will simply call it `printStuff` and pass in an `int` variable via a parameter to be printed.

Insert this method after the closing } of the `onCreate` method but before the closing } of the `MainActivity` class. Remember to import the `Log` class in the usual way:

```
void printStuff(int myInt){
    Log.i("info", "This is the int only version");
    Log.i("info", "myInt = "+ myInt);
}
```

In this second method, we will also call it `printStuff` but pass in a `String` variable to be printed. Insert this method after the closing } of the `onCreate` method but before the closing } of the `MainActivity` class:

```
void printStuff(String myString){
    Log.i("info", "This is the String only version");
```

```
    Log.i("info", "myString = "+ myString);
}
```

In this third method, we will call it printStuff yet again but pass in a String variable and an int value to be printed. Insert this method after the closing } of onCreate but before the closing } of the MainActivity class:

```
void printStuff(int myInt, String myString){
    Log.i("info", "This is the combined int and String
    version");
    Log.i("info", "myInt = "+ myInt);
    Log.i("info", "myString = "+ myString);
}
```

Finally, insert this code just before the closing } of the onCreate method to call the methods and print some values to the logcat window:

```
// Declare and initialize a String and an int
int anInt = 10;
String aString = "I am a string";

// Now call the different versions of printStuff
// The name stays the same, only the parameters vary
printStuff(anInt);
printStuff(aString);
printStuff(anInt, aString);
```

Now we can run the app on the emulator or a real device. Here is the output:

```
Info: This is the int only version
Info: myInt = 10
Info: This is the String only version
Info: myString = I am a string
Info: This is the combined int and String version
Info: myInt = 10
Info: myString = I am a string
```

As you can see, Java has treated three methods with the same name as different methods. This, as we have just shown, can be useful. It is called **method overloading**.

> **Method overloading and overriding confusion**
>
> **Overloading** is when we have more than one method with the same name but different parameters.
>
> **Overriding** is when we replace a method with the same name and the same parameter list.
>
> We know enough about overloading and overriding to complete this book; but if you are brave and your mind is wandering, yes, you can override an overloaded method, but that is something for another time.

This is how it all works. In each of the steps where we wrote code, we created a method called printStuff. But each printStuff method has different parameters, so each is actually a different method that can be called individually:

```
void printStuff(int myInt){
    ...
}


void printStuff(String myString){
    ...
}


void printStuff(int myInt, String myString){
    ...
}
```

The body of each of the methods is trivial and just prints out the passed-in parameters and confirms which version of the method is being called.

The next important part of our code is when we make it plain which version of the method we mean to call by using the specific arguments that match the parameters in the signature. In the final step, we call each method in turn, using the matching parameters so that Java knows the exact method required:

```
printStuff(anInt);
printStuff(aString);
printStuff(anInt, aString);
```

We now know all we need to know about methods, so let's take a quick second look at the relationship between methods and variables. Then, we'll get our heads around this scope phenomenon a bit more.

Scope and variables revisited

You might remember in the `Real World Methods` project the slightly disturbing anomaly was that variables in one method were not apparently the same as those from another even if they do have the same name. If you declare a variable in a method, whether that is one of the life cycle methods or one of our own methods, it can only be used within that method.

It is no use if we do this in `onCreate`:

```
int a = 0;
```

And then, following that, we try to do this in `onPause` or some other method:

```
a++;
```

We will get an error because `a` is only visible within the method it was declared. At first, this might seem like a problem, but surprisingly, it is actually an especially useful feature of Java.

I have already mentioned that the term used to describe this is **scope**. A variable is said to be in scope when it is usable and out of scope when it is not. The topic of scope is best discussed along with classes, and we will do so in *Chapter 10, Object-Oriented Programming*, and *Chapter 11, More Object-Oriented Programming*, but as a sneak look at what lies ahead, you might like to know that a class can have its very own variables and when it does, they have scope for the whole class; that is, all its methods can "see" and use them. We call them **member** variables or **fields**.

To declare a member variable, you simply use the usual syntax after the start of the class, outside of any method declared in the class. Say our app started like this:

```
public class MainActivity extends AppCompatActivity {

    int mSomeVariable = 0;
    // Rest of code and methods follow as usual
    // ...
```

We could use mSomeVariable anywhere, inside any method in this class. Our new variable, mSomeVariable, has **class scope**. We append an m to the variable name simply to remind us when we see it that it is a **member** variable. This is not required by the compiler, but it is a useful convention.

Let's look at one more method topic before we move on to classes.

Method recursion

Method recursion is when a method calls itself. This might at first seem like something that happens by mistake but is an efficient technique for solving some programming problems.

Here is some code that shows a recursive method in its most basic form:

```
void recursiveMethod() {
    recursiveMethod();
}
```

If we call the recursiveMethod method, its only line of code will then call itself, which will then call itself, which will then call itself, and so on. This process will go on forever until the app crashes, giving the following error in Logcat:

```
java.lang.StackOverflowError: stack size 8192KB
```

When the method is called, its instructions are moved to an area of the processor called the stack, and when it returns, its instructions are removed. If the method never returns and yet more and more copies of the instructions are added, eventually the stack will run out of memory (or overflow) and we get StackOverflowError.

We can attempt to visualize the first four method calls using the next screenshot. Also, in the next screenshot, I have crossed out the call to the method to show that if we were able to, at some point, prevent the method call, eventually all the methods would return and be cleared from the stack:

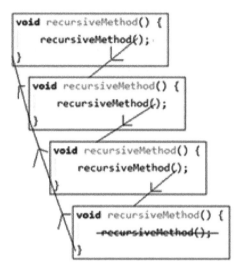

Figure 9.2 – Method calls

To make our recursive methods worthwhile, we need to enhance two aspects. We will look at the second aspect shortly. First and most obviously, we need to give it a purpose. How about we ask our recursive method to sum (add up) the values of numbers in a range from 0 to a given target value, say 10, 100, or more? Let's modify the preceding method by giving it this new purpose and renaming it accordingly. We will also add a variable with class scope (outside the method) called `answer`:

```java
int answer = 0;

void computeSum(int target) {
answer += target;
    computeSum(target-1);
}
```

Now we have a method called computeSum that takes an int as a parameter. If we wanted to compute the sum of all the digits between 0 and 10, we could call the method like this:

```
computeSum(10);
```

Here are the values of the answer variable at each function call:

First call of computeSum: answer = 10

Second call of computeSum: answer = 19

...

Tenth call of computeSum: answer = 55

Apparent success – until you realize that the method continues to call itself beyond the target variable reaching 0. In fact, we still have the same problem as our first recursive method and after tens of thousands of method calls, the app will crash with StackOverflowError again.

What we need is a way to stop the method calling itself once target is equal to 0. The way we solve this problem is to check whether the value of target is 0 and if it is, we quit calling the method. Have a look at the additional highlighted code shown next:

```
void computeSum(int target) {
    answer += target;
    if(target > 0) {
        Log.d("target = ", "" + target);
        computeSum(target - 1);
    }
    Log.d("answer = ", "" + answer);
```

We have used an if statement to check whether the target variable is greater than 0. We also have an additional Log.d code to output the value of answer when the method has been called for the last time. See whether you can work out what is happening before reading the explanation following the output.

The output of calling computeSum(10) would be as follows:

```
target =: 10
target =: 9
target =: 8
target =: 7
```

```
target =: 6
target =: 5
target =: 4
target =: 3
target =: 2
target =: 1
answer =: 55
```

`if(target > 0)` tells the code to first check whether the `target` variable is above 0. If it is, only then does it call the method again and pass in the value of `target - 1`. If it isn't, then it stops the whole process.

> **Important Note**
>
> We won't be using method recursion in this book, but it is an interesting concept to understand.

We know more than enough about methods to complete all the projects in the book. Let's have a quick recap with some questions and answers.

Questions

1. What is wrong with this method definition?

    ```
    doSomething() {
        // Do something here
    }
    ```

    No return type is declared. You do not have to return a value from a method, but its return type must be `void` in this case. This is how the method should look:

    ```
    void doSomething() {
        // Do something here
    }
    ```

2. What is wrong with this method definition?

```
float getBalance(){
    String customerName = "Linus Torvalds";
    float balance = 429.66f;
    return userName;
}
```

The method returns a string (userName) but the signature states that it must return a float type. With a method name like getBalance, this code is what was likely intended:

```
float getBalance(){
    String customerName = "Linus Torvalds";
    float balance = 429.66f;
    return balance;
}
```

3. When do we call the onCreate method? (Trick question alert!)

We don't. Android decides when to call the onCreate method, as well as all the other methods that make up the lifecycle of an Activity. We just override the ones that are useful to us. We do, however, call super.onCreate so that our overridden version and the original version both get executed.

> **Important Note**
> For the sake of complete disclosure, it is technically possible to call the lifecycle methods from our code, but we will never need to in the context of this book. It is best to leave these things to Android.

Summary

In the first five chapters, we got quite proficient with a whole array of widgets and other UI elements. We also built a broad selection of UI layouts. In this chapter and the previous three, we have explored Java and the Android activity lifecycle in quite significant depth, especially considering how quickly we have done it.

We have, to a small extent, created interaction between our Java code and our UI. We have called our methods by setting the onClick attribute and we have loaded our UI layouts using the setContentView method. We haven't, however, really made a proper connection between our UI and our Java code.

What we really need to do now is to bring these things together, so we can begin to display and manipulate our data using the Android UI. To achieve this, we need to understand a bit more about classes.

Classes have been lurking in our code since *Chapter 1, Beginning Android and Java*, and we have even used them a bit. Up until now, however, we haven't tackled them properly other than constantly referring to *Chapter 10, Object-Oriented Programming*. In the next chapter, *Chapter 10, Object-Oriented Programming*, we will quickly get to grips with classes, and then we can finally start to build apps where the UI designs and our Java code work in perfect harmony.

Further reading

We have learned enough Java to proceed with the book. It is always beneficial, however, to see more examples of Java in action and to go beyond the minimum necessary knowledge to proceed. If you want a good source to learn Java in greater depth, then the official Oracle website is good. Note that you do not need to study this website to continue with this book. Also, note that the tutorials on the Oracle website are not set in an Android context. The site is a useful resource to bookmark and browse all the same:

- The official Java tutorials: `https://docs.oracle.com/javase/tutorial/`
- The official Android developer site: `https://developer.android.com/training/basics/firstapp`

10
Object-Oriented Programming

In this chapter, we will discover that in Java, classes are fundamental to just about everything. We will also begin to understand why the software engineers at Sun Microsystems back in the early 1990s made Java the way they did.

We have already talked about reusing other people's code, specifically the Android API, but in this chapter, we will really get to grips with how this works and learn about object-oriented programming and how to use it.

In summary, we will cover the following topics:

- What object-oriented programming is, including **encapsulation**, **inheritance**, and **polymorphism**
- Writing and using our first class in an app

Technical requirements

You can find the code files present in this chapter on GitHub at `https://github.com/PacktPublishing/Android-Programming-for-Beginners-Third-Edition/tree/main/chapter%2010`.

Important memory management warning

I'm referring to our brains' memories for a change. If you tried to memorize this chapter (or the next), you would have to make a lot of room in your brain and you would probably forget something really important – like going to work or thanking the author for telling you not to try and memorize this stuff.

A good goal will be to try and *just-about get it*. This way, your understanding will become more rounded. You can then refer to this chapter (or the next) for a refresher when needed.

> **Tip**
> It doesn't matter if you don't completely understand everything in this chapter straight away! Keep on reading and make sure to complete all the apps.

Object-oriented programming

In *Chapter 1, Beginning Android and Java*, we mentioned that Java was an object-oriented language. An object-oriented language requires us to use **object-oriented programming (OOP)**. It isn't an optional extra like a racing spoiler on a car or pulsating LEDs in a gaming PC. It's part of Java and therefore Android as well.

Let's find out a little bit more.

What is OOP exactly?

OOP is a way of programming that involves breaking our requirements down into chunks that are more manageable than the whole.

Each chunk is self-contained yet potentially reusable by other programs, while working together as a whole with the other chunks.

These chunks are what we refer to as objects. When we plan/code an object, we do so with a class. A class can be thought of as the blueprint of an object.

We implement an object *of* a class. This is called an **instance** of a class. Think about a house blueprint. You can't live in it, but you can build a house from it; you build an instance of it. Often when we design classes for our apps, we write them to represent real-world *things*.

However, OOP is more than this. It is also a *way* of doing things – a methodology that defines best practices.

The three core principles of OOP are **encapsulation**, **polymorphism**, and **inheritance**. This might sound complex but, when taken a step at a time, is reasonably straightforward.

Encapsulation

Encapsulation means keeping the internal workings of your code safe from interference from the code that uses it, by allowing only the variables and methods you choose to be accessed.

This means your code can always be updated, extended, or improved without affecting the programs that use it, as long as the exposed parts are still accessed in the same way.

Remember this line of code from *Chapter 1, Beginning Android and Java*?

```
locationManager.getLastKnownLocation(LocationManager.GPS_
PROVIDER)
```

With proper encapsulation, it doesn't matter if the satellite company or the Android API team needs to update the way their code works. Provided the getLastKnownLocation method signature remains the same, we don't have to worry about what goes on inside. Our code written before the update will still work after the update.

If the manufacturer of a car gets rid of the wheels and makes it an electrically powered hovercar, as long as it still has a steering wheel, accelerator, and brake pedal, driving it should not be too challenging.

> **Important Note**
>
> When we use the classes of the Android API, we are doing so in the way the Android developers designed their classes to allow us to.

Polymorphism

Polymorphism allows us to write code that is less dependent on the *types* we are trying to manipulate, making our code clearer and more efficient. Polymorphism means *different forms*. If the objects that we code can be more than one type of thing, then we can take advantage of this. Some examples in the next chapter will make this clear, and the analogy coming next will give you a real-world perspective.

If we have a car factory that can make vans and small trucks just by changing the instructions given to the robots and the parts that go onto the production line, then the factory is using polymorphism.

Wouldn't it be useful if we could write code that could handle different types of data without starting again? We will see some examples of this in *Chapter 11, More Object-Oriented Programming.*

Inheritance

Just like it sounds, **inheritance** means we can harness all the features and benefits of other peoples' classes, including the encapsulation and polymorphism, while further refining their code specifically to our situation. Actually, we have done this already, every time we have used the extends keyword:

```
public class MainActivity extends AppCompatActivity {
```

The AppCompatActivity class itself inherits from Activity. So, we inherited from Activity every time we created a new Android project. We can go further than this and see how it is useful.

Imagine if the strongest man in the world gets together with the smartest woman in the world. There is a good chance that their children will have serious benefits from gene inheritance. Inheritance in Java lets us do the same thing with another person's code and our own, creating a class more specific to our needs.

Why do it like this?

When written properly, all this OOP allows you to add new features without worrying as much about how they interact with existing features. When you do have to change a class, its self-contained (encapsulated) nature means fewer or perhaps even zero consequences for other parts of the program. This is the encapsulation part.

You can use other people's code (such as the Android API) without knowing or perhaps even caring how it works: think about the Android lifecycle, Toast, Log, all the UI widgets, listening to satellites, and so on. For example, the Button class has nearly 50 methods – do we really want to write all that ourselves, just for a button? Much better to use someone else's Button class.

OOP allows you to write apps for highly complex situations without breaking a sweat.

You can create multiple similar-yet-different versions of a class without starting the class from scratch, by using inheritance; and you can still use the methods intended for the original type of object with your new object because of polymorphism.

It makes sense really. And Java was designed from the start with all of this in mind, so we are forced into using all this OOP; however, this is a good thing.

Let's have a quick class recap.

Class recap

A class is a collection of lines of code that can contain methods, variables, loops, and all the other Java syntax we have learned about. A class is part of a Java package and most packages will normally have multiple classes. Usually, although not always, each new class will be defined in its own .java code file with the same name as the class – as with all of our Activity classes so far.

Once we have written a class, we can use it to make as many objects from it as we want. Remember, the class is the blueprint and we make objects based on the blueprint. The house isn't the blueprint just as the object isn't the class; it is an object made from the class. An object is a reference variable, as is a String variable, and later we will discover exactly what being a reference variable means. For now, let's look at some actual code.

Looking at the code for a class

Let's say we are making an app for the military. It is for use by senior officers to micro-manage their troops in battle. Among others, we would probably need a class to represent a soldier.

Class implementation

Here is the real code for our hypothetical class. We call it a class **implementation**. As the class is called Soldier, if we implement this for real, we would do so in a file called Soldier.java:

```java
public class Soldier {

    // Member variables
    int health;
    String soldierType;

    // Method of the class
    void shootEnemy(){
            // Bang! Bang!
    }

}
```

The preceding is a class implementation for a class called `Soldier`. There are two **member variables**, or **fields**, an `int` variable called `health`, and a `String` variable called `soldierType`.

There is also a method called `shootEnemy`. The method has no parameters and a `void` return type, but class methods can be of any shape or size that we discussed in *Chapter 9, Learning Java Methods*.

To be precise about member variables and fields, when the class is instantiated into a real object, the fields become variables of the object itself and we call them **instance** or **member** variables.

They are just variables of the class, whatever fancy name they are referred to by. However, the difference between fields and variables declared in methods (called **local** variables) does become more important as we progress.

We briefly discussed variable scope at the end of *Chapter 9, Learning Java Methods* We will look at all types of variables again later in the next chapter. Let's concentrate on coding and using a class.

Declaring, initializing, and using an object of the class

Remember that `Soldier` is just a class, not an actual usable object. It is a blueprint for a soldier, not an actual soldier object, just as `int`, `String`, and `boolean` are not variables; they are just types we can make variables of. This is how we make an object of type `Soldier` from our `Soldier` class:

```
Soldier mySoldier = new Soldier();
```

In the first part of the code, `Soldier mySoldier` declares a new variable of type `Soldier` called `mySoldier`. The last part of the code, `new Soldier()`, calls a special method called a **constructor** that is automatically made for all classes by the compiler.

It is this constructor method that creates an actual `Soldier` object. As you can see, the constructor method has the same name as the class. We will look at constructors in more depth later in this chapter.

And of course, the assignment operator = in the middle of the two parts assigns the result of the second part to that of the first. The next figure summarizes all this information:

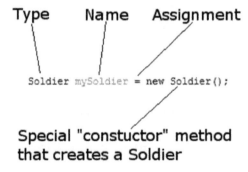

Figure 10.1 – Declaring, initializing, and using an object of the class

This is not far from how we deal with a regular variable except for the constructor/method call instead of a value on the end of the line of code. To create and use a very basic class, we have done enough.

> **Important Note**
>
> As we will see when we explore further, we can write our own constructors rather than relying on the auto-generated constructor. This gives us lots of power and flexibility, but we will just continue to explore the simplest case for now.

Just like regular variables, we could also have done it in two parts like this.

```
Soldier mySoldier;
mySoldier = new Soldier();
```

This is how we might assign to and use the variables of our hypothetical class:

```
mySoldier.health = 100;
mySoldier.soldierType = "sniper";

// Notice that we use the object name mySoldier.
// Not the class name Soldier.
// We didn't do this:
// Soldier.health = 100;
// ERROR!
```

Here, the dot operator . is used to access the variables of the class. And this is how we would call the method – again, by using the object name, not the class name, followed by the dot operator:

```
mySoldier.shootEnemy();
```

We can summarize the use of the dot operator with a diagram:

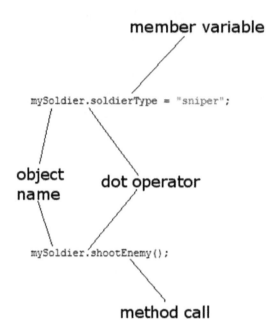

Figure 10.2 – dot operator

Tip

We can think of a class' method as what it can *do* and its instance/member variables as what it *knows* about itself.

We can also go ahead and make another `Soldier` object and access its methods and variables:

```
Soldier mySoldier2 = new Soldier();
mySoldier2.health = 150;
mySoldier2.soldierType = "special forces";
mySoldier2.shootEnemy();
```

It is important to realize that mySoldier2 is a totally separate object with completely distinct instance variables to mySoldier:

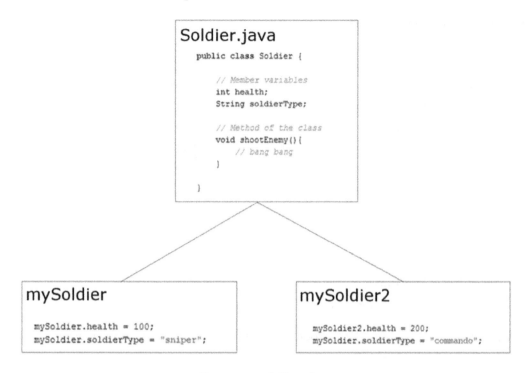

Figure 10.3 – Soldier object

What is also key here is that this preceding code would not be written within the class itself. For example, we could create the Soldier class in an external file called Soldier.java and then use the code that we have just seen, perhaps in the MainActivity class.

This will become clearer when we write our first class in an actual project in a minute.

Also notice that everything is done *on* the object itself. We must create objects of classes to make them useful.

> **Important Note**
>
> As always, there are exceptions to this rule. But they are in the minority, and we will look at the exceptions in the next chapter. In fact, we have already seen two exceptions in the book so far. The exceptions we have seen are the Toast and Log classes. Exactly what is going on with them will be explained soon.

Let's explore basic classes a little more deeply by writing one for real.

Basic classes app

The generals who will be using our app will need more than one Soldier object. In the app that we are about to build, we will instantiate and use multiple objects. We will also demonstrate using the dot operator on variables and methods to show that different objects have their very own instance variables.

You can get the completed code for this example in the code download. It is in the chapter 10/Basic Classes folder. But it is most useful to read on to create your own working example.

Create a project with the **Empty Activity** template. Call the application Basic Classes. Now we will create a new class called Soldier:

1. Right-click the com.yourdomain.basicclasses (or whatever your package name is) folder in the project explorer window.
2. Select **New | Java Class**.
3. In the **Name:** field, type Soldier and press the *Enter* key.

The new class is created for us with a code template ready to put our implementation within, just as the next code shows.

```
package com.yourdomain.basicclasses;


public class Soldier {
}
```

Notice that Android Studio has put the class in the same package/folder as the rest of our app's Java files.

And now we can write its implementation.

Write the following class implementation code within the opening and closing curly braces of the `Soldier` class as shown. The new code to type is highlighted:

```java
public class Soldier {
    int health;
    String soldierType;

    void shootEnemy(){
        //let's print which type of soldier is shooting
        Log.i(soldierType, " is shooting");
    }
}
```

Now that we have a class, a blueprint for our future objects of type `Soldier`, we can start to build our army. In the editor window, left-click the **MainActivity.java** tab. We will write this next code, as so often, within the `onCreate` method just after the call to the `setContentView` method. Type this code:

```java
// First, we make an object of type soldier
Soldier rambo = new Soldier();
rambo.soldierType = "Green Beret";
rambo.health = 150;
// It takes a lot to kill Rambo


// Now we make another Soldier object
Soldier vassily = new Soldier();
vassily.soldierType = "Sniper";
vassily.health = 50;
// Snipers have less health


// And one more Soldier object
Soldier wellington = new Soldier();
wellington.soldierType = "Sailor";
wellington.health = 100;
// He's tough but no green beret
```

Now we have our extremely varied and unlikely army, we can use it and verify the identity of each object.

Type this code below the code in the previous step:

```
Log.i("Rambo's health = ", "" + rambo.health);
Log.i("Vassily's health = ", "" + vassily.health);
Log.i("Wellington's health = ", "" + wellington.health);

rambo.shootEnemy();
vassily.shootEnemy();
wellington.shootEnemy();
```

Now we can run our app. All the output will be in the logcat window.

This is how it works. First, we created our new `Soldier` class. Then we implemented our class including declaring two fields (member variables), an `int` variable and a `String` variable called `health` and `soldierType`.

We also have a method in our class called `shootEnemy`. Let's look at it again and examine what is going on:

```
void shootEnemy(){
        //let's print which type of soldier is shooting
        Log.i(soldierType, " is shooting");
}
```

In the body of the method, we print to the logcat window: first `soldierType` and then the text `" is shooting"`. What's neat here is that the string `soldierType` will be different depending on which object we call the `shootEnemy` method on.

Next, we declared and created three new objects of type `Soldier`. They were `rambo`, `vassily`, and `wellington`.

Finally, we initialized each with a different value for `health` as well as `soldierType`.

Here is the output:

```
Rambo's health =: 150
Vassily's health =: 50
Wellington's health =: 100
Green Beret: is shooting
Sniper: is shooting
Sailor: is shooting
```

Notice that each time we access the `health` variable of each `Soldier` object, it prints the value we assigned it, proving that although the three objects are of the same type, they are completely separate, individual instances/objects.

Perhaps more interesting is the three calls to `shootEnemy`. One by one, each of our `Soldier` object's `shootEnemy` methods is called and we print the `soldierType` variable to the logcat window. The method has the proper value for each individual object, further proving that we have three distinct objects (instances of the class), albeit created from the same `Soldier` class.

We saw how each object is completely independent of the other objects. However, if we imagine whole armies of `Soldier` objects in our app, then we realize that we are going to need to learn new ways of handling large numbers of objects (and regular variables too).

Think about managing just 100 separate `Soldier` objects. What about when we have thousands of objects? In addition, this isn't very dynamic. The way we are writing the code now relies on us (the developers) knowing the exact details of the soldiers that the generals (the user) will be commanding. We will see the solution for this in *Chapter 15, Arrays, Maps, and Random Numbers.*

More things we can do with our first class

We can treat a class much as we can other variables. We can use a class as a parameter in a method signature, as here:

```
public void healSoldier(Soldier soldierToBeHealed){
    // Use soldierToBeHealed here


    // And because it is a reference the changes
    // are reflected in the actual object passed into
    // the method.
    // Oops! I just mentioned what
    // a reference variable can do
    // More info in the FAQ, chapter 11, and onwards
}
```

And when we call the method we must of course pass an object of that type. Here is a hypothetical call to the `healSoldier` method:

```
healSoldier(rambo);
```

Of course, the preceding example might raise questions, such as, should the healSoldier method be a method of a class?

```
fieldhospital.healSoldier(rambo);
```

It could be or it could not. It would depend on what the best solution for the situation was. We will look at more OOP, and then the best solutions for lots of similar conundrums should present themselves more easily.

And, as you might guess, we can also use an object as the return value of a method. Here is what the updated hypothetical healSoldier signature and implementation might look like now:

```
Soldier healSoldier(Soldier soldierToBeHealed) {
    soldierToBeHealed.health++;

    return soldierToBeHealed;
}
```

In fact, we have already seen classes being used as parameters. For example, here is our topClick method from *Chapter 2, First Contact: Java, XML, and the UI Designer*. It receives an object called v of type View:

```
public void topClick(View v) {
```

However, in the case of the topClick method we didn't do anything with the passed-in object of type View. Partly, this was because we didn't need to, and partly it was because we don't know what we can do with an object of type View – yet.

As I mentioned at the start of the chapter, you don't need to understand or remember everything in this chapter. The only way to get good at OOP is to keep using it. Like learning a spoken language – studying it and poring over grammatical rules will help but nowhere near as much as having a conversation verbally (or in writing). If you just about get it, move on with the next chapter.

Frequently asked questions

1. I just can't wait any longer. What is a reference already!?

    It literally is the same thing as a reference in normal (non-programming) language. It is a value that identifies/points to data rather than the actual data itself. One way of thinking about it is that a reference is a memory location/address. It identifies and gives access to the actual data at that location/address in memory.

2. If it is not the actual object but just a reference, how come we can do things like call methods on it, such as `mySoldier.shootEnemy()`?

    Java works out the exact details under the hood, but you can think of a reference as being the controller of an object, and anything you want to do to the object you must do through the controller, because the actual object/memory itself cannot be directly accessed. More on this in *Chapter 12, The Stack, the Heap, and the Garbage Collector.*

Summary

We have at last written our first class. We have seen that we can implement a class in a Java file of the same name as the class. The class itself doesn't do anything until we instantiate an object/instance of the class. Once we have an instance of the class, we can use its variables and methods. As we proved in the basic classes app, each and every instance of a class has its own distinct variables, just as when you buy a car made in a factory, you get your very own steering wheel, satnav, and go-faster stripes.

All this information will raise more questions. OOP is like that. So, let's try and consolidate all this class stuff by taking another look at variables and encapsulation, polymorphism, and inheritance in action in the next chapter. We can then go further with classes and explore topics such as static classes (such as Log and Toast) as well as the more advanced concepts of abstract classes and interfaces.

11
More Object-Oriented Programming

This chapter is the second part of our whirlwind tour (theoretical and practical) into OOP. We have already briefly discussed the concepts of encapsulation, inheritance, and polymorphism, but in this chapter, we will get to see them more in action in some demo apps. While the working examples will show these concepts in their simplest forms, it will still be a significant stepping stone towards taking control of our layouts via our Java code.

In this chapter, we will explore the following:

- Encapsulation in depth and how it helps us

- Inheritance in depth and how to take full advantage

- Polymorphism explained in greater detail

- Static classes and how we have been using them already

- Abstract classes and interfaces

First, we will handle encapsulation.

Technical requirements

You can find the code files present in this chapter on GitHub at `https://github.com/PacktPublishing/Android-Programming-for-Beginners-Third-Edition/tree/main/chapter%2011`.

Remember that encapsulation thing?

So far, what we have really seen is what amounts to a kind of code-organizing convention where we write classes, full of variables and methods. We did discuss the wider goals of all this OOP stuff but now we will take things further and begin to see how we actually manage to achieve encapsulation with OOP.

> **Definition of encapsulation**
>
> Encapsulation describes the ability of an object to hide its data and methods from the rest of the world, allowing only the variables and methods you choose to be accessed. This means your code can always be updated, extended, or improved without affecting the programs that use it – provided the exposed parts are still made accessible in the same way. It also allows the code that uses your encapsulated code to be much simpler and easier to maintain because much of the complexity of the task is encapsulated within your code.

But didn't you say we don't have to know what is going on inside? So you might question what we have seen so far like this: If we are constantly setting the instance variables like this `rambo.health = 100;`, isn't it possible that, eventually, things could start to go wrong, perhaps like this?

```
rambo.soldierType = "fluffy bunny";
```

Encapsulation protects the objects of your class from being used in a way that they weren't meant to be. By controlling the way that your classes' code is used, it can only ever do what you want it to do and with value ranges that you can control.

It can't be forced into errors or crashes. Also, you are then free to make changes to the way your code works internally, without breaking the rest of your program or any programs that are using an older version of the code:

```
weightlifter.legstrength = 100;
weightlifter.armstrength = 1;
weightlifter.liftHeavyWeight();

// one typo and weightlifter rips own arms off
```

Encapsulation is not just vital for writing code that other people will use (such as the Android API that we use), it is also essential when writing code we will reuse ourselves as it will save us from our own mistakes. Furthermore, a team of programmers will use encapsulation extensively so that different members of the team can work on the same program without all members of the team knowing how the other team members' code works. We can encapsulate our classes for this same advantage and here is how.

Controlling class use with access modifiers

The designer of the class controls what can be seen and manipulated by any program that uses their class. We can add an **access modifier** before the `class` keyword like this:

```
public class Soldier{
    //Implementation goes here
}
```

Class access modifiers

There are two main access modifiers for classes in the context we have discussed so far. Let's briefly look at each in turn:

- `public`: This is straightforward. A class declared as public can be seen by all other classes.

- `default`: A class has default access when no access modifier is specified. This will make it public but only to classes in the same package and inaccessible to all others.

So now we can make a start on this encapsulation thing. But even at a glance, the access modifiers described are not very fine-grained. We seem to be limited to complete lockdown to anything outside the package or a complete free-for-all.

Actually, the benefits here are easily taken advantage of. The idea would be to design a package of classes that fulfills a set of tasks. Then, all the complex inner workings of the package, the stuff that shouldn't be messed with by anybody but our package, should be default access (only accessible to classes within the package). We can then make available a careful choice of public classes that can be used by others (or other distinct parts of our program).

> **Important note**
>
> For the size and complexity of the apps in this book, creating multiple packages is overkill. We will of course be using other people's packages and classes (the public parts), so this stuff is worth knowing.

Class access in summary

A well-designed app will probably consist of one or more packages, each containing only default or default and public classes.

In addition to class-level privacy controls, Java gives us programmers very fine-grained controls, but to use these controls, we have to look into variables with a little more detail.

Controlling variable use with access modifiers

To build on the class visibility controls, we have variable access modifiers. Here is a variable with the `private` access modifier being declared:

```
private int myInt;
```

Note also that all of our discussion of variable access modifiers applies to object variables too. For example, here is an instance of our `Soldier` class being declared, created, and assigned. As you can see, the access specified in this case is public:

```
public Soldier mySoldier = new Soldier();
```

Before you apply a modifier to a variable, you must first consider the class visibility. If class *a* is not visible to class *b*, say because class *a* has default access and class *b* is in another package, then it doesn't make any difference what access modifiers you use on the variables in class *a* – class *b* can't see any of them anyway.

So, it makes sense to show a class to another class when necessary but only to expose the variables that are directly needed – not everything.

Here is an explanation of the different variable access modifiers.

Variable access modifiers

Variable access modifiers are more numerous and finely grained than class access modifiers. The depth and complexity of access modification are not so much in the range of modifiers but rather in the smart ways we can combine them to achieve the worthy goals of encapsulation. Here are the variable access modifiers:

- `public`: You guessed it, any class or method from any package can see this variable. Use `public` only when you are sure this is what you want.

- `protected`: This is the next least restrictive after `public`. `protected` variables can be seen by any class and any method as long as they are in the same package.

- `default`: `default` doesn't sound as restrictive as `protected` but it is more so. A variable has `default` access when no access is specified. The fact that `default` is restrictive perhaps implies we should be thinking of hiding our variables more than we should be exposing them. At this point, we need to introduce a new concept. Do you remember we briefly discussed inheritance and how we can quickly take on the attributes of a class and yet refine it by using the `extends` keyword? Just for the record, default access variables are not visible to subclasses; that is, when we extend a class as we did with an Activity, we cannot see its default variables. We will look at inheritance in more detail later in the chapter.

- `private`: `private` variables can only be seen within the class they are declared. This means, like default access, they cannot be seen by subclasses (classes that inherit from the class in question).

Variable access summary

A well-designed app will probably consist of one or more packages, each containing only `default` or `default` and `public` classes. Within these classes, variables will have carefully chosen and varied access modifiers, chosen with a view to achieving our goal of encapsulation.

One more twist in all this access modification stuff before we get practical with it.

Methods can have access modifiers too

We already briefly mentioned in *Chapter 9, Learning Java Methods*, that methods can have access modifiers. It makes sense because methods are the things that our classes can *do*. We will want to control what users of our classes can and can't do.

The general idea here is that some methods will do things internally only and are therefore not needed by users of the class and some methods will be fundamental to how users of the class use the class.

Method access modifiers

The access modifiers for methods are the same as for the class variables. This makes things easy to remember but suggests, again, that successful encapsulation is a matter of design rather than of following any specific set of rules.

As an example, this method, provided it is in a public class, could be used by any other class:

```
public useMeEverybody() {
    //do something everyone needs to do here
}
```

Whereas this method could only be used internally by the class that it is part of:

```
private secretInternalTask() {
    /*
            do something that helps the class function
            internally
            Perhaps, if it is part of the same class,
            useMeEverybody could use this method...
            On behalf of the classes outside of this class.
            Neat!
    */
}
```

And this next method with no access specified has default visibility. It can be used only by other classes in the same package. If we extend the class holding this `default` access method, the child class will not have access to this parent class's method:

```
fairlySecretTask() {
    // allow just the classes in the package
    // Not for external use
}
```

As the last example before we move on, here is a `protected` method, only visible to the package, but usable by our classes that extend it – just like `onCreate`:

```
protected packageTask() {
    // Allow just the classes in the package
    // And you can use me if you extend me too
}
```

Let's have a quick recap of method encapsulation, but remember that you don't need to memorize everything.

Method access summary

Method access should be chosen to best enforce the principles we have already discussed. It should provide the users of your class with just the access they need and preferably nothing more. Thereby we achieve our encapsulation goals, such as keeping the internal workings of your code safe from interference from the programs that use it, for all the reasons we have discussed.

Accessing private variables with getters and setters

Now, if it is best practice to hide our variables away as private, we need to consider how we allow access to them without spoiling our encapsulation. What if an object of the Hospital class wanted access to the health member variable from an object of type Soldier, so it could increase it? The health variable should be private because we don't want just any piece of code changing it.

To be able to make as many member variables as possible private and yet still allow some kind of limited access to some of them, we use **getters** and **setters**. Getters and setters are just methods that get and set variable values.

This is not some special new Java thing we have to learn. It is just a convention for using what we already know. Let's have a look at getters and setters using our Soldier class and Hospital class examples.

In this example, each of our two classes is created in its own file but the same package. First of all, here is our hypothetical Hospital class:

```
class Hospital{

    private void healSoldier(Soldier soldierToHeal){
        int health = soldierToHeal.getHealth();
        health = health + 10;
        soldierToHeal.setHealth(health);
    }

}
```

Our implementation of the Hospital class has just one method, healSoldier. It receives a reference to a Soldier object as a parameter. So, this method will work on whichever Soldier object is passed in: vassily, wellington, rambo, or whoever.

It also has a local `health` variable, which it uses to temporarily hold and increase the soldier's health. In the same line, it initializes the `health` variable to the `Soldier` object's current health. The `Soldier` object's health is private so the public `getHealth` getter method is used instead.

Then `health` is increased by 10 and the `setHealth` setter method loads up the new revived health value, back to the `Soldier` object.

The key here is that although a `Hospital` object can change a `Soldier` object's health, it only does so within the bounds of the getter and setter methods. The getter and setter methods can be written to control and check for potentially mistaken, or even harmful, values.

Next, look at our hypothetical `Soldier` class we have just been using with the simplest implementation possible of its getter and setter methods:

```
public class Soldier{

    private int health;

    public int getHealth(){
        return health;
    }

    public void setHealth(int newHealth){
        // Check for bad values of newHealth
        health = newHealth;
    }
}
```

We have one instance variable called `health` and it is private. Private means it can only be changed by methods of the `Soldier` class. We then have a public `getHealth` method that returns the value held in the private `health` int variable. As this method is public, any code with access to an object of type `Soldier` can use it.

Next, the `setHealth` method is implemented. Again, it is public but this time it takes an `int` as a parameter and assigns whatever is passed in to the private `health` variable. In a more life-like example, we would write some more code here to make sure the value passed in is within the bounds we expect.

Now we declare, create, and assign to make an object of each of our two new classes and see how our getters and setters work:

```
Soldier mySoldier = new Soldier();
// mySoldier.health = 100;//Doesn't work, private


// we can use the public setter setHealth() instead
mySoldier.setHealth(100); //That's better


Hospital militaryHospital = new Hospital();


// Oh no mySoldier has been wounded
mySoldier.setHealth(10);


/*
    Take him to the hospital.
    But my health variable is private
    And Hospital won't be able to access it
    I'm doomed - tell Laura I love her

    No wait- what about my public getters and setters?
    We can use the public getters and setters
    from another class
*/


militaryHospital.healSoldier(mySoldier);


// mySoldiers private variable health has been increased
// by 10. I'm feeling much better thanks!
```

We see that we can call our public setHealth and getHealth methods directly on our object of type Soldier. Not only that, we can call the healSoldier method of the Hospital object, passing in a reference to the Soldier object, which too can use the public getters and setters to manipulate the private health variable.

We see that the private health variable is simply accessible, yet totally within the control of the designer of the Soldier class.

If you want to play around with this example, there is the code for a working app in the code bundle in the `Chapter 11` folder called `GettersAndSetters`. I have added a few lines of code to print to the console.

> **Important note**
>
> Getters and setters are sometimes referred to by their more correct names, **Accessors** and **Mutators**. We will stick to getters and setters. I just thought you might like to know the jargon.

Yet again, our example and the explanation are probably raising more questions. That's good.

By using encapsulation features (such as access control), it is like signing a really important deal about how to use and access a class, its methods, and variables. The contract is not just an agreement about now, but an implied guarantee for the future. We will see that as we go ahead through this chapter, there are more ways in which we'll refine and strengthen this contract.

> **Tip**
>
> Use encapsulation where it is needed or, of course, if you are being paid to use it by an employer. Often encapsulation is overkill on small learning projects, such as some of the examples in this book. Except, of course, when the topic you are learning is encapsulation itself.
>
> We are learning this Java OOP stuff under the assumption that you will one day want to write much more complex apps, whether on Android or some other platform that uses OOP. In addition, we will be using classes from the Android API that use it extensively and it will help us understand what is happening then as well. Typically, throughout this book, we will use encapsulation when implementing full projects and often overlook it when showing small code samples to demonstrate a single idea or topic.

Setting up our objects with constructors

With all these private variables and their getters and setters, does it mean that we need a getter and a setter for every private variable? What about a class with lots of variables that need initializing at the start. Think about the following:

```
mySoldier.name
mysoldier.type
mySoldier.weapon
```

```
mySoldier.regiment
...
```

Some of these variables might need getters and setters, but what if we just want to set things up when the object is first created, to make the object function correctly?

Surely, we don't need two methods (a getter and a setter) for each?

Fortunately, this is unnecessary. To solve this potential problem there is a special method called a **constructor**. We briefly mentioned the existence of a constructor when we discussed instantiating an object of a class in *Chapter 10, Object-Oriented Programming*. Let's look again at constructors.

Here, we create an object of type Soldier and assign it to an object called mySoldier:

```
Soldier mySoldier = new Soldier();
```

Nothing new here but look at the last part of that line of code:

```
...Soldier();
```

This looks suspiciously like a method.

All along, we have been calling a special method called a constructor that has been created behind the scenes, automatically, by the compiler.

However, and this is getting to the point now, like a method, we can *override* the constructor, which means we can do useful things to set up our new object *before* it is used. This next code shows how we could do this:

```
public Soldier(){
    // Someone is creating a new Soldier object

    health = 200;
    // more setup here
}
```

The constructor has a lot of syntactical similarities to a method. It can, however, only be called with the use of the new keyword, and it is created for us automatically by the compiler – unless we create our own like in the previous code.

Constructors have the following features:

- They have no return type
- They have the exact same name as the class
- They can have parameters
- They can be overloaded

One more piece of Java syntax that it is useful to introduce at this point is the Java this keyword.

The this keyword is used when we want to be explicit about exactly which variables we are referring to. Look at this example constructor, again for a hypothetical variation of the Soldier class:

```java
public class Soldier{

    String name;
    String type;
    int health;

    // This is the constructor
    // It is called when a new instance is created
    public Soldier(String name, String type, int health){

        // Someone is creating a new Soldier object

        this.name = name;
        this.type = type;
        this.health = health;

        // more setup here
    }
}
```

This time, the constructor has a parameter for each of the variables we want to initialize. By using the this keyword, it is clear when we mean the member variable or the parameter.

There are more twists and turns to be learned about variables and this and they make much more sense when applied to a practical project. In the next app, we will explore all we have learned so far in this chapter and some more new ideas too.

First, a bit more OOP.

Static methods

We know quite a lot about classes already. For example, we know how to turn them into objects and use their methods and variables. But something isn't quite right. Since the very start of the book, we have been using two classes more than any other. We have repeatedly used Log and Toast to output to logcat or the user's screen but have not instantiated them once! How can this be? We never did this:

```
Log myLog  = new Log();
Toast myToast = new Toast();
```

We just went ahead and used the classes directly, like this:

```
Log.i("info","our message here");
Toast.makeText(this, "our message",
Toast.LENGTH_SHORT).show();
```

The **static** methods of classes can be used *without* first instantiating an object of the class. We can think of this as a static method belonging to the class and all other methods belonging to an object/instance of a class.

And as you have probably realized by now, Log and Toast both contain static methods. To be clear: Log and Toast *contain* static methods; they themselves are still classes.

Classes can have both static and regular methods as well, but the regular methods would need to be used in a regular way, via an instance/object of the class.

Take another look at Log.i in action:

```
Log.i("info","our message here");
```

Here, i is the method being statically accessed and the method takes two parameters, both of type String.

Next, we see the static method `makeText` of the `Toast` class in use:

```
Toast.makeText(this, "our message",
Toast.LENGTH_SHORT).show();
```

The `makeText` method of the `Toast` class takes three arguments.

The first is `this`, which is a reference to the current class. We saw when talking about constructors that to explicitly refer to the member variables of the current instance of an object, we can use `this.health`, `this.regiment`, and so on.

When we use `this` as we do in the previous line of code, we are referring to the instance of the class itself; not the `Toast` class but the `this` in the previous line of code is a reference to the class the method is being used *from*. In our case, we have used it from the `MainActivity` class.

Many things in Android require a reference to an instance of `Activity` to do their job. We will fairly regularly throughout this book pass in `this` (a reference to `Activity`) in order to enable a class/object from the Android API to do its work. We will also write classes that need `this` as an argument in one or more of its methods. So, we will see how to handle `this` when it is passed in as well.

The second argument of the `makeText` method is of course a `String`.

The third argument is accessing a `final` variable, `LENGTH_SHORT`, again via the class name not an instance of the class. If we declare a variable like this next line of code:

```
public static final int LENGTH_SHORT = 1;
```

If the variable was declared in a class called `MyClass`, we could access the variable like this: `MyClass.LENGTH_SHORT` and use it like any other variable, but the `final` keyword makes sure that the value of the variable can never be changed. This type of variable is called a **constant**.

The `static` keyword also has another consequence for a variable, especially when it is not a constant (can be changed) and we will see this in action in our next app.

Now if you look carefully at the very end of the line of code that shows a `Toast` message to the user, you will see something else new, `.show()`.

This is called **chaining** and what we are doing is calling a second method of the `Toast` class but using just one line of code. It is the `show` method that actually triggers the message.

We will look at chaining more closely as we proceed through the book, such as in *Chapter 14, Android Dialog Windows*, when we make a pop-up dialog.

> **Tip**
>
> If you want to read about the `Toast` class and some of its other methods in detail, you can do so here: `http://developer.android.com/reference/android/widget/Toast.html`.

Static methods are often provided in classes that have uses that are so generic it doesn't make sense to create an object of the class. Another really useful class with static methods is `Math`. This class is actually a part of the Java API, not the Android API.

> **Tip**
>
> Want to write a calculator app? It's easier than you think with the static methods of the `Math` class. You can look at them here: `http://docs.oracle.com/javase/7/docs/api/java/lang/Math.html`.

If you try this out, you will need to import the `Math` class the same way you imported all the other classes we have used. Next, we can try out a practical mini app to understand encapsulation and static methods.

Encapsulation and static methods mini-app

We have looked at the intricate way that access to variables and their scope is controlled and it would serve us well to look at an example of them in action. These will not so much be practical real-world examples of variable use, more a demonstration to help understand access modifiers for classes, methods, and variables alongside the different types of variables such as reference or primitive and local or instance, along with the new concepts of static and final variables and the `this` keyword.

The completed code is in the `chapter 11` folder of the download bundle. It is called `Access Scope This And Static`.

Create a new Empty Activity project and call it `Access Scope This And Static`.

Create a new class by right-clicking on the existing `MainActivity` class in the project explorer and clicking **New | Java Class**. Name the new class `AlienShip`.

Now we will declare our new class and some member variables. Note that numShips is private and static. We will see how this variable is the same across all instances of the class soon. The shieldStrength variable is private and shipName is public:

```
public class AlienShip {

    private static int numShips;
    private int shieldStrength;
    public String shipName;
```

Next is the constructor. We can see that the constructor is public, has no return type, and has the same name as the class – as per the rules. In it, we increment the private static numShips variable. Remember this will happen each time we create a new object of type AlienShip. Also, the constructor sets a value for the private variable shieldStrength using the private setShieldStrength method:

```
public AlienShip(){
    numShips++;

    /*
            Can call private methods from here because I am
            part of the class.
            If didn't have "this" then this call
            might be less clear
            But this "this" isn't strictly necessary
            Because of "this" I am sure I am setting
            the correct shieldStrength
    */

    this.setShieldStrength(100);

}
```

Here is the public static getter method so classes outside of AlienShip can find out how many AlienShip objects there are. We will also see the way in which we use static methods:

```
    public static int getNumShips(){
        return numShips;

    }
```

And this is our private `setShieldStrength` method. We could have just set `shieldStrength` directly from within the class, but the code below shows how we distinguish between the `shieldStrength` local variable/parameter and the `shieldStrength` member variable by using the `this` keyword:

```
private void setShieldStrength(int shieldStrength){

    // "this" distinguishes between the
    // member variable shieldStrength
    // And the local variable/parameter of the same name
    this.shieldStrength = shieldStrength;

}
```

This next method is the getter so other classes can read but not alter the shield strength of each `AlienShip` object:

```
public int getShieldStrength(){
    return this.shieldStrength;
}
```

Now we have a public method that can be called every time an `AlienShip` object is hit. It just prints to the console and then detects whether that object's `shieldStrength` is zero. If it is, it calls the `destroyShip` method, which we'll look at next:

```
public void hitDetected(){

    shieldStrength -=25;
    Log.i("Incomiming: ","Bam!!");
    if (shieldStrength == 0){
```

```
        destroyShip();
    }


}
```

And lastly for our `AlienShip` class, we will code the `destroyShip` method. We print a message that indicates which ship has been destroyed based on its `shipName` as well as decrementing the `numShips` static variable so we can keep track of how many objects of type `AlienShip` we have:

```
private void destroyShip(){
    numShips--;
    Log.i("Explosion: ", ""+this.shipName + "
    destroyed");
}
} // End of the class
```

Now we switch over to our `MainActivity` class and write some code that uses our new `AlienShip` class. All the code goes in the `onCreate` method after the call to `setContentView`. First, we create two new `AlienShip` objects called `girlShip` and `boyShip`:

```
// every time we do this the constructor runs
AlienShip girlShip = new AlienShip();
AlienShip boyShip = new AlienShip();
```

In the next code, look at how we get the value in `numShips`. We use the `getNumShips` method as we might expect. However, look closely at the syntax. We are using the class name and not an object. We can also access static variables with methods that are not static. We did it this way to see a static method in action:

```
// Look no objects but using the static method
Log.i("numShips: ", "" + AlienShip.getNumShips());
```

Now we assign names to our public `shipName` String variables:

```
// This works because shipName is public
girlShip.shipName = "Corrine Yu";
boyShip.shipName = "Andre LaMothe";
```

In this next code, we try to assign a value directly to a private variable. It won't work. Then we use the public getter method `getShieldStrength` to print out the `shieldStrength`, which was assigned in the constructor:

```
// This won't work because shieldStrength is private
// girlship.shieldStrength = 999;

// But we have a public getter
Log.i("girl shields: ", "" + girlShip.getShieldStrength());

Log.i("boy shields: ", "" + boyShip.getShieldStrength());

// And we can't do this because it's private
// boyship.setShieldStrength(1000000);
```

Finally, we get to blow some stuff up by playing with the `hitDetected` method and occasionally checking the `shieldStrength` of our two objects:

```
// let's shoot some ships
girlShip.hitDetected();
Log.i("girl shields: ", "" + girlShip.getShieldStrength());

Log.i("boy shields: ", "" + boyShip.getShieldStrength());

boyShip.hitDetected();
boyShip.hitDetected();
boyShip.hitDetected();

Log.i("girl shields: ", "" + girlShip.getShieldStrength());

Log.i("boy shields: ", "" + boyShip.getShieldStrength());

boyShip.hitDetected();//Ahhh!

Log.i("girl shields: ", "" + girlShip.getShieldStrength());

Log.i("boy shields: ", "" + boyShip.getShieldStrength());
```

When we think we have destroyed a ship, we again use our static `getNumShips` method to see if our static variable `numShips` was changed by the `destroyShip` method:

```
Log.i("numShips: ", "" + AlienShip.getNumShips());
```

Run the demo and look at the console output:

```
numShips: 2
girl shields: 100
boy shields: 100
Incomiming: Bam!!
girl shields:: 75
boy shields:: 100
Incomiming: Bam!!
Incomiming: Bam!!
girl shields:: 75
boy shields:: 25
Incomiming: Bam!!
Explosion: Andre LaMothe destroyed
girl shields: 75
boy shields: 0
numShips: 1
boy shields: 0
numShips: 1
```

In the previous example, we saw that we can distinguish between local and member variables of the same name by using the `this` keyword. We can also use the `this` keyword to write code that refers to whatever the current object being acted upon is.

We saw that a static variable – in this case, `numShips` – is consistent across all instances; moreover, by incrementing it in the constructor and decrementing it in our `destroyShip` method, we can keep track of the number of `AlienShip` objects we currently have.

We also saw that we can use static methods by using the class name with the dot operator instead of an actual object.

Tip
Yes, I know it is like living in the blueprint of a house – but it's quite useful too.

Finally, we proved how we could hide and expose certain methods and variables using an access specifier.

Next, we will look at the topic of inheritance.

OOP and inheritance

We have seen how we can use other people's code by instantiating/creating objects from the classes of an API like Android. But this whole OOP thing goes even further than that.

What if there is a class that has loads of useful functionality in it but not exactly what we want? We can inherit from the class and then further refine or add to how it works and what it does.

You might be surprised to hear that we have done this already. In fact, we have done this with every single app we have created. When we use the `extends` keyword, we are inheriting. Remember this:

```
public class MainActivity extends AppCompatActivity ...
```

Here, we are inheriting the `AppCompatActivity` class along with all its functionality – or more specifically, all the functionality that the class designers want us to have access to. Here are some of the things we can do to classes we have extended.

We can even override a method *and* still rely in part on the overridden method in the class we inherit from. For example, we overrode the `onCreate` method every time we extended the `AppCompatActivity` class. But we also called on the default implementation provided by the class designers when we did this:

```
super.onCreate(...
```

And in *Chapter 6, The Android Lifecycle*, we overrode just about all of the Activity class lifecycle methods.

We discuss inheritance mainly so that we understand what is going on around us and as the first step towards being able to eventually design useful classes that we or others can extend.

With this in mind, let's look at some example classes and see how we can extend them, just to see the syntax and as a first step, and also to be able to say we have done it.

When we look at the final major topic of this chapter, polymorphism, we will also dig a little deeper into inheritance at the same time. Here is some code using inheritance.

This code would go in a file named `Animal.java`:

```java
public class Animal{

    // Some member variables
    public int age;
    public int weight;
    public String type;
    public int hungerLevel;

    public void eat(){
        hungerLevel--;
    }

    public void walk(){
        hungerLevel++;
    }

}
```

Then in a separate file named `Elephant.java`, we could do this:

```java
public class Elephant extends Animal{

    public Elephant(int age, int weight){
        this.age = age;
        this.weight = weight;
        this.type = "Elephant";
        int hungerLevel = 0;
    }

}
```

We can see in the previous code that we have implemented a class called `Animal` and it has four member variables: `age`, `weight`, `type`, and `hungerLevel`. It also has two methods, `eat` and `walk`.

We then extended `Animal` with `Elephant`. `Elephant` can now do anything an `Animal` can and it also has all its variables.

We initialized the variables from `Animal` that `Elephant` has in the `Elephant` constructor. Two variables (`age` and `weight`) are passed into the constructor when an `Elephant` object is created and two variables (`type` and `hungerLevel`) are assigned the same for all `Elephant` objects.

We could go ahead and write a bunch of other classes that extend `Animal`, perhaps `Lion`, `Tiger`, and `ThreeToedSloth`. Each would have an `age`, `weight`, `type`, and `hungerLevel` and each would be able to `walk` and `eat`.

As if OOP were not useful enough already, we can now model real-world objects. We have also seen that we can make OOP even more useful by subclassing/extending/inheriting from other classes. The terminology we might like to learn here is that the class that is extended from is the **super class** and the class that inherits from the super class is the **subclass**. We can also say the parent and child class.

> **Tip**
>
> As usual, we might find ourselves asking this question about inheritance. Why? The reason is something like this: we can write common code once, in the parent class; we can update that common code and all classes that inherit from it are also updated. Furthermore, a subclass only gets to use public/protected instance variables and methods. So, designed properly, this also further enhances the goals of encapsulation.

Let's build another small app to play about with inheritance.

Inheritance example app

We have looked at the way we can create hierarchies of classes to model a system that fits our app. So, let's try out some simple code that uses inheritance. The completed code is in the `chapter 11` folder of the code download. It is called `Inheritance Example`.

Create a new project called `Inheritance Example` using the **Empty Activity** template and then add three new classes in the usual way. Name one `AlienShip`, another `Fighter`, and the last one `Bomber`.

Here is the code for the `AlienShip` class. It is very similar to our previous class demo, `AlienShip`. The differences are that the constructor now takes an `int` parameter, which it uses to set the shield strength.

The constructor also outputs a message to the logcat window, so we can see when it is being used. The AlienShip class also has a new method, fireWeapon, that is declared as abstract.

Declaring a class as abstract guarantees that any class that subclasses AlienShip must implement its own version of fireWeapon. Notice the class has the abstract keyword as part of its declaration. We have to do this because one of its methods also uses the abstract keyword. We will explain the abstract method when discussing this demo and the abstract class when we talk about polymorphism in the next section.

Add the following code to the AlienShip class:

```
public abstract class AlienShip {
    private static int numShips;
    private int shieldStrength;
    public String shipName;

    public AlienShip(int shieldStrength){
        Log.i("Location: ", "AlienShip constructor");
        numShips++;
        setShieldStrength(shieldStrength);
    }

    public abstract void fireWeapon();
    // Ahh my body where is it?

    public static int getNumShips(){
        return numShips;
    }

    private void setShieldStrength(int shieldStrength){
        this.shieldStrength = shieldStrength;
    }


    public int getShieldStrength(){
        return this.shieldStrength;
    }
```

```
    public void hitDetected(){
        shieldStrength -=25;
        Log.i("Incomiming: ", "Bam!!");
        if (shieldStrength == 0){
            destroyShip();
        }


    }

    private void destroyShip(){
        numShips--;
        Log.i("Explosion: ", "" + this.shipName + "
        destroyed");
    }


}
```

Now we will implement the Bomber class. Notice the call to super(100). This calls the constructor of the super class with the value for shieldStrength. We could do further specific Bomber initialization in this constructor, but for now, we just print out the location so we can see when the Bomber constructor is being executed. We also, because we must, implement a Bomber specific version of the abstract fireWeapon method. Add the following code to the Bomber class:

```
public class Bomber extends AlienShip {

    public Bomber(){
        super(100);
        // Weak shields for a bomber
        Log.i("Location: ", "Bomber constructor");
    }

    public void fireWeapon(){
        Log.i("Firing weapon: ", "bombs away");
    }
}
```

Now we will implement the Fighter class. Notice the call to super(400). This calls the constructor of the super class with the value for shieldStrength. We could do further specific Fighter initialization in this constructor but for now, we just print out the location so we can see when the Fighter constructor is being executed. We also must implement a Fighter specific version of the abstract fireWeapon method. Add the following code to the Fighter class:

```
public class Fighter extends AlienShip{

    public Fighter(){
        super(400);
        // Strong shields for a fighter
        Log.i("Location: ", "Fighter constructor");
    }

    public void fireWeapon(){
        Log.i("Firing weapon: ", "lasers firing");
    }

}
```

Next, we will code the onCreate method of MainActivity. As usual, enter this code after the call to the setContentView method. This is the code that uses our three new classes. The code looks quite ordinary – nothing new. It is the output that is interesting:

```
Fighter aFighter = new Fighter();
Bomber aBomber = new Bomber();

// Can't do this AlienShip is abstract -
// Literally speaking as well as in code
// AlienShip alienShip = new AlienShip(500);

// But our objects of the subclasses can still do
// everything the AlienShip is meant to do

aBomber.shipName = "Newell Bomber";
```

```
aFighter.shipName = "Meier Fighter";


// And because of the overridden constructor
// That still calls the super constructor
// They have unique properties
Log.i("aFighter Shield:", ""+ aFighter.getShieldStrength());
Log.i("aBomber Shield:", ""+ aBomber.getShieldStrength());


// As well as certain things in certain ways
// That are unique to the subclass
aBomber.fireWeapon();
aFighter.fireWeapon();


// Take down those alien ships
// Focus on the bomber it has a weaker shield
aBomber.hitDetected();
aBomber.hitDetected();
aBomber.hitDetected();
aBomber.hitDetected();
```

Run the app and you will get the following output in the logcat window:

```
Location:: AlienShip constructor
Location:: Fighter constructor
Location:: AlienShip constructor
Location:: Bomber constructor
aFighter Shield:: 400
aBomber Shield:: 100
Firing weapon:: bombs away
Firing weapon:: lasers firing
Incomiming:: Bam!!
Incomiming:: Bam!!
Incomiming:: Bam!!
Incomiming:: Bam!!
Explosion:: Newell Bomber destroyed
```

We can see how the constructor of the subclass calls the constructor of the super class. We can also clearly see that the individual implementations of the `fireWeapon` method work exactly as expected.

Let's take a closer look at the final major OOP concept, polymorphism. Then we will be able to do some more practical things with the Android API.

Polymorphism

We already know that polymorphism means *different forms*. But what does it mean to us?

Boiled down to its simplest:

> *Any subclass can be used as part of the code that uses the super class.*

This means we can write code that is simpler and easier to understand, and easier to change.

Also, we can write code for the super class and rely on the fact that no matter how many times it is sub-classed, within certain parameters, the code will still work. Let's discuss an example.

Suppose we want to use polymorphism to help to write a zoo management app. We will probably want to have a method such as `feed`. We will probably want to pass a reference to the animal to be fed into the `feed` method. This might seem like we need to write a `feed` method for each and every type of `Animal`.

However, we can write polymorphic methods with polymorphic return types and arguments:

```
Animal feed(Animal animalToFeed){
    // Feed any animal here
    return animalToFeed;
}
```

The preceding method has `Animal` as a parameter, which means that any object that is built from a class that extends `Animal` can be passed into it. And as you can see in the preceding code, the method also returns `Animal`, which has exactly the same benefits.

There is a small gotcha with polymorphic return types and that is that we need to be aware of what is being returned and make it explicit in the code that calls the method.

For example, we could handle `Elephant` being passed into the `feed` method like this:

```
someElephant = (Elephant) feed(someElephant);
```

Notice the highlighted (`Elephant`) in the previous code. This makes it plain that we want `Elephant` from the returned `Animal`. This is called **casting**. We will use casting occasionally throughout the rest of the book.

So, you can even write code *today* and make another subclass in a week, month, or year, and the very same methods and data structures will still work.

Also, we can enforce upon our subclasses a set of rules as to what they can and cannot do, as well as how they do it. So, clever design in one stage can influence it at other stages.

But will we ever really want to instantiate an actual `Animal`?

Abstract classes

We played with an abstract class in the inheritance example app but let's dig a little deeper. An abstract class is a class that cannot be instantiated; it cannot be made into an object. So, it's a blueprint that will never be used then? But that's like paying an architect to design your home and then never building it? You might be saying to yourself, "I kind of got the idea of an abstract method but abstract classes are just silly."

If we or the designer of a class wants to force us to inherit *before* we use their class, they can declare a class **abstract**. Then, we cannot make an object from it; therefore, we must extend it first and make an object from the subclass.

We can also declare a method `abstract` and then that method must be overridden in any class that extends the class with the abstract method.

Let's look at an example – it will help. We make a class `abstract` by declaring it with the `abstract` keyword like this:

```
abstract class someClass{
    /*
            All methods and variables here.
            As usual!
            Just don't try and make
            an object out of me!
    */
}
```

Yes, but why?

Sometimes we want a class that can be used as a polymorphic type, but we need to guarantee it can never be used as an object. For example, "animal" doesn't really make sense on its own.

We don't talk about animals; we talk about *types* of animals. We don't say, "Ooh, look at that lovely fluffy, white animal." Or, "Yesterday we went to the pet shop and got an animal and an animal bed." It's just too, well, *abstract*.

So, an abstract class is kind of like a template to be used by any class that `extends` it (inherits from it).

We might want a `Worker` class and extend it to make `Miner`, `Steelworker`, `OfficeWorker`, and of course `Programmer`. But what exactly does a plain `Worker` do? Why would we ever want to instantiate one?

The answer is we probably wouldn't want to instantiate one; but we might want to use it as a polymorphic type, so we can pass multiple worker subclasses between methods and have data structures that can hold all types of `Worker`.

We call this type of class an abstract class and when a class has even one abstract method, it must be declared abstract itself. And all abstract methods must be overridden by any class that extends it.

This means that the abstract class can give some of the common functionality that would be available in all its subclasses. For example, the `Worker` class might have the `height`, `weight`, and `age` member variables.

It might also have the `getPayCheck` method, which is not abstract and is the same in all the subclasses, but a `doWork` method is abstract and must be overridden, because all the different types of worker `doWork` differently.

This leads us neatly to another area of polymorphism that is going to make life easier for us throughout this book.

Interfaces

An interface is like a class. Phew! Nothing complicated here then. But it's like a class that is always abstract and has only abstract methods.

We can think of an interface as an entirely abstract class with all its methods abstract and no member variables either.

OK, so you can just about wrap your head around an abstract class because at least it can pass on some functionality in its methods that are not abstract and serve as a polymorphic type. But seriously, this interface seems a bit pointless.

Let's look at the simplest possible generic example of an interface, then we can discuss it further.

To define an interface, we type the following:

```
public interface someInterface{
    void someAbstractMethod();
    // omg I've got no body

    int anotherAbstractMethod();
    // Ahh! Me too

    // Interface methods are always abstract and public
    // implicitly but we could make it explicit if we prefer

    public abstract void
    explicitlyAbstractAndPublicMethod();
    // still no body though


}
```

The methods of an interface have no body because they are abstract, but they can still have return types and parameters, or not.

To use an interface, we use the `implements` keyword after the class declaration:

```
public class someClass implements someInterface{

    // class stuff here

    /*
        Better implement the methods of the interface
        or we will have errors.
        And nothing will work
    */

    public void someAbstractMethod(){
        // code here if you like
```

```
            // but just an empty implementation will do
    }


    public int anotherAbstractMethod(){
            // code here if you like
            // but just an empty implementation will do

            // Must have a return type though
            // as that is part of the contract
            return 1;
    }


    Public void explicitlyAbstractAndPublicMethod(){


    }


}
```

This enables us to use polymorphism with multiple different objects that are from completely unrelated inheritance hierarchies. If a class implements an interface, the whole thing can be passed along or used as if it is that thing – because it is that thing. It is polymorphic (many things).

We can even have a class implement multiple different interfaces at the same time. Just add a comma between each interface and list them after the `implements` keyword. Just be sure to implement all the necessary methods.

In this book, we will use the interfaces of the Android API more often than we write our own. In *Chapter 13, Anonymous Classes - Bringing Android Widgets to Life*, one such interface we will use in the Java Meet UI app is the `OnClickListener` interface.

Many things might like to know when they are being clicked. Perhaps a `Button` or a `TextView` widget, and so on. So, using an interface we don't need different methods for every type of UI element we might like to click.

Frequently asked questions

1. What is wrong with this class declaration?

```
private class someClass{
        // class implementation goes here
}
```

   There are no private classes. Classes can be public or default. Public classes are public; default classes are private within their own package.

2. What is encapsulation?

   Encapsulation is how we contain our variables, code, and methods in a manner that exposes just the parts and functionality we want to other code.

Summary

In this chapter, we covered more theory than in any other chapter. If you haven't memorized everything or some of the code seemed a bit too in-depth, then you have still succeeded completely.

If you just understand that OOP is about writing reusable, extendable, and efficient code through encapsulation, inheritance, and polymorphism, then you have the potential to be a Java master.

Simply put, OOP enables us to use other peoples' code even when those other people were not aware of exactly what we would be doing at the time they wrote the code.

All you must do is keep practicing because we will constantly be using these same concepts over and over again throughout the book, so you do not need to have even begun to have mastered them at this point.

In the next chapter, we will be revisiting some concepts from this chapter as well as looking at some new aspects of OOP and how it enables our Java code to interact with our XML layouts.

But first, there is an important incoming news flash!

> **Important note**
>
> All the UI elements – TextView, ConstraintLayout,
> CalenderView, and Button – are classes too. Their attributes are
> member variables and they have loads of methods that we can use to do all
> sorts of things with the UI. This could prove useful.

There will much more on this revelation in the next two chapters, but first, we will see how Android handles trash.

12

The Stack, the Heap, and the Garbage Collector

By the end of this chapter, the missing link between Java and our XML layouts will be fully revealed, leaving us with the power to add all kinds of widgets to our apps as we have done before, but this time, we will be able to control them through our Java code.

In this chapter, we will get to take control of some simple UI elements such as `Button` and `TextView` and in the next chapter, we will take things further and manipulate a whole range of UI elements.

To enable us to understand what is happening, we need to find out a bit more about the memory in an Android device and two areas of it – the **Stack** and the **Heap**.

In this chapter, we will learn about the following:

- Android UI elements are classes
- Garbage collection

- Our UI is on the heap?

- Special types of classes, including inner and anonymous

Back to that news flash.

Technical requirements

You can find the code files present in this chapter on GitHub at `https://github.com/PacktPublishing/Android-Programming-for-Beginners-Third-Edition/tree/main/chapter%2012`.

All the Android UI elements are classes too

When our app is run and the `setContentView` method is called from the `onCreate` method, the layout is `inflated` from the XML and instances of the UI classes are loaded into memory as usable objects. They are stored in a part of the memory called the heap. The heap is managed by the **Android Runtime (ART)** system.

Re-introducing references

But where are all these UI objects/classes? We certainly can't see them in our code. And how on earth do we get our hands on them?

The ART inside every Android device takes care of memory allocation to our apps. In addition, it stores different types of variables in different places.

Variables that we declare and initialize in methods are stored on the area of memory known as the **Stack**. We can stick to our existing warehouse analogy when talking about the Stack. We already know how we can manipulate variables on the Stack with straightforward expressions. So, let's talk about the heap and what is stored there.

> **Important fact**
>
> All objects of classes are reference type variables and are just references to the actual objects that are stored on the heap – they are not the actual objects.

Think of the heap as a separate area of the same warehouse. The heap has lots of floor space for odd-shaped objects, racks for smaller objects, lots of long rows with smaller-sized cubby holes, and so on. This is where objects are stored. The problem is we have no direct access to the heap. Think of it as a restricted access part of the warehouse. You can't actually go there but you can *refer* to what is stored there. Let's look at what exactly a reference variable is.

It is a variable that we refer to and use via a reference. A reference can be loosely but usefully defined as an address or location. The reference (address or location) of the object is on the Stack.

So, when we use the dot operator, we are asking Android to perform a task *at* a specific location, a location that is stored in the reference.

Why would we ever want a system like this? Just give me my objects on the Stack already. Here is why.

A quick break to throw out the trash

This is what the whole stack and heap thing does for us.

As we know, the ART system keeps track of all our objects for us and stores them in a devoted area of our warehouse called the heap. Regularly, while our app is running, ART will scan the stack, the regular racks of our warehouse, and match up references to objects that are on the heap. And any objects it finds without a matching reference, it destroys. Or in Java terminology, it **garbage collects**.

Think of a very discerning refuse vehicle driving through the middle of our heap, scanning objects to match up to references (on the stack). No reference? You're garbage now.

If an object has no reference variable, we can't possibly do anything with it anyway because we have no way to access it/refer to it. This system of garbage collection helps our apps run more efficiently by freeing up unused memory.

If this task was left to us, our apps would be much more complicated to code.

So, variables declared in a method are local, on the stack, and only visible within the method they were declared in. A member variable (in an object) is on the heap and can be referenced from anywhere there is a reference to it and the access specification (encapsulation) allows.

Seven facts about the stack and the heap

Let's take a quick look at what we learned about the stack and the heap:

1. Local variables and methods are on the stack and local variables are local to the specific method within which they were declared.
2. Instance/class variables are on the heap (with their objects) but the reference *to* the object (its address), is a local variable on the stack.

3. We control what goes on the stack. We can use the objects on the heap but only by referencing them.

4. The heap is kept clear and up to date by the garbage collector.

5. You don't delete objects but the ART system sends the garbage collector when it thinks it is appropriate. An object is garbage collected when there is no longer a valid reference to it. So, when a reference variable, either local or instance, is removed from the stack, then its related object becomes viable for garbage collection. And when the ART system decides the time is right (usually very promptly), it will free up the RAM memory to avoid running out.

6. If we try to reference an object that doesn't exist, we will get a **NullPointerException** and the app will crash.

Let's move on and see exactly what this information buys us in terms of taking control of our UI.

So how does this heap thing help me?

Any UI element that has its `id` attribute set in the XML layout can have its reference retrieved from the heap using the `findViewById` method, which is part of the Activity/ `AppCompatActivity` class. As it is part of the class that we extend in all our apps, we have access to it, as this code shows:

```
Button myButton = findViewById(R.id.myButton);
```

The preceding code assumes that within the XML layout there is a `Button` widget with its `id` attribute set to `myButton`. The `myButton` object now directly refers to the widget in the XML layout with the `id` attribute set to `myButton`.

Note that the `findViewById` method is also polymorphic and any class that extends the `View` class can be retrieved from the UI and it just so happened that *everything* in the UI palette extends `View`.

The sharp-minded reader might notice that we don't use a cast to make sure we are getting a `Button` object (as opposed to a `TextView` or some other `View` descendant) as we did when retrieving an `Elephant` instance descended from an abstract `Animal`:

```
someElephant = (Elephant) feed(someElephant);
```

The reason for this is that the `View` class uses Java's **generics automatic type inference**. This is an advanced topic that we won't be covering in this book, but it means that the cast is automatic, and we don't need to write more lengthy code like this:

```
Button myButton = (Button) findViewById(R.id.myButton);
```

This ability to grab a reference to anything in the UI is exciting because it means we can start using all the methods that these objects have. Here are some examples of the methods we can use for `Button` objects:

```
myButton.setText
```
```
myButton.setHeight
```
```
myButton.setOnCLickListener
```
```
myButton.setVisibility
```

> **Important note**
> The `Button` class alone has around 50 methods!

If you think, after 11 chapters, we are finally going to start doing some neat stuff with Android, you are right!

Using buttons and TextView widgets from our layout

To follow along with this project, create a new Android Studio project, call it `Java Meet UI`, choose the Empty Activity template, and leave all the other options at their defaults. As usual, you can find the Java code and the XML layout code in the `Chapter 12/Java Meet UI` folder.

First, let's build a simple UI by following these steps:

1. In the editor window of Android Studio, switch to `activity_main.xml` and make sure you are on the **Design** tab.

2. Delete the autogenerated **TextView**, the one that reads "Hello world!".

3. Add a **TextView** widget at the top center of the layout.

4. Set its **text** property to 0, its **id** property to **txtValue**, and its **textSize** property to 40sp. Pay careful attention to the case of the id property's value. It has an uppercase V.

5. Now drag and drop six buttons on the layout so it looks as close as possible to this next screenshot. The exact layout isn't important:

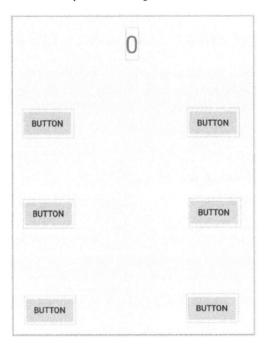

Figure 12.1 – Layout setup

6. When the layout is how you want it, click the **Infer Constraints** button to constrain all the UI items.

7. Edit the properties of each button in turn (left to right, then top to bottom) and set the text and id properties as shown in the next table. The image that follows the table should make it clear which button has which values.

The text property	The id property
Add	btnAdd
Take	btnTake
Grow	btnGrow
Shrink	btnShrink
Hide	btnHide
Reset	btnReset

When you're done, your layout should look like the next screenshot:

Figure 12.2 – Final layout

The precise position and text on the buttons are not very important but the values given to the id properties must be the same as those in the table. The reason for this is we will be using these IDs to get a reference to the buttons and the TextView in this layout, from our Java code.

Switch to the **MainActivity.java** tab in the editor and we will write the code.

Amend this line:

```
public class MainActivity extends AppCompatActivity{
```

to

```
public class MainActivity extends AppCompatActivity implements
    View.OnClickListener{
```

> **Tip**
>
> You will need to import the `View` class. Be sure to do this before continuing with the next step or you will get confusing results.

```
import android.view.View;
```

Notice that the entire line we just amended is underlined in red showing an error. Now, because we have made `MainActivity` into an `OnClickListener` by adding it as an interface, we must implement the abstract method required by `OnClickListener`. The method is called `onClick`. When we add the `onClick` method, the error will be gone.

We can get Android Studio to add it for us by left-clicking anywhere on the line with an error and then using the keyboard combination *Alt + Enter*. Left-click the **Implement methods** option as shown in the next screenshot.

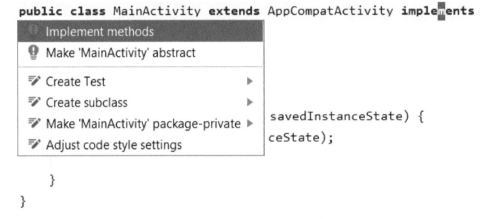

Figure 12.3 – Implement methods

Now, left-click **OK** to confirm we want Android Studio to automatically add the `onClick` method. The error is gone, and we can carry on adding code. We also have an empty `onClick` method and we will soon see what we will do with that.

Now we will declare an `int` type variable called `value` and initialize it to `0`. We will also declare six `Button` objects and a `TextView` object. We will give them the exact same Java variable names we gave the `id` property values in our UI layout. This name association is not needed but it is useful to keep track of which `Button` in our Java code will be holding a reference to which `Button` from our XML UI layout.

Furthermore, we are declaring them all with the `private` access specification because we know they will not be needed outside of this class.

Before you go ahead and type the code, note that all these variables are members of the MainActivity class. This means we enter all the code shown next, immediately after the class declaration (which we amended in the previous step).

Making all these variables into members/fields means they have a class scope and we can access them from anywhere within the MainActivity class. This will be essential for this project because we will need to use them in the onCreate method and in our new onClick method.

Enter this next code that we have just discussed, after the opening curly brace { of the MainActivity class and before the onCreate method:

```
// An int variable to hold a value
private int value = 0;


// A bunch of Buttons and a TextView
private Button btnAdd;
private Button btnTake;
private TextView txtValue;
private Button btnGrow;
private Button btnShrink;
private Button btnReset;
private Button btnHide;
```

> **Tip**
>
> Remember to use the *ALT + Enter* keyboard combination to import new classes.
>
> ```
> import android.widget.Button;
> import android.widget.TextView;
> ```

Next, we want to prepare all our variables ready for action. The best place for this to happen is in the onCreate method because we know that will be called by Android just before the app is shown to the user. This code uses the findViewById method to associate each of our Java objects with an item from our UI layout.

It does so by returning a reference to the object associated with the UI widget on the heap. It "knows" which one we are after because we use the id attribute value as an argument. For example, . . . (R.id.btnAdd) will return the Button widget with the text **ADD** that we created in our layout.

Enter the following code, just after the call to setContentView in the onCreate method:

```
// Get a reference to all the buttons in our UI
// Match them up to all our Button objects we declared earlier
btnAdd = findViewById(R.id.btnAdd);
btnTake = findViewById(R.id.btnTake);
txtValue = findViewById(R.id.txtValue);
btnGrow = findViewById(R.id.btnGrow);
btnShrink = findViewById(R.id.btnShrink);
btnReset = findViewById(R.id.btnReset);
btnHide = findViewById(R.id.btnHide);
```

Now we have a reference to all our Button widgets and our TextView widget so now we can start using their methods. In the code that follows, we use the setOnClickListener method on each of the Button references to make Android pass any clicks from the user onto our onClick method.

This works because when we implemented the View.OnClickListener interface, our MainActivity class effectively *became* an OnClickListener.

So, all we have to do is call setOnClickListener on each button in turn. As a reminder, the this argument is a reference to MainActivity. So, the method call says, "Hey Android, I want an OnClickListener and I want it to be the MainActivity class."

Android now knows which class to call onClick on. This next code wouldn't work if we hadn't implemented the interface first. Also, we must set up these listeners before the Activity starts, which is why we do it in onCreate.

Soon, we will add code to the onClick method to handle what happens when a button is clicked and we will see how we differentiate between all the different buttons.

Add this code after the previous code, inside the onCreate method:

```
// Listen for all the button clicks
btnAdd.setOnClickListener(this);
btnTake.setOnClickListener(this);
txtValue.setOnClickListener(this);
btnGrow.setOnClickListener(this);
btnShrink.setOnClickListener(this);
btnReset.setOnClickListener(this);
```

```
btnHide.setOnClickListener(this);
```

Now scroll down to the `onClick` method that Android Studio added for us after we implemented the `OnClickListener` interface. Add the `float size;` variable declaration and an empty `switch` block inside it so it looks like this next code. The new code to add is highlighted:

```
public void onClick(View view){


        // A local variable to use later
    float size;

    switch(view.getId()){



    }
}
```

Remember that `switch` will check for a `case` to match the condition inside the `switch` statement.

In the previous code, the `switch` condition is `view.getId()`. Let's step through and explain this. The `view` variable is a reference to an object of type `View`, which was passed into the `onClick` method by Android:

```
public void onClick(View view)
```

`View` is the parent class for `Button`, `TextView`, and more. So, perhaps as we might expect, calling `view.getId()` will return the `id` attribute of the UI widget that has been clicked and triggered the call to `onClick` in the first place.

All we need to do then is provide a `case` statement (and appropriate action) for each of the `Button` references we want to respond to.

The next code we will see is the first three `case` statements. They handle `R.id.btnAdd`, `R.id.btnTake`, and `R.id.btnReset` cases:

- The code in the `R.id.btnAdd` case simply increments the `value` variable, then it does something new.

It calls the setText method on the txtValue object. Here is the argument: (""+ value). This argument uses an empty string and adds (concatenates) whatever value is stored in value to it. This has the effect of causing our TextView txtValue to display whatever value is stored in value.

- The **TAKE** button (R.id.btnTake) does exactly the same, only subtracts one from value instead of adding one.

- The third case statement handles the **RESET** button and sets value to zero and again updates the text attribute of txtValue.

Then, at the end of each case, there is a break statement. At this point, the switch block is exited, the onClick method returns, and life goes back to normal – until the user's next click.

Enter this code that we have just discussed inside the switch block after the opening curly brace {:

```
case R.id.btnAdd:
    value ++;
    txtValue.setText(""+ value);

    break;

case R.id.btnTake:
    value--;
    txtValue.setText(""+ value);

    break;

case R.id.btnReset:
    value = 0;
    txtValue.setText(""+ value);

    break;
```

The next two case statements handle the **SHRINK** and **GROW** buttons from our UI. We can confirm this from the IDs R.id.btnGrow and R.id.btnShrink. What is new and more interesting are the two new methods that are used.

The getTextScaleX method returns the horizontal scale of the text within the object it is used on. We can see that the object it is used on is our TextView txtValue. The size = at the start of the line of code assigns that returned value to our float variable size.

The next line of code in each case statement changes the horizontal scale of the text using setTextScaleX. When the **GROW** button is pressed, the scale is set to size + 1, and when the **SHRINK** button is pressed, the scale is set to size - 1.

The overall effect is to allow these two buttons to grow and shrink the text in the txtValue widget by a scale of 1 on each click.

Enter the next two case statements that we have just discussed below the previous code:

```
case R.id.btnGrow:
    size = txtValue.getTextScaleX();
    txtValue.setTextScaleX(size + 1);


    break;


case R.id.btnShrink:
    size = txtValue.getTextScaleX();
    txtValue.setTextScaleX(size - 1);


    break;

```

In our final case statement, which we will code next, we have an if-else block. The condition takes a little bit of explaining so let's have sight of it in advance:

```
if(txtValue.getVisibility() == View.VISIBLE)
```

The condition to be evaluated is txtValue.getVisibility() == View.VISIBLE. The first part of that condition before the == operator returns the visibility attribute of our txtValue TextView. The return value will be one of three possible constant values as defined in the View class. They are View.VISIBLE, View.INVISIBLE, and View.GONE.

If TextView is visible to the user on the UI, the method returns View.VISIBLE, the condition is evaluated as true, and the if block is executed.

Inside the `if` block, we use the `setVisibility` method on the `txtValue` object and make it invisible to the user with the `View.INVISIBLE` argument.

In addition to this, we change the text on the `btnHide` widget to **SHOW** using the `setText` method.

After the `if` block has executed, `txtValue` is invisible and we have a button on our UI that says **SHOW**. When the user clicks it in this state, the `if` statement will be false and the `else` block will execute. In the `else` block, we reverse the situation. We set `txtValue` back to `View.VISIBLE` and the `text` property on `btnHide` back to **HIDE**.

If this is in any way unclear, just enter the code, run the app, and revisit this last code and explanation once you have seen it in action:

```
case R.id.btnHide:
    if(txtValue.getVisibility() == View.VISIBLE)
    {
            // Currently visible so hide it
            txtValue.setVisibility(View.INVISIBLE);

            // Change text on the button
            btnHide.setText("SHOW");

    }else{
            // Currently hidden so show it
            txtValue.setVisibility(View.VISIBLE);

            // Change text on the button
            btnHide.setText("HIDE");
    }


    break;
```

We have the UI and the code in place, so it is time to run the app and try out all the buttons.

Running the app

Run the app in the usual way. Notice that the **ADD** and **TAKE** buttons change the value of value by one in either direction and then display the result in the TextView widget. In this next screenshot, I have clicked the **ADD** button three times.

Figure 12.4 – Add button example

Notice that the **SHRINK** and **GROW** buttons increase the width of the text and **RESET** sets the `value` variable to 0 and displays it on the `TextView` widget. In this next screenshot, I have clicked the **GROW** button eight times.

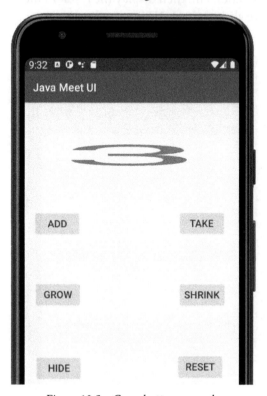

Figure 12.5 – Grow button example

Finally, the **HIDE** button not only hides the `TextView` but changes its own text to **SHOW** and will indeed re-show the `TextView` if tapped again.

> **Tip**
> I will not bother you by showing you an image of something that is hidden. Be sure to try the app.

Notice that there was no need for the `Log` or `Toast` classes in this app as we are finally manipulating the UI using our Java code. Let's dig even deeper into manipulating the UI with our code by exploring inner and anonymous classes.

Inner and anonymous classes

Before we go ahead to the next chapter and build apps with loads of different widgets that will put into practice and reinforce everything we have learned in this chapter, we will have a very brief introduction to **Anonymous** and **Inner** classes.

When we implemented our basic classes demo app in *Chapter 10, Object-Oriented Programming*, we declared and implemented the class in a separate file to our `MainActivity` class. That file had to have the same name as the class. This is the way to create a regular class.

We can also declare and implement classes within a class. Other than *how* we do this, the only question remaining, of course, is why would we do this?

When we implement an inner class, the inner class can access the member variables of the enclosing class and the enclosing class can access the members of the inner class.

This often makes the structure of our code more straightforward. So inner classes are sometimes the way to go.

In addition, we can also declare and implement an entire class within a method of one of our classes. When we do so, we use a slightly different syntax and do not use a name with the class. This is an **anonymous** class.

We will see both inner and anonymous classes in action throughout the rest of the book and we will thoroughly discuss them when we use them.

Frequently asked questions

1. I don't get it all and actually I have more questions now than I had at the start of the chapter. What should I do?

    You know enough about OOP to make considerable progress with Android and any other type of Java programming. If you are desperate to know more about OOP right now, there are plenty of books that discuss nothing but OOP. However, practice and familiarity with the syntax will go a long way to achieving the same thing and will be more fun. This is exactly what we will do for the rest of the book.

Summary

In this chapter, we finally had some real interaction between our code and our UI. It turns out that every time we add a widget to our UI, we are adding an instance of a class that we can access with a reference in our Java code. All these objects are stored in a separate area of memory called the heap – along with any classes of our own.

We are now in a position where we can learn about and do cool things with some of the more interesting widgets. We will look at loads of them in the next chapter, and then keep introducing further new widgets throughout the rest of the book as well.

13
Anonymous Classes – Bringing Android Widgets to Life

This chapter could have been called *Even More OOP*, as anonymous classes are very much still part of that subject. However, as you will see, anonymous classes offer us so much flexibility, especially when it comes to interacting with the **User Interface (UI)**, that I thought they deserved a chapter dedicated to them and their key use in Android.

Now that we have a good overview of both the layout and coding of an Android app, along with our newly acquired insight into **Object-Oriented Programming (OOP)**, and how we can manipulate the UI from our Java code, we are ready to experiment with more widgets from the palette alongside anonymous classes.

OOP is a tricky thing at times, and anonymous classes are known to be a bit awkward for beginners. However, by gradually learning these new concepts and then practicing them repeatedly, over time, they will become our friends.

In this chapter, we will diversify a lot by going back to the Android Studio palette and looking at half a dozen widgets that we have either not seen at all or have not fully used yet.

Once we have done this, we will put them all into a layout and practice manipulating them with Java code.

In this chapter, we will focus on the following topics:

- Declaring and initializing layout widgets
- Creating widgets with just Java code
- The EditText, ImageView, RadioButton (and RadioGroup), Switch, CheckBox, and TextClock widgets
- Using WebView
- How to use an anonymous class
- Making a widget demo mini app using all of the preceding widgets and some anonymous classes

Let's begin with a quick recap.

Technical requirements

You can find the code files present in this chapter on GitHub at https://github.com/PacktPublishing/Android-Programming-for-Beginners-Third-Edition/tree/main/chapter%2013.

Declaring and initializing the objects

We know that when we call the setContentView method from the onCreate method, Android inflates all the widgets and layouts and turns them into *real* Java objects on the heap.

Additionally, we know that to use a widget from the heap, we must first declare an object of the correct type and then use it to get a reference to the UI widget object on the heap by using its unique id property.

For example, we get a reference to a TextView widget with an id property of txtTitle and assign it to a new Java object, called myTextView, as follows:

```
// Grab a reference to an object on the heap
TextView myTextView = findViewById(R.id.txtTitle);
```

Now, using our `myTextView` instance variable, we can do anything that the `TextView` class was designed to do. For example, we can set the text to show the following:

```
myTextView.setText("Hi there");
```

Additionally, we can make it disappear as follows:

```
// Bye bye
myTextView.setVisibility(View.GONE)
```

We can change its text again and make it reappear:

```
myTextView.setText("BOO!");

// Surprise
myTextView.setVisibility(View.VISIBLE)
```

It is worth mentioning we can manipulate any property in Java that we set using XML in the previous chapters. Furthermore, we have hinted at – but not actually seen – the creation of widgets from nothing, using just Java code.

Creating UI widgets from pure Java without XML

We can also create widgets from Java objects that are not a reference to an object in our layout. We can declare, instantiate, and set a widget's attributes all in code, as follows:

```
Button myButton = new Button();
```

The preceding code creates a new `Button` by using the `new()` keyword. The only caveat is that the `Button` has to be part of a layout before it can be seen by the user. So, we could either get a reference to a layout element from our XML layout or create a new one, in code.

If we assume that we have a `LinearLayout` in our XML with an `id` property equal to `linearLayout1`, we could put our `Button` from the earlier line of code into it, as follows:

```
// Get a reference to the LinearLayout
LinearLayout linearLayout = (LinearLayout)
```

```
    findViewById(R.id.linearLayout);

// Add our Button to it
linearLayout.addView(myButton);
```

We could even create an entire layout in pure Java code by, first, creating a new layout and then all the widgets we want to add. Then, finally, we call the setContentView method on the layout that has our widgets.

In the following code, we have created a layout in pure Java, albeit a very simple one with a single Button inside a LinearLayout:

```
// Create a new LinearLayout
LinearLayout linearLayout = new LinearLayout();

// Create a new Button
Button myButton = new Button();

// Add myButton to the LinearLayout
linearLayout.addView(myButton);

// Make the LinearLayout the main view
setContentView(linearLayout);
```

It is probably obvious – but well worth pointing out – that designing a detailed and nuanced layout using only Java is significantly more awkward, harder to visualize, and not the way it is usually done. However, there are times when we will find it useful to do things this way.

We are getting quite advanced now with layouts and widgets. However, it is evident that there are a whole bunch of other widgets from the palette that we have not explored or interacted with. So, let's fix that.

Exploring the palette – part 1

Let's take a whirlwind tour of some of those previously unexplored/unused items from the palette. Then, we can drag a bunch of them onto a layout and see some of the methods they have that might be useful. We can then implement a project to put them all to use.

We already explored the Button and TextView widgets in the last chapter. Let's take a closer look at some additional widgets.

The EditText widget

The EditText widget does as its name suggests. If we make an EditText widget available to our users, then they will indeed be able to *edit* the *text* inside it. We looked at this in an earlier chapter; however, we didn't actually achieve anything with it. What we didn't explore was how to capture the information from within it, or where we would type this text-capturing code.

The following block of code assumes that we have declared an object of the EditText type and used it to get a reference to an EditText widget in our XML layout. We might write code similar to the following code for a button click, for example, a submit button for a form. However, it could go anywhere we deem necessary for our app:

```
String editTextContents = editText.getText()
// editTextContents now contains whatever the user entered
```

We will use this in a real-life context in the next mini-app.

The ImageView widget

We have already put an image onto our layout a couple of times so far, but we have never got a reference to one from our Java code or done anything with it before. The process of getting a reference to an ImageView widget is the same as any other widget:

- Declare an object.
- Get a reference using the findViewById method and a valid id property, such as the following:

```
ImageView imageView = findViewById(R.id.imageView);
```

Then, we can go on to do some quite neat things with our image by using code that is similar to the following:

```
// Make the image 50% TRANSPARENT
imageView.setAlpha(.5f);
```

> **Important note**
> The odd-looking f simply lets the compiler know the value is of the float type, as required by the setAlpha method.

In the preceding, we use the setAlpha method on imageView. The setAlpha method takes a value between 0 and 1. An image that is completely see-through is 0, while an image with no transparency at all is 1.

> **Tip**
> There is also an overloaded setAlpha method that takes an integer value from 0 (completely see-through) to 255 (no transparency). We can choose whichever is the most appropriate at the time. If you want a reminder about method overloading, please refer back to *Chapter 9, Learning Java Methods.*

We will use some of the ImageView class' methods in our next app.

Radio buttons and groups

A RadioButton widget is used when there are two or more mutually exclusive options for the user to choose from. This means that when one option is chosen, the other options are not – just like on an old-fashioned radio. Take a look at a simple RadioGroup with a few RadioButton widgets in the following screenshot:

Figure 13.1 – RadioButton widget

As the user selects a choice, the other options will automatically be deselected. We control RadioButton widgets by placing them within a RadioGroup in our UI layout. We can, of course, use the visual designer to simply drag a bunch of RadioButtons onto a RadioGroup. When we do so within a ConstraintLayout layout, the XML will look similar to the following:

```
<RadioGroup
    android:layout_width="wrap_content"
    android:layout_height="wrap_content"
    tools:layout_editor_absoluteX="122dp"
    tools:layout_editor_absoluteY="222dp" >

    <RadioButton
```

```
                android:id="@+id/radioButton1"
        android:layout_width="match_parent"
        android:layout_height="wrap_content"
        android:text="Option 1" />


    <RadioButton
        android:id="@+id/radioButton2"
        android:layout_width="match_parent"
        android:layout_height="wrap_content"
        android:text="Option 2" />


    <RadioButton
        android:id="@+id/radioButton3"
        android:layout_width="match_parent"
        android:layout_height="wrap_content"
        android:text="Option 3" />


</RadioGroup>
```

Note, as highlighted in the previous code, that each `RadioButton` instance has an appropriate `id` attribute set. We can then get a reference to them, as we might expect, as this code shows us:

```
// Get a reference to all our widgets
RadioButton rb1 = findViewById(R.id.radioButton1);


RadioButton rb2 = findViewById(R.id.radioButton2);


RadioButton rb3 = findViewById(R.id.radioButton3);
```

In practice, however, as you will see, we can manage almost everything from the `RadioGroup` reference alone. Additionally, you will learn that we can assign an `id` property to the `RadioGroup` widget for this purpose.

You might be thinking, how do we know when they have been clicked on? Or, you might wonder whether keeping track of the one that has been selected might be awkward. We will need some help from the Android API and Java in the form of anonymous classes.

Anonymous classes

In *Chapter 12, The Stack, the Heap, and the Garbage Collector*, we briefly introduced anonymous classes. Here, we will discuss it in a little more detail and examine how they can help us. When a `RadioButton` widget is part of a `RadioGroup` widget, the visual appearance of them all is coordinated for us. All we need to do is react when any given `RadioButton` widget is pressed. Of course, as with any other button, we need to know when they have been clicked on.

A `RadioButton` widget behaves differently to a regular `Button`, and simply listening for clicks in `onClick` (after implementing `OnClickListener`) will not work because `RadioButton` is not designed that way.

What we need to do is use another Java feature. We need to implement a class, that is, an anonymous class, for the sole purpose of listening for clicks on the `RadioGroup` widget. The next block of code assumes that we have a reference to a `RadioGroup` widget, called `radioGroup`. Here is the code:

```
radioGroup.setOnCheckedChangeListener(
    new RadioGroup.OnCheckedChangeListener() {

        @Override
        public void onCheckedChanged(RadioGroup group,
                int checkedId) {

            // Handle clicks here
        }
    }
);
```

The preceding code, specifically, `RadioGroup.OnCheckedChangedListener` from its opening { to closing }, is what is known as an **anonymous** class. This is because it has no name.

If we place the preceding code in the onCreate method, then, surprisingly, the code does not run when onCreate is called. It simply prepares the new anonymous class to be ready to handle any clicks on radioGroup. We will now discuss this in more detail.

This class is more technically known as an **anonymous inner** class because it is inside another class. Inner classes can be anonymous or have names. We will learn about inner classes with names in *Chapter 16, Adapters and Recyclers*.

I remember the first time I saw an anonymous class, and it made me want to hide in a cupboard. However, it is not as complex as it might appear at first.

What we are doing is adding a listener to radioGroup. This has, very much, the same effect as when we implemented View.OnClickListener in *Chapter 12, The Stack, the Heap, and the Garbage Collector*. However, this time, we are declaring and instantiating a listener class, preparing it to listen to radioGroup, while simultaneously overriding the required method, which, in this case, is onCheckedChanged. This is like the RadioGroup equivalent of onClick.

Let's step through the process:

1. First, we call the setOnCheckedChangedListener method on our radioGroup instance:

    ```
    radioGroup.setOnCheckedChangeListener(
    ```

2. We then provide a new anonymous class implementation that includes the details of this class' overridden method as an argument to the setOnCheckedChangedListener method:

    ```
    new RadioGroup.OnCheckedChangeListener() {

        @Override
        public void onCheckedChanged(RadioGroup group,
                int checkedId) {

            // Handle clicks here
        }
    }
    ```

3. Finally, we have the closing parenthesis of the method along with, of course, the semicolon to mark the end of the line of code. The only reason we present it on multiple lines is to make it more readable. As far as the compiler is concerned, it could be all lumped together:

```
);
```

If we use the preceding code to create and instantiate a class that listens for clicks to our RadioGroup, perhaps in the onCreate method, it will listen and respond for the entire life of the Activity. All we need to learn now is how to handle the clicks in the onCheckedChanged method that we override.

Notice that one of the parameters of the onCheckedChanged method, which is passed in when radioGroup is pressed, is int checkedId. This holds the id property of the currently selected RadioButton widget. This is just what we need – well, almost.

It might be surprising to know that checkedId is an int. Android stores all IDs as int, even though we declare them with alphanumeric characters such as radioButton1 and radioGroup.

All our human-friendly names are converted into integers when the app is compiled. So, how do we know which integer value refers to which id attribute value such as radioButton1 or radioButton2?

What we need to do is to get a reference to the actual object that the integer is an identifier for. We can do so by using the int CheckedId parameter and then asking the object for its human-friendly id attribute value. We do this as follows:

```
RadioButton rb = group.findViewById(checkedId);
```

Now, we can retrieve the familiar id attribute value that we used for the currently selected RadioButton widget, for which we now have a reference stored in rb, using the getId method, as follows:

```
rb.getId();
```

We could, therefore, handle any RadioButton widget clicks by using a switch block with a case, for each possible RadioButton widget that could be pressed, and rb.getId(), as the switch block's expression.

Th following code shows the entire contents of the onCheckedChanged method that we just discussed:

```
// Get a reference to the RadioButton
// that is currently checked
RadioButton rb = group.findViewById(checkedId);

// Switch based on the 'friendly' id from the XML layout
switch (rb.getId()) {

    case R.id.radioButton1:
            // Do something here
            break;

    case R.id.radioButton2:
            // Do something here
            break;


    case R.id.radioButton3:
            // Do something here
            break;



}
// End switch block
```

To make this clearer, we will view this in action in the next working app, where we can press the buttons in real time.

Let's continue with our palette exploration.

Exploring the palette and more anonymous classes – part 2

Now that we have seen how anonymous classes work, specifically with RadioGroup and RadioButton, we can continue to explore the palette and examine how anonymous classes work with some more UI widgets.

Switch

The Switch (not to be confused with the lowercase switch Java keyword) widget is just like a Button widget, except it has two possible states that can be read and responded to.

One obvious use for the Switch widget is to show or hide something. Remember that in our Java Meet UI app, in *Chapter 12, The Stack, the Heap, and the Garbage Collector*, we used a Button widget to show and hide a TextView widget.

Each time we hid or showed the TextView widget, we changed the text property on the Button widget to make it clear what would happen if it was clicked on again. What might have been more intuitive for the user, and more straightforward for us as programmers, would have been to use a Switch widget, as follows:

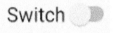

Figure 13.2 – Switch widget

The following code assumes that we already have an object called mySwitch, which is a reference to the Switch object in the layout. We could show and hide a TextView widget just like we did in our Java Meet UI app in *Chapter 12, The Stack, the Heap, and the Garbage Collector*.

To listen for and respond to clicks, we, again, use an anonymous class. However, this time, we use the CompoundButton version of OnCheckedChangedListener instead of the RadioGroup version.

We need to override the onCheckedChanged method, and that method has a Boolean parameter, called isChecked. The isChecked variable is simply false for off and true for on.

Here is how we could, more intuitively, replace that text hiding/showing code from *Chapter 12, The Stack, the Heap, and the Garbage Collector*:

```
mySwitch.setOnCheckedChangeListener(
    new CompoundButton.OnCheckedChangeListener() {

        public void onCheckedChanged(
                CompoundButton buttonView, boolean
                isChecked) {

            if(isChecked){
                    // Currently visible so hide it
                    txtValue.setVisibility(View.
                    INVISIBLE);

            }else{
                    // Currently hidden so show it
                    txtValue.setVisibility(View.
                    VISIBLE);
            }
        }
    }
);
```

If the anonymous class code still looks a little odd, don't worry because it will become more familiar as you keep using it. We will do so now when we look at the CheckBox widget.

CheckBox

This is a CheckBox widget. It is either checked or unchecked. In the following screenshot, it is checked:

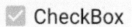

Figure 13.3 – CheckBox widget

With a `CheckBox` widget, we can simply detect its state (checked or unchecked) at a given moment – for example, at the moment when a specific button is clicked on. The following code gives us a glimpse at how this might happen, again using an inner class to act as a listener:

```
myCheckBox.setOnCheckedChangeListener(
    new CompoundButton.OnCheckedChangeListener() {

        public void onCheckedChanged(
                CompoundButton buttonView, boolean
                isChecked) {

                if (myCheckBox.isChecked()) {
                        // It's checked so do something
                } else {
                        // It's not checked do something else
                }

        }
    }
);
```

In the previous code, we assume that `myCheckBox` has been declared and initialized. Then, we use the same type of anonymous class that we did for `Switch`, in order to detect and respond to clicks.

TextClock

In our next app, we will use the `TextClock` widget to show off some of its features. We will need to add the XML directly, as this widget is not available to drag and drop from the palette. The `TextClock` widget looks similar to the following screenshot:

4:28 PM

Figure 13.4 – TextClock widget

Let's look at an example of using `TextClock`. This is how we would set its time to the same time as it is in Brussels, Europe:

```
tClock.setTimeZone("Europe/Brussels");
```

The preceding code assumes that `tClock` is a reference to a `TextClock` widget in the layout.

Using WebView

WebView is quite a powerful widget. It can be used to show a web page in your app's UI. You can even implement a basic web browser app with just half a dozen lines of code.

> **Tip**
> Normally, you wouldn't implement an entire web browser; rather, you would use the user's preferred web browser.

To simply get a reference to a `WebView` widget that is present in the XML and display a website, you would only need two lines of code. This code loads my website – `https://gamecodeschool.com` – assuming that there is a `WebView` widget in the layout with the `id` property set to `webView`:

```
WebView webView = findViewById(R.id.webView);
webView.loadUrl("https://gamecodeschool.com");
```

With all of this extra information, let's make an app that uses the Android widgets more extensively than we have so far.

The Widget Exploration app

So far, we have discussed seven widgets: `EditText`, `ImageView`, `RadioButton` (and `RadioGroup`), `Switch`, `CheckBox`, `TextClock`, and `WebView`. Let's make a working app and do something real with each of them. We will also use a `Button` widget and a `TextView` widget again.

Remember that you can refer to the completed code in the download bundle. This app can be found in `Chapter 13/Widget Exploration`.

Setting up the Widget Exploration project and UI

First, we will set up a new project and prepare the UI layout. These steps will arrange all the widgets on the screen and set the id properties, ready to grab a reference to them. It is useful to look at the target layout – while it is up and running – before we get started. Take a look at the following screenshot:

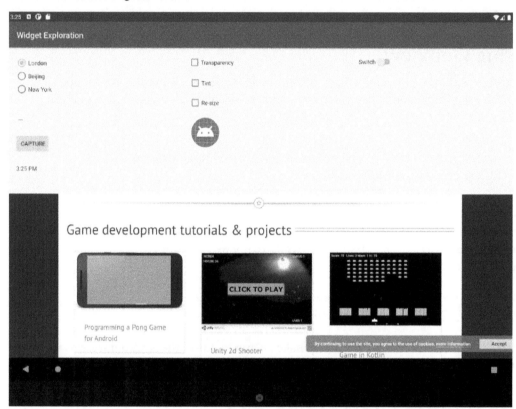

Figure 13.5 – Widget exploration layout

Here is how this app will demonstrate these widgets:

- The radio buttons allow the user to change the time displayed on the clock to a choice of three time zones.

- The **Capture** button, when clicked on, will change the text of the TextView widget (which is on the right) to whatever is currently in the EditText widget (which is on the left).

- The three CheckBox widgets will add and remove visual effects from the Android robot image.

- The Switch widget will turn on and off the TextView widget, which displays information entered in the EditText widget and is captured at the push of a button.

- The WebView widget will occupy the full width and bottom half of the app. Keep this in mind when adding widgets to the layout; try and get them all in the top half.

The exact layout positions are not essential, but the id properties that are specified must match exactly. If you just want to view/use the code, you can find all of the files in the Chapter 13/Widget Exploration folder of the download bundle.

So, let's perform the following steps to set up a new project and prepare the UI layout:

1. Create a new project, called Widget Exploration. Set the **Minimum SDK** to API 17:Android 4.2 (Jelly Bean). Then, use an Empty Activity and keep all the other settings at their defaults. We are using API 17 because one of the features of the TextClock widget requires us to. We can still support in excess of 99% of all Android devices.

2. Switch to the activity_main.xml layout file and make sure you are in the design view. Delete the default **Hello World!** TextView widget.

3. Using the drop-down controls that are displayed above the design view (as shown in the following screenshot), select a tablet in landscape orientation. I chose the **Pixel C** option:

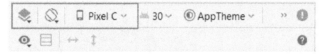

Figure 13.6 – Selecting the orientation options

> **Important note**
>
> For a reminder of how to make a tablet emulator, please refer to *Chapter 3, Exploring Android Studio and the Project Structure*. For additional advice on how to manipulate the orientation of the emulator, please refer to *Chapter 5, Beautiful Layouts with CardView and ScrollView*.

4. Drag a **Switch** widget from the **Button** category of the palette to near the upper-right corner of the layout. Then, just below this, add a **TextView** widget. The upper-right corner of your layout should now look similar to the following screenshot:

Figure 13.7 – Switch widget to the layout

5. Drag three **CheckBox** widgets, one above the other. Then, drag an **ImageView** widget below them onto the central area of the layout. In the resulting pop-up **Resources** dialog window, choose sym_def_app_icon to use the Android icon as the image for the ImageView. The central portion of the layout should now look similar to the following screenshot. For more context on the final layout, please refer back to the screenshot showing the completed app:

Figure 13.8 – CheckBox widget

6. Drag **RadioGroup** to the upper-left corner of the layout.

7. Add three **RadioButton** widgets within the **RadioGroup**. This step can be easily done using the **Component Tree** window.

8. Underneath **RadioGroup**, drag a **Plain Text** widget from the **Text** category of the palette. Remember, despite its name, this is a widget that allows the user to type some text into it. Later, we will learn how to capture and use the entered text.

9. Add a **Button** widget underneath the **Plain Text** widget. The left-hand side of your layout should look similar to the following screenshot:

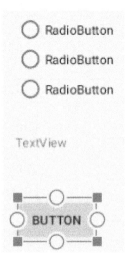

Figure 13.9 – Adding a Button widget

10. Now, add the following attributes to the widgets we have just laid out:

> **Important note**
> Note that some of the attributes might already be correct by default.

Widget type	Property	Value to set to
RadioGroup	ID	`radioGroup`
RadioButton (top)	ID	`radioButtonLondon`
RadioButton (top)	Text	`London`
RadioButton (top)	Checked	Select the tick icon for `true`
RadioButton (second)	ID	`radioButtonBeijing`
RadioButton (second)	Text	`Beijing`
RadioButton (third)	ID	`radioButtonNewYork`
RadioButton (third)	Text	`New York`
EditText (underneath the RadioButton widgets)	ID	`editText`
Button	ID	`Button`
Button	Text	`Capture`
CheckBox (top)	Text	`Transparency`
CheckBox (top)	ID	`checkBoxTransparency`
CheckBox (middle)	Text	`Tint`
CheckBox (middle)	ID	`checkBoxTint`
CheckBox (bottom)	Text	`Re-Size`
CheckBox (bottom)	ID	`checkBoxReSize`
ImageView	ID	`imageView`
Switch	ID	`switch1`
Switch	Enabled	Select the tick icon for `true`
Switch	Clickable	Select the tick icon for `true`
TextView (underneath the Switch widget)	ID	`textView`
TextView	`textSize`	`24sp`
TextView	`layout_width`	`wrap_content`
TextView	`layout_height`	`wrap_content`

11. The penultimate widget is a bit different, so I thought we would handle it separately. Add another regular `TextView` widget underneath the `Button` widget on the left-hand side, and set its `id` property to `textClock`. Remember to keep this widget, as with all of the other widgets, above the approximate halfway point vertically. Readjust some of the widgets above it if required.

12. Switch to the code view and find the `TextView` widget that we are working on – the one with `textClock` as its `id` property value.

13. Observe the start of the XML code, as shown in the following code snippet, with a couple of key parts highlighted:

```
<TextView
        android:id="@+id/textClock"
        android:layout_width="wrap_content"
        android:layout_height="wrap_content"
        android:text="TextView"

        . . .

        . . .
```

Change the preceding highlighted code to the following:

```
<TextClock
        android:id="@+id/textClock"
        android:layout_width="wrap_content"
        android:layout_height="wrap_content"
        android:format12Hour="hh:mm:ss a"

        . . .

        . . .
```

Notice that we have changed the type of widget from `TextView` to `TextClock`, and we have deleted the `text` property and replaced it with the format that we would like for our clock.

14. Switch to the **Design** tab.

15. Now it's time for the final widget. Drag a `WebView` widget from the **Widgets** section of the palette and add it to the bottom of the layout in the center. All might not be as you expect. The `WebView` widget is apparently missing. In fact, if you look very carefully, you can see a tiny indication that the widget is in the upper-left corner of the layout. We will configure the position and size of the `WebView` widget slightly differently.

16. Make sure that the WebView widget is selected in the component tree window.

17. Change the id attribute to webView (if it isn't this value already).

18. For this next step to work correctly, all the other widgets must be constrained. Therefore, click on the **Infer Constraints** button to secure all of the other widgets.

19. At the moment, our WebView widget is not constrained to anything, and it is not possible to grab the constraint handles that we need. Now, find the **Layout** section in the attributes window, as shown in the following screenshot:

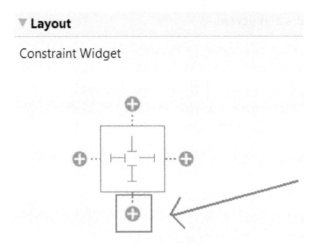

Figure 13.10 – Adding constraint

20. Left-click on the add constraint to the bottom button, as highlighted in the previous screenshot. Now, we have a constraint where the bottom of the WebView widget is constrained to the bottom of the layout. This is almost perfect, but the default margin is set very high.

21. Find the layout_margin_bottom property in the properties window and change it to 0dp.

22. Change the layout_height property in the properties window to 400dp. Note that when this project is complete, if your WebView widget is too tall or too short, then you can come back and tweak this value.

23. Tweak your layout to resemble the following reference diagram as much as possible. However, if you have the appropriate types of UI with the correct id attributes, then the code will still work even if the layout isn't identical. Remember that the WebView widget is not visible, but it will take up the entire bottom half of the screen once we have done some coding:

Figure 13.11 – Tweaking layout

We have just laid out and set the required attributes for our layout. There is nothing here that we haven't done before, except that some of the widget types are new to us and the layout is slightly more intricate.

Now we can get on with using all of these widgets in our Java code.

Coding the Widget Exploration app

There are many `import` statements needed for this app. So, let's add them all now to save us from having to mention them all the time. Add the following `import` statements:

```
import android.graphics.Color;
import android.graphics.PorterDuff;
import androidx.appcompat.app.AppCompatActivity;
import android.os.Bundle;
import android.util.Log;
import android.view.Menu;
import android.view.MenuItem;
import android.view.View;
import android.widget.AnalogClock;
import android.widget.Button;
import android.widget.CheckBox;
import android.widget.CompoundButton;
import android.widget.EditText;
import android.widget.ImageView;
import android.widget.RadioButton;
import android.widget.RadioGroup;
import android.widget.Switch;
```

```
import android.widget.TextClock;
import android.widget.TextView;
```

Let's get a reference to all the parts of the UI that we will be using in the Java code.

Getting a reference to all the parts of the UI

This next block of code looks quite long and sprawling, but all we are doing is getting a reference to each of the widgets in our layout. When we come to use them, we will discuss the code in more detail.

The only thing that is new in this next block of code is that some of the objects are declared as final. This is needed as they are going to be used within an anonymous class.

> **But doesn't final mean that the object cannot be changed?**
>
> If you recall *Chapter 11, More Object-Oriented Programming*, we learned that variables declared as final could not be changed, that is, they are a constant. So, how are we going to change the attributes of these objects? Remember that objects are reference type variables. This means that they refer to an object on the heap. They are not the object themselves. We can think of them as holding an address of an object. It is the address that cannot change. We can still use the address to reference the object on the heap and change the actual object as much as we like. Let's take the address analogy further. If you live at a particular address and if the address is final, then you cannot move to a new house. However, you are unrestricted in what you can do at that address. For example, you can still rearrange your house, perhaps repaint the living room, and put the bath in the kitchen and the sofa on the roof.

Enter the following code just after the call to the setContentView method in the onCreate method:

```
// Get a reference to all our widgets


RadioGroup radioGroup =
findViewById(R.id.radioGroup);


final EditText editText =
findViewById(R.id.editText);
```

```
final Button button =
findViewById(R.id.button);


final TextClock tClock =
findViewById(R.id.textClock);


final CheckBox cbTransparency =
findViewById(R.id.checkBoxTransparency);


final CheckBox cbTint =
findViewById(R.id.checkBoxTint);
final CheckBox cbReSize =
findViewById(R.id.checkBoxReSize);


final ImageView imageView =
findViewById(R.id.imageView);


Switch switch1 = (Switch) findViewById(R.id.switch1);
final TextView textView =
findViewById(R.id.textView);


// Hide the TextView at the start of the app
textView.setVisibility(View.INVISIBLE);
```

We now have a reference, in our Java code, to all of the UI elements in our layout that we need to manipulate.

Coding the checkboxes

Now, we can create an anonymous class to listen for and handle clicks on the checkboxes. The next three blocks of code each implement an anonymous class for each of the checkboxes in turn. However, what is different in each of the following three blocks of code is how we respond to a click; we will discuss each in turn.

Changing the transparency

The first checkbox is labeled **Transparency**, and we use the setAlpha method in imageView to change how transparent (or see-through) it is. The setAlpha method takes a floating-point value between 0 and 1 as an argument.

0 is invisible, and 1 refers to no transparency at all. So, when this checkbox is checked, we set the alpha to .1, which means that the image is barely visible. And when it is unchecked, we set it to 1, which means that it is completely visible with no transparency. The boolean isChecked parameter of onCheckedChanged contains true or false to show whether the checkbox is checked or not.

Add this code after the previous block of code in the onCreate method:

```
/*
    Now we need to listen for clicks
    on the button, the CheckBoxes
    and the RadioButtons
*/


// First the check boxes using an anonymous class
cbTransparency.setOnCheckedChangeListener(new
CompoundButton.OnCheckedChangeListener(){

    public void onCheckedChanged(
    CompoundButton buttonView, boolean isChecked){

        if(cbTransparency.isChecked()){
            // Set some transparency
            imageView.setAlpha(.1f);
        }else{
            imageView.setAlpha(1f);
        }


    }
});
```

In the next anonymous class, we will handle the checkbox labeled **Tint.**

Changing the color

In the onCheckedChanged method, we use the setColorFilter method in imageView to overlay a color layer on the image. When isChecked is true, we layer a color, and when isChecked is false, we remove it.

The setColorFilter method takes a color in **ARGB** (**Alpha**, **Red**, **Green**, and **Blue**) format as an argument. The color is provided by the static method, argb, of the Color class. The four arguments of the argb method are, as you might expect, values for alpha, red, green, and blue. These four values create a color. In our case, the value of 150, 255, 0, 0 creates a strong red tint. Alternatively, the value of 0, 0, 0, 0 creates no tint at all.

> **Important note**
>
> To understand more about the Color class, check out the Android developer site at http://developer.android.com/reference/ android/graphics/Color.html. Additionally, to understand the RGB color system in more detail, please refer to the following Wikipedia page: https://en.wikipedia.org/wiki/RGB_color_model.

Add this code after the previous block of code in the onCreate method:

```
// Now the next checkbox
cbTint.setOnCheckedChangeListener(new
CompoundButton.OnCheckedChangeListener() {

    public void onCheckedChanged(CompoundButton
    buttonView, boolean isChecked) {

        if (cbTint.isChecked()) {
            // Checked so set some tint
            imageView.setColorFilter(
            Color.argb(150, 255, 0, 0));

        } else {
            // No tint needed
            imageView.setColorFilter(Color.argb(0, 0,
            0, 0));
        }
```

```
        }
    });
```

Now we will look at how to scale the UI.

Changing the size

In the anonymous class that handles the labeled **Resize** checkbox, we use the setScaleX method to resize the robot image. When we call setScaleX(2) and setScaleY(2) in imageView, we will double the size of the image, and setScaleX(1) and setScaleY(1) will return it to normal.

Add this code after the previous block of code in the onCreate method:

```
// And the last check box
cbReSize.setOnCheckedChangeListener(
new CompoundButton.OnCheckedChangeListener() {

    public void onCheckedChanged(
    CompoundButton buttonView, boolean isChecked) {

        if (cbReSize.isChecked()) {
            // It's checked so make bigger
            imageView.setScaleX(2);
            imageView.setScaleY(2);
        } else {
            // It's not checked make regular size
            imageView.setScaleX(1);
            imageView.setScaleY(1);
        }

    }
});
```

Now we will handle the three radio buttons.

Coding the radio buttons

As they are part of a `RadioGroup` widget, we can handle them much more succinctly than we did the `CheckBox` objects. Here is how we do it.

First, we make sure they are clear to start with, by calling `clearCheck()` in `radioGroup`. Then, we create our anonymous class of the `OnCheckedChangedListener` type and override the `onCheckedChanged` method.

This method will be called when any `RadioButton` widget from `RadioGroup` is clicked on. All we need to do is get the `id` property of the `RadioButton` widget that was clicked on and respond accordingly. We can achieve this by using a `switch` statement with three possible cases, one for each `RadioButton`.

You will remember that when we first talked about `RadioButton` widgets, we mentioned that the value supplied in the `checkedId` parameter of the `onCheckedChanged` method is an integer. This is why we must first create a new `RadioButton` instance from the `checkedId` parameter:

```
RadioButton rb =
(RadioButton) group.findViewById(checkedId);
```

Then, we can call `getId` on the new `RadioButton` instance as the condition for the `switch` block:

```
switch (rb.getId())
```

Then, in each `case` option, we use the `setTimeZone` method with the proper Android time zone code as an argument.

> **Tip**
> You can view all the Android time zone codes at `https://gist.github.com/arpit/1035596`.

Take a look at the following code, which incorporates everything we just discussed. Add it to the `onCreate` method after the previous code that we entered to handle the checkboxes:

```
// Now for the radio buttons
// Uncheck all buttons
radioGroup.clearCheck();

radioGroup.setOnCheckedChangeListener(new RadioGroup.
```

```java
OnCheckedChangeListener() {
@Override
public void onCheckedChanged(
RadioGroup group, int checkedId) {

        RadioButton rb =
        group.findViewById(checkedId);


                switch (rb.getId()) {

                        case R.id.radioButtonLondon:
                                tClock.setTimeZone(
                                "Europe/London");
                                break;

                        case R.id.radioButtonBeijing:
                                tClock.setTimeZone("Etc/GMT-
                                8");
                                break;

                        case R.id.radioButtonNewYork:

                                tClock.setTimeZone(
                                "America/New_York");
                                break;

                }// End switch block
    }
});
```

Now for something a little bit new.

Using an anonymous class for a regular Button

In the next block of code, we will write and use an anonymous class to handle the clicks on a regular Button. We call button.setOnclickListener just as we have done so before. However, this time, instead of passing this as an argument, we create a brand-new class of the View.OnClickListener type and override the onClick method as the argument – just like we did with our other anonymous classes.

> **Tip**
> This method is preferable in this situation because there is only one button. If we had lots of buttons, then having MainActivity implement View. OnClickListener, and then overriding the onClick method to handle all clicks in one method, would probably be preferable, as we have done previously.

In the onClick method, we use the setText method to set the text property on textView and the getText method of editText to get whatever text is currently in the EditText widget.

Add the following code after the previous block of code in the onCreate method:

```
/*
    Let's listen for clicks on our "Capture" Button.
    We can do this with an anonymous class as well.
    An interface seems a bit much for one button.
*/
button.setOnClickListener(new View.OnClickListener() {
    @Override
    public void onClick(View v) {
        // We only handle one button
        // So, no switching required

        // Change the text on the TextView
        // to whatever is currently in the EditText
        textView.setText(editText.getText());
    }
});
```

Coding the Switch widget

Next, we will create yet another anonymous class to listen for and handle changes to our `Switch` widget.

When the `isChecked` variable is `true`, we show `textView`; when it is `false`, we hide it.

Add the following code after the previous block of code in the `onCreate` method:

```
// Show or hide the TextView
switch1.setOnCheckedChangeListener(
    new CompoundButton.OnCheckedChangeListener() {

    public void onCheckedChanged(
        CompoundButton buttonView, boolean isChecked) {

        if(isChecked){
            textView.setVisibility(View.VISIBLE);
        }else{
            textView.setVisibility(View.INVISIBLE);
        }
    }
});
```

Now we can move on to the `WebView` widget.

Using WebView

Your manifest must include the `INTERNET` permission. This is how we add it.

Open the `AndroidManifest.xml` file, and add the following line of highlighted code, which is shown with a bit of context:

```
<?xml version="1.0" encoding="utf-8"?>
<manifest xmlns:android="http://schemas.android.com/apk/res/
android"
    package="com.gamecodeschool.widgetexploration">

    <uses-permission android:name="android
```

```
        .permission.INTERNET" />


    <application

        ...

        ...
```

Finally, we will add two more lines of code in order to grab a reference to the `WebView` widget and load up a website. It should be a relatively straightforward process to modify the code in order to load any website that you like. Add the following lines of code to the end of the `onCreate` method:

```
WebView webView = (WebView) findViewById(R.id.webView);
webView.loadUrl("https://gamecodeschool.com");
```

Now we can run our app and try out all the features.

Running the Widget Exploration app

Run the app in the usual way, making sure that you use your tablet emulator.

> **Tip**
> The Android emulators can be rotated into landscape mode by pressing the *Ctrl + F11* keyboard combination on a PC or *Ctrl + fn+ F11* on a Mac.

Here is the entire app, including the `WebView` widget, which is now visible:

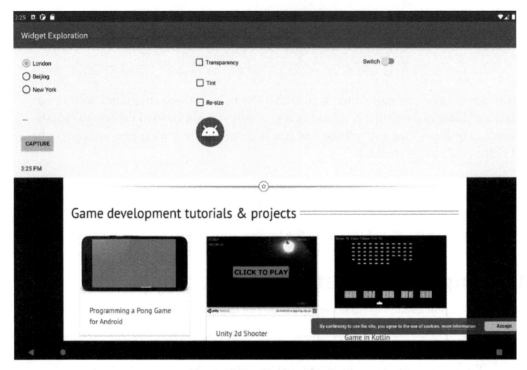

Figure 13.12 – Final app layout

Try checking the radio buttons to see the time zone change on the clock. In the following diagram, I have Photoshopped a few cropped screenshots together to show that the time changes when a new time zone is selected:

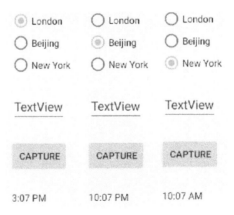

Figure 13.13 – Time zones

To test out the **CAPTURE** button, the editable text, and the switch, follow these steps (we have also listed them in the adjoining screenshot):

1. Enter different values into the `EditText` widget (which is on the left).

2. Click on the **CAPTURE** button.

3. Make sure that the `Switch` widget is on.

4. View the message:

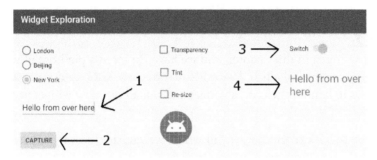

Figure 13.14 – Testing the CAPTURE button

You can change what the preceding diagram looks like with different combinations of checked and unchecked checkboxes, and you can hide and show the `TextView` widget by using the switch above it. The following screenshot shows what happens to the `ImageView` widget when you have the **Tint** and **Re-size** options selected:

Figure 13.15 – Testing the ImageView widget

Oops! The size of the icon has been increased so much that it overlaps with the **Re-size** checkbox.

> **Tip**
> Transparency doesn't show very clearly in a printed book, so I haven't shown a visual example of the **Transparency** box being checked. Be sure to try this out on an emulator or real device.

Summary

We have learned so much in this chapter, and we have explored a plethora of widgets. We learned how to implement widgets in Java code without any XML, and we used our first anonymous classes to handle clicks on a widget and put all our new widget prowess into a working app.

Now, let's move on to look at another way in which we can significantly enhance our UIs.

In the next chapter, we will look at a totally new UI element that we can't simply drag and drop from the palette, but we will still have plenty of help from the Android API. Next up are dialog windows. Additionally, we will also make a start on our most significant app so far, the Note to Self app, for memos, to-do lists, and personal notes.

14
Android Dialog Windows

In this chapter, we will look at how to present the user with a pop-up dialog window. We can then put all that we know into the first phase of our first app, **Note to Self**. We will then explore the latest Android and Java features in this chapter and the next four (up to *Chapter 18, Localization*), and use our newly acquired knowledge to enhance the Note to Self app at each stage.

Each chapter will also build a selection of smaller apps that are separate from this main app. So, what does this chapter hold in store for you? Well, we will cover the following topics:

- Implementing a simple app with a pop-up dialog box
- Using the `DialogFragment` class to begin the Note to Self app
- Adding string resources in our projects instead of hardcoding text in our layouts
- Using Android naming conventions for the first time to make our code more readable
- Implementing more complex dialog boxes to capture input from the user

Let's get started.

Technical requirements

You can find the code files present in this chapter on GitHub at https://github.com/PacktPublishing/Android-Programming-for-Beginners-Third-Edition/tree/main/chapter%2014.

Dialog windows

On many occasions, in our apps, we will want to show the user some information or even ask for confirmation of an action in a pop-up window. This is known as a **dialog** window. If you quickly scan the palette in Android Studio, then you might be surprised to see that there is no mention whatsoever of dialogs.

Dialogs in Android are more advanced than a simple widget or even a whole layout. They are classes that can have layouts and other **User Interface** (**UI**) elements of their own.

The best way to create a dialog window in Android is to use the FragmentDialog class.

> **Note**
> Fragments are a wide and vital topic in Android, and we will spend much of the second half of this book exploring and using them.

Creating a neat pop-up dialog (using FragmentDialog) for our user to interact with is a great introduction to fragments, and it's not overly complicated at all.

Creating the Dialog Demo project

We previously mentioned that the best way to create a dialog in Android is via the FragmentDialog class.

To do this, create a new project in Android Studio using the Empty Activity template and call it Dialog Demo. As you have come to expect, the completed code for this project is in the Chapter 14/Dialog Demo folder of the download bundle.

Coding a DialogFragment class

Create a new class in Android Studio by right-clicking on the folder with the name of your package (the same one that has the MainActivity.java file). Select **New | Java class** and name it MyDialog. Press the *Enter* key to create the class.

The first thing to do is to change the class declaration to extend DialogFragment. When you have done so, your new class should look similar to the following code block:

```java
public class MyDialog extends DialogFragment {
}
```

Now, let's add code to this class, a little bit at a time, and explain what is happening at each step. Now, we need to import the DialogFragment class. You can do this by holding down the *Alt* key and then tapping on *Enter* or by adding the following line of highlighted code after the package declaration at the top of the MyDialog.java file:

```java
package com.gamecodeschool.dialogdemo;

import androidx.fragment.app.DialogFragment;

public class MyDialog extends DialogFragment {
}
```

Just like so many classes in the Android API, DialogFragment provides us with methods that we can override in order to interact with the different events that will occur with the class.

Add the following highlighted code to override the onCreateDialog method. Study it carefully, and we will examine what is happening next:

```java
public class MyDialog extends DialogFragment {

    @Override
    public Dialog onCreateDialog(Bundle savedInstanceState) {

        // Use the Builder class because this dialog
        // has a simple UI
        AlertDialog.Builder builder =
                new AlertDialog.Builder(getActivity());
    }
}
```

You will need to import the `Dialog`, `Bundle`, and `AlertDialog` classes in the usual way or by adding the following highlighted code manually:

```
import android.app.Dialog;
import android.os.Bundle;


import androidx.appcompat.app.AlertDialog;
import androidx.fragment.app.DialogFragment;
```

> **Note**
>
> There is still one error in the code because we are missing the `return` statement for the `onCreateDialog` method. We will add this later on when we have finished coding the rest of the method.

In the preceding code, we first added the overridden `onCreateDialog` method. This will be called by Android when we later show the dialog to the user via code in the `MainActivity` class.

Then, inside the `onCreateDialog` method, we get our hands on a new class. We declare and initialize an object of the `AlertDialog.Builder` type, which needs a reference to `MainActivity` passed into its constructor. This is why we use the `getActivity()` method as the argument.

The `getActivity` method is part of the `Fragment` class (and, therefore, `DialogFragment` too), and it returns a reference to `Activity`, which will create `DialogFragment`. In this case, that is our `MainActivity` class.

Let's examine what we can do with `builder` now that we have declared and initialized it.

Using chaining to configure DialogFragment

Now we can use our `builder` object to do the remainder of the work. There is something slightly odd in the following code snippet. If you quickly scan the next three blocks of code, you will notice that there is a distinct lack of semicolons, `;`. These three blocks of code are, in fact, just one line to the compiler.

We have seen this before but in a less pronounced situation; that is, when we created a `Toast` message and added a `.show()` method to the end of it. This is called **chaining**. This is where we call more than one method, in sequence, on the same object. This is equivalent to writing multiple lines of code; it is just more succinct this way.

Add the following code (which uses chaining) inside the onCreateDialog method right after the previous code we added. Examine the new code, and we will discuss it next:

```
// Dialog will have "Make a selection" as the title
builder.setMessage("Make a selection")


// An OK button that does nothing
.setPositiveButton("OK", new DialogInterface.OnClickListener()
{

    public void onClick(DialogInterface dialog, int id) {

        // Nothing happening here
    }
})

// A "Cancel" button that does nothing
.setNegativeButton("Cancel", new DialogInterface.
OnClickListener() {

    public void onClick(DialogInterface dialog, int id) {
        // Nothing happening here either

    }

});
```

At this point, you will need to import the DialogInterface class. Use the *Alt* | *Enter* technique, or add this line of code among the other import statements:

```
import android.content.DialogInterface;
```

Here is an explanation for each of the three parts of the code that we just added:

1. In the first of the three blocks (which uses chaining), we call builder. setMessage. This sets the main message that the user will see in the dialog box. Additionally, note that it is fine to have comments between parts of the chained method calls since these are ignored by the compiler.

2. Then, we add a button to our dialog with the `.setPositiveButton` method, and the first argument of this method sets the text of the button to OK. The second argument is an anonymous class, called `DialogInterface.OnClickListener`, which handles any clicks on the button. Notice that we are not going to add any code to the `onClick` method. Here, we just want to see this simple dialog; we will take things a step further in the next project.

3. Next, we call yet another method on the same `builder` object. This time, it's the `setNegativeButton` method. Again, the two arguments set `Cancel` as the text for the button and an anonymous class to listen for clicks. Again, for the purpose of this demonstration, we are not taking any action in the overridden `onClick` method. After the call to the `setNegativeButton` method, we finally see a semicolon marking the end of the line of code.

We will finally code the `return` statement to complete the method and remove the error that we have had from the start. Add the `return` statement, as shown in the following snippet, to the end (but inside the final curly brace) of the `onCreateDialog` method:

```
...
// Create the object and return it
return builder.create();


}// End of onCreateDialog
```

This last line of code has the effect of returning to the `MainActivity` class (which calls the `onCreateDialog` method in the first place) our new, fully configured, dialog window. We will examine and add this calling code later on.

Now, we have our `MyDialog` class that extends `FragmentDialog`. All we need to do is to declare an instance of `MyDialog`, instantiate it, and call its overridden `createDialog` method.

Using the DialogFragment class

Before we turn to the code, let's add a button to our layout. Perform the following steps:

1. Switch to the `activity_main.xml` tab and then switch to the **Design** tab.

2. Drag a **Button** onto the layout and make sure its `id` attribute is set to `button`.

3. Click on the **Infer Constraints** button to constrain the button exactly where you want to place it. Note that the position isn't important – how we will use it to create an instance of our `MyDialog` class is the key lesson for now.

Now switch to the `MainActivity.java` tab, and we will handle a click on this new button by using an anonymous class just as we did in *Chapter 13, Anonymous Classes – Bringing Android Widgets to Life*, during the Widget Exploration app. We do it this way because we only have one button in the layout, and it seems sensible and more compact than implementing the more complicated `OnClickListener` interface alternative (as we did for the Java Meet UI demo app in *Chapter 12, The Stack, the Heap, and the Garbage Collector*).

Notice, in the following code block, that the anonymous class is exactly the same type that we previously implemented an interface for. Add this code to the `onCreate` method:

```
/*
    Let's listen for clicks on our regular Button.
    We can do this with an anonymous class.
*/

Button button = (Button) findViewById(R.id.button);

button.setOnClickListener(
    new View.OnClickListener() {

        @Override
        public void onClick(View v) {
            // We only handle one button
            // Therefor no switching required
            MyDialog myDialog = new MyDialog();
            myDialog.show(getSupportFragmentManager(),
            "123");
            // This calls onCreateDialog
            // Don't worry about the strange looking
                123
            // We will find out about this in chapter
                18
        }
    }
);
```

> **Note**
>
> The following `import` statements are needed for this code:
>
> `import android.view.View;`
>
> `import android.widget.Button;`

Notice that the only thing that happens in the code is that the `onClick` method creates a new instance of `MyDialog` and calls its `show` method. This, unsurprisingly, will show our dialog window just as we configured it in the `MyDialog` class.

The `show` method needs a reference to `FragmentManager`, which we can get with `getSupportFragmentManager`. This is the class that tracks and controls all `Fragment` instances for an activity. We also pass in an identifier: `"123"`.

More details on the `FragmentManager` will be revealed when we look more closely at fragments. We will do so in the *Android Fragments* section in *Chapter 20, Drawing Graphics*.

> **Note**
>
> The reason we use the `getSupportFragmentManager` method is that we are supporting older devices by extending `AppCompatActivity`. If we simply extended `Activity`, then we could use the `getFragmentManager` class. The downside is that the app wouldn't run on as many devices.

Now we can run the app and admire our new dialog window, which appears when we click on the button in the layout. Notice that clicking on either of the buttons in the dialog window will close it. This is the default behavior. The following screenshot shows our dialog in action on the Pixel C tablet emulator:

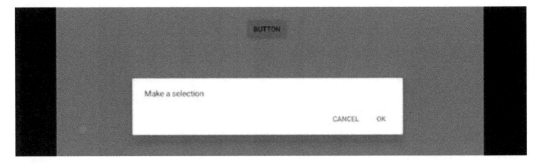

Figure 14.01 – Dialog in action

Next, we will make two more classes that implement dialogs, as part of the first phase of our multi-chapter Note to Self app. We will learn that a dialog window can have almost any layout we choose and that we don't have to rely on simple layouts like those that the `Dialog.Builder` class gave us.

The Note to Self app

Welcome to the first of three major apps that we will implement in this book. When we carry out these projects, we will execute them more professionally than the smaller apps. We will use Android naming conventions, string resources, and proper encapsulation.

Sometimes, these things can be overkill when you are trying to learn a new Android/Java topic. However, they are useful, and it is important to start using them as soon as possible in real projects. Eventually, they become second nature, and the quality of our apps will benefit.

Using naming conventions and string resources

In *Chapter 3, Exploring Android Studio and the Project Structure*, we talked about using string resources instead of hardcoding text in our layout files. There are a few benefits to doing things this way, but it is also relatively long-winded.

As this is our first real-world project, it would be a good time to do things the right way so that we can get the experience of doing so. If you want a quick refresher on the benefits of string resources, check back to *Chapter 3, Exploring Android Studio and the Project Structure*.

Naming conventions are the conventions or rules used for naming the variables, methods, and classes in our code. Throughout this book, we have loosely applied Android's naming conventions. As this is our first real-world app, we will be slightly stricter in applying these naming conventions.

Most notably, when a variable is a member of a class, we will prefix the name with a lowercase m.

> **Note**
> You can find more information about Android's naming conventions and code styles at `https://source.android.com/source/code-style.html`.

How to get the code files for the Note to Self app

The fully completed app, including all the code and resources, can be found in the `Chapter 18/Note to self` folder within the download bundle. As we are implementing this app over the next five chapters, it will probably be useful to view the part-completed, runnable app at the end of every chapter as well. The part-completed runnable apps and all their associated code and resources can be found in their respective folders:

`Chapter 14/Note to self`

`Chapter 16/Note to self`

`Chapter 17/Note to self`

`Chapter 18/Note to self`

> **Note**
>
> There is no Note to Self code in *Chapter 15, Arrays Maps, and Random Numbers*. This is because, even though we will learn about topics we use in Note to Self, we won't make any changes until *Chapter 16, Adapters and Recyclers*.

If you are following along and intend to build the Note to Self app from start to finish, we will build a project simply called `Note to self`. However, there is still nothing stopping you from dipping into the code files of the projects from each chapter to do a bit of copying and pasting at any time. Just be aware that at various points in the instructions, you will be asked to remove or replace the occasional line of code from a previous chapter.

So, even if you are copying and pasting more than you are typing in code, be sure to read the instructions in full, and refer to the code in the book for extra comments that might be useful.

In each chapter, the code will be presented as if you have completed the last chapter in full, showing code from earlier chapters, where necessary, as useful context for our new code.

Each chapter will not be solely devoted to the Note to Self app – we will learn about other, usually related, things and build some smaller/simpler apps as well. So, when we come to the Note to Self implementation, we will, in theory, be prepared for it.

The completed app

The following screenshots are from the completed app. It will, of course, look slightly different at the various stages of development. Where necessary, we will refer to more screenshots either as a reminder or to see the differences throughout the development process.

The completed app will allow the user to tap on the floating action button in the lower-right corner of the app to open a dialog window to add a new note. The following screenshot shows this feature highlighted:

Figure 14.02 – Floating action button

On the left, you can view the button to tap on, and on the right, you can view the dialog window where the user can add a new note.

Eventually, as the user adds more notes, they will have a list of all the notes they have added on the main screen of the app, as shown in the following screenshot. The user can select whether the note is **Important**, an **Idea**, and/or a **Todo**:

Figure 14.03 – Notes on the main screen

You will be able to scroll down the list and tap on a note to see it shown in another dialog window that is dedicated to that note. The following screenshot shows a dialog window displaying a note:

Figure 14.04 – Display of the selected note

There will also be a simple (that is, very simple) **Settings** screen, which will be accessible from the menu. It will allow the user to configure whether the note list is formatted with a dividing line. Here is the **Settings** menu option in action:

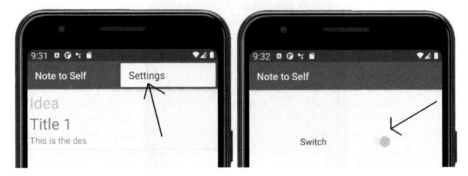

Figure 14.05 –Settings menu option

Now that we know exactly what we are going to build, we can go ahead and start to implement it.

Building the project

Let's create our new project now. Use the Basic Activity template. As we discussed in *Chapter 3, Exploring Android Studio and the Project Structure*, this template will generate a simple menu and a floating action button, which are both used in this project. Call the project Note to Self.

Preparing the string resources

Here, we will create all the string resources that we will refer to from our layout files instead of hardcoding the text property of the UI widgets, which we have been doing up until now.

To get started, open the strings.xml file from the res/values folder in the project explorer. You will see the autogenerated resources. Add the following highlighted string resources that we will use in our app throughout the rest of the project. Add the code before the closing </resources> tag:

```
...
<resources>
    <string name="app_name">Note to Self</string>
    <string name="action_settings">Settings</string>
    <!-- Strings used for fragments for navigation -->
    <string name="first_fragment_label">First
```

```xml
                    Fragment</string>
<string name="second_fragment_label">Second
                    Fragment</string>
<string name="next">Next</string>
<string name="previous">Previous</string>


<string name="hello_first_fragment">Hello first
                    fragment</string>
<string name="hello_second_fragment">Hello second
                    fragment. Arg: %1$s</string>


<string name="action_add">add</string>
<string name="title_hint">Title</string>
<string name="description_hint">Description</string>
<string name="idea_text">Idea</string>
<string name="important_text">Important</string>
<string name="todo_text">To do</string>
<string name="cancel_button">Cancel</string>
<string name="ok_button">OK</string>


<string name="settings_title">Settings</string>
<string name="theme_title">Theme</string>
<string name="theme_light">Light</string>
<string name="theme_dark">Dark</string>


</resources>
```

In the preceding code, notice that each string resource has a name attribute that is unique and distinguishes it from all the others while also providing a meaningful and, hopefully, memorable clue as to the actual string value it represents. It is these name values that we will use to refer to from within our layout files.

We will not need to revisit this file for the rest of the app.

Coding the Note class

This is the fundamental data structure of the app. It is a class that we will write ourselves from scratch and has all the member variables we need to represent one of the user's notes. In *Chapter 15*, *Arrays Maps, and Random Numbers*, we will learn some new Java in order to understand how we can let the user have dozens, hundreds, or even thousands of notes.

Create a new class by right-clicking on the folder with the same name as your package. As expected, it is the one that also contains the MainActivity.java file. Select **New | Java class** and name it Note. Press the *Enter* key to create the class.

Add the following highlighted code to the new Note class:

```
public class Note {


    private String mTitle;
    private String mDescription;
    private boolean mIdea;
    private boolean mTodo;
    private boolean mImportant;


}
```

Notice that our member variable names are prefixed with m as per the Android convention. Additionally, we don't want any other class to access these variables directly, so they are all declared private.

Therefore, we will need a getter and a setter method for each of our members. Add the following getter and setter methods to the Note class:

```
public String getTitle() {
    return mTitle;
}


public void setTitle(String mTitle) {
    this.mTitle = mTitle;
}

```

```java
public String getDescription() {
    return mDescription;
}

public void setDescription(String mDescription) {
    this.mDescription = mDescription;
}

public boolean isIdea() {
    return mIdea;
}

public void setIdea(boolean mIdea) {
    this.mIdea = mIdea;
}

public boolean isTodo() {
    return mTodo;
}

public void setTodo(boolean mTodo) {
    this.mTodo = mTodo;
}

public boolean isImportant() {
    return mImportant;
}

public void setImportant(boolean mImportant) {
    this.mImportant = mImportant;
}
```

There is quite a lot of code in this preceding list, but there is nothing complicated. Each of the methods has `public` access specified, so it can be used by any other class that has a reference to an object of the `Note` type. Furthermore, for each variable, there is a method with the name of `get...` and a method with the name of `set....` The getters for the Boolean type variables are named `is....` This is a logical name if you think about it because the returned answer will be either true or false.

Each of the getters simply returns the value of the related variable. And each of the setters sets the value of the related variable to whatever value is passed into the method.

> **Note**
>
> In fact, we should really enhance our setters a little to do a bit of checking to make sure that the values passed in are within reasonable limits. For example, we might want to check on and enforce a maximum or minimum length for `String mTtile` and `String mDescription`. This is left as an exercise for the reader to come back to.

Let's design the layout of the two dialog windows.

Implementing the dialog designs

Now, we will do something that we have done many times before, but this time, for a new reason. As we know, we will have two dialog windows: one for the user to enter a new note and one for the user to view a note of their choice.

We can design the layouts of these two dialog windows in the same way that we designed all our previous layouts. When we come to create the Java code for the `FragmentDialog` classes, we will then learn how to incorporate these layouts.

First, let's add a layout for our "new note" dialog. Perform the following steps:

1. Right-click on the **layout** folder in the project explorer, and select **New | Layout resource file**. Enter `dialog_new_note` for the **File name:** field.

2. Left-click on **OK** to generate the new layout file that will have the `ConstraintLayout` type, by default, as its root element.

3. Refer to the target design, in the following diagram, as you follow the rest of these instructions. I have Photoshopped the finished layout, including the constraints that we will soon autogenerate, next to the layout with the constraints hidden for extra clarity:

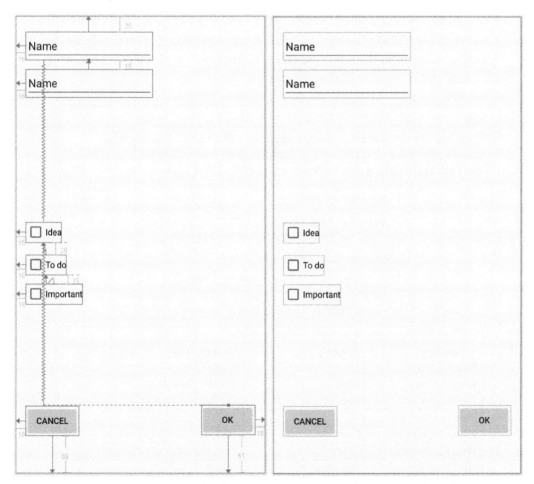

Figure 14.06 – Finished layout for new note

4. Drag and drop a **Plain Text** widget (from the **Text** category) to the upper-left corner of the layout. Then, add another **Plain Text** widget below it. Don't worry about any of the attributes for now.

5. Drag and drop three **CheckBox** widgets from the **Button** category, one below the other. Look at the earlier reference diagram for guidance. Again, don't worry about any attributes for now.

6. Drag and drop two **Buttons** onto the layout. The first will go directly below the last **CheckBox** widget from the previous step; the second will fall horizontally, in line with the first **Button**, but to the right of the layout.

7. Tidy up the layout so that it looks as close to the reference diagram as possible. Then, click on the **Infer Constraints** button to fix the positions you have chosen.

8. Now, we can set up all of our `text`, `id`, and `hint` properties. You can do this by using the values from the following table. Remember that we are using our string resources for the `text` and `hint` properties:

Note

When you edit the first `id` property (which we will do next), you might be shown a pop-up window asking for a confirmation of your changes. Check the **Don't ask again during this session** box and click on **Yes** to continue:

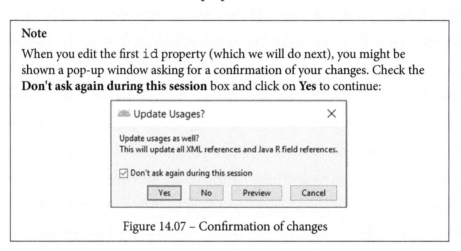

Figure 14.07 – Confirmation of changes

Widget type	Property	Value to set to
Plain Text (top)	ID	editTitle
Plain Text (top)	Hint	@string/title_hint
Plain Text (top)	Text	@string/title_hint
Plain Text (bottom)	ID	editDescription
Plain Text (bottom)	Hint	@string/description_hint
Plain Text (bottom)	Text	@string/description_hint
Plain Text (bottom)	inputType	textMultiLine
CheckBox (top)	ID	checkBoxIdea
CheckBox (top)	Text	@string/idea_text
CheckBox (middle)	ID	checkBoxTodo
CheckBox (middle)	Text	@string/todo_text
CheckBox (bottom)	ID	checkBoxImportant
CheckBox (bottom)	Text	@string/important_text
Button (left)	ID	btnCancel
Button (left)	Text	@string/cancel_button
Button (right)	ID	btnOK
Button (right)	Text	@string/ok_button

We now have an organized layout that is ready for our Java code to display. Make sure that you keep the id property values of the different widgets in mind. We will see them in action when we write our Java code. The important thing is that our layout looks nice and has an id property value for every relevant item, so we can get a reference to it.

Let's create the layout for the "show note" dialog:

1. Right-click on the **layout** folder in the project explorer and select **New | Layout resource file**. Enter dialog_show_note for the **File name:** field.

2. Left-click on **OK** to generate the new layout file that will have the ConstraintLayout type as its root element by default.

3. Refer to the target design, in the following diagram, as you follow the rest of these instructions. I have Photoshopped the finished layout, including the constraints we will soon autogenerate, next to the layout with the constraints hidden for extra clarity:

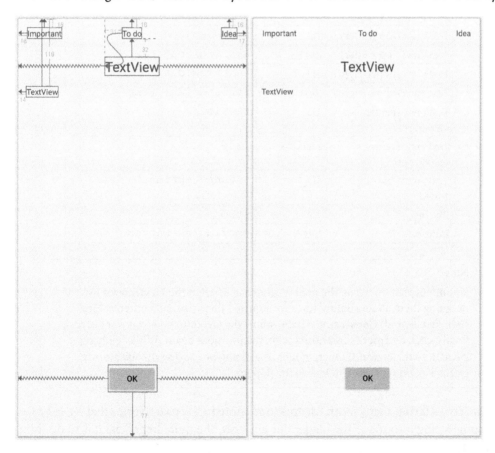

Figure 14.08 – Finished layout for the show note dialog

4. First of all, drag and drop three **TextView** widgets so that they are vertically aligned across the top of the layout.

5. Next, drag and drop another **TextView** widget just below the center of the three previous TextView widgets.

6. Add another **TextView** widget just below the previous widget but over to the left.

7. Now add a **Button** horizontally in the center, but near the bottom of the layout.

8. Tidy up the layout so that it looks as close to the reference diagram as possible, Then, click on the **Infer Constraints** button to fix the positions you have chosen.

9. Configure the attributes from the following table:

Widget type	Attribute	Value to set to
TextView (upper-left)	ID	`textViewImportant`
TextView (upper-left)	Text	`@string/important_text`
TextView (top-center)	ID	`textViewTodo`
TextView (top-center)	Text	`@string/todo_text`
TextView (upper-right)	ID	`textViewIdea`
TextView (upper-right)	Text	`@string/idea_text`
TextView (center, second row)	ID	`txtTitle`
TextView (center, second row)	textSize	`24sp`
TextView (last one added)	ID	`txtDescription`
Button	ID	`btnOK`
Button	Text	`@string/ok_button`

> **Note**
>
> You might want to tweak the final positions of some of the UI elements by dragging them about slightly since we adjusted their size and contents. First, click on **Clear all Constraints**. Then, adjust the layout to how you want it, and, finally, click on **Infer Constraints** to fix the positions again. While applying `btnOK` to the button ID there might be a dialog box saying this ID already exist, click on **Continue** to ignore the pop up.

Now we have a layout that we can use to show a note to the user. Notice that we get to reuse some string resources. The bigger our apps get, the more beneficial it is to do things in this way.

Coding the dialog boxes

Now we have a design for both of our dialog windows ("show note" and "new note"), we can use what we know about the `FragmentDialog` class to implement a class to represent each of the dialog windows that the user can interact with.

We will start with the "new note" screen.

Coding the DialogNewNote class

Create a new class by right-clicking on the project folder that has all the `.java` files and choose **New | Java class**. Name the class `DialogNewNote`.

First, change the class declaration and extend `DialogFragment`. Then, override the `onCreateDialog` method, which is where all the rest of the code in this class will go. To achieve this, make your code is the same as the following snippet:

```
public class DialogNewNote extends DialogFragment {

    @Override
    public Dialog onCreateDialog(Bundle savedInstanceState) {

        // All the rest of the code goes here

    }
}
```

> **Note**
> You will also need to add these new imports:
> ```
> import androidx.fragment.app.DialogFragment;
> import android.app.Dialog;
> import android.os.Bundle;
> ```

We temporarily have an error in the new class because we need a `return` statement; however, we will get to that in just a moment.

In the next block of code, first, we declare and initialize an `AlertDialog.Builder` object, in the same way we did earlier when creating dialog windows. However, this time, we will rely on this object far less than we previously did.

Next, we initialize a `LayoutInflater` object, which we will use to inflate our XML layout. By "inflate," we are simply referring to how we turn our XML layout into a Java object. Once this has been done, we can then access all our widgets in the usual way. We can think of the `inflater.inflate` method as replacing the `setContentView` method for our dialog. Then, in the second line, we do just that using the `inflate` method.

Add the three lines of code that we just discussed:

```
AlertDialog.Builder builder =
    new AlertDialog.Builder(getActivity());


LayoutInflater inflater =
    getActivity().getLayoutInflater();


View dialogView =
    inflater.inflate(R.layout.dialog_new_note, null);
```

> **Note**
>
> To use the new classes in the preceding three lines of code, you will need to add the following `import` statements:
>
> `import androidx.appcompat.app.AlertDialog;`
>
> `import android.view.View;`
>
> `import android.view.LayoutInflater;`

We now have a `View` object, called `dialogView`, that has all of the UI elements from our `dialog_new_note.xml` layout file.

Immediately after the previous block of code, we will add the following block of code, which we explain next.

This code will get a reference to each of the UI widgets in the usual way. Many of the objects in the following code are declared as `final` because they will be used in an anonymous class, and as we learned previously, this is necessary. Remember that it is the reference that is `final` (that is, it cannot change); we can still change the objects on the heap to which they are a reference.

Add the following code just after the previous block of code:

```
final EditText editTitle =
dialogView.findViewById(R.id.editTitle);
```

```
final EditText editDescription =
dialogView.findViewById(R.id.editDescription);
final CheckBox checkBoxIdea =
dialogView.findViewById(R.id.checkBoxIdea);
final CheckBox checkBoxTodo =
dialogView.findViewById(R.id.checkBoxTodo);
final CheckBox checkBoxImportant =
dialogView.findViewById(R.id.checkBoxImportant);
Button btnCancel =
dialogView.findViewById(R.id.btnCancel);
Button btnOK =
dialogView.findViewById(R.id.btnOK);
```

> **Note**
>
> Add the following `import` code statements to make the code that you just added error-free:
>
> ```
> import android.widget.Button;
>
> import android.widget.CheckBox;
>
> import android.widget.EditText;
> ```

In the next code block, we will set the message of the dialog using `builder`, which is our builder instance. Then, we will write an anonymous class to handle clicks on the `btnCancel` button. In the overridden `onClick` method, we will simply call `dismiss()`, which is a public method of `DialogFragment`, to close the dialog window. This is just what we need if the user clicks on **Cancel**.

Add the following code that we have just discussed:

```
builder.setView(dialogView).setMessage("Add a new note");

// Handle the cancel button
btnCancel.setOnClickListener( new View.OnClickListener() {
    @Override
    public void onClick(View v) {
        dismiss();
    }
});
```

Now, we will add an anonymous class to handle what happens when the user clicks on the **OK** button (btnOK).

First, we create a new Note instance, called newNote. Then, we set each of the member variables from newNote to the appropriate contents of the form.

After this, we do something new. We create a reference to the MainActivity class using the getActivity method. Then, we use that reference to call the createNewNote method in MainActivity.

> **Note**
>
> Note that we have not written this createNewNote method yet, and it will show up as an error until we do so later in this chapter.

The argument sent in this method is our newly initialized newNote object. This has the effect of sending the user's new note back to MainActivity. We will learn what to do with this later on in the chapter.

Finally, we call dismiss to close the dialog window.

Add the following code that we have been discussing after the preceding code:

```
btnOK.setOnClickListener(new View.OnClickListener() {

    @Override
    public void onClick(View v) {

        // Create a new note
        Note newNote = new Note();

        // Set its variables to match the
        // user's entries on the form
        newNote.setTitle(editTitle.
                getText().toString());

        newNote.setDescription(editDescription.
                getText().toString());

        newNote.setIdea(checkBoxIdea.isChecked());
        newNote.setTodo(checkBoxTodo.isChecked());
```

```
        newNote.setImportant(checkBoxImportant.
            isChecked());


        // Get a reference to MainActivity
        MainActivity callingActivity =
            (MainActivity) getActivity();


        // Pass newNote back to MainActivity
        callingActivity.createNewNote(newNote);


        // Quit the dialog
        dismiss();
    }
});


return builder.create();
```

That's our first dialog done. We haven't wired it up to appear in MainActivity yet, and we still need to implement the createNewNote method too. We will do this straight after we create the next dialog.

Coding the DialogShowNote class

Create a new class by right-clicking on the project folder that contains all of the .java files and choose **New | Java class**. Name the class DialogShowNote.

First, change the class declaration and extend DialogFragment. Then, override the onCreateDialog method. As most of the code for this class goes in the onCreateDialog method, implement the signature and empty body, as shown in the following code snippet, and we will revisit it later.

Notice that we declare a member variable, mNote, of the Note type. Add the sendNoteSelected method and the one line of code that initializes mNote. This method will be called by MainActivity, and it will pass to the Note object the user has clicked on.

Add the code we just discussed. Then, we can view and code the details of
onCreateDialog:

```
public class DialogShowNote extends DialogFragment {


    private Note mNote;


    @Override
    public Dialog onCreateDialog(Bundle savedInstanceState) {


        // All the other code goes here



    }



    // Receive a note from the MainActivity
    public void sendNoteSelected(Note noteSelected) {
        mNote = noteSelected;
    }


}
```

Note

At this point, you will need to import the following classes:

import android.app.Dialog;

import android.os.Bundle;

import androidx.fragment.app.DialogFragment;

Next, we declare and initialize an instance of AlertDialog.Builder. Additionally,
as we did for the DialogNewNote class, we declare and initialize a LayoutInflater
instance and then use it to create a View object that has the layout for the dialog. In this
case, it is the layout from dialog_show_note.xml.

Finally, in the following code, we get a reference to each of the UI widgets and set the `text` attributes to `txtTitle` and `textDescription` from the appropriate member variables of `mNote`, which was initialized in the `sendNoteSelected` method.

Add the code that we just discussed to the `onCreateDialog` method:

```
// All the other code goes here
AlertDialog.Builder builder =
        new AlertDialog.Builder(getActivity());


LayoutInflater inflater =
        getActivity().getLayoutInflater();


View dialogView =
        inflater.inflate(R.layout.dialog_show_note, null);


TextView txtTitle =
        dialogView.findViewById(R.id.txtTitle);


TextView txtDescription =
        dialogView.findViewById(R.id.txtDescription);


txtTitle.setText(mNote.getTitle());
txtDescription.setText(mNote.getDescription());


TextView txtImportant =
        dialogView.findViewById(R.id.textViewImportant);


TextView txtTodo =
        dialogView.findViewById(R.id.textViewTodo);


TextView txtIdea =
        dialogView.findViewById(R.id.textViewIdea);
```

> **Note**
>
> Add the following import statements so that all of the classes in the preceding code are available:
>
> ```
> import android.view.LayoutInflater;
> ```
>
> ```
> import android.view.View;
> ```
>
> ```
> import android.widget.TextView;
> ```
>
> ```
> import androidx.appcompat.app.AlertDialog;
> ```

The following code that we will add is also in the onCreateDialog method. It checks whether the note being shown is "important" and then shows or hides the txtImportant TextView accordingly. We then do the same for txtTodo and txtIdea.

Add this code after the previous block of code while you are still in the onCreateDialog method:

```
if (!mNote.isImportant()){
    txtImportant.setVisibility(View.GONE);
}


if (!mNote.isTodo()){
    txtTodo.setVisibility(View.GONE);
}


if (!mNote.isIdea()){
    txtIdea.setVisibility(View.GONE);
}
```

All we need to do now is dismiss (close) the dialog window when the user clicks on the **OK** button. This is done via an anonymous class, as we have discussed on several occasions by now. The onClick method simply calls the dismiss method, which closes the dialog window.

Add this code to the onCreateDialog method after the previous block of code:

```
Button btnOK = (Button) dialogView.findViewById(R.id.btnOK);


builder.setView(dialogView).setMessage("Your Note");
```

```
btnOK.setOnClickListener(new View.OnClickListener() {
    @Override
    public void onClick(View v) {
        dismiss();
    }
});


return builder.create();
```

> **Note**
>
> Import the Button class using this line of code:
>
> ```
> import android.widget.Button;
> ```

We now have two dialog windows ready to roll. We just need to add some code to the MainActivity class to finish the job. First, let's do a bit of project housekeeping.

Removing the unwanted autogenerated fragments

We will now tidy up the files and structure of our project. Remember that the Basic Activity template we used to generate this project has quite a few features. Some of these we need, while some we don't. We want the floating action button to be in the lower-right corner of the layout, and we want the main menu with the **Settings** option in the upper-right corner. We don't, however, want multiple fragments for the user to navigate between. To effectively remove all the fragments and have just one simple main layout in the content_main.xml file, we will delete the reference to the fragment along with all of its navigation options.

Open the content_main.xml layout file. In the **Component tree** window in the **Design** tab of the content_main.xml file, find the **nav_host_fragment** element. Select it and then press the *Delete* key on the keyboard. Now, we have a cleaner UI that is ready for future development.

Showing our new dialogs

Open the MainActivity.java file. Add a new temporary member variable just after the MainActivity class declaration. This won't be in the final app; it is so we can test our dialog windows as soon as possible:

```
// Temporary code
Note mTempNote = new Note();
```

Now, add this method to the `MainActivity` class so that we can receive a new note from the `DialogNewNote` class:

```
public void createNewNote(Note n) {
    // Temporary code
    mTempNote = n;
}
```

To send a note to the `DialogShowNote` method, we need to add a button with an ID of `button` to the `content_main.xml` layout file. Open the `content_main.xml` layout file.

Just so that it is clear what this button is for, we will change its `text` attribute to `Show Note`, as follows:

- Drag a button onto the `content_main.xml` layout and configure the `id` property as `button` and the `text` property as `Show Note`.

- Click on the **Infer Constraints** button so that the button stays where you put it. The exact position of this button is not important at this stage.

> **Note**
>
> Just to clarify, this is a temporary button for testing purposes and will not be in the final app. At the end of development, we will be able to click on a note's title from a scrolling list.

In the `onCreate` method, we will set up an anonymous class to handle clicks on our temporary button. The code in the `onClick` method will do the following:

- Create a new `DialogShowNote` instance that is simply called `dialog`.

- Call the `sendNoteSelected` method on `dialog` to pass in `mTempNote` as a parameter, which is our `Note` object.

- Finally, it will call `show`, which breathes life into our new dialog and reveals it to the user.

Add the code that we just described to `onCreate`:

```java
// Temporary code
Button button = findViewById(R.id.button);
button.setOnClickListener(new View.OnClickListener() {
    @Override
    public void onClick(View v) {

        // Create a new DialogShowNote called dialog
        DialogShowNote dialog = new DialogShowNote();

        // Send the note via the sendNoteSelected method
        dialog.sendNoteSelected(mTempNote);

        // Create the dialog
        dialog.show(getSupportFragmentManager(), "123");
    }
});
```

> **Note**
>
> Add the Button class using this line of code:
>
> `import android.widget.Button;`

We can now summon our `DialogShowNote` dialog window at the click of a button. Run the app and click on the **SHOW NOTE** button to view the `DialogShowNote` dialog with the `dialog_show_note.xml` layout:

Figure 14.09 – DialogShowNote dialog

Admittedly, this is not much to look at considering how much coding we have done in this chapter. However, when we get the `DialogNewNote` class working, we will be able to see how the `MainActivity` class interacts and shares data between the two dialogs.

Next, let's make the `DialogNewNote` dialog useable.

Coding the floating action button

This is going to be easy. The floating action button is provided for us in the layout. As a reminder, the floating action button is the round icon with an envelope image on it, as pictured in the lower-right corner of the preceding screenshot.

It is in the `activity_main.xml` file. This is the XML code that positions and defines its appearance. Notice that just before the code for the floating action button, there is a line of code (highlighted) that includes the `content_main.xml` file. This currently contains our **Show Note** button and will eventually contain our sophisticated scrolling list:

```
...

...

<include layout="@layout/content_main" />


<com.google.android.material
    .floatingactionbutton.FloatingActionButton

    android:id="@+id/fab"
    android:layout_width="wrap_content"
    android:layout_height="wrap_content"
    android:layout_gravity="bottom|end"
    android:layout_margin="@dimen/fab_margin"
    app:srcCompat="@android:drawable/ic_dialog_email" />

...

...
```

Android Studio has even provided an anonymous class to handle any clicks on the floating action button. All we need to do is add some code to the `onClick` method of this already provided class, and we can use the `DialogNewNote` class.

The floating action button is usually used for a core action within an app. For example, in an email app, it would probably be used to start a new email. Alternatively, in a note-keeping app, it would probably be used to add a new note. So, let's do that now.

In the `MainActivity.java` file, find the autogenerated code provided by Android Studio in the `MainActivity` class of the `onCreate` method. Here it is in its entirety:

```
fab.setOnClickListener(new View.OnClickListener() {
   @Override
   public void onClick(View view) {
            Snackbar.make(view, "Replace with your own
            action",
                        Snackbar.LENGTH_LONG)
                    .setAction("Action",
```

```
                              null).show();


    }
});
```

In the preceding code snippet, note the highlighted line and delete it. Now, add the following code in place of the deleted code:

```
DialogNewNote dialog = new DialogNewNote();
dialog.show(getSupportFragmentManager(), "");
```

The new code creates a new dialog window of the `DialogNewNote` variety and then shows it to the user.

We can now run the app. Tap on the floating action button, and add a note that is similar to the following screenshot:

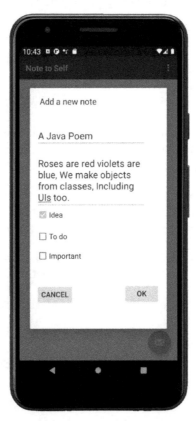

Figure 14.10 – Add new note

Next, we can tap on the **Show Note** button in order to view it in a dialog window, as follows:

Figure 14.11 – Show note dialog window

Note that if you add a second note, it will overwrite the first because we only have one Note object. We will need to learn some more Java in order to solve this problem.

Summary

In this chapter, we discussed and implemented a common UI design with dialog windows using the DialogFragment class.

Then, we went a step further and started the Note to Self app by implementing more complicated dialogs that can capture information from the user. We saw that the DialogFragment class enables us to have any UI we design inside a dialog box.

In the next chapter, we will deal with the obvious problem that the user can only have one note. We will solve this problem by exploring Java arrays and their close cousin, ArrayList, along with another data-related Java class, Map.

15
Arrays, Maps, and Random Numbers

In this chapter, we will learn about Java arrays, which allow us to manipulate a potentially huge amount of data in an organized and efficient manner. We will also use a close Java relation to arrays, `ArrayList`, and look at the differences between them.

Once we are comfortable handling substantial amounts of data, we will see what the Android API has to offer to help us easily connect our newfound data-handling skills to the user interface without breaking a sweat.

The topics in this chapter include the following:

- The `Random` class

- Handling data with arrays

- Arrays mini-app

- Dynamic arrays including a mini-app

- Multidimensional arrays including a mini-app

- The `ArrayList` class

- The enhanced `for` loop

- The Java HashMap

First, let's learn about the `Random` class.

Technical requirements

You can find the code files present in this chapter on GitHub at `https://github.com/PacktPublishing/Android-Programming-for-Beginners-Third-Edition/tree/main/chapter%2015`.

A random diversion

Sometimes in our apps we will want a random number, and Java provides us with the `Random` class for these occasions. There are many possible uses for this class. For instance, maybe our app wants to show a random tip of the day, or is a game that has to choose between scenarios, or is a quiz that asks random questions.

The `Random` class is part of the Java API and is fully compatible with our Android apps.

Let's have a look at how we can create random numbers, and later in the chapter we will put it to practical use. All the hard work is done for us by the `Random` class. First, we need to create an object of type `Random`:

```
Random randGenerator = new Random();
```

Then we use our new object's `nextInt` method to generate a random number in a certain range. This next line of code generates the random number using our `Random` object and stores the result in the `ourRandomNumber` variable:

```
int ourRandomNumber = randGenerator.nextInt(10);
```

The number that we enter for the range starts from zero. So, the preceding line will generate a random number between 0 and 9. If we want a random number between 1 and 10, we just do this:

```
ourRandomNumber ++;
```

We can also use the `Random` object to get other types of random numbers using the `nextLong`, `nextFloat`, and `nextDouble` methods.

We will put the `Random` class to practical use later in the chapter with a quick geography quiz app.

Handling large amounts of data with arrays

You might be wondering what happens when we have an app with lots of variables to keep track of. What about our Note to Self app with 100 notes or a high score table in a game with the top 100 scores? We could declare and initialize 100 separate variables like this:

```
Note note1;
Note note2;
Note note3;
// 96 more lines like the above
Note note100;
```

Or we could do this:

```
int topScore1;
int topScore2;
int topScore3;
// 96 more lines like the above
int topScore100;
```

Straight away, this might seem unwieldy, but what about when someone gets a new top score or we want to let our users sort the order that their notes are displayed in? Using the high scores scenario, we must shift the scores in every variable down one place. A nightmare begins:

```
topScore100 = topScore99;
topScore99 = topScore98;
topScore98 = topScore97;
// 96 more lines like the above
topScore1 = score;
```

There must be a better way. When we have a whole array of variables, what we need is a Java array. An array is a reference variable that holds up to a pre-determined, fixed maximum number of elements. Each element is a variable with a consistent type.

The following code declares an array that can hold `int` type variables, perhaps a high score table or a series of exam grades:

```
int [] intArray;
```

We could also declare arrays of other types, including classes such as Note, like this:

```
String [] classNames;
boolean [] bankOfSwitches;
float [] closingBalancesInMarch;
Note [] notes;
```

Each of these arrays would need to have a fixed maximum amount of storage space allocated before it was used. Just like other objects, we must initialize arrays before we use them:

```
intArray = new int [100];
```

The preceding code allocates up to a maximum of 100 int-sized storage spaces. Think of a long aisle of 100 consecutive storage spaces in our memory warehouse analogy. The spaces would probably be labeled intArray[0], intArray[1], intArray[2], and so on, with each space holding a single int value. Perhaps the slightly surprising thing here is that the storage spaces start off at zero, not 1. Therefore, in a 100-*wide* array, the storage spaces would run from 0 to 99.

We could initialize the values in some of these storage spaces like this:

```
intArray[0] = 5;
intArray[1] = 6;
intArray[2] = 7;
```

But note that we can only ever put the pre-declared type into an array, and the type that an array holds can never change:

```
intArray[3]= "John Carmack"; // Won't compile String not int
```

So, when we have an array of int types, what are each of these int variables called? What are the names of these variables and how do we access the values stored in them? The array notation syntax replaces the variable names. And we can do anything with a variable in an array that we could do with a regular variable with a name:

```
intArray [3] = 123;
```

The preceding code assigns the value 123 into the fourth position of intArray. Here is another example:

```
intArray[10] = intArray[9] - intArray[4];
```

The preceding code subtracts the value in the fifth position of `intArray` from the value in the tenth position and stores the answer in the eleventh position. We can also assign the value from an array to a regular variable of the same type, like this:

```
int myNamedInt = intArray [3];
```

Note, however, that `myNamedInt` is a separate and distinct primitive variable and any changes to it do not affect the value stored in the `intArray` reference. It has its own space in the warehouse and is unconnected to the array. To be more specific, the array is on the heap and the `int` variable is on the stack.

Arrays are objects

We said that arrays are reference variables. Think of an array variable as an address to a group of variables of a given type. Perhaps, using the warehouse analogy, `someArray` is an aisle number. So, `someArray[0]`, `someArray[1]`, and so on are the aisle numbers followed by the position number in the aisle.

Arrays are also objects; that is, they have methods and properties that we can use. See this, for example:

```
int lengthOfSomeArray = someArray.length;
```

In the preceding code, we assigned the length of `someArray` to the `int` variable called `lengthOfSomeArray`.

We can even declare an array of arrays. This is an array where in each of its elements lurks another array, as follows:

```
String[][] countriesAndCities;
```

In the preceding array, we could hold a list of cities within each country. Let's not go array crazy just yet, though. Just remember that an array holds up to a pre-determined number of variables of any pre-determined type, and those values are accessed using this syntax:

```
someArray[someLocation];
```

Let's use some arrays in a real app to try and get an understanding of how to use them in real code and what we might use them for.

Simple array example mini-app

Let's make a simple working array example. You can get the completed code for this example in the downloadable code bundle. It's at `Chapter 15/Simple Array Example/MainActivity.java`.

Create a project using the Empty Activity template and call it `Simple Array Example`.

First, we declare our array, allocate five spaces, and initialize values for each of the elements. Then we output each of the values to the logcat console. Add this code to the `onCreate` method just after the call to `setContentView`:

```java
// Declaring an array
int[] ourArray;


// Allocate memory for a maximum size of 5 elements
ourArray = new int[5];


// Initialize ourArray with values
// The values are arbitrary, but they must be int
// The indexes are not arbitrary. 0 through 4 or crash!

ourArray[0] = 25;
ourArray[1] = 50;
ourArray[2] = 125;
ourArray[3] = 68;
ourArray[4] = 47;


//Output all the stored values
Log.i("info", "Here is ourArray:");
Log.i("info", "[0] = "+ourArray[0]);
Log.i("info", "[1] = "+ourArray[1]);
Log.i("info", "[2] = "+ourArray[2]);
Log.i("info", "[3] = "+ourArray[3]);
Log.i("info", "[4] = "+ourArray[4]);
```

Next, we add each of the elements of the array together, just as we could regular `int` type variables. Notice that when we add the array elements together, we are doing so over multiple lines. This is fine as we have omitted a semicolon until the last operation, so the Java compiler treats the lines as one statement. Add the code we have just discussed to `MainActivity.java`:

```java
/*
    We can do any calculation with an array element
    provided it is appropriate to the contained type
    Like this:
*/
int answer = ourArray[0] +
ourArray[1] +
ourArray[2] +
ourArray[3] +
ourArray[4];

Log.i("info", "Answer = "+ answer);
```

Run the example and see the output in the logcat window.

Remember that nothing will happen on the emulator display as all the output will be sent to our logcat console window in Android Studio. Here is the output:

```
info: Here is ourArray:
info: [0] = 25
info: [1] = 50
info: [2] = 125
info: [3] = 68
info: [4] = 47
info: Answer = 315
```

We declared an array called `ourArray` to hold `int` variables, then allocated space for up to five of that type.

Next, we assigned a value to each of the five spaces in our array. Remember that the first space is `ourArray[0]` and the last space is `ourArray[4]`.

Next, we simply printed the value in each array location to the console, and from the output, we can see they hold the values we initialized them to be in the previous step. Then we added together each of the elements in `ourArray` and initialized their values to the `answer` variable. We then printed `answer` to the console and we can see that indeed all the values were added together, just as if they were plain old `int` types, which they are, just stored and accessed in a different manner.

Getting dynamic with arrays

As we discussed at the beginning of all this array stuff, if we need to declare and initialize each element of an array individually, there isn't a huge amount of benefit to an array over regular variables. Let's look at an example of declaring and initializing arrays dynamically.

Dynamic array example

Let's make a simple dynamic array example. You can get the working project for this example in the download bundle. It is at `Chapter 15/Dynamic Array Example/ MainActivity.java`.

Create a project using the Empty Activity template and call it `Dynamic Array Example`.

Type the following code just after the call to the `setContentView` method in the `onCreate` method. See whether you can work out what the output will be before we discuss it and analyze the code:

```
// Declaring and allocating in one step
int[] ourArray = new int[1000];


// Let's initialize ourArray using a for loop
// Because more than a few variables is allot of typing!


for(int i = 0; i < 1000; i++){


    // Put the value of our value into ourArray
    // At the position decided by i.
    ourArray[i] = i*5;


    //Output what is going on
    Log.i("info", "i = " + i);
```

```
    Log.i("info", "ourArray[i] = " + ourArray[i]);
}
```

Run the example app, remembering that nothing will happen on the screen as all the output will be sent to our logcat console window in Android Studio. Here is the output:

```
info: i = 0
info: ourArray[i] = 0
info: i = 1
info: ourArray[i] = 5
info: i = 2
info: ourArray[i] = 10

... 994 iterations of the loop removed for brevity.
info: ourArray[i] = 4985
info: i = 998
info: ourArray[i] = 4990
info: i = 999
info: ourArray[i] = 4995
```

First, we declared and allocated an array called ourArray to hold up to 1,000 int values. Notice that this time we did the two steps in one line of code:

```
int[] ourArray = new int[1000];
```

Then we used a for loop that was set to loop 1,000 times:

```
(int i = 0; i < 1000; i++){
```

We initialized the spaces in the array, from 0 through to 999, with the value of i multiplied by 5, like this:

```
ourArray[i] = i*5;
```

Then, to demonstrate the value of i and the value held in each position of the array, we output the value of i followed by the value held in the corresponding position in the array, like so:

```
Log.i("info", "i = " + i);
Log.i("info", "ourArray[i] = " + ourArray[i]);
```

And all this happened 1,000 times, producing the output we have seen. Of course, we have yet to use this technique in a real-world app, but we will use it soon to make our Note to Self app hold an almost infinite number of notes.

Entering the nth dimension with arrays

We very briefly mentioned that an array can even hold other arrays at each position. But if an array holds lots of arrays that hold lots of some other type, how do we access the values in the contained arrays? And why would we ever need this anyway? Look at this next example of where multidimensional arrays can be useful.

Multidimensional array mini-app

Let's make a simple multidimensional array example. You can get the working project for this example in the download bundle. It is in `Chapter 15/Multidimensional Array Example/MainActivity.java`.

Create a project using the Empty Activity template and call it `Multidimensional Array Example`.

After the call to `setContentView` in `onCreate`, add the following code, including declaring and initializing a two-dimensional array (highlighted):

```
// Random object for generating question numbers
Random randInt = new Random();
// a variable to hold the random value generated
int questionNumber;


// declare and allocate in separate stages for clarity
// but we don't have to
String[][] countriesAndCities;
// Now we have a 2 dimensional array


countriesAndCities = new String[5][2];
// 5 arrays with 2 elements each
// Perfect for 5 "What's the capital city" questions


// Now we load the questions and answers into our arrays
// You could do this with less questions to save typing
// But don't do more or you will get an exception
```

```
countriesAndCities [0][0] = "United Kingdom";
countriesAndCities [0][1] = "London";


countriesAndCities [1][0] = "USA";
countriesAndCities [1][1] = "Washington";


countriesAndCities [2][0] = "India";
countriesAndCities [2][1] = "New Delhi";


countriesAndCities [3][0] = "Brazil";
countriesAndCities [3][1] = "Brasilia";


countriesAndCities [4][0] = "Kenya";
countriesAndCities [4][1] = "Nairobi";
```

Now we output the contents of the array using a `for` loop and our `Random` object. Note how we ensure that although the question is random, we can always pick the correct answer. Add the following code after the previous code:

```
/*
        Now we know that the country is stored at element 0
        The matching capital at element 1
        Here are two variables that reflect this
*/
int country = 0;
int capital = 1;


// A quick for loop to ask 3 questions
for(int i = 0; i < 3; i++){
    // get a random question number between 0 and 4
    questionNumber = randInt.nextInt(5);


    // and ask the question and in this case just
    // give the answer for the sake of brevity
    Log.i("info", "The capital of "
    +countriesAndCities[questionNumber][country]);
```

```
    Log.i("info", "is "
    +countriesAndCities[questionNumber][capital]);


} // end of for loop
```

Run the example, remembering that nothing will happen on the screen as all the output will be sent to our logcat console window in Android Studio. Here is the output:

```
info: The capital of USA
info: is Washington
info: The capital of India
info: is New Delhi
info: The capital of United Kingdom
info: is London
```

What just happened? Let's go through this chunk by chunk so we know exactly what is going on.

We make a new object of type `Random` called `randInt`, ready to generate random numbers later in the program:

```
Random randInt = new Random();

```

There's a simple `int` variable to hold a question number:

```
int questionNumber;
```

And here we declare our array of arrays called `countriesAndCities`. The outer array holds arrays:

```
String[][] countriesAndCities;

```

Now we allocate space within our arrays. The first outer array will now be able to hold five arrays and each of the inner arrays will be able to hold two strings:

```
countriesAndCities = new String[5][2];
```

Now we initialize our arrays to hold countries and their corresponding capital cities. Notice with each pair of initializations that the outer array number stays the same, indicating that each country/capital pair is within one inner array, a `String` array. And of course, each of these inner arrays is held in one element of the outer array (which holds arrays):

```
countriesAndCities [0][0] = "United Kingdom";
countriesAndCities [0][1] = "London";


countriesAndCities [1][0] = "USA";
countriesAndCities [1][1] = "Washington";


countriesAndCities [2][0] = "India";
countriesAndCities [2][1] = "New Delhi";


countriesAndCities [3][0] = "Brazil";
countriesAndCities [3][1] = "Brasilia";


countriesAndCities [4][0] = "Kenya";
countriesAndCities [4][1] = "Nairobi";
```

To make the upcoming `for` loop clearer, we declare and initialize `int` variables to represent the country and the capital from our arrays. If you glance back at the array initialization, all the countries are held in position 0 of the inner array and all the corresponding capital cities are at position 1:

```
int country = 0;
int capital = 1;
```

Now we set up a `for` loop to run three times. Note that this does not simply access the first three elements of our array; it just determines the number of times we go through the loop. We could make it loop one time or a thousand times; the example would still work:

```
for(int i = 0; i < 3; i++){
```

Next, we determine which question to ask – or more specifically, which element of our outer array. Remember that `randInt.nextInt(5)` returns a number between 0 and 4 – just what we need, as we have an outer array with five elements, 0 through 4:

```
questionNumber = randInt.nextInt(5);
```

Now we can ask a question by outputting the strings held in the inner array, which in turn is held by the outer array that was chosen in the previous line by the randomly generated number:

```
    Log.i("info", "The capital of "
    +countriesAndCities[questionNumber][country]);
```

```
    Log.i("info", "is "
    +countriesAndCities[questionNumber][capital]);
```

```
}//end of for loop
```

For the record, we will not be using any multidimensional arrays in the rest of this book. So, if there is still a little bit of murkiness around these arrays inside arrays, then that doesn't matter. You know they exist, what they can do, and you can revisit them if necessary.

Array-out-of-bounds exceptions

An array-out-of-bounds exception occurs when we attempt to access an element of an array that does not exist. Sometimes the compiler will catch it for us to prevent the error going into a working app. For example, see this code:

```
int[] ourArray = new int[1000];
int someValue = 1; // Arbitrary value
ourArray[1000] = someValue;
// Won't compile as compiler knows this won't work.
// Only locations 0 through 999 are valid
```

But what if we do something like this:

```
int[] ourArray = new int[1000];
int someValue = 1;// Arbitrary value
int x = 999;
if(userDoesSomething){
    x++; // x now equals 1000
}

ourArray[x] = someValue;
// Array out of bounds exception if userDoesSomething
```

```
// evaluates to true! This is because we end up referencing
// position 1000 when the array only has positions 0
// through 999
// Compiler can't spot it. App will crash!
```

The only way we can avoid this problem is to know the rule: the rule that arrays start at zero and go up to their length – 1. We can also use clear, readable code where it is easy to evaluate what we have done and spot problems more easily.

ArrayList

ArrayList is like a regular Java array on steroids. It overcomes some of the shortfalls of arrays, such as having to predetermine the size. It adds some useful methods to make its data easy to manage and it uses an enhanced version of a for loop that is clearer to use than a regular for loop.

Let's look at some code that uses an ArrayList instance:

```
// Declare a new ArrayList called myList to hold int variables
ArrayList<int> myList;
```

```
// Initialize the myList ready for use
myList = new ArrayList<int>();
```

In the previous code, we declared and initialized a new ArrayList called myList. We can also do this in a single step like this code shows:

```
ArrayList<int> myList = new ArrayList<int>();
```

Nothing especially interesting so far, so let's take a look at what we can actually do with ArrayList. Let's use a String ArrayList instance this time:

```
// declare and initialize a new ArrayList
ArrayList<String> myList = new ArrayList<String>();
```

```
// Add a new String to myList in the next available location
myList.add("Donald Knuth");
// And another
myList.add("Rasmus Lerdorf");
// And another
```

```
myList.add("Richard Stallman");
// We can also choose 'where' to add an entry
myList.add(1, "James Gosling");


// Is there anything in our ArrayList?
if(myList.isEmpty()){
    // Nothing to see here
}else{
    // Do something with the data
}


// How many items in our ArrayList?
int numItems = myList.size();


// Now where did I put James Gosling?
int position = myList.indexOf("James Gosling");
```

In the previous code, we saw that we can use some really useful methods of the ArrayList class on our ArrayList object; those methods are listed as follows:

- We can add an item (myList.add).

- Add at a specific location (myList.add(x, value)).

- Check whether ArrayList is empty (myList.isEmpty).

- See how many elements it has (myList.size()).

- Get the current position of a given item (myList.indexOf).

> **Note**
>
> There are even more methods in the ArrayList class and you can read about them here: http://docs.oracle.com/javase/7/docs/api/java/util/ArrayList.html. What we have seen so far is enough to complete this book, however.

With all this functionality, all we need now is a way to handle ArrayList instances dynamically.

The enhanced for loop

This is what the condition of an enhanced `for` loop looks like:

```
for (String s : myList)
```

The previous example would iterate (step through) all of the items in `myList` one at a time. At each step, `s` would hold the current `String` value.

So, this code would print to the console all of our eminent programmers from the previous section's `ArrayList` code sample:

```
for (String s : myList){
    Log.i("Programmer: ","" + s);
}
```

We can also use the enhanced `for` loop with regular arrays too:

```
int [] anArray = new int [];
// We can initialize arrays quickly like this
anArray {0, 1, 2, 3, 4, 5}

for (int s : anArray){
    Log.i("Contents = ","" + s);
}
```

There's another incoming news flash!

Arrays and ArrayList instances are polymorphic

We already know that we can put objects into arrays and `ArrayList`. But being polymorphic means they can handle objects of multiple distinct types as long as they have a common parent type all within the same array or `ArrayList`.

In *Chapter 10, Object-Oriented Programming*, we learned that polymorphism means *different forms*. But what does it mean to us in the context of arrays and `ArrayList`?

Boiled down to its simplest: any subclass can be used as part of the code that uses the superclass.

For example, if we have an array of `Animal` instances, we could put any object that is a type that is a subclass of `Animal` in the `Animal` array – perhaps `Cat` and `Dog` instances.

This means we can write code that is simpler and easier to understand, and easier to change:

```
// This code assumes we have an Animal class
// And we have a Cat and Dog class that extends Animal
Animal myAnimal =  new Animal();
Dog myDog = new Dog();
Cat myCat = new Cat();
Animal [] myAnimals = new Animal[10];
myAnimals[0] = myAnimal; // As expected
myAnimals[1] = myDog; // This is OK too
myAnimals[2] = myCat; // And this is fine as well
```

Also, we can write code for the superclass and rely on the fact that no matter how many times it is sub-classed, within certain parameters the code will still work. Let's continue our previous example:

```
// 6 months later we need elephants
// with its own unique aspects
// If it extends Animal we can still do this
Elephant myElephant = new Elephant();
myAnimals[3] = myElephant; // And this is fine as well
```

But when we remove an object from a polymorphic array, we must remember to cast it to the type we want:

```
Cat newCat = (Cat) myAnimals[2];
```

All we have just discussed is true for `ArrayList` as well. Armed with this new tool kit of arrays, `ArrayList`, and the fact that they are polymorphic, we can move on to learn about some more Android classes that we will soon use to enhance our Note to Self app.

More Java collections – meet the Java HashMap

The Java `HashMap` is neat. It's part of the Java collections framework and a kind of cousin of the `ArrayList` class that we will use in the Note to Self project in the next chapter. They basically encapsulate useful data storage techniques that would otherwise be quite technical for us to code successfully for ourselves.

I thought it would be worth taking a first look at `HashMap` on its own. Suppose we want to store the data of lots of characters from a role-playing game and each different character is represented by an object of type `Character`.

We could use some of the Java tools we already know about, such as arrays or `ArrayList`. The Java `HashMap` is also like these things, but with `HashMap` we can give a unique key/identifier to each `Character` object and access any such object using that key/identifier.

The term hash comes from the process of turning our chosen key/identifier into something used internally by the `HashMap` class. The process is called hashing.

Any of our `Character` instances can then be accessed with our chosen key/identifier. A good candidate for a key/identifier in the `Character` class scenario would be the character's name.

Each key/identifier has a corresponding object; in this case, it is of type `Character`. This is known as a key-value pair.

We just give `HashMap` a key and it gives us the corresponding object. No need to worry about in which index we stored our characters, whether it's Geralt, Ciri, or Triss; just pass the name to `HashMap` and it will do the work for us.

Let's look at some examples. You don't need to type any of this code – just get familiar with how it works.

We can declare a new `HashMap` to hold keys and `Character` instances like this code:

```
Map<String, Character> characterMap;
```

The previous code assumes we have coded a class called `Character`.

We can initialize `HashMap` like this:

```
characterMap = new HashMap();
```

We can add a new key and its associated object like this:

```
characterMap.put("Geralt", new Character());
```

We can also use this:

```
characterMap.put("Ciri", new Character());
```

And we can use this:

```
characterMap.put("Triss", new Character());
```

> **Note**
>
> All the example code assumes that we can somehow give the `Character` instances their unique properties to reflect their internal differences elsewhere.

We can then retrieve an entry from `HashMap` like this:

```
Character ciri = characterMap.get("Ciri");
```

Or perhaps we can use the `Character` class's methods directly like this:

```
characterMap.get("Geralt").drawSilverSword();
```

```
// Or maybe call some other hypothetical method
characterMap.get("Triss").openFastTravelPortal("Kaer Morhen");
```

The previous code calls the hypothetical `drawSilverSword` and `openFastTravelPortal` methods on the `Character` class.

> **Note**
>
> The HashMap class also has lots of useful methods, such as `ArrayList`. See the official Java page for HashMap here: `https://docs.oracle.com/javase/tutorial/collections/interfaces/map.html`.

Let's talk about the Note to Self app.

The Note to Self app

Despite all we have learned, we are not quite ready to apply a solution to the Note to Self app. We could update our code to store lots of notes in an `ArrayList` instance, but before we do, we also need a way to display the contents of `ArrayList` in the UI. It wouldn't look good to throw the whole `ArrayList` contents into a `TextView` widget, for example.

The solution is adapters and a special UI layout called `RecyclerView`. We will get to them in the next chapter.

Frequently asked questions

1. How does a computer that can only make *real* calculations possibly generate a genuinely random number?

    In reality, a computer cannot create a number that is truly random, but the `Random` class uses a seed that produces a number that would stand up as genuinely random under close statistical scrutiny. To find out more about seeds and generating random numbers, look at this article: `https://en.wikipedia.org/wiki/Random_number_generation`.

Summary

In this chapter, we looked at how to use simple Java arrays to store substantial amounts of data provided it is of the same type. We also used the `ArrayList` class, which is like an array with loads of extra features. Furthermore, we found out that both arrays and `ArrayList` instances are polymorphic, which means that a single array (or `ArrayList`) can hold multiple different objects as long as they are all derived from the same parent class.

In addition, we learned about the `HashMap` class, which is also a data storage solution but allows access in different ways.

In the next chapter, we will learn about the `Adapter` and `RecyclerView` classes to put our theory into practice and enhance the Note to Self app.

16
Adapters and Recyclers

In this brief chapter, we will achieve a lot. We will first go through the theory of adapters and lists – how we can extend the `RecyclerAdapter` class in Java code and add a `RecyclerView` instance that acts as a list to our UI – and then through the apparent magic of how the Android API binds them together so that `RecyclerView` displays the contents of `RecyclerAdapter` and allows the user to scroll through the contents. You have probably guessed that we will be using this technique to display our list of notes in the Note to Self app.

In this chapter, we will cover the following:

- Looking at the theory of adapters and binding them to our UI
- Implementing the layout with `RecyclerView`
- Laying out a list item for use in `RecyclerView`
- Implementing the adapter with `RecyclerAdapter`
- Binding the adapter to `RecyclerView`
- Storing notes in `ArrayList` and displaying them in `RecyclerView`
- Discussing how we can improve the Note to Self app further

Soon we will have a self-managing layout that holds and displays all of our notes, so let's get started.

Technical requirements

You can find the code files present in this chapter on GitHub at `https://github.com/PacktPublishing/Android-Programming-for-Beginners-Third-Edition/tree/main/chapter%2016`.

RecyclerView and RecyclerAdapter

In *Chapter 5, Beautiful Layouts with CardView and ScrollView*, we used `ScrollView` and we populated it with a few `CardView` widgets so we could see it scrolling. We could take what we have just learned about arrays and `ArrayList` and create an array of `TextView` widgets, use them to populate a `ScrollView`, and within each `TextView` place the title of a note. This sounds like a perfect solution for showing each note so that it is clickable in the Note to Self app.

We could create the `TextView` widgets dynamically in Java code, set their `text` property to be the title of a note, and then add the `TextView` widgets to a `LinearLayout` contained in a `ScrollView`. However, this is imperfect.

The problem with displaying lots of widgets

This might seem fine, but what if there were dozens, hundreds, or even thousands of notes? We couldn't have thousands of `TextView` widgets in memory because the Android device might simply run out of memory or at the very least grind to a halt as it tries to handle the scrolling of such a vast amount of widgets and their data.

Now, also imagine that we wanted (which we do) each note in the `ScrollView` to show whether it was important, a to-do, or an idea. And how about a short snippet from the text of the note as well?

We would need to devise some clever code that loads and destroys `Note` objects and multiple `TextView` widgets per note from multiple `ArrayList` instances. It can be done, but doing it efficiently is far from straightforward.

The solution to the problem of displaying lots of widgets

Fortunately, this is a problem faced so commonly by mobile developers that the Android API has a solution built in.

We can add a single widget called `RecyclerView` (like an environmentally friendly `ScrollView` but with boosters too) to our UI layout. The `RecyclerView` class was designed precisely as a solution to the problem we have been discussing. In addition, we need to interact with `RecyclerView` with a special type of class that understands how `RecyclerView` works.

We will interact with it using an adapter. We will use the `RecyclerAdapter` class, extend it, customize it, and then use it to control the data from our `ArrayList` instance (which will hold our `Note` instances) and display it in `RecyclerView`.

Let's find out a bit more about how the `RecyclerView` and `RecyclerAdapter` classes work.

How to use RecyclerView and RecyclerAdapter

We already know how to store almost unlimited notes; we can do so in an `ArrayList` instance, although we haven't implemented it yet. We also know that there is a UI layout called `RecyclerView` that is specifically designed to display potentially long lists of data from an `ArrayList` instance. We just need to see how to put it all into action.

To add a `RecyclerView` widget to our layout, we can simply drag and drop it, from the palette onto our UI, in the usual way. Don't do it yet. Let's just discuss it for a bit first.

The RecyclerView widget will look like this in the UI designer if you added one underneath the button in content_main.xml, for example:

Figure 16.1 – RecyclerView widget

This appearance, however, is more a representation of the possibilities than the actual appearance of an app. If we run the app straight after adding a RecyclerView widget, we just get a blank area where the RecyclerView widget is.

The first thing we need to do, to make practical use of RecyclerView, is to decide what each item in the list will look like. It could be just a single TextView widget or it could be an entire layout. We will use LinearLayout. To be clear and specific, we will use a LinearLayout that holds three TextView widgets for each item in our RecyclerView. This will allow us to display the note status (important, idea, or to-do), the note title, and a short snippet of text from the actual note contents.

A list item needs to be defined in its own XML file, then RecyclerView can hold multiple instances of this list item layout.

Of course, none of this explains how we overcome the complexity of managing what data is shown in which list item and how it is retrieved from an `ArrayList`.

This data handling is taken care of by our own customized implementation of the `RecyclerAdapter` class. The `RecyclerAdapter` class implements the `Adapter` interface. We don't need to know how `Adapter` works internally; we just need to override the necessary methods, and then `RecyclerAdapter` will do all the work of communicating with our `RecyclerView` widget.

Wiring up an implementation of `RecyclerAdapter` to `RecyclerView` is certainly more complicated than dragging 20 `TextView` instances onto a `ScrollView` – but once it is done, we can forget about it and it will keep on working and manage itself regardless of how many notes we add to the `ArrayList`. It also has built-in features for handling things such as neat formatting and detecting which item in a list was clicked.

We will need to override some methods of the `RecyclerAdapter` class and add a little code of our own.

What we will do to set up RecyclerView with RecyclerAdapter and an ArrayList of notes

Let's look at an outline of the required steps so we know what to expect. To get the whole thing up and running, we would do the following:

1. Delete the temporary button and related code, and then add a `RecyclerView` widget to our layout with a specific `id` property.

2. Create an XML layout to represent each item in the list. We have already mentioned each item in the list will be a `LinearLayout` that contains three `TextView` widgets.

3. Create a new class that extends `RecyclerAdapter` and add code to several overridden methods to control how it looks and behaves, including using our list item layout and `ArrayList` full of `Note` instances.

4. Add code to the `MainActivity` class to use the `RecyclerAdapter` class and the `RecyclerView` widget and bind it to our `ArrayList` instance.

5. Add an `ArrayList` to `MainActivity` to hold all our notes and update the `createNewNote` method to add any new notes created in the `DialogNewNote` class to this `ArrayList`.

Let's walk through each of these steps in detail.

Adding RecyclerView, RecyclerAdapter, and ArrayList to the Note to Self project

Open the Note to Self project. As a reminder, if you want to see the completed code and working app as a result of completing this chapter, it can be found in the Chapter 16/ Note to self folder.

> **Note**
>
> As the required actions in this chapter jump around between different files, classes, and methods, I encourage you to follow along with the files from the download bundle by keeping it open for reference in your preferred text editor.

Removing the temporary "Show Note" button and adding RecyclerView

These next few steps will get rid of the temporary code we added in *Chapter 14, Android Dialog Windows*, and set up our RecyclerView widget ready for binding to RecyclerAdapter later in the chapter:

1. In the content_main.xml file, remove the temporary Button with an ID of button, which we added previously for testing purposes.

2. In the onCreate method of the MainActivity.java file, delete the Button instance declaration and initialization along with the anonymous class that handles its clicks as this code now creates an error. We will delete some more temporary code later in this chapter. Delete the following code:

```
// Temporary code
Button button = (Button) findViewById(R.id.button);
button.setOnClickListener(new View.OnClickListener() {
    @Override
    public void onClick(View v) {

        // Create a new DialogShowNote called dialog
        DialogShowNote dialog = new DialogShowNote();

        // Send the note via the sendNoteSelected
        method
```

```
            dialog.sendNoteSelected(mTempNote);

            // Create the dialog
            dialog.show(getSupportFragmentManager(),
            "123");
        }
    });
```

3. Now switch back to the content_main.xml file in design view and drag a **RecyclerView** widget from the **Containers** category of the palette onto the layout.

4. Set its id property to recyclerView.

Now we have removed the temporary UI aspects from our project and we have a RecyclerView widget complete with a unique id value ready to be referenced from our Java code.

Creating a list item for RecyclerView

Next, we need a layout to represent each item in our RecyclerView widget. As previously mentioned, we will use a LinearLayout that holds three TextView widgets.

Use the following steps to create a list item for use within our RecyclerView:

1. Right-click on the **layout** folder in the project explorer and select **New | Layout resource file**. Enter listitem in the **Name** field and set **Root element** to LinearLayout.

2. Make sure you are on the **Design** tab and set the orientation attribute to vertical.

3. Look at the next screenshot to see what we are trying to achieve with the remaining steps of this section. I have annotated it to show what each part will be in the finished app:

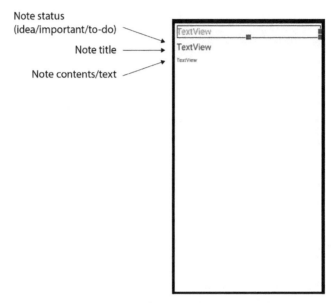

Figure 16.2 – List item for use within our RecyclerView

4. Drag three TextView widgets onto the layout, one above the other, as per the reference image. The first (top) will hold the note status/type (idea, important, or to-do). The second (middle) will hold the note title and the third (bottom) the snippet of text from the note itself.

5. Configure the various attributes of the LinearLayout and TextView widgets as shown in the following table:

Widget type	Property	Value to set to
LinearLayout	layout_height	wrap_contents
LinearLayout	Layout_Margin all	5dp
TextView (top)	Id	textViewStatus
TextView (top)	textSize	24sp
TextView (top)	textColor	@color/colorAccent
TextView (middle)	Id	textViewTitle
TextView (middle)	textSize	24sp
TextView (bottom)	Id	textViewDescription

Now we have a `RecylerView` widget for the main layout and a layout to use for each item in the list of `RecyclerView`. We can go ahead and code our `RecyclerAdapter` class implementation.

Coding the RecyclerAdapter class

We will now create and code a brand-new class. Let's call our new class `NoteAdapter`. Create a new class called `NoteAdapter` in the same folder as the `MainActivity` class (and all the other classes).

Edit the code for the `NoteAdapter` class by adding these `import` statements and extending it with the `RecyclerView.Adapter` class, and then add these two important member variables. Edit the `NoteAdapter` class to be the same as the following code that we have just discussed:

```
import android.view.LayoutInflater;
import android.view.View;
import android.view.ViewGroup;
import android.widget.TextView;

import java.util.List;

import androidx.recyclerview.widget.RecyclerView;

public class NoteAdapter extends
    RecyclerView.Adapter<NoteAdapter.ListItemHolder> {

    private List<Note> mNoteList;
    private MainActivity mMainActivity;
}
```

Notice the class declaration is underlined in red showing there is an error in our code. The error is there because the `RecylerView.Adapter` class (that we are extending) needs us to override some of its abstract methods.

Note

We discussed abstract classes and their methods in *Chapter 11, More Object-Oriented Programming*.

The quickest way to do this is to click the class declaration, hold the *Alt* key, and then tap the *Enter* key. Choose **Implement methods**, as shown in the following screenshot:

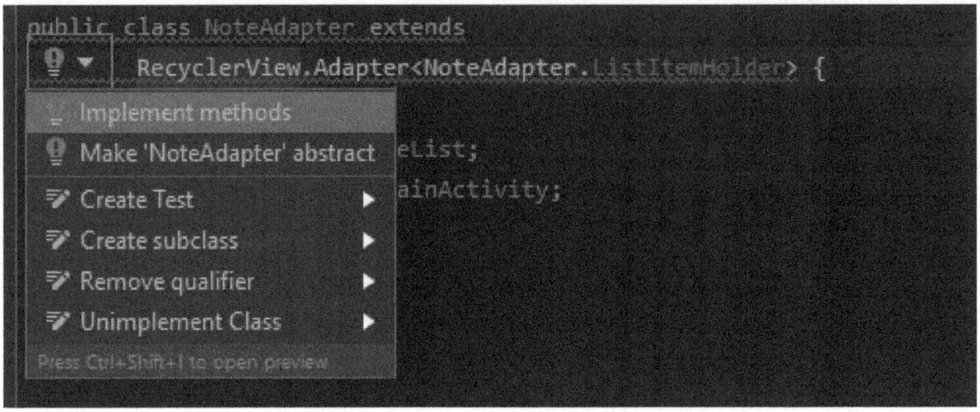

Figure 16.3 – Selecting Implement methods

Then, click **OK** to have Android Studio auto-generate the required methods.

This process adds the following three methods:

- The `onCreateViewHolder` method, which is called when a layout for a list item is required.

- The `onBindViewHolder` method, which is called when `RecyclerAdapter` is bound to (connected/associated with) `RecyclerView` in the layout.

- The `getItemCount` method, which will be used to return the number of `Note` instances in `ArrayList`. Now it just returns `0`.

We will soon add code to each of these methods to do the required work at the specified time.

Note, however, that we still have multiple errors in our code, including in the auto-generated methods as well as the class declaration. A screenshot of the code editor at this stage might be useful:

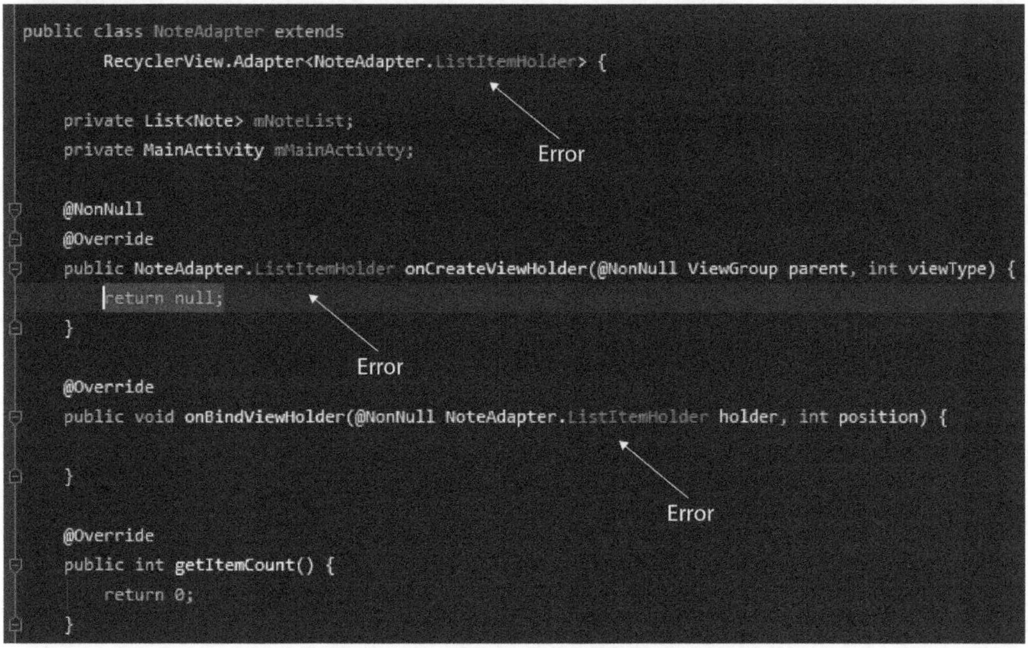

```
public class NoteAdapter extends
        RecyclerView.Adapter<NoteAdapter.ListItemHolder> {

    private List<Note> mNoteList;
    private MainActivity mMainActivity;              Error

    @NonNull
    @Override
    public NoteAdapter.ListItemHolder onCreateViewHolder(@NonNull ViewGroup parent, int viewType) {
        return null;
    }
                            Error
    @Override
    public void onBindViewHolder(@NonNull NoteAdapter.ListItemHolder holder, int position) {

    }
                                            Error
    @Override
    public int getItemCount() {
        return 0;
    }
}
```

Figure 16.4 – Multiple errors in our code

The errors are there because the `NoteAdapter.ListItemHolder` class does not exist. `ListItemHolder` was added by us when we extended `NoteAdapter`. It is our chosen class type that will be used as the holder for each list item. At the moment, it doesn't exist, hence the error. The two methods that also have the same error for the same reason were auto-generated when we asked Android Studio to implement the missing methods.

Let's solve the problem by making a start on the required `ListItemHolder` class. It is useful to us if `ListItemHolder` instances share data/variables with `NoteAdapter`, therefore we will create `ListItemHolder` as an inner class.

Click the error in the class declaration and select **Create class 'ListItemHolder'**, as shown in the following screenshot:

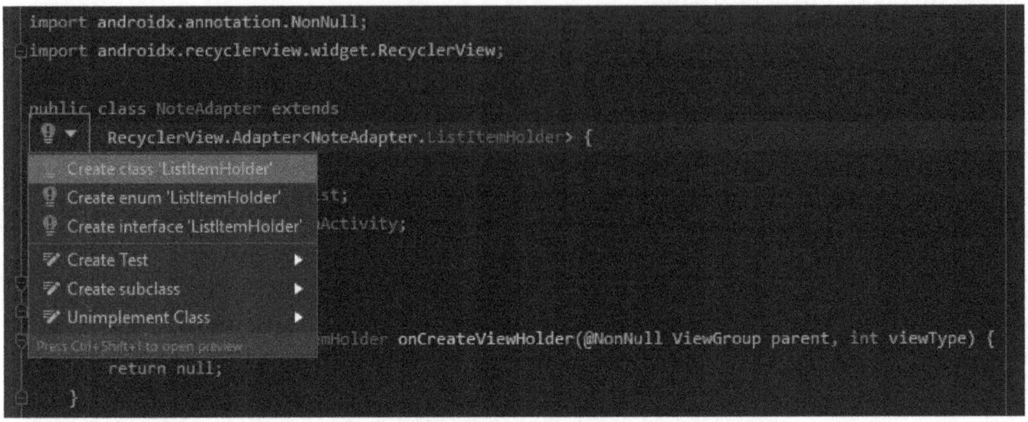

```
import androidx.annotation.NonNull;
import androidx.recyclerview.widget.RecyclerView;

public class NoteAdapter extends
        RecyclerView.Adapter<NoteAdapter.ListItemHolder> {
    Create class 'ListItemHolder'
    Create enum 'ListItemHolder'          st;
    Create interface 'ListItemHolder'    Activity;
    Create Test                     ▶
    Create subclass                 ▶
    Unimplement Class               ▶
    Press Ctrl+Shift+I to open preview    mHolder onCreateViewHolder(@NonNull ViewGroup parent, int viewType) {
        return null;
    }
}
```

Figure 16.5 – Selecting Create class 'ListItemHolder'

The following code has been added to the `NoteAdapter` class:

```
public class ListItemHolder {
}
```

But there is still one error with the class declaration, as shown in this screenshot:

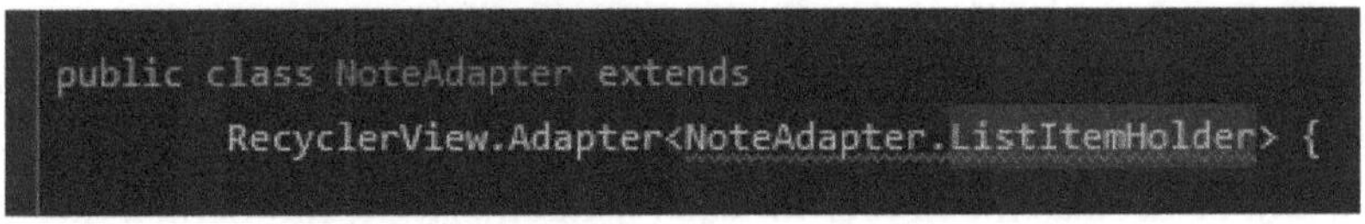

```
public class NoteAdapter extends
        RecyclerView.Adapter<NoteAdapter.ListItemHolder> {
```

Figure 16.6 – Error with the class declaration

The error message reads **...should extend 'android.recylerview.widget.RecyclerView. ViewHolder'** because we may have added `ListItemHolder` but `ListItemHolder` must also extend `RecyclerView.ViewHolder` in order to be used as the parameterized type.

Amend the declaration of the `ListItemHolder` class to match this code:

```
public class ListItemHolder extends
    RecyclerView.ViewHolder
    implements View.OnClickListener {


}
```

Now the error is gone from the `NoteAdapter` class declaration but because we implemented `View.OnClickListener`, we need to implement the `onClick` method. Furthermore, `ViewHolder` doesn't provide a default constructor, so we need to do it. Add the following `onClick` method (empty for now) and this constructor method (empty for now) to the `ListItemHolder` class:

```
public ListItemHolder(View view) {
    super(view);
}


@Override
public void onClick(View view) {
}
```

> **Note**
>
> Be sure you added the code to the inner `ListItemHolder` class and not the `NoteAdapter` class.

After much tinkering and auto-generating, we finally have an error-free `NoteAdapter` class complete with overridden methods and an inner class that we can code to get our `RecyclerAdapter` class working. In addition, we can write code to respond to clicks (in the `onClick` method) on each of our `ListItemHolder` instances.

Coding the NoteAdapter constructor

Next, we will code the `NoteAdapter` constructor method, which will initialize the members of the `NoteAdapter` class. Add this constructor to the `NoteAdapter` class:

```
public NoteAdapter(MainActivity mainActivity,
                            List<Note> noteList) {

    mMainActivity = mainActivity;
    mNoteList = noteList;
}
```

First, notice the parameters of the constructor. It receives a `MainActivity` instance as well as a `List`. This implies that when we use this class, we will need to send in a reference to the main activity of this app (`MainActivity`) as well as a `List`/ `ArrayList`. We will see what use we put the `MainActivity` reference to shortly, but we can sensibly guess that the reference to a `List` with the parameterized `<Note>` type will be a reference to our `ArrayList` of `Note` instances that we will soon code in the `MainActivity` class. `NoteAdapter` will then hold a permanent reference to all the user's notes.

Coding the onCreateViewHolder method

Next, we will adapt the auto-generated `onCreateViewHolder` method. Add the two highlighted lines of code to the `onCreateViewHolder` method and study the parameters that were auto-generated:

```
@NonNull
@Override
public NoteAdapter.ListItemHolder onCreateViewHolder(
        @NonNull ViewGroup parent, int viewType) {

    View itemView = LayoutInflater.from(parent.getContext())
                .inflate(R.layout.listitem, parent,
                false);

    return new ListItemHolder(itemView);
}
```

This code works by initializing `itemView` using `LayoutInflater` and our newly designed `listitem` layout. It then returns a new `ListItemHolder` instance complete with an inflated and ready-to-use layout.

Coding the onBindViewHolder method

Next, we will adapt the `onBindViewHolder` method. Add the highlighted code to make the method the same as this code and also make sure to study the method's parameters as well:

```java
@Override
public void onBindViewHolder(
@NonNull NoteAdapter.ListItemHolder holder, int position) {

    Note note = mNoteList.get(position);
    holder.mTitle.setText(note.getTitle());
    // Show the first 15 characters of the actual note
    // Unless a short note then show half
if(note.getDescription().length() > 15) {
holder.mDescription.setText(note.getDescription()
.substring(0, 15));
}
else{
        holder.mDescription.setText(note.getDescription()
        .substring(0, note.getDescription().length() /2 ));
}

    // What is the status of the note?
    if(note.isIdea()){
        holder.mStatus.setText(R.string.idea_text);
    }
    else if(note.isImportant()){
        holder.mStatus.setText(R.string.important_text);
    }
    else if(note.isTodo()){
        holder.mStatus.setText(R.string.todo_text);
    }
}
```

First, the code checks whether the note is longer than 15 characters and if it is, it truncates it so it looks sensible in the list.

Then, it checks what type of note it is (idea, to-do, or important) and assigns the appropriate label from the string resources.

This new code has left some errors in the code with the `holder.mTitle`, `holder.mDescription`, and `holder.mStatus` variables because we need to add them to our `ListItemHolder` inner class. We will do this very soon.

Coding getItemCount

Amend the `return` statement in this auto-generated method to be the same as the highlighted line of code shown next:

```
@Override
public int getItemCount() {
    return mNoteList.size();
}
```

This code is used internally by the class and it supplies the current number of items in `ArrayList`.

Coding the ListItemHolder inner class

Now we can turn our attention to the inner class, `ListItemHolder`. Adapt the `ListItemHolder` inner class by adding the following highlighted code:

```
public class ListItemHolder
    extends RecyclerView.ViewHolder
    implements View.OnClickListener {

    TextView mTitle;
    TextView mDescription;
    TextView mStatus;

    public ListItemHolder(View view) {
        super(view);
        mTitle =
            view.findViewById(R.id.textViewTitle);

        mDescription =
            view.findViewById(R.id.textViewDescription);

        mStatus =
            view.findViewById(R.id.textViewStatus);

        view.setClickable(true);
        view.setOnClickListener(this);
```

```
    }

    @Override
    public void onClick(View view) {
        mMainActivity.showNote(getAdapterPosition());
    }
}
```

The `ListItemHolder` constructor just gets a reference to each of the `TextView` widgets in the layout. The final two lines of code set the whole view as clickable so that the operating system will call the next method we discuss, `onClick`, when a holder is clicked.

In the `onClick` method, the call to the `mMainActivity.showNote` method has an error because the method doesn't exist yet, but we will fix that in the next section. The call will show the clicked note in its appropriate `DialogFragment` instance.

Coding MainActivity to use the RecyclerView and RecyclerAdapter classes

Now, switch over to the `MainActivity` class in the editor window. Add these three new members to the `MainActivity` class and remove the temporary code shown commented out next:

```
// Temporary code
//Note mTempNote = new Note();

private List<Note> noteList = new ArrayList<>();
private RecyclerView recyclerView;
private NoteAdapter mAdapter;
```

Add the following `import` directives if you haven't already:

```
import androidx.recyclerview.widget.RecyclerView;
import java.util.ArrayList;
import java.util.List;
```

These three members are our `ArrayList` for all our `Note` instances, our `RecyclerView` instance, and an instance of our class, `NoteAdapter`.

Adding code to the onCreate method

Add the following highlighted code to the `onCreate` method after the code that handles presses on the floating action button (shown again for context):

```
fab.setOnClickListener(new View.OnClickListener() {
    @Override
    public void onClick(View view) {
        DialogNewNote dialog = new DialogNewNote();
        dialog.show(getSupportFragmentManager(), "");
    }
});


recyclerView =
    findViewById(R.id.recyclerView);

mAdapter = new NoteAdapter(this, noteList);
RecyclerView.LayoutManager mLayoutManager =
    new LinearLayoutManager(getApplicationContext());

recyclerView.setLayoutManager(mLayoutManager);
recyclerView.setItemAnimator(new DefaultItemAnimator());

// Add a neat dividing line between items in the list
recyclerView.addItemDecoration(
    new DividerItemDecoration(this, LinearLayoutManager.
VERTICAL));

// set the adapter
recyclerView.setAdapter(mAdapter);
```

The preceding code will need the following three `import` directives:

```
import androidx.recyclerview.widget.LinearLayoutManager;
import androidx.recyclerview.widget.DefaultItemAnimator;
import androidx.recyclerview.widget.DividerItemDecoration;
```

In the preceding code, we initialize the `recyclerView` reference with the `RecyclerView` instance in the layout. Our `NoteAdapter` (`mAdapter`) is initialized by calling the constructor we coded and note that a reference to `MainActivity` (`this`) and the `ArrayList` instance is passed in, just as required by the class we have coded previously.

Next, we create a new object, `LayoutManager`. In the next line of code, we call `setLayoutManager` on `recyclerView` and pass in this new `LayoutManager` instance. Now we can configure some properties of `recyclerView`.

The `setItemAnimator` and `addItemDecoration` methods make each list item a little more visually enhanced with a separator line between each item in the list. Later, when we build a settings screen, we will give the user the option to add and remove this separator.

The last thing we do is call the `setAdapter` method, which combines our adapter with our view.

Now we will make some changes to the `addNote` method.

Modifying the addNote method

In the `addNote` method, delete the temporary code we added in *Chapter 14, Android Dialog Windows*, (shown commented out) and add the new highlighted code shown next:

```
public void createNewNote(Note n) {
    // Temporary code
    //mTempNote = n;
    noteList.add(n);
    mAdapter.notifyDataSetChanged();
}
```

The new highlighted code adds a note to `ArrayList` instead of simply initializing a solitary `Note` object, which has now been commented out. Then, we need to call the `notifyDataSetChanged` method, which lets our adapter know that a new note has been added.

Coding the showNote method

Add this new method, which is called from the `NoteAdapter` class using the reference to this class that was passed into the `NoteAdapter` constructor. More specifically, it is called from the `ListerItemHolder` inner class when one of the items in `RecyclerView` is tapped by the user. Add the `showNote` method to the `MainActivity` class:

```java
public void showNote(int noteToShow) {
    DialogShowNote dialog = new DialogShowNote();
    dialog.sendNoteSelected(noteList.get(noteToShow));
    dialog.show(getSupportFragmentManager(), "");
}
```

> **Note**
> All the errors in the `NoteAdapter.java` file are now gone.

The code just added will launch a new instance of `DialogShowNote` and pass in the specific, required note as pointed to by `noteToShow`.

Running the app

You can now run the app and enter a new note as shown in the following screenshot:

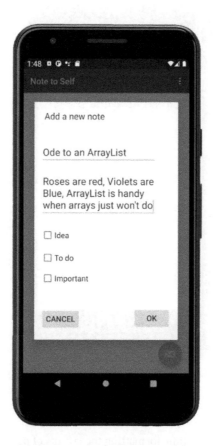

Figure 16.7 – Adding a new note

After you have entered several notes of several types, the list (`RecyclerView`) will look something like this:

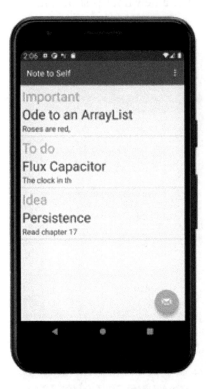

Figure 16.8 – List of notes

Reader challenge

We could have spent more time formatting the layouts of our two dialog windows. Why not refer to *Chapter 5, Beautiful Layouts with CardView and ScrollView*, as well as the Material Design website and do a better job than we have done so far? Furthermore, you could enhance the `RecyclerView` class/list of notes by using `CardView` instead of `LinearLayout`.

Don't spend too long adding new notes, however, because there is a slight problem. Close and restart the app. Uh oh, all the notes are gone!

Frequently asked questions

1. I still don't understand how `RecyclerAdapter` works – why?

    That's because we haven't really discussed it. The reason we have not discussed the behind-the-scenes details is that we don't need to know them. If we override the required methods, as we have just seen, everything will work. This is how `RecyclerAdapter` and most other classes we use are meant to be: hidden implementations with public methods to expose the necessary functionality.

2. Do I need to know what is going on inside the `RecyclerAdapter` class and other classes as well?

    It is true that there are more details about `RecyclerAdapter` (and almost every class that we use in this book) that we don't have the space to discuss. It is good practice to read the official documentation of the classes you use. You can read more about all the classes from the Android API here: `https://developer.android.com/reference`.

Summary

Now we have added the ability to hold multiple notes and implemented the ability to display them.

We achieved this by learning about and using the `RecyclerAdapter` class, which implements the `Adapter` interface, which allows us to bind together `RecyclerView` and `ArrayList`, allowing the seamless display of data without us (the programmer) having to worry about the complex code that is part of these classes and that we don't even see.

In the next chapter, we will start with making the user's notes persist when they quit the app or switch off their device. In addition, we will create a settings screen and see how we can make the settings persist as well. We will use different techniques to achieve each of these goals.

17
Data Persistence and Sharing

In this chapter, we will look at a couple of different ways to save data to an Android device's permanent storage. Also, for the first time, we will add a second `Activity` to our app. It often makes sense when implementing a separate "screen" in our app, such as a settings screen, to do so in a new `Activity`. We could go to the trouble of hiding the original UI and then showing the new UI, but this would quickly lead to confusing and error-prone code. So, we will see how to add an `Activity` class and navigate the user between them.

In summary, in this chapter, we will do the following:

- Learn about using Android intents to switch between `Activity` classes and pass data

- Create a simple (very simple) settings screen in a new `Activity` class for the Note to Self project

- Persist the settings screen data using the `SharedPreferences` class

- Learn about **JavaScript Object Notation (JSON)** for serialization

- Explore Java's `try-catch-finally` syntax

- Implement saving data in our Note to Self app

Technical requirements

You can find the code files present in this chapter on GitHub at `https://github.com/PacktPublishing/Android-Programming-for-Beginners-Third-Edition/tree/main/chapter%2017`.

Android intents

The `Intent` class is appropriately named. It is a class that demonstrates the intent of an `Activity` class from our app. It makes an intent clear and it also facilitates it.

All our apps so far have had just one `Activity`, but many Android apps comprise more than one.

In perhaps its most common use, an `Intent` class allows us to switch between `Activity` instances. But of course, `Activity` instances are made from classes with member variables. So, what happens to the variable's value – the data – when we switch between them? Intents handle this problem for us by allowing us to pass data between `Activity` instances.

Intents aren't just about wiring up the `Activity` instances of our app. They also make it possible to interact with other apps too. For example, we could provide a link in our app for the user to send an email, make a phone call, interact with social media, or open a web page in a browser and have the email app, phone call app, social media app, or web browser do all the work.

There aren't enough pages in this book to really dig deep into interacting with other apps, and we will mainly focus on switching between activities and passing data.

Switching Activity

Let's say we have an app with two `Activity`-based classes, because we will soon. We can assume that as usual, we have an `Activity` class called `MainActivity`, which is where the app starts, and a second `Activity` called `SettingsActivity`. This is how we can swap from `MainActivity` to `SettingsActivity`:

```
// Declare and initialize a new Intent object called myIntent
Intent myIntent = new Intent(this, SettingsActivity.class);

// Switch to the SettingsActivity
startActivity(myIntent);
```

Look carefully at how we initialized the `Intent` object. `Intent` has a constructor that takes two arguments. The first is a reference to the current `Activity`, `this`. And the second parameter is the name of the `Activity` class we want to open, `SettingsActivity.class`. The `.class` part on the end of `SettingsActivity` makes it the full name of the `Activity` class as declared in the `AndroidManifest. xml` file, and we will look at that when we experiment with intents shortly.

The only problem is that `SettingsActivity` doesn't share any of the data of `MainActivity`. In a way, this is a good thing because if you need all the data from `MainActivity`, then it is a reasonable indication that switching activities might not be the best way of proceeding with your app's design. It is, however, unreasonable to have encapsulation so thorough that the two `Activity` instances know absolutely nothing about each other.

Passing data between activities

What if we have a sign-in screen for the user and we want to pass the user's credentials to each `Activity` of our app? We could do so using intents.

We can add data to an `Intent` class like this:

```
// Create a String called username
// and set its value to bob
String username = "Bob";


// Create a new Intent as we have already seen
Intent myIntent = new Intent(this, SettingsActivity.class);


// Add the username String to the Intent
// using the putExtra method of the Intent class
myIntent.putExtra("USER_NAME", username);


// Start the new Activity as we did before
startActivity(myIntent);
```

In `SettingsActivity`, we could then retrieve the string like this:

```
// Here we need an Intent also
// But the default constructor will do
// as we are not switching Activity
Intent myIntent = new Intent();

// Initialize username with the passed in String
String username = intent.getExtra().getStringKey("USER_NAME");
```

In the previous two blocks of code, we switched `Activity` in the same way as we have already seen. But before we called the `startActivity` method, we used the `putExtra` method to load a string into the intent.

We add data using **key-value pairs**. Each piece of data needs to be accompanied by an `identifier` instance that can be used in the retrieving `Activity` to identify and retrieve the data.

The identifier name is up to you, but useful/memorable values should be used.

Then, in the receiving `Activity`, we simply create an intent using the default constructor:

```
Intent myIntent = new Intent();
```

And we can then retrieve the data using the `getExtras` method and the appropriate identifier from the key-value pair.

Once we want to start sending more than a few values, it is worth considering different tactics.

The `Intent` class can help us when sending more complex data than this, but the `Intent` class has its limits. For example, we wouldn't be able to send a `Note` object.

Adding a settings page to Note to Self

Now that we are armed with all this knowledge about the Android `Intent` class, we can add another screen (`Activity`) to our Note to Self app. We will add a settings screen.

We will first create a new `Activity` for our settings screen and see what effect that has on the `AndroidManifest.xml` file; we will then create a very simple layout for our settings screen and add the Java code to switch from `MainActivity` to the new one. We will, however, defer wiring up our settings screen with Java until we have learned how to save the settings to disk. We will do this later in this chapter and then come back to the settings screen to make its data persist.

First, let's create that new `Activity` class. We will call it `SettingsActivity`.

Creating SettingsActivity

This will be a screen where the user can turn on or off the decorative divider between each note in the `RecyclerView` widget. This will not be a comprehensive settings screen but it will be a useful exercise, and we will learn how to switch between activities as well as saving data to disk. Follow these steps to get started:

1. In the project explorer, right-click the folder that contains all your `.java` files and has the same name as your package. From the pop-up context menu, select **New | Activity | Empty Activity**.

2. In the **Activity Name** field, enter `SettingsActivity`.

3. Leave all the other options at their defaults and left-click **Finish**.

Android Studio has created a new `Activity`-based class for us and its associated `.java` file. Let's take a quick peek at some of the work that was done behind the scenes for us because it is useful to know what is going on.

Open the `AndroidManifest.xml` file from within the `manifests` folder in the project explorer. Notice the following line of code about halfway through this file:

```
<activity android:name=".SettingsActivity"></activity>
```

This is how an `Activity` class is **registered** with the operating system. If an `Activity` class is not registered, then an attempt to run it will crash the app. We could create an `Activity` class simply by creating a class that extends `Activity` (or `AppCompatActivity`) in a new `.java` file. However, we would then have to add the preceding code ourselves. Also, by using the new `Activity` wizard, we got a layout XML file (`activity_settings.xml`) automatically generated for us.

Designing the settings screen layout

We will quickly build a UI for our settings screen, and the following steps and figure should make this straightforward:

1. Open the `activity_settings.xml` file, switch to the **Design** tab, and we will quickly lay out our settings screen. Use this next figure as a guide while following the rest of the steps:

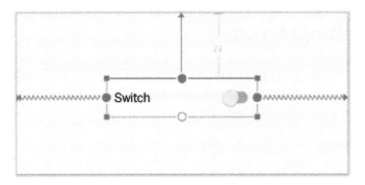

Figure 17.1 – Designing the settings screen

2. Drag and drop a **Switch** widget onto the center top of the layout. I stretched mine by dragging the edges to make it larger.

3. Add an `id` attribute of `switch1` (if it isn't already by default) so we can interact with it using Java code from `SettingsActivity.java`.

4. Use the constraint handles to fix the position of the switch or click the **Infer Constraints** button to fix it automatically.

We now have a simple new layout for our settings screen and the `id` property is in place, ready for when we wire it up with our Java code later in the chapter.

Enabling the user to switch to the settings screen

We already know how to switch to `SettingsActivity`. Also, as we won't be passing any data to it or from it, we can get this working with just two lines of Java code.

You might have noticed in the action bar of our app that there is a menu icon. It is a default part of the Basic Activity template that we used when we created the project. It is indicated in the following figure:

Figure 17.2 – Menu icon

If you tap it, there is already a menu option in there for **Settings**, provided by default when we first created the app. This is what you will see when you tap the menu icon:

Figure 17.3 – Settings option

All we need to do is place our code to switch to the SettingsActivity class within the onOptionsItemSelected method in the MainActivity class. Android Studio even provided an if block by default for us to paste our code into, on the assumption that we would one day want to add a settings screen. How thoughtful.

Switch to MainActivity.java in the editor window and find the following block of code in the onOptionsItemSelected method:

```
//noinspection SimplifiableIfStatement
if (id == R.id.action_settings) {
    return true;
}
```

Add this code into the if block shown previously, just before the return true statement:

```
Intent intent = new Intent(this, SettingsActivity.class);
startActivity(intent);
```

You will need to import the `Intent` class using your preferred technique to add this line of code:

```
import android.content.Intent;
```

You can now run the app and visit the new settings screen by tapping the **Settings** menu option. This screenshot shows the settings screen running on the emulator:

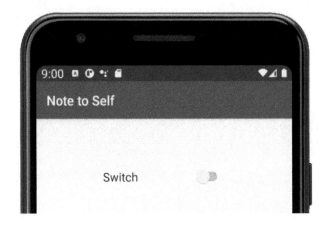

Figure 17.4 – Settings screen

To return from `SettingsActivity` to `MainActivity`, you can tap the back button on the device.

Persisting data with SharedPreferences

In Android, there are a few ways to make data persist. By persist, I mean that if the user quits the app, then when they come back to it, their data is still available. Which method is the correct one to use is dependent upon the app and the type of data.

In this book, we will look at three ways to make data persist. For saving our users' settings, we only need a simple method. After all, we just need to know whether they want the decorative divider between each of the notes in the `RecyclerView` widget.

Let's look at how we can make our apps save and reload variables to the internal storage of the device. We need to use the `SharedPreferences` class. `SharedPreferences` is a class that provides access to data that can be accessed and edited by all `Activity` classes of an app. Let's look at how we can use it:

```
// A SharedPreferences for reading data
SharedPreferences prefs;
```

```
// A SharedPreferences.Editor for writing data
SharedPreferences.Editor editor;
```

As with all objects, we need to initialize them before we can use them. We can initialize the prefs object by using the getSharedPreferences method and passing in a string that will be used to refer to all the data read and written using this object. Typically, we could use the name of the app as the value for this string. In the next code, MODE_PRIVATE means that any class, in this app only, can access it:

```
prefs = getSharedPreferences("My App", MODE_PRIVATE);
```

We then use our newly initialized prefs object to initialize our editor object by calling the edit method:

```
editor = prefs.edit();
```

Let's say we wanted to save the user's name that we have in a string called username. We can then write the data to the internal memory of the device like this:

```
editor.putString("username", username);
editor.commit();
```

The first argument used in the putString method is a label that can be used to refer to the data; the second is the actual variable that holds the data we want to save. The second line in the previous code initiates the saving process. So, we could write multiple variables to disk like this:

```
editor.putString("username", username);
editor.putInt("age", age);
editor.putBoolean("newsletter-subscriber", subscribed);

// Save all the above data
editor.commit();
```

The previous code demonstrates that you can save other variable types, and it of course assumes that the username, age, and subscribed variables have previously been declared and then initialized with appropriate values.

Once editor.commit() has executed, the data is stored. We can quit the app, even turn off the device, and the data will persist.

Reloading data with SharedPreferences

Let's see how we can reload our data the next time the app is run. This code will reload the three values that the previous code saved. We could even declare our variables and initialize them with the stored values:

```
String username   =
    prefs.getString("username", "new user");

int age   = prefs.getInt("age", -1);

boolean subscribed =
    prefs.getBoolean("newsletter-subscriber", false)
```

In the previous code, we load the data from disk using the method appropriate for the data type and the same label we used to save the data in the first place. What is less clear is the second argument to each of the method calls.

The `getString`, `getInt`, and `getBoolean` methods require a default value as the second parameter. If there is no data stored with that label, it will then return the default value.

We could then check for these default values in our code and go about trying to obtain the real values. See here, for example:

```
if (age == -1){
    // Ask the user for his age
}
```

We now know enough to save our users' settings in the Note to Self app.

Making the Note to Self settings persist

We have already learned how to save data to the device's memory. As we implement saving the users' settings, we will also see again how we handle `Switch` input and where exactly the code we have just seen will go to make our app work the way we want it to.

Coding the SettingsActivity class

Most of the action will take place in the `SettingsActivity.java` file. So, click on the appropriate tab and we will add the code a bit at a time.

First, we need some member variables that will give us working `SharedPreferences` and `Editor` instances. We also want a member variable to represent the user's settings option: whether they want decorative dividers or not.

Add the following member variables to the `SettingsActivity` class just after the class declaration:

```
private SharedPreferences mPrefs;
private SharedPreferences.Editor mEditor;


private boolean mShowDividers;
```

Import the `SharedPreferences` class:

```
import android.content.SharedPreferences;
```

Now in the `onCreate` method, add the code to initialize `mPrefs` and `mEditor`:

```
mPrefs = getSharedPreferences("Note to self", MODE_PRIVATE);
mEditor = mPrefs.edit();
```

Next, still in the `onCreate` method, let's get a reference to our `Switch` widget and load up the saved data that represents our user's previous choice for whether to show the dividers.

We get a reference to the switch in the same way that we did in *Chapter 13, Anonymous Classes – Bringing Android Widgets to Life*. Notice the default value is `true` – to show the dividers. We will also set the switch to either on or off as appropriate:

```
mShowDividers  = mPrefs.getBoolean("dividers", true);


Switch switch1 = findViewById(R.id.switch1);
// Set the switch on or off as appropriate
switch1.setChecked(mShowDividers);
```

You will need to import the `Switch` class:

```
import android.widget.Switch;
```

Next, we create an anonymous class to listen for and handle changes to our `Switch` widget.

When the isChecked variable is true, we use the prefs object to set the dividers label and the mShowDividers variable to true; when it is not checked, we set them both to false.

Add the following code to the onCreate method that we have just discussed:

```
switch1.setOnCheckedChangeListener(
        new CompoundButton.OnCheckedChangeListener() {

            public void onCheckedChanged(
                    CompoundButton buttonView,
                        boolean isChecked) {

                if(isChecked){
                    mEditor.putBoolean(
                            "dividers", true);

                    mShowDividers = true;

                }else{
                    mEditor.putBoolean(
                            "dividers", false);

                    mShowDividers = false;
                }
            }
        }
);
```

You will need to import the CompoundButton class:

```
import android.widget.CompoundButton;
```

You might have noticed that at no point in any of that code did we call the mEditor.
commit method to save the user's settings. We could have placed it after we detected
a change to the switch, but it is much simpler to put it where it is guaranteed to be called,
but only once.

We will use our knowledge of the `Activity` lifecycle and override the `onPause` method. When the user leaves the `SettingsActivity` screen either to go back to `MainActivity` or to quit the app, the `onPause` method will be called by the operating system and the settings will be saved. Add this code to override the `onPause` method and save the user's settings. Add the code just before the closing curly brace of the `SettingsActivity` class:

```
@Override
protected void onPause() {
    super.onPause();

    // Save the settings here
    mEditor.commit();
}
```

Finally, we can add some code to the `MainActivity` class to load the settings when the app starts or when the user switches back from the settings screen to the main screen.

Coding the MainActivity class

Add this highlighted code to add some member variables after our `NoteAdapter` instance is declared:

```
private List<Note> noteList = new ArrayList<>();
private RecyclerView recyclerView;
private NoteAdapter mAdapter;
private boolean mShowDividers;
private SharedPreferences mPrefs;
```

Import the `SharedPreferences` class:

```
import android.content.SharedPreferences;
```

Now we have a `boolean` member to decide whether to show the dividers and a `SharedPreferences` instance to read the settings from disk.

Now we will override the `onResume` method to initialize our `mPrefs` variable and load the settings into the `mShowDividers` variable.

Add the overridden `onResume` method as shown next to the `MainActivity` class:

```
@Override
protected void onResume(){
    super.onResume();

    mPrefs = getSharedPreferences(
            "Note to self", MODE_PRIVATE);

    mShowDividers  = mPrefs.getBoolean(
            "dividers", true);
}
```

The user is now able to choose their settings. The app will both save and reload them as necessary, but we need to make the `MainActivity` class respond to the user's choice.

Find this code in the `onCreate` method and delete it:

```
// Add a neat dividing line between items in the list
recyclerView.addItemDecoration(
    new DividerItemDecoration(
    this, LinearLayoutManager.VERTICAL));
```

The previous code is what sets the dividers between each note in the list. Add this new code to the `onResume` method, which is the same line of code surrounded by an `if` statement, to selectively use dividers only when `mShowDividers` is `true`. Add the code after the previous code in the `onResume` method:

```
if(mShowDividers) {
    // Add a neat dividing line between list items
    recyclerView.addItemDecoration(
            new DividerItemDecoration(
            this, LinearLayoutManager.VERTICAL));
}else{
    // check there are some dividers
    // or the app will crash
    if(recyclerView.getItemDecorationCount() > 0) {
            recyclerView.removeItemDecorationAt(0);
```

```
    }
    }
```

Run the app and notice that the dividers are gone; go to the settings screen, switch on the dividers, and return to the main screen (with the back button) – and behold: there are now separators. This next figure shows the list with and without separators side by side to illustrate that the code we have added works and the settings persist between the two Activity classes:

Figure 17.5 – List with and without separators

Be sure to try quitting the app and restarting to verify that the setting is saved to disk. You can even turn the emulator off and back on again and the setting will persist.

Now we have a neat settings screen and we can permanently save the user's choice of decorative preference. Of course, the big missing link regarding persistence is that the user's fundamental data, their notes, still does not persist.

More advanced persistence

Let's think about what we need to do. We want to save a bunch of notes to the internal storage. Being more specific, we want to store a selection of strings and related Boolean values. These strings and Boolean values represent the user's note title, the note's text, and whether it is a to-do, important, or an idea.

Given what we already know about the `SharedPreferences` class, at first glance this might not seem especially challenging – until we dig a little deeper into our requirements. What if the user loves our app and ends up with 100 notes? We would need 100 identifiers for key-value pairs. Not impossible, but starting to get awkward.

Now consider that we want to enhance the app and give the user the ability to add dates to them. Android has a `Date` class that is perfect for this. It would be reasonably straightforward to then add neat features such as reminders to our app. But when it comes to saving data, suddenly, things start to get complicated.

How would we store a date using `SharedPreferences`? It wasn't designed for this. We could convert it to a string when we save it and convert it back again when we load it, but this is far from simple.

And as our app grows in features and our users get more and more notes, the whole persistence thing becomes a nightmare. What we need is a way to save and load objects, actual Java objects. If we can simply save and load objects, including their internal data (strings, Booleans, dates, or anything else), our apps can have any kind of data we can think of to suit our users.

The process of converting data objects into bits and bytes to store on a disk is called **serialization**; the reverse process is called **de-serialization**. Serialization on its own is a vast topic and far from straightforward. Fortunately, as we are coming to expect, there is a class to handle most of the complexity for us.

What is JSON?

JSON stands for **JavaScript Object Notation** and it is widely used in fields beyond Android and the Java language. It is perhaps most frequently used to send data between web applications and servers.

Fortunately, there are JSON classes available for Android that almost entirely hide the complexity of the serialization process. By learning about a few more Java concepts, we can quickly begin to use these classes and start writing entire Java objects to the device storage rather than worrying ourselves about what primitive types make up the objects.

The JSON classes when compared with other classes we have seen so far undertake operations that have a higher-than-normal probability of failure that is beyond their control. To find out why this is so and what can be done about it, let's look at Java exceptions.

Java exceptions – try, catch, and finally

All this talk of JSON requires us to learn a new Java concept: **exceptions**. When we write a class that performs operations that have a possibility of failure, especially for reasons beyond our control, it is advisable to make this plain in our code so that anyone using our class is prepared for the possibility.

Saving and loading data is one such scenario where failure is possible beyond our control. Think about trying to load data when the SD card has been removed or has been corrupted. Another instance where code might fail is perhaps when we write code that relies on a network connection – what if the user goes offline partway through a data transfer?

Java exceptions are the solution and JSON classes use them, so it is a good time to learn about them.

When we write a class that uses code with a chance of failure, we can prepare the users of our class by using exceptions with `try`, `catch`, and `finally`.

We can write methods in our classes using the `throws` Java keyword at the end of the signature – a bit like this perhaps:

```
public void somePrecariousMethod() throws someException{
    // Risky code goes here
}
```

Now any code that uses the `somePrecariousMethod` method will need to **handle** the exception. The way that we handle exceptions is by wrapping code in `try` and `catch` blocks – perhaps like this:

```
try{
    ...
    somePrecariousMethod();
    ...
}catch(someException e){
    Log.e("Exception:" + e, "Uh ohh")
    // Take action if possible
}
```

Optionally, we can also add a `finally` block if we want to take any further action after the `try` and `catch` blocks:

```
finally{
    // More action here
}
```

In our Note to Self app, we will take the minimum amount of action to handle exceptions and simply output an error to logcat, but you could do things such as notify the user, retry the operation, or put into action some clever back-up plan.

Backing up user data in Note to Self

So, with our newfound insight into exceptions, let's modify our Note to Self code, and then we can be introduced to the `JSONObject` and `JSONException` classes.

First, let's make some minor modifications to our `Note` class. Add some more members that will act as the key in a key-value pair for each aspect of our `Note` class:

```
private static final String JSON_TITLE = "title";
private static final String JSON_DESCRIPTION = "description";
private static final String JSON_IDEA = "idea";
private static final String JSON_TODO = "todo";
private static final String JSON_IMPORTANT = "important";
```

Now add a constructor and an empty default constructor that receives `JSONObject` and throws `JSONException`. The body of the constructor initializes each of the members that defines the properties of a single `Note` object by calling the `getString` or `getBoolean` method of `JSONObject`, passing in the key as an argument. We also provide an empty default constructor, which is required now that we are providing our specialized constructor:

```
// Constructor
// Only used when new is called with a JSONObject
public Note(JSONObject jo) throws JSONException {

    mTitle =  jo.getString(JSON_TITLE);
    mDescription = jo.getString(JSON_DESCRIPTION);
    mIdea = jo.getBoolean(JSON_IDEA);
```

```
    mTodo = jo.getBoolean(JSON_TODO);
    mImportant = jo.getBoolean(JSON_IMPORTANT);
}


// Now we must provide an empty default constructor
// for when we create a Note as we provide a
// specialized constructor.
public Note (){


}
```

You will need to import the JSONException and JSONObject classes:

```
import org.json.JSONException;
import org.json.JSONObject;
```

The next code we will see will load the member variables of a given Note object into JSONObject. This is where the Note object's members are packed up as a single JSONObject ready for when the actual serialization takes place.

All we need to do is call the put method with the appropriate key and the matching member variable. This method returns JSONObject (we will see where in a minute) and it also throws a JSONObject exception. Add the code we have just discussed:

```
public JSONObject convertToJSON() throws JSONException{


    JSONObject jo = new JSONObject();


    jo.put(JSON_TITLE, mTitle);
    jo.put(JSON_DESCRIPTION, mDescription);
    jo.put(JSON_IDEA, mIdea);
    jo.put(JSON_TODO, mTodo);
    jo.put(JSON_IMPORTANT, mImportant);


    return jo;
}
```

Now let's make a `JSONSerializer` class that will perform the actual serialization and deserialization. Create a new class and call it `JSONSerializer`.

Let's split it up into a few chunks and talk about what we are doing as we code each chunk.

First, the declaration and a couple of member variables: a string to hold the filename where the data will be saved and a `Context` object that is necessary in Android to write data to a file. Add the highlighted code inside the class you just created:

```
public class JSONSerializer {

    private String mFilename;
    private Context mContext;

    // All the rest of the code for the class goes here

}// End of class
```

> **Note**
>
> You will need to import the `Context` class:
>
> `import android.content.Context;`

The previous code shows that the closing curly brace of the class and all the code that follows for this class should be entered inside of it. Here is the very straightforward constructor where we initialize the two member variables that are passed in as parameters. Add the constructor for `JSONSerializer`:

```
public JSONSerializer(String fn, Context con){
    mFilename = fn;
    mContext = con;
}
```

Now we can start coding the real guts of the class. The `save` method is next. It first creates a `JSONArray` object, which is a specialized `ArrayList` class for handling JSON objects.

Next, the code uses an enhanced `for` loop to go through all the `Note` objects in the `notes` array list and convert them to JSON objects using the `convertToJSON` method from the `Note` class, which we added previously. Then, we load these converted `JSONObject` instances into `jArray`.

Next, the code uses a `Writer` instance and an `OutputStream` instance combined to write the data to an actual file. Notice the `OutputStream` instance needed the `mContext` object to be initialized. Add the code we have just discussed:

```java
public void save(List<Note> notes)
    throws IOException, JSONException{

    // Make an array in JSON format
    JSONArray jArray = new JSONArray();

    // And load it with the notes
    for (Note n : notes)
        jArray.put(n.convertToJSON());

    // Now write it to the private disk space of our app
    Writer writer = null;
    try {
        OutputStream out =
        mContext.openFileOutput(mFilename,
                mContext.MODE_PRIVATE);

        writer = new OutputStreamWriter(out);
        writer.write(jArray.toString());
    } finally {
        if (writer != null) {

            writer.close();
        }
    }
}
```

You will need to add the following `import` statements for these new classes:

```java
import org.json.JSONArray;
import org.json.JSONException;
import java.io.IOException;
import java.io.OutputStream;
import java.io.OutputStreamWriter;
```

```
import java.io.Writer;
import java.util.List;
```

Now for the de-serialization – loading the data. This time, as we might expect, the method receives no parameters but instead returns an `ArrayList` instance. An `InputStream` instance is created using `mContext.openFileInput` and our file containing all our data is opened.

We use a `while` loop to append all the data to a string and use our new `Note` constructor, which extracts JSON data to regular primitive variables to unpack each `JSONObject` into a `Note` object and add it to the `ArrayList` that is returned to the calling code:

```
public ArrayList<Note> load() throws IOException,
JSONException{
    ArrayList<Note> noteList = new ArrayList<Note>();
    BufferedReader reader = null;
    try {

        InputStream in =
        mContext.openFileInput(mFilename);
        reader = new BufferedReader(new
        InputStreamReader(in));
        StringBuilder jsonString = new StringBuilder();
        String line = null;

        while ((line = reader.readLine()) != null) {

            jsonString.append(line);
        }


        JSONArray jArray = (JSONArray) new
            JSONTokener(jsonString.toString()
            ).nextValue();

        for (int i = 0; i < jArray.length(); i++) {
            noteList.add(new
```

```
                    Note(jArray.getJSONObject(i)));
        }
    } catch (FileNotFoundException e) {
        // we will ignore this one, since it happens
        // when we start fresh. You could add a log here.
    } finally {// This will always run
        if (reader != null)
            reader.close();
    }


    return noteList;
}
```

You will need to add these imports:

```
import org.json.JSONTokener;
import java.io.BufferedReader;
import java.io.FileNotFoundException;
import java.io.InputStream;
import java.io.InputStreamReader;
import java.util.ArrayList;
```

Now all we need to do is put our new class to work in the MainActivity class. Add
a new member after the MainActivity declaration as highlighted next. Also, remove
the initialization of noteList to leave just the declaration as we will now initialize it
with some new code in the onCreate method. I have commented out the line you need
to delete:

```
public class MainActivity extends AppCompatActivity {


    private JSONSerializer mSerializer;


    //private List<Note> noteList = new ArrayList<>();
    private List<Note> noteList;
```

Now, in the onCreate method, we initialize mSerializer by calling the
JSONSerializer constructor with the filename and getApplicationContext(),
which returns the Context instance of the application and is required. We can then use
the JSONSerializer load method to load any saved data. Add this new, highlighted
code after the code that handles the floating action button. This new code must come
before we handle the RecyclerView instance:

```java
...
FloatingActionButton fab =
        (FloatingActionButton) findViewById(R.id.fab);

fab.setOnClickListener(new View.OnClickListener() {
        @Override
        public void onClick(View view) {
                DialogNewNote dialog = new DialogNewNote();
                dialog.show(getSupportFragmentManager(), "");
        }
});

    mSerializer = new JSONSerializer("NoteToSelf.json",
    getApplicationContext());

    try {
            noteList = mSerializer.load();
    } catch (Exception e) {
            noteList = new ArrayList<Note>();
            Log.e("Error loading notes: ", "", e);
    }

    recyclerView =
            findViewById(R.id.recyclerView);

mAdapter = new NoteAdapter(this, noteList);
    ...
```

> **Note**
>
> You need to import the Log class at this point:
>
> ```
> import android.util.Log;
> ```
>
> I have shown a great deal of context in the previous code because its positioning is essential for it to work. If you are having any problems getting this to run, be sure to compare it to the code in the download bundle in the Chapter 17/java folder.

Now we can add a new method to our MainActivity class so that that we can call it to save all our user's data. All this new method does is call the save method of the JSONSerializer class, passing in the required list of Note objects:

```
public void saveNotes(){
    try{
        mSerializer.save(noteList);

    }catch(Exception e){
        Log.e("Error Saving Notes","", e);
    }
}
```

Now, just as we did when saving our user's settings, we will override the onPause method to save our user's note data. Be sure to add this code in the MainActivity class:

```
@Override
protected void onPause(){
    super.onPause();

    saveNotes();

}
```

That's it. We can now run the app and add as many notes as we like. ArrayList will store them all in our running app, our RecyclerAdapter will manage displaying them in RecyclerView, and now JSON will take care of loading them to disk and loading them back as well.

Frequently asked questions

1. I didn't understand everything in this chapter – am I not cut out to be
    a programmer?

    This chapter introduced many new classes, concepts, and methods. If your
    head is aching a little, that is to be expected. If some of the detail is unclear,
    don't let that hold you back. Proceed with the next couple of chapters (they are
    much more straightforward), then revisit this one and examine the completed
    code files.

2. So, how does serialization work in detail?

    Serialization really is a vast topic. It is possible to write apps your whole life and
    never really need to understand it. It is the type of topic that might be the subject
    of a computer science degree. If you are curious to know more, have a look at this
    article: `https://en.wikipedia.org/wiki/Serialization`.

Summary

At this point in our journey through the Android API, it is worth taking stock of what
we know. We can lay out our own UI designs and choose from a wide and diverse range
of widgets to allow the user to interact with the UI. We can create multiple screens as well
as pop-up dialogs and we can capture comprehensive user data. Furthermore, we can now
make this data persist.

Certainly, there is a lot more to the Android API still to learn, even beyond what this
book will teach you, but the point is that we know enough now to plan and implement
a working app. You could just get started on your own app right now.

If you have the urge to start your own project right away, then my advice is to go ahead
and do it. Don't wait until you consider yourself an "expert" or more ready. Reading this
book and, more importantly, implementing the apps will make you a better Android
programmer, but nothing will teach you faster than designing and implementing your
own app! It is perfectly possible to read through this book and work on your own
project(s) simultaneously.

In the next chapter, we will add the finishing touches to this app by making it multilingual.
This is quite quick and easy.

18
Localization

This chapter is quick and simple and what we will learn to do here can make your app accessible to millions more potential users. We will see how to add additional languages. We will also see how adding text the correct way via string resources benefits us when it comes to adding multiple languages.

In this chapter, we will cover the following:

- Making the Note to Self app multilingual by adding the Spanish and German languages
- Learning how to use string resources more fully

Let's get started.

Technical requirements

You can find the code files present in this chapter on GitHub at `https://github.com/PacktPublishing/Android-Programming-for-Beginners-Third-Edition/tree/main/chapter%2018`.

Making the Note to Self app accessible for Spanish and German speakers

First, we need to add some folders to our project – one for each new language. The text is classed as a **resource** and consequently needs to go in the `res` folder. Follow these steps to add Spanish and German support to the project.

> **Important Note**
>
> While the source files for this project are provided in the `Chapter 18` folder, they are just for reference. You need to go through the processes described next to achieve multilingual functionality.

Adding Spanish language support

Follow the next steps to add Spanish language support:

1. Right-click on the **res** folder, and then select **New | Android resource directory**. In the **Directory name** field, type `values-es`.

2. Left-click **OK**.

3. Now we need to add a file in which we can place all our Spanish translations. Right-click on **res**, and then select **New | Android resource file** and type `strings.xml` in the **File name** field. Type `values-es` in the **Directory name** field.

4. Left-click **OK**.

At this stage, we have a new folder for Spanish translations with a `strings.xml` file inside for the string resources. Let's do the same for the German language.

Adding German language support

Follow these steps to add German language support:

1. Right-click on the **res** folder, and then select **New | Android resource directory**. In the **Directory name** field, type `values-de`.

2. Left-click **OK**.

3. Now we need to add a file in which we can place all our German translations. Right-click on **res**, and then select **New | Android resource file** and type `strings.xml` in the **File name** field. Type `values-de` in the **Directory name** field.

4. Left-click **OK**.

This is what the `strings.xml` folder looks like. You are probably wondering where the `strings.xml` folder came from as it doesn't correspond to the structure we seemed to be creating in the previous steps. Android Studio is helping us (apparently) to organize our files and folders as is required by the Android operating system. You can, however, see the Spanish and German files indicated by their country-specific extensions, **es** and **de**, respectively:

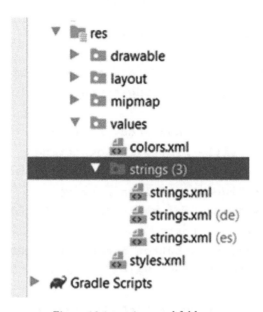

Figure 18.1 – strings.xml folder

Now we can add the translations to the files.

Adding the string resources

As we know, the `strings.xml` file contains the words that the app will display – words such as "important," "to do," "idea," and more. By having a `strings.xml` file for each language we want to support, we can then leave Android to choose the appropriate text depending on the language settings of the user.

As you go through the following, notice that although we place the translation of whatever word we are translating as the value, the `name` attribute remains the same. If you think about it, this is logical because it is the `name` attribute that we refer to in our layout files.

Let's provide the translations, see what we have achieved, and then come back and discuss what we will do about the text in our Java code. The simplest way to achieve this code is to copy and paste the code from the original `strings.xml` file and then edit the values of each of the `name` attributes:

1. Open the `strings.xml` file by double-clicking it. Be sure to choose the one next to the **(es)** postfix. Edit the file to look like this:

```xml
<?xml version="1.0" encoding="utf-8"?>
<resources>
<string name="app_name">Nota a sí mismo</string>
<string name="action_settings">Configuración</string>

<string name="action_add">add</string>
<string name="title_hint">Título</string>
<string name="description_hint">Descripción</string>
<string name="idea_text">Idea</string>
<string name="important_text">Importante</string>
<string name="todo_text">Que hacer</string>
<string name="cancel_button">Cancelar</string>
<string name="ok_button">Vale</string>

<string name="settings_title">Configuración</string>

</resources>
```

2. Open the `strings.xml` file by double-clicking it. Be sure to choose the one next to the **(de)** postfix. Edit the file to look like this:

```xml
<?xml version="1.0" encoding="utf-8"?>
<resources>
<string name="app_name">Hinweis auf selbst</string>
<string name="action_settings">Einstellungen</string>

<string name="action_add">add</string>
<string name="title_hint">Titel</string>
<string name="description_hint">Beschreibung</string>
<string name="idea_text">Idee</string>
<string name="important_text">Wichtig</string>
```

```xml
<string name="todo_text">zu tun</string>
<string name="cancel_button">Abbrechen</string>
<string name="ok_button">Okay</string>


<string name="settings_title">Einstellungen</string>
</resources>
```

> **Note**
> If you don't provide all the string resources in the extra (Spanish and German) `strings.xml` files, then the missing resources will be taken from the default file.

What we have done is provided two translations. Android knows which translation is for which language because of the folders they are placed in. Furthermore, we have used a **string identifier** (the `name` attribute) to refer to the translations. Look back at the previous code and you will see that the same identifier is used for both translations as well as in the original `strings.xml` file.

You can even localize to different versions of a language, for example, US or UK English. The complete list of codes can be found here: `http://stackoverflow.com/questions/7973023/what-is-the-list-of-supported-languages-locales-on-android`. You can even localize resources such as images and sound. Find out more about this here: `http://developer.android.com/guide/topics/resources/localization.html`.

The translations were copy and pasted from Google Translate, so it is very likely that some of the translations are far from correct. Doing translation on the cheap like this can be an effective way to get an app with a basic set of string resources onto the devices of users who speak different languages to yourself. Once you start needing any depth of translation, perhaps in the case of the lines of a story-driven game or a social media app, you will certainly benefit from having the translation done by a human professional.

The purpose of this exercise is to show how Android works, not how to translate.

> **Note**
> My sincere apologies to any Spanish or German speakers who can likely see the limitations of the translations provided here.

Now that we have the translations, we can see them in action, up to a point.

Running Note to Self in German or Spanish

Run the app to see whether it is working as normal. Now we can change the localization settings to see it in Spanish. Different devices vary slightly in how to do this, but the Pixel 3 emulator options are as follows:

1. Choose **Settings | System | Languages and input | Add a language**. Next, select **Español** and you will then be able to switch between Spanish and English from a list.

2. Left-click and drag **Español (Estados Unidos)** so that it is at the top of the list.

Congratulations, your emulator is now defaulting to Spanish. Once you are done with this chapter, you can drag your preferred language back to the top of the list.

Now you can run the app in the usual way. Here are some screenshots of the app running in Spanish. I have photoshopped a couple of screenshots side by side to show different screens of the Note to Self app:

Figure 18.2 – The app running in Spanish

In the screenshots, you can clearly see that our app is translated to Spanish, mainly. Obviously, the text that the user enters will be in whatever language they speak; that is not a flaw of our app. However, look at the screenshots closely and notice that I have pointed out a couple of places where the text is still in English. We still have some untranslated text in each of our dialog windows.

This is because the text is contained within our Java code directly. As we have seen, it is easy to use string resources in multiple languages and then refer to them in our layouts, but how do we refer to string resources from our Java code?

Making the translations work in Java code

The first thing to do is create the resources in each of the three `strings.xml` files. Here are the two resources that need adding to the three different files.

In `strings.xml` (without any country postfix), add these two resources within the `<resources></resources>` tags:

```
<string name="add_new_note">Add a new note</string>
<string name="your_note">Your note</string>
```

In `strings.xml` with the **(es)** postfix, add these two resources within the `<resources></resources>` tags:

```
<string name="add_new_note">Agregar una nueva nota</string>
<string name="your_note">Su nota</string>
```

In `strings.xml` with the **(de)** postfix, add these two resources within the `<resources></resources>` tags:

```
<string name="add_new_note">Eine neue Note hinzufügen</string>
<string name="your_note">Ihre Notiz</string>
```

Next, we need to edit some Java code to refer to a resource instead of a hardcoded string.

Open the `DialogNewNote.java` file and find this line of code:

```
builder.setView(dialogView).setMessage("Add a new note");
```

Edit it as shown next to use the string resource we just added instead of the hardcoded text:

```
builder.setView(dialogView).setMessage(getResources().
getString(R.string.add_new_note));
```

The new code uses the chained getResources.getString methods to replace the previously hardcoded "Add a new note" text. Look closely and you will see that the argument sent to the getString method is the R.string.add_new_note string identifier.

The R.string code refers to the string resources in the res folder and add_new_note is our identifier. Android will then be able to decide which version (default, Spanish, or German) is appropriate based on the locale of the device on which the app is running.

We have one more hardcoded string to change.

Open the DialogShowNote.java file and find this line of code:

```
builder.setView(dialogView).setMessage("Your Note");
```

Edit it as shown next to use the string resource we just added instead of the hardcoded text:

```
builder.setView(dialogView).setMessage(getResources().
getString(R.string.your_note));
```

The new code again uses the chained getResources.getString methods to replace the previously hardcoded "Your note" text. Again, the argument sent to getString is the string identifier, in this case, R.string.your_note.

Android can now decide which version (default, Spanish, or German) is appropriate based upon the locale of the device on which the app is running. The next screenshot shows that the **New note** screen now has the opening text in the appropriate language:

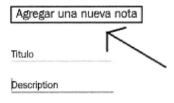

Figure 18.3 – New note screen

You can add as many string resources as you like. As a reminder from *Chapter 3, Exploring Android Studio and the Project Structure*, note that using string resources is the recommended way to add any text to all projects. The tutorials in this book (apart from Note to Self) will tend to hardcode them to make a more compact tutorial.

Summary

We have seen how we can cater to regions of the world that speak a different language to us. We can now go global with our apps, as well as adding more flexible string resources instead of hardcoding all the text.

In the next chapter, we will see how we can add cool animations to our apps using animations and interpolators.

19
Animations and Interpolations

Here, we will see how we can use the `Animation` class to make our UI a little less static and a bit more interesting. As we have come to expect, the Android API will allow us to do some quite advanced things with relatively straightforward code, and the `Animation` class is no different.

This chapter can be approximately divided into these parts:

- An introduction to how animations in Android work and are implemented
- An introduction to a UI widget we haven't explored yet, `SeekBar`
- Creating a working animation app

First, let's explore how animations in Android work.

Technical requirements

You can find the code files present in this chapter on GitHub at `https://github.com/PacktPublishing/Android-Programming-for-Beginners-Third-Edition/tree/main/chapter%2019`.

Animations in Android

The normal way to create an animation in Android is through XML. We can write XML animations and then load and play them in Java, on a specified UI widget. So, for example, we can write an animation that fades in and out five times over 3 seconds, then play that animation on an `ImageView` or any other widget. We can think of these XML animations as a script as they define the type, order, and timing.

Let's explore some of the different properties we can assign to our animations, then how to use them in our Java code, and finally, we can make a neat animations app to try it all out.

Designing cool animations in XML

We have learned that XML can be used to describe animations as well as UI layouts, but let's find out exactly how. We can state the properties of an animation that describe the starting and ending appearance of a widget. The XML can then be loaded by our Java code by referencing the name of the XML file that contains it and turning it into a usable Java object, again not unlike a UI layout.

Here is a quick look at some of the animation property pairs we can state to create an animation. Straight after we have looked at some XML, we will see how to use it in our Java.

Fading in and out

Alpha is the measure of transparency. So, by stating the starting `fromAlpha` and ending `toAlpha` values, we can fade items in and out. A value of `0.0` is invisible and `1.0` is an object's normal appearance. Steadily moving between the two makes a fading-in effect:

```
<alpha
    android:fromAlpha="0.0"
    android:toAlpha="1.0" />
```

Moving

We can move an object within our UI by using a similar technique. `fromXDelta` and `toXDelta` can have their values set as a percentage of the size of the object being animated.

The following code moves an object from left to right at a distance equal to the width of the object itself:

```
<translate
    android:fromXDelta="-100%"
    android:toXDelta="0%"/>
```

In addition, there are the `fromYDelta` and `toYDelta` properties for animating up and down.

Scaling or stretching

`fromXScale` and `toXScale` will increase or decrease the scale of an object. As an example, the following code will change the object, running the animation from normal size to invisible:

```
<scale
    android:fromXScale="1.0"
    android:fromYScale="0.0"/>
```

As another example, we could shrink the object to a tenth of its usual size using `android:fromYScale="0.1"` or make it 10 times bigger using `android:fromYScale="10.0"`.

Controlling the duration

Of course, none of these animations would be especially interesting if they just instantly arrived at their conclusion. To make our animations more interesting, we can, therefore, set their duration in milliseconds. A millisecond is one-thousandth of a second. We can also make the timing easier, especially in relation to other animations, by setting `startOffset`, also in milliseconds.

The next code would begin an animation one-third of a second after we started it and it would take two-thirds of a second to complete:

```
    android:duration="666"
    android:startOffset="333"
```

Rotating animations

If you want to spin something around, just use `fromDegrees` and `toDegrees`. This next code, probably predictably, will spin a widget around in a complete circle because, of course, there are 360 degrees in a circle:

```
<rotate android:fromDegrees="360"
        android:toDegrees="0"
/>
```

Repeating animations

Repetition might be important in some animations, perhaps a wobble or shake effect, so we can add a `repeatCount` property. In addition, we can specify how the animation is repeated by setting `repeatMode`.

The following code would repeat an animation 10 times, each time reversing the direction of the animation. The `repeatMode` property is relative to the current state of the animation. What this means is that if you, for example, rotated a button from 0 to 360 degrees, the second part of the animation (the first repeat) would rotate the other way from 360 back to 0. The third part of the animation (the second repeat) would again reverse and rotate from 0 to 360:

```
android:repeatMode="reverse"
android:repeatCount="10"
```

Using the 360-degree spin example, the preceding code would spin a widget through 360 degrees to the right, then back 360 degrees to the left, five times. This is 10 repeats, reversing after each.

Combining an animation's properties with set

To combine groups of these effects, we need to use `set`. This code shows how we can combine all the previous code snippets we have just seen into an actual XML animation that will compile:

```
<?xml version="1.0" encoding="utf-8"?>
<set xmlns:android="http://schemas.android.com/apk/res/android"
            ...All our animations go here
</set>
```

We still haven't seen any Java with which to bring these animations to life. Let's fix that now.

Instantiating animations and controlling them with Java code

This next snippet of Java code shows how we would declare an object of the `Animation` type, initialize it with an animation contained in an XML file named `fade_in.xml`, and start the animation on an `ImageView` widget. Soon we will do this in a project and see where to put the XML animations as well:

```java
// Declare an Animation object
Animation animFadeIn;

// Initialize it
animFadeIn = AnimationUtils.loadAnimation(
getApplicationContext(), R.anim.fade_in);

// Get an ImageView from the UI in the usual way
ImageView findViewById(R.id.imageView);

// Start the animation on the ImageView
imageView.startAnimation(animFadeIn);
```

We already have quite a powerful arsenal of animations and control features for things such as timing. But the Android API gives us a little bit more than this as well.

More animation features

We can listen for the status of animations much as we can listen for clicks on a button. We can also use **interpolators** to make our animations more life-like and pleasing. Let's look at listeners first.

Listeners

If we implement the `AnimationListener` interface, we can indeed listen to the status of animations by overriding the three methods that tell us when something has occurred. We could then act based on these events.

OnAnimationEnd announces the end of an animation, onAnimationRepeat is called each and every time an animation begins a repeat, and perhaps predictably, onAnimationStart is called when an animation has started animating. This might not be the same time as when startAnimation is called if startOffset is set in the animation's XML:

```
@Override
public void onAnimationEnd(Animation animation) {
    // Take some action here

}

@Override
public void onAnimationRepeat(Animation animation) {

    // Take some action here
}

@Override
public void onAnimationStart(Animation animation) {

    // Take some action here

}
```

We will see how AnimationListener works in the animation demo app, as well as putting another widget, SeekBar, into action.

Animation interpolators

If you can think back to high school, you might remember exciting lessons about calculating acceleration. If we animate something at a constant speed, then at first glance, things might seem OK. If we then compare the animation to another that uses gradual acceleration, then the latter will almost certainly be more pleasing to watch.

It is possible that if we were not told that the only difference between the two animations was that one used acceleration and the other didn't, we wouldn't be able to say why we preferred it. Our brains are more receptive to things that conform to the norms of the world around us. This is why adding a bit of real-world physics such as acceleration and deceleration improves our animations.

The last thing we want to do, however, is start doing a bunch of mathematical calculations just to slide a button onto the screen or spin some text in a circle.

This is where **interpolators** come in. They are animation modifiers that we can set in a single line of code within our XML.

Some examples of interpolators are `accelerate_interpolator` and `cycle_interpolator`:

```
android:interpolator="@android:anim/accelerate_
interpolator"android:interpolator="@android:anim/cycle_
interpolator"/>
```

We will put some interpolators, along with some XML animations and the related Java code, into action next.

> **Note**
>
> You can learn more about interpolators and the Android `Animation` class on the developer website here: `http://developer.android.com/guide/topics/resources/animation-resource.html`.

Animation demo app – introducing SeekBar

That's enough theory, especially with something that should be visual. Let's build an animation demo app that explores everything we have just discussed and a bit more.

This app involves small amounts of code in lots of different files. Therefore, I have tried to make it plain which code is in which file, so you can keep track of what is going on. This will make the Java we write for this app more understandable as well.

The app will demonstrate rotations, fades, translations, animation events, interpolations, and controlling duration with a `SeekBar` widget. The best way to explain what the `SeekBar` widget does is to build it and then watch it in action.

Laying out the animation demo

Create a new project called `Animation Demo` using the **Empty Activity** template, leaving all the other settings at their defaults. As usual, should you wish to speed things up by copy and pasting the layout, the Java code, or the animation XML, it can all be found in the `Chapter 19` folder.

Use the following reference screenshot of the finished layout to help guide you through the next steps:

Figure 19.1 – Finished layout

Here is how to lay out the UI for this app:

1. Open `activity_main.xml` in the design view of the editor window.

2. Delete the default **Hello world!** `TextView`.

3. Add an `ImageView` widget to the top-center of the layout. Use the previous reference screenshot to guide you. Use `@mipmap/ic_launcher` to show the Android robot in the `ImageView` widget when prompted to do so by selecting **Project | ic_launcher** in the pop-up **Resources** window.

4. Set the `id` property of the `ImageView` widget to `imageView`.

    Directly below the `ImageView` widget, add a `TextView` widget. Set the `id` attribute to `textStatus`. I made my `TextView` widget a little bigger by dragging its edges and changed its `textSize` attribute to `40sp`.

5. Now we will add a large selection of **Button** widgets to the layout. The exact positioning is not vital but the exact id property values we add to them later in the tutorial will be. Follow this next screenshot to lay out 12 buttons. Alter the text attribute on each so that your buttons have the same text as those in the next screenshot. The text attributes are detailed specifically in the next step in case the screenshot isn't clear enough:

Figure 19.2 – text attributes

> **Note**
>
> To make the process of laying out the buttons quicker, lay them out just approximately at first, then add the text attributes from the next step, and then fine-tune the button positions to get a neat layout.

6. Add the text values as they are in the screenshot. Here are all the values from left to right and top to bottom: FADE IN, FADE OUT, FADE IN OUT, ZOOM IN, ZOOM OUT, LEFT RIGHT, RIGHT LEFT, TOP BOT, BOUNCE, FLASH, ROTATE LEFT, and ROTATE RIGHT.

7. Add a SeekBar widget from the **Widgets** category of the palette, on the left, below the buttons. Set the id property to seekBarSpeed and the max property to 5000. This means that the seek bar will hold a value between 0 and 5000 as it is dragged by the user from left to right. We will see how we can read and use this data soon.

8. We want to make the SeekBar widget much wider. To achieve this, you use the exact same technique as with any widget; just drag the edges of the widget. However, as the seek bar is quite small, it is hard to increase its size without accidentally selecting the constraint handles. To overcome this problem, zoom in to the design by holding the *Ctrl* key and rolling the middle mouse wheel forward. You can then grab the edges of the seek bar without touching the constraint handles. I have shown this in action in the next screenshot:

Figure 19.3 – Grab the edges of the seek bar

9. Now add a TextView widget just to the right of the SeekBar widget and set its id property to textSeekerSpeed.

10. Tweak the positions to look like the reference image at the start of these steps, and then click the **Infer Constraints** button to lock the positions. Of course, you can do this manually if you want the practice.

11. Next add the following id properties to the buttons, as identified by the text property that you have already set. If you are asked whether you want to **Update usages…** as you enter these values, select **Yes**:

Existing text property	Value of id property to set
Fade In	btnFadeIn
Fade Out	btnFadeOut
Fade In Out	btnFadeInOut
Zoom In	btnZoomIn
Zoom Out	btnZoomOut
Left Right	btnLeftRight
Right Left	btnRightLeft
Top Bot	btnTopBottom
Bounce	btnBounce
Flash	btnFlash
Rotate Left	btnRotateLeft
Rotate Right	btnRotateRight

We will see how to use this newcomer to our UI (SeekBar) when we get to coding the MainActivity class in a few sections time.

Coding the XML animations

Right-click on the **res** folder and select **New | Android resource directory**. Enter anim in the **Directory name** field and left-click **OK**.

Now, right-click on the new **anim** directory and select **New | Animation resource file**. In the **File name** field, type fade_in, and then left-click **OK**. Delete the entire contents and add this code to create the animation:

```xml
<?xml version="1.0" encoding="utf-8"?>
<set xmlns:android="http://schemas.android.com/apk/res/android"
android:fillAfter="true" >

<alpha
android:fromAlpha="0.0"
android:interpolator="
@android:anim/accelerate_interpolator"

android:toAlpha="1.0" />
</set>
```

Right-click on the **anim** directory and select **New | Animation resource file**. In the **File name** field, type fade_out, and then left-click **OK**. Delete the entire contents and add this code to create the animation:

```xml
<?xml version="1.0" encoding="utf-8"?>
<set xmlns:android="http://schemas.android.com/apk/res/android"
android:fillAfter="true" >

    <alpha
        android:fromAlpha="1.0"
        android:interpolator="
        @android:anim/accelerate_interpolator"
        android:toAlpha="0.0" />
</set>
```

Right-click on the **anim** directory and select **New | Animation resource file**. In the
File name field, type `fade_in_out`, and then left-click **OK**. Delete the entire contents
and add this code to create the animation:

```xml
<?xml version="1.0" encoding="utf-8"?>
<set xmlns:android="http://schemas.android.com/apk/res/android"
    android:fillAfter="true" >

<alpha
android:fromAlpha="0.0"
android:interpolator="
@android:anim/accelerate_interpolator"

android:toAlpha="1.0" />

<alpha
android:fromAlpha="1.0"
android:interpolator="
@android:anim/accelerate_interpolator"

android:toAlpha="0.0" />

</set>
```

Right-click on the **anim** directory and select **New | Animation resource file**. In the
File name field, type `zoom_in`, and then left-click **OK**. Delete the entire contents and
add this code to create the animation:

```xml
<set xmlns:android="http://schemas.android.com/apk/res/android"
    android:fillAfter="true" >

    <scale
        android:fromXScale="1"
        android:fromYScale="1"
        android:pivotX="50%"
        android:pivotY="50%"
        android:toXScale="6"
        android:toYScale="6" >
```

```
        </scale>

    </set>
```

Right-click on the **anim** directory and select **New** | **Animation resource file**. In the **File name** field, type zoom_out, and then left-click **OK**. Delete the entire contents and add this code to create the animation:

```
<?xml version="1.0" encoding="utf-8"?>
<set xmlns:android="http://schemas.android.com/apk/res/
android">
    <scale
        android:fromXScale="6"
        android:fromYScale="6"
        android:pivotX="50%"
        android:pivotY="50%"
        android:toXScale="1"
        android:toYScale="1" >
    </scale>

</set>
```

Right-click on the **anim** directory and select **New** | **Animation resource file**. In the **File name** field, type left_right, and then left-click **OK**. Delete the entire contents and add this code to create the animation:

```
<?xml version="1.0" encoding="utf-8"?>
<set xmlns:android="http://schemas.android.com/apk/res/
android">
    <translate

        android:fromXDelta="-500%"
        android:toXDelta="0%"/>
</set>
```

Right-click on the **anim** directory and select **New | Animation resource file**. In the **File name** field, type `right_left`, and then left-click **OK**. Delete the entire contents and add this code to create the animation:

```xml
<?xml version="1.0" encoding="utf-8"?>
<set xmlns:android="http://schemas.android.com/apk/res/
android">
    <translate
        android:fillAfter="false"
        android:fromXDelta="500%"
        android:toXDelta="0%"/>
</set>
```

Right-click on the **anim** directory and select **New | Animation resource file**. In the **File name** field, type `top_bot`, and then left-click **OK**. Delete the entire contents and add this code to create the animation:

```xml
<?xml version="1.0" encoding="utf-8"?>
<set xmlns:android="http://schemas.android.com/apk/res/
android">
    <translate
        android:fillAfter="false"
        android:fromYDelta="-100%"
        android:toYDelta="0%"/>
</set>
```

Right-click on the **anim** directory and select **New | Animation resource file**. In the **File name** field, type `flash`, and then left-click **OK**. Delete the entire contents and add this code to create the animation:

```xml
<?xml version="1.0" encoding="utf-8"?>
<set xmlns:android="http://schemas.android.com/apk/res/
android">
    <alpha android:fromAlpha="0.0"
        android:toAlpha="1.0"
        android:interpolator="
        @android:anim/accelerate_interpolator"

        android:repeatMode="reverse"
```

```
            android:repeatCount="10"/>
</set>
```

Right-click on the **anim** directory and select **New | Animation resource file**. In the **File name** field, type bounce, and then left-click **OK**. Delete the entire contents and add this code to create the animation:

```
<?xml version="1.0" encoding="utf-8"?>
<set xmlns:android="http://schemas.android.com/apk/res/android"
    android:fillAfter="true"
    android:interpolator="
    @android:anim/bounce_interpolator">

    <scale
        android:fromXScale="1.0"
        android:fromYScale="0.0"
        android:toXScale="1.0"
        android:toYScale="1.0" />

</set>
```

Right-click on the **anim** directory and select **New | Animation resource file**. In the **File name** field, type rotate_left, and then left-click **OK**. Delete the entire contents and add this code to create the animation. Here we see something new, pivotX="50%" and pivotY="50%". This makes the rotate animation central on the widget that will be animated. We can think of this as setting the pivot point of the animation:

```
<?xml version="1.0" encoding="utf-8"?>
<set xmlns:android="http://schemas.android.com/apk/res/
android">
    <rotate android:fromDegrees="360"
        android:toDegrees="0"
        android:pivotX="50%"
        android:pivotY="50%"
        android:interpolator="
        @android:anim/cycle_interpolator"/>

</set>
```

Right-click on the **anim** directory and select **New | Animation resource file**. In the **File name** field, type `rotate_right`, and then left-click **OK**. Delete the entire contents and add this code to create the animation:

```xml
<?xml version="1.0" encoding="utf-8"?>
<set xmlns:android="http://schemas.android.com/apk/res/
android">
    <rotate android:fromDegrees="0"
        android:toDegrees="360"
        android:pivotX="50%"
        android:pivotY="50%"
        android:interpolator="
        @android:anim/cycle_interpolator"/>

</set>
```

Now we can write the Java code to add our animations to our UI.

Wiring up the animation demo app with Java

Open the `MainActivity.java` file. Now, below the class declaration, we can declare the following member variables for the animations:

```java
Animation animFadeIn;
Animation animFadeOut;
Animation animFadeInOut;

Animation animZoomIn;
Animation animZoomOut;

Animation animLeftRight;
Animation animRightLeft;
Animation animTopBottom;

Animation animBounce;
Animation animFlash;

Animation animRotateLeft;
Animation animRotateRight;
```

Now add these member variables below for the UI widgets after the previous code:

```
ImageView imageView;
TextView textStatus;


Button btnFadeIn;
Button btnFadeOut;
Button btnFadeInOut;
Button zoomIn;
Button zoomOut;
Button leftRight;
Button rightLeft;
Button topBottom;
Button bounce;
Button flash;
Button rotateLeft;
Button rotateRight;
SeekBar seekBarSpeed;
TextView textSeekerSpeed;
```

> **Note**
>
> You will need to add the following import statements at this point:
>
> import android.view.animation.Animation;
>
> import android.widget.Button;
>
> import android.widget.ImageView;
>
> import android.widget.SeekBar;
>
> import android.widget.TextView;

Next, we add an int member variable that will be used to track the current value/position of the seek bar:

```
int seekSpeedProgress;
```

Now let's call two new methods from the `onCreate` method after the call to the `setContentView` method:

```
@Override
protected void onCreate(Bundle savedInstanceState) {
    super.onCreate(savedInstanceState);
    setContentView(R.layout.activity_main);

    loadAnimations();
    loadUI();
}
```

At this point, the two new lines of code will have errors until we implement the two new methods.

Now we will implement the `loadAnimations` method. Although the code in this method is quite extensive, it is also very straightforward. All we are doing is using the static `loadAnimation` method of the `AnimationUtils` class to initialize each of our `Animation` references with one of our XML animations. Notice also that for the `animFadeIn` `Animation` reference, we also call `setAnimationListener` on it. We will write the methods to listen for events shortly.

Add the `loadAnimations` method:

```
private void loadAnimations(){
    animFadeIn = AnimationUtils.loadAnimation(
    this, R.anim.fade_in);
    animFadeIn.setAnimationListener(this);
    animFadeOut = AnimationUtils.loadAnimation(
    this, R.anim.fade_out);
    animFadeInOut = AnimationUtils.loadAnimation(
    this, R.anim.fade_in_out);

    animZoomIn = AnimationUtils.loadAnimation(
    this, R.anim.zoom_in);
    animZoomOut = AnimationUtils.loadAnimation(
    this, R.anim.zoom_out);

    animLeftRight = AnimationUtils.loadAnimation(
```

```
        this, R.anim.left_right);
    animRightLeft = AnimationUtils.loadAnimation(
        this, R.anim.right_left);
    animTopBottom = AnimationUtils.loadAnimation(
        this, R.anim.top_bot);

    animBounce = AnimationUtils.loadAnimation(
        this, R.anim.bounce);
    animFlash = AnimationUtils.loadAnimation(
        this, R.anim.flash);

    animRotateLeft = AnimationUtils.loadAnimation(
        this, R.anim.rotate_left);
    animRotateRight = AnimationUtils.loadAnimation(
        this, R.anim.rotate_right);
}
```

> **Note**
> You will need to import one new class at this point:
>
> `import android.view.animation.AnimationUtils;`

Implement the `loadUI` method in three sections. First, let's get a reference to the parts of our XML layout in the usual way:

```
private void loadUI(){

    imageView = findViewById(R.id.imageView);
    textStatus = findViewById(R.id.textStatus);

    btnFadeIn = findViewById(R.id.btnFadeIn);
    btnFadeOut = findViewById(R.id.btnFadeOut);
    btnFadeInOut = findViewById(R.id.btnFadeInOut);
    zoomIn = findViewById(R.id.btnZoomIn);
    zoomOut = findViewById(R.id.btnZoomOut);
    leftRight = findViewById(R.id.btnLeftRight);
    rightLeft = findViewById(R.id.btnRightLeft);
```

```
topBottom = findViewById(R.id.btnTopBottom);
bounce = findViewById(R.id.btnBounce);
flash = findViewById(R.id.btnFlash);
rotateLeft = findViewById(R.id.btnRotateLeft);
rotateRight = findViewById(R.id.btnRotateRight);
```

Now we will add a click listener for each button. Add this code immediately after the last block within the loadUI method:

```
btnFadeIn.setOnClickListener(this);
btnFadeOut.setOnClickListener(this);
btnFadeInOut.setOnClickListener(this);
zoomIn.setOnClickListener(this);
zoomOut.setOnClickListener(this);
leftRight.setOnClickListener(this);
rightLeft.setOnClickListener(this);
topBottom.setOnClickListener(this);
bounce.setOnClickListener(this);
flash.setOnClickListener(this);
rotateLeft.setOnClickListener(this);
rotateRight.setOnClickListener(this);
```

> **Note**
>
> The code we just added creates errors in all the lines of code. We can ignore them for now as we will fix them shortly and discuss what happened.

The third and last section of the loadUI method sets up an anonymous class to handle the SeekBar widget. We could have added this as an interface to the MainActivity class as we did with listening for button clicks and animation events, but with a single SeekBar widget like this, it makes sense to handle it directly.

We will override three methods as is required by the interface when implementing OnSeekBarChangeListener:

- A method that detects a change in the position of the seek bar called onProgressChanged

- A method that detects the user starting to change the position called onStartTrackingTouch

- A method that detects when the user has finished using the seek bar called onStopTrackingTouch

To achieve our goals, we only need to add code to the onProgressChanged method but we must still override them all.

All we do in the onProgressChanged method is assign the current value of the seek bar to the seekSpeedProgress member variable so it can be accessed from elsewhere. Then we use this value along with the maximum possible value of the SeekBar widget, obtained by calling seekBarSpeed.getMax(), and output a message to the textSeekerSpeed TextView widget.

Add the code we have just discussed into the loadUI method:

```java
seekBarSpeed = findViewById(R.id.seekBarSpeed);
textSeekerSpeed = findViewById(R.id.textSeekerSpeed);


seekBarSpeed.setOnSeekBarChangeListener(new SeekBar.
OnSeekBarChangeListener() {

    @Override
    public void onProgressChanged(SeekBar seekBar,
    int value, boolean fromUser) {

            seekSpeedProgress = value;
            textSeekerSpeed.setText(""
            + seekSpeedProgress
            + " of "
            + seekBarSpeed.getMax());
    }

    @Override
    public void onStartTrackingTouch(SeekBar seekBar) {
    }

    @Override
    public void onStopTrackingTouch(SeekBar seekBar) {
```

```
        }


    });


    }
```

Now we need to alter the `MainActivity` class declaration to implement two interfaces. In this app, we will be listening for clicks and animation events, so the two interfaces we will be using are `View.OnClickListener` and `Animation.AnimationListener`. Notice that to implement more than one interface, we simply separate the interfaces with a comma.

Alter the `MainActivity` class declaration by adding the following highlighted code we have just discussed:

```
public class MainActivity extends AppCompatActivity
    implements View.OnClickListener,
    Animation.AnimationListener {
```

At this stage, we can add and implement the required methods for those interfaces – first, the following methods of `AnimationListener`: `onAnimationEnd`, `onAnimationRepeat`, and `onaAnimationStart`. We only need to add a little code to two of these methods. In `onAnimationEnd`, we set the `text` property of `textStatus` to `STOPPED`, and in the `onAnimationStart` method, we set the `text` property of `textStatus` to `RUNNING`. This will demonstrate our animation listeners are indeed listening and working:

```
@Override
public void onAnimationEnd(Animation animation) {
    textStatus.setText("STOPPED");

}


@Override
public void onAnimationRepeat(Animation animation) {



}
```

```
@Override
public void onAnimationStart(Animation animation) {
    textStatus.setText("RUNNING");


}
```

The onClick method is quite long but not anything complicated. Each case that handles each button from the UI simply sets the duration of the animation based on the current position of the seek bar, sets up the animation so it can be listened to for events, and then starts the animation.

> **Note**
>
> You will need to use your preferred technique to import the View class:
>
> import android.view.View;

Add the onClick method we have just discussed, and we have then completed this mini-app:

```
@Override
public void onClick(View v) {


switch(v.getId()){
    case R.id.btnFadeIn:
            animFadeIn.setDuration(seekSpeedProgress);
            animFadeIn.setAnimationListener(this);
            imageView.startAnimation(animFadeIn);

        break;

    case R.id.btnFadeOut:

            animFadeOut.setDuration(seekSpeedProgress);
            animFadeOut.setAnimationListener(this);
            imageView.startAnimation(animFadeOut);

        break;
```

```
case R.id.btnFadeInOut:

    animFadeInOut.setDuration(seekSpeedProgress);
    animFadeInOut.setAnimationListener(this);
    imageView.startAnimation(animFadeInOut);

    break;

case R.id.btnZoomIn:
    animZoomIn.setDuration(seekSpeedProgress);
    animZoomIn.setAnimationListener(this);
    imageView.startAnimation(animZoomIn);

    break;

case R.id.btnZoomOut:
    animZoomOut.setDuration(seekSpeedProgress);
    animZoomOut.setAnimationListener(this);
    imageView.startAnimation(animZoomOut);

    break;


case R.id.btnLeftRight:
    animLeftRight.setDuration(seekSpeedProgress);
    animLeftRight.setAnimationListener(this);
    imageView.startAnimation(animLeftRight);

    break;

case R.id.btnRightLeft:
    animRightLeft.setDuration(seekSpeedProgress);
    animRightLeft.setAnimationListener(this);
    imageView.startAnimation(animRightLeft);
```

```
        break;

    case R.id.btnTopBottom:
        animTopBottom.setDuration(seekSpeedProgress);
        animTopBottom.setAnimationListener(this);
        imageView.startAnimation(animTopBottom);

        break;

    case R.id.btnBounce:
        /*
            Divide seekSpeedProgress by 10 because with
            the seekbar having a max value of 5000 it
            will make the animations range between
            almost instant and half a second
            5000 /  10 = 500 milliseconds
        */
        animBounce.setDuration(seekSpeedProgress / 10);
        animBounce.setAnimationListener(this);
        imageView.startAnimation(animBounce);

        break;

    case R.id.btnFlash:
        animFlash.setDuration(seekSpeedProgress / 10);
        animFlash.setAnimationListener(this);
        imageView.startAnimation(animFlash);

        break;

    case R.id.btnRotateLeft:
        animRotateLeft.setDuration(seekSpeedProgress);
        animRotateLeft.setAnimationListener(this);
        imageView.startAnimation(animRotateLeft);
```

```
        break;


    case R.id.btnRotateRight:
        animRotateRight.setDuration(seekSpeedProgress);
        animRotateRight.setAnimationListener(this);
        imageView.startAnimation(animRotateRight);


        break;
}


}
```

Now run the app. Move the seek bar to roughly the center so the animations run for a reasonable amount of time, as shown in the next screenshot:

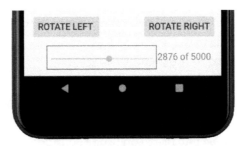

Figure 19.4 – Move the seek bar to roughly the center

Click the **ZOOM IN** button to see the effect, as shown in this next screenshot:

Figure 19.5 – ZOOM IN effect

Notice how the text on the Android robot changes from **RUNNING** to **STOPPED** at the appropriate time. Now click one of the **ROTATE** buttons to see this effect shown next:

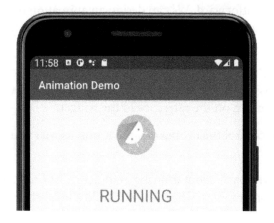

Figure 19.6 – Rotate button

Most of the other animations don't do themselves justice in a screenshot, so be sure to try them all out for yourself.

Frequently asked questions

1. I know how to animate widgets now but what about shapes or images that I create myself?

    An `ImageView` can hold any image you like. Just add the image to the `drawable` folder and then set the appropriate `src` attribute on the `ImageView` widget. You can then animate whatever image is being shown in the `ImageView`.

2. But what if I want more flexibility than this, such as for a drawing app or even a game?

    To implement this kind of functionality, we will need to learn about another general computing concept (**threads**) as well as some more Android classes (such as `Paint`, `Canvas`, and `SurfaceView`). We will learn how to draw anything from a single pixel to shapes and then move them around the screen starting in the next chapter, *Chapter 20, Drawing Graphics*.

Summary

Now we have another app-enhancing trick up our sleeves and we know that animations in Android are quite straightforward. We can design an animation in XML and add the file to the `anim` folder. After that, we can get a reference to the animation in XML with an `Animation` object in our Java code.

We can then use a reference to a widget in our UI and set an animation to it using `setAnimation` and passing in the `Animation` object. We commence the animation by calling `startAnimation` on the reference to the widget.

We also saw that we can control the timing of animations, as well as listening for animation events.

In the next chapter, we will learn about drawing graphics in Android. This will be the start of several chapters on graphics, where we will build a kids'-style drawing app.

20
Drawing Graphics

This entire chapter will be about the Android `Canvas` class and some related classes, including `Paint`, `Color`, and `Bitmap`. These classes combined bring great power when it comes to drawing to the screen. Sometimes the default UI provided by the Android API isn't what we need. If we want to make a drawing app, draw graphs, or perhaps create a game, we need to take control of every pixel that the Android device has to offer.

In this chapter, we will cover the following:

- Understanding `Canvas` and related classes
- Writing a `Canvas`-based demo app
- Looking at the Android coordinate system so we know where to do our drawing
- Learning about drawing and manipulating bitmaps
- Writing a bitmap-based demo app

Let's draw!

Technical requirements

You can find the code files present in this chapter on GitHub at https://github. com/PacktPublishing/Android-Programming-for-Beginners-Third- Edition/tree/main/chapter%2020.

Understanding the Canvas class

The Canvas class is part of the android.graphics package. In the next two chapters, we will be using all the following import statements from the android.graphics package and one more from the now-familiar View package. They give us access to some powerful drawing methods from the Android API:

```
import android.graphics.Bitmap;
import android.graphics.Canvas;
import android.graphics.Color;
import android.graphics.Paint;
import android.widget.ImageView;
```

First, let's talk about Bitmap, Canvas, and ImageView, as highlighted in the previous code.

Getting started drawing with Bitmap, Canvas, and ImageView

As Android is designed to run all types of mobile apps, we can't immediately start typing our drawing code and expect it to work. We need to do a bit of preparation (coding) to consider the specific device our app is running on. It is true that some of this preparation can be slightly counterintuitive, but we will go through it a step at a time.

Canvas and Bitmap

Depending on how you use the Canvas class, the term can be slightly misleading. While the Canvas class *is* the class to which you draw your graphics, like a painting canvas, you still need a surface to transpose the canvas to.

The surface, in this case (and in our first two demo apps), will be from the Bitmap class. We can think of it like this: we get a Canvas object and a Bitmap object and then set the Bitmap object as the part of the Canvas object to draw upon.

This is slightly counterintuitive if you take the word canvas in its literal sense but once it is all set up, we can forget about it and concentrate on the graphics we want to draw.

> **Note**
>
> The Canvas class supplies the *ability* to draw. It has all the methods for doing things such as drawing shapes, text, lines, and image files (including other bitmaps), and even plotting individual pixels.
>
> The Bitmap class is used by the Canvas class and is the surface that gets drawn upon. You can think of the Bitmap instance as being inside a picture frame on the Canvas instance.

Paint

In addition to the Canvas and Bitmap classes, we will be using the Paint class. This is much more easily understood. Paint is the class used to configure specific properties such as the color that we will draw on Bitmap (within Canvas).

There is still another piece of the puzzle to cover before we can start drawing.

ImageView and Activity

The ImageView class is the class that the Activity class will use to display output to the user. The reason for this third layer of abstraction is that as we have seen throughout the book, the Activity class needs to pass a View to the setContentView method to display something to the user. Throughout the book so far, this has been a layout that we created in the visual designer or in XML code.

This time, we don't want a regular UI; we want to draw lines, pixels, and shapes.

There are multiple types of classes that extend the View class, enabling many different types of apps to be made, and they will all be compatible with the Activity class, which is the foundation of all regular Android apps (including drawing apps and games).

It is, therefore, necessary to associate the Bitmap class that gets drawn on (through its association with Canvas) with ImageView, once the drawing is done. The last step will be telling Activity that our ImageView class represents the content for the user to see by passing it to the setContentView method.

Canvas, Bitmap, Paint, and ImageView quick summary

If the theory of the code structure we need to set up seems like it is not simple, you will breathe a sigh of relief when you see the relatively simple code shortly.

A quick summary of what we know so far:

- Every app needs an `Activity` class to interact with the user and the underlying operating system. Therefore, we must conform to the required hierarchy if we want to succeed.

- We will use the `ImageView` class, which is a type of the `View` class. The `View` class is what `Activity` needs to display our app to the user.

- The `Canvas` class supplies the *ability* to draw lines, pixels, and other graphics too. It has all the methods for doing things such as drawing shapes, text, lines, and image files, and even plotting individual pixels.

- The `Bitmap` class will be associated with the `Canvas` class and it is the surface that actually gets drawn upon.

- The `Canvas` class uses the `Paint` class to configure details such as the color.

Finally, once the bitmap has been drawn upon, we must associate it with the `ImageView` instance, which in turn is set as the view for `Activity` via the `setContentView` method.

The result will be what we draw on the `Bitmap` instance in the `Canvas` instance, which is displayed to the user through the `ImageView` instance via the call to the `setContentView` method. Phew!

> **Note**
>
> It doesn't matter if that isn't 100% clear. It is not that you aren't seeing things clearly – it simply isn't a clear relationship. Writing the code and using the techniques over and over will cause things to become clearer. Look at the code, do the demo apps in this chapter and the next, and then re-read this section.

Let's look at how to set up this relationship in code. Don't worry about typing the code; just study it first.

Using the Canvas class

Let's look at the code and the different stages required to get drawing, and then we can quickly move on to drawing something for real, with the `Canvas` demo app.

Preparing the instances of the required classes

The first step is to declare the instances of the classes we require:

```
// Here are all the objects(instances)
// of classes that we need to do some drawing
ImageView myImageView;
Bitmap myBlankBitmap;
Canvas myCanvas;
Paint myPaint;
```

The previous code declares references of the ImageView, Bitmap, Canvas, and Paint types. They are named myImageView, myBlankBitmap, myCanvas, and myPaint, respectively.

Initializing the objects

Next, we need to initialize our new objects before using them:

```
// Initialize all the objects ready for drawing
// We will do this inside the onCreate method
int widthInPixels = 800;
int heightInPixels = 800;

myBlankBitmap = Bitmap.createBitmap(widthInPixels,
        heightInPixels,
        Bitmap.Config.ARGB_8888);

myCanvas = new Canvas(myBlankBitmap);
myImageView = new ImageView(this);
myPaint = new Paint();
// Do drawing here
```

Notice this comment in the previous code:

```
// Do drawing here
```

This is where we would configure our color and draw stuff. Also, notice at the top of the code we declare and initialize two int variables called widthInPixels and heightInPixels. When we code the Canvas demo app, I will go into greater detail about some of those lines of code.

We are now ready to draw. All we must do is assign the ImageView instance to Activity.

Setting the Activity content

Finally, before we can see our drawing, we tell Android to use our ImageView instance called myImageView as the content to display to the user:

```
// Associate the drawn upon Bitmap with the ImageView
myImageView.setImageBitmap(myBlankBitmap);


// Tell Android to set our drawing
// as the view for this app
// via the ImageView
setContentView(myImageView);
```

As we have already seen in every app so far, the setContentView method is part of the Activity class and we pass in myImageView as an argument, instead of an XML layout as we have been doing throughout the book so far. That's it. All we must learn now is how to actually draw on that Bitmap instance.

Before we do some drawing, I thought it would be useful to start a real project, copy and paste the code we have just discussed, a step at a time, into the correct place, and then actually see something drawn to the screen.

Let's do some drawing.

Canvas demo app

We will create a new project just to explore the topic of drawing with Canvas. We will reuse what we have just learned and this time, we will also draw to the Bitmap instance.

Creating a new project

Create a new project and call it Canvas Demo. Choose the **Empty Activity** template.

In addition, we are going to be using the vanilla version of the Activity class and the MainActivity class will therefore extend Activity instead of AppCompatActivity as we have been using previously. This is simply because we no longer need the extra features provided by the AppCompatActivity class.

> **Note**
> The complete code for this app can be found in the download bundle in the Chapter 20/Canvas Demo folder.

Coding the Canvas demo app

To get started, edit the code in MainActivity.java, including adding the import directives and changing the version of the Activity class that the MainActivity class inherits from. Also notice in the next code that the call to the setContentView method has also been deleted. We will replace it soon:

```java
import android.app.Activity;
import android.graphics.Bitmap;
import android.graphics.Canvas;
import android.graphics.Color;
import android.graphics.Paint;
import android.os.Bundle;
import android.widget.ImageView;


public class MainActivity extends Activity {

    // Here are all the objects(instances)
    // of classes that we need to do some drawing
    ImageView myImageView;
    Bitmap myBlankBitmap;
    Canvas myCanvas;
    Paint myPaint;



    @Override
    protected void onCreate(Bundle savedInstanceState) {
        super.onCreate(savedInstanceState);
```

```
        }

    }
```

Now that we have declared instances of the required classes, we can initialize them. Add the following code to the onCreate method after the call to super.onCreate..., as shown in this next code:

```
@Override
protected void onCreate(Bundle savedInstanceState) {
    super.onCreate(savedInstanceState);

    // Initialize all the objects ready for drawing
    // We will do this inside the onCreate method
    int widthInPixels = 800;
    int heightInPixels = 600;

    // Create a new Bitmap
    myBlankBitmap = Bitmap.createBitmap(widthInPixels,
                heightInPixels,
                Bitmap.Config.ARGB_8888);

    // Initialize the Canvas and associate it
    // with the Bitmap to draw on
    myCanvas = new Canvas(myBlankBitmap);

    // Initialize the ImageView and the Paint
    myImageView = new ImageView(this);
    myPaint = new Paint();
}
```

This code is the same as we saw when we were discussing Canvas earlier. It is worth exploring the Bitmap class initialization as it is not straightforward.

Exploring the Bitmap initialization

Bitmaps, more typically in graphics-based apps and games, are used to represent objects such as different brushes to paint with, the player, backgrounds, game objects, and so on. Here we are simply using it to draw upon. In the next project, we will use bitmaps to represent the subject of our drawing, not just the surface to draw upon.

The method that needs explaining is the `createBitmap` method. The parameters from left to right are as follows:

- The width (in pixels)
- The height (in pixels)
- The bitmap configuration

Bitmaps can be configured in several different ways. The `ARGB_8888` configuration means that each pixel is represented by 4 bytes of memory.

There are a few bitmap formats that Android can use. This one is perfect for a good range of colors and will ensure that the bitmaps we use and the colors we request will be drawn as intended. There are higher and lower configurations but `ARGB_8888` is perfect for the entirety of this chapter.

Now we can do the actual drawing.

Drawing on the screen

Add this next highlighted code after the initialization of `myPaint` and inside the closing curly brace of the `onCreate` method:

```
myPaint = new Paint();


// Draw on the Bitmap
// Wipe the Bitmap with a blue color
myCanvas.drawColor(Color.argb(255, 0, 0, 255));


// Re-size the text
myPaint.setTextSize(100);
// Change the paint to white
myPaint.setColor(Color.argb(255, 255, 255, 255));
// Draw some text
myCanvas.drawText("Hello World!",100, 100, myPaint);


// Change the paint to yellow
myPaint.setColor(Color.argb(255, 212, 207, 62));
// Draw a circle
myCanvas.drawCircle(400,250, 100, myPaint);
}
```

The previous code uses the `myCanvas.drawColor` method to fill the screen with color.

The `myPaint.setTextSize` method defines the size of the text that will be drawn next. The `myPaint.setColor` method determines what color any future drawing will be. The `myCanvas.drawText` method actually draws the text to the screen.

Analyze the arguments passed into the `drawText` method and we can see that the text will say "Hello World!" and will be drawn 100 pixels from the left and 100 pixels from the top of our bitmap (`myBitmap`).

Next, we use the `setColor` method again to change the color that will be used for drawing. Finally, we use the `drawCircle` method to draw a circle that is 400 pixels from the left and 100 pixels from the top. The circle will have a radius of 100 pixels.

I reserved explaining the `Color.argb` method until now.

Explaining Color.argb

The `Color` class, unsurprisingly, helps us to manipulate and represent color. The `argb` method used previously returns a color constructed using the **alpha (opacity/ transparency), red, green, blue (argb)** model. This model uses values ranging from 0 (no color) to 255 (full color) for each element. It is important to note, although on reflection it might seem obvious, that the colors mixed are intensities of light and are quite different to what happens when we mix paint, for example.

> **Note**
>
> To devise an argb value and explore this model further, look at this handy website: `https://www.rapidtables.com/web/color/ RGB_Color.html`. The site helps you pick the RGB values; you can then experiment with the alpha values.

The values used to clear the drawing surface were `255, 0, 0, 255`. These values mean full opacity (solid color), no red, no green, and full blue. This makes a blue color.

The next call to the `argb` method is in the first call to `setColor` where we are setting the required color for the text. The values `255, 255, 255, 255` mean full opacity, full red, full green, and full blue. When you combine light with these values, you get white.

The final call to the `argb` method is in the final call to the `setColor` method when we are setting the color to draw the circle. `255, 21, 207, 62` makes a sun-yellow color.

The last step before we can run the code is to add the call to the `setContentView` method that places our `ImageView` (`myImageView`) as the `View` instance to be set as the content for this app. Here are the final lines of code to be added before the closing curly brace of the `onCreate` method:

```
// Associate the drawn upon Bitmap with the ImageView
myImageView.setImageBitmap(myBlankBitmap);
// Tell Android to set our drawing
// as the view for this app
// via the ImageView
setContentView(myImageView);
```

Finally, we tell the `Activity` class to use `myImageView` by calling the `setContentView` method.

This is what the `Canvas` demo looks like when you run it. We can see an 800 by 800-pixel drawing. In the next chapter, we will use more advanced techniques to utilize the entire screen and we will also learn about threads to make the graphics move in real time:

Figure 20.1 – Canvas demo

It will help to understand the result of the coordinates we use in our `Canvas` class drawing methods if we better understand the Android coordinate system.

The Android coordinate system

As we can see, drawing a bitmap is trivial. But the coordinate system that we use to draw our graphics onto needs a brief explanation.

Plotting and drawing

When we draw a `Bitmap` object to the screen, we pass in the coordinates we want to draw the object at. The available coordinates of a given Android device depend upon the resolution of its screen.

For example, the Google Pixel phone has a screen resolution of 1,920 pixels (across) by 1,080 pixels (down) when held in landscape view.

The numbering system of these coordinates starts in the top left-hand corner at `0, 0` and proceeds down and to the right until the bottom-right corner, which is pixel `1919, 1079`. The apparent 1-pixel disparity between `1920` and `1919` and `1080` and `1079` is because the numbering starts at 0.

So, when we draw a bitmap or anything else to the screen (such as `Canvas` circles and rectangles), we must specify an `x, y` coordinate.

Furthermore, a bitmap (or `Canvas` shape) of course comprises many pixels. So, which pixel of a given bitmap is drawn at the `x, y` screen coordinate that we will be specifying?

The answer is the top-left pixel of the `Bitmap` object. Look at the next figure, which should clarify the screen coordinates using the Google Pixel phone as an example. As a graphical means for explaining the Android coordinate drawing system, I will use a cute spaceship graphic:

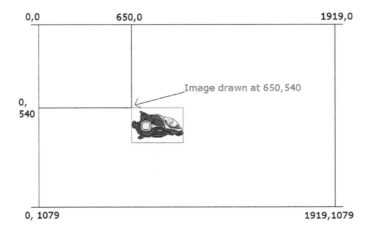

Figure 20.2 – Screen coordinates

Furthermore, the coordinates are relative to what you draw upon. So, in the Canvas demo app we just coded, as well as the next demo, the coordinates are relative to the bitmap (myBitmap). In the next chapter, we will use the entire screen and the previous figure will be an accurate representation of what is happening.

Let's do some more drawing, this time with bitmaps from a graphics file. We will use the same starting code as we have seen in this app.

Creating bitmaps

Let's do a little bit of theory before we dive into the code and consider exactly how we are going to bring images to life on the screen. To draw a bitmap, we will use the drawBitmap method of the Canvas class.

First, we would need to add a bitmap to the project in the res/drawable folder; we will do this for real in the Bitmap demo app coming up shortly. For now, assume the graphics file/bitmap has the name myImage.png.

Next, we declare an object of the Bitmap type, just the same as we did for the Bitmap object we used for our background in the previous demo:

```
Bitmap mBitmap;
```

Next, we need to initialize the mBitmap object using our preferred image that we previously added to the project's drawable folder:

```
mBitmap = BitmapFactory.decodeResource
                (getResources(), R.drawable.myImage);
```

The static decodeResource method of the BitmapFactory method is used to initialize mBitmap. It takes two parameters. The first is a call to getResources, which is made available by the Activity class. This method, as the name suggests, gives access to the project resources, and the second parameter, R.drawable.myImage, points to the myImage.png file in the drawable folder. The bitmap (mBitmap) is now ready to be drawn by the Canvas class.

You could then draw the bitmap with the following code:

```
// Draw the bitmap at coordinates 100, 100
mCanvas.drawBitmap(mBitmap,
                100, 100, mPaint);
```

Here is what the spaceship graphic from the previous section looks like when drawn to the screen as a reference for when we talk about rotating bitmaps:

Figure 20.3 – Spaceship graphic

Manipulating bitmaps

Quite often, however, we need to draw bitmaps in a rotated or otherwise-altered state. It would be quite easy to use Photoshop or whatever your favorite image editing software happens to be to create more bitmaps from the original bitmap to face in other directions. Then, when we come to draw our bitmap, we can simply decide which way to face and draw the appropriate pre-loaded bitmap.

However, I thought it would be much more interesting and instructive if we worked with just one single source image and learned about the class that Android provides to manipulate images in our Java code. You will then be able to add rotating and inverting graphics to your app developer's toolkit.

What is a bitmap exactly?

A bitmap is called a bitmap because that is exactly what it is: a *map of bits*. While there are many bitmap formats that use different ranges and values to represent colors and transparency, they all amount to the same thing. They are a grid/map of values and each value represents the color of a single pixel.

Therefore, to rotate, scale, or invert a bitmap, we must perform the appropriate mathematical calculation upon each pixel/bit of the image/grid/map of the bitmap. The calculations are not terribly complicated, but they are not especially simple either. If you took math to the end of high school, you will probably understand the math without too much bother.

Unfortunately, understanding the math isn't enough. We would also need to devise efficient code, as well as understanding the bitmap format, and then modify our code for each format. This would not be trivial. Fortunately, the Android API has done it all for us. Meet the `Matrix` class.

The Matrix class

The class is named `Matrix` because it uses the mathematical concept and rules to perform calculations on a series of values known as matrices – the plural of matrix.

> **Note**
>
> The Android `Matrix` class has nothing to do with the movie series of the same name. However, the author advises that all aspiring app developers take the red pill.

You might be familiar with matrices but don't worry if you're not because the `Matrix` class hides all the complexity away. Furthermore, the `Matrix` class not only allows us to perform calculations on a series of values, but it also has some pre-prepared calculations that enable us to do things such as rotating a point around another point by a specific number of degrees. All this without knowing anything about trigonometry.

> **Note**
>
> If you are intrigued by how the math works and want an absolute beginner's guide to the mathematics of rotating game objects, then look at this series of Android tutorials on my website that ends with a flyable and rotatable spaceship:
>
> http://gamecodeschool.com/essentials/calculating-heading-in-2d-games-using-trigonometric-functions-part-1/
>
> http://gamecodeschool.com/essentials/rotating-graphics-in-2d-games-using-trigonometric-functions-part-2/
>
> http://gamecodeschool.com/android/2d-rotation-and-heading-demo/

This book will stick to using the Android `Matrix` class, but we will do slightly more advanced math when we create a particle system in the next chapter.

Inverting a bitmap to face the opposite direction

First, we need to create an instance of the `Matrix` class. This next line of code does so in a familiar way by calling new on the default constructor:

```
Matrix matrix = new Matrix();
```

> **Note**
>
> Note that you don't need to add any of this code to a project right now; it will all be shown again shortly with much more context. I just thought it would be easier to see all the `Matrix`-related code on its own beforehand.

Now we can use one of the many neat methods of the `Matrix` class. The `preScale` method takes two parameters: one for the horizontal change and one for the vertical change. Look at this line of code:

```
matrix.preScale(-1, 1);
```

What the `preScale` method will do is loop through every pixel position and multiply all the horizontal coordinates by `-1` and all the vertical coordinates by `1`.

The effect of these calculations is that all the vertical coordinates will remain the same because if you multiply by 1, then the number doesn't change. However, when you multiply by -1, the horizontal position of the pixel will be inverted. Take the following example:

Horizontal positions 0, 1, 2, 3, and 4 will become 0, -1, -2, -3, and -4.

At this stage, we have created a matrix that can perform the necessary calculations on a bitmap. We haven't actually done anything with the bitmap yet. To use the matrix, we call the `createBitmap` method of the `Bitmap` class such as this line of code shown next:

```
mBitmapLeft = Bitmap
.createBitmap(mBitmap,
            0, 0, 25, 25, matrix, true);
```

The previous code assumes that `mBitmapLeft` is already initialized as well as `mBitmap`. The parameters of the `createBitmap` method are explained as follows:

- `mBitmapHeadRight` is a `Bitmap` object that has already been created and scaled and has the image of a spaceship (facing the right) loaded into it. This is the image that will be used as the source for creating the new bitmap. The source bitmap will not actually be altered at all.

- `0, 0` is the horizontal and vertical starting position that we want the new bitmap to be mapped into.

- The `25, 25` parameters are values that set the size that the bitmap is scaled to.

- The next parameter is our pre-prepared `Matrix` instance, `matrix`.

- The final parameter, `true`, instructs the `createBitmap` method that filtering is required to correctly handle the creation of the bitmap.

This is what `mBitmapLeft` will look like when drawn to the screen:

Figure 20.4 – mBitmapLeft

We can also create the bitmap facing up or down using a rotation matrix.

Rotating the bitmap to face up or down

Let's look at rotating a bitmap, and then we can build the demo app. We already have an instance of the `Matrix` class, so all we must do is call the `preRotate` method to create a matrix capable of rotating every pixel by a specified number of degrees in the single argument to `preRotate`. Look at this line of code:

```
// A matrix for rotating
matrix.preRotate(-90);
```

How simple was that? The `matrix` instance is now ready to rotate any series of numbers we pass to it, anti-clockwise (`-`), by `90` degrees.

This next line of code has exactly the same parameters as the previous call to `createBitmap` that we previously dissected, except that the new `Bitmap` instance is assigned to `mBitmapUp` and the effect of `matrix` is to perform the rotation instead of `preScale`:

```
mBitmapUp = Bitmap
 .createBitmap(mBitmap,
            0, 0, ss, ss, matrix, true);
```

This is what `mBitmapUp` will look like when drawn:

Figure 20.5 – mBitmapUp

You can also use the same technique but a different value in the argument to `preRotate` to turn the bitmap downward. Let's get on with the demo app to see all this stuff in action.

Bitmap manipulation demo app

Now that we have studied the theory, let's draw and spin some bitmaps. Create a new project using the **Empty Activity** template and call it `Manipulating Bitmaps`.

Adding the graphic to the project

Right-click and select **Copy** to copy the `bob.png` graphics file from the download bundle in the `Chapter 20/Manipulating Bitmaps/drawable` folder.

In Android Studio, locate the `app/res/drawable` folder in the project explorer window. This next screenshot makes clear where this folder can be located and what it will look like with the `bob.png` image in it:

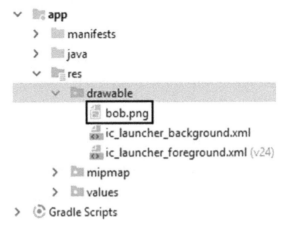

Figure 20.6 – app/res/drawable folder with bob.png

Right-click on the **drawable** folder and select **Paste** to add the bob.png file to the project. Click **OK** twice to confirm the default options for importing the file into the project.

Edit the code of the MainActivity class to include all the required import directives, the basic version of the Activity class, and a selection of member variables so we can get started. The state of the MainActivity class at this stage is shown next:

```
import android.app.Activity;
import android.graphics.Bitmap;
import android.graphics.Canvas;
import android.graphics.Paint;
import android.os.Bundle;
import android.widget.ImageView;
import android.graphics.BitmapFactory;
import android.graphics.Color;
import android.graphics.Matrix;


public class MainActivity extends Activity {

    // Here are all the objects(instances)
    // of classes that we need to do some drawing
    ImageView myImageView;
    Bitmap myBlankBitmap;
    Bitmap bobBitmap;
    Canvas myCanvas;
    Paint myPaint;



    @Override
    protected void onCreate(Bundle savedInstanceState) {
        super.onCreate(savedInstanceState);

    }
}
```

Now we can initialize all the members in onCreate:

```
// Initialize all the objects ready for drawing
int widthInPixels = 2000;
int heightInPixels = 1000;

// Create a new Bitmap
myBlankBitmap = Bitmap.createBitmap(widthInPixels,
        heightInPixels,
        Bitmap.Config.ARGB_8888);

// Initialize Bob
bobBitmap = BitmapFactory.decodeResource
        (getResources(), R.drawable.bob);

// Initialize the Canvas and associate it
// with the Bitmap to draw on
myCanvas = new Canvas(myBlankBitmap);

// Initialize the ImageView and the Paint
myImageView = new ImageView(this);
myPaint = new Paint();

// Draw on the Bitmap
// Wipe the Bitmap with a blue color
myCanvas.drawColor(Color.argb(255, 0, 0, 255));
```

Next, we add calls to three methods that we will write soon and set our new drawing as the view for the app:

```
// Draw some bitmaps
drawRotatedBitmaps();
drawEnlargedBitmap();
drawShrunkenBitmap();

// Associate the drawn upon Bitmap with the ImageView
myImageView.setImageBitmap(myBlankBitmap);
// Tell Android to set our drawing
```

```
// as the view for this app
// via the ImageView
setContentView(myImageView);
```

Now add the `drawRotatedBitmap` method that does the bitmap manipulation:

```
void drawRotatedBitmaps(){
    float rotation = 0f;
    int horizontalPosition =350;
    int verticalPosition = 25;
    Matrix matrix = new Matrix();

    Bitmap rotatedBitmap = Bitmap.createBitmap(100,
                200,
                Bitmap.Config.ARGB_8888);

    for(rotation = 0; rotation < 360; rotation += 30){
        matrix.reset();
        matrix.preRotate(rotation);
        rotatedBitmap = Bitmap
                .createBitmap(bobBitmap,
                        0, 0, bobBitmap
                        .getWidth()-1,
                        bobBitmap.getHeight()-1,
                        matrix, true);

        myCanvas.drawBitmap(rotatedBitmap,
                    horizontalPosition,
                    verticalPosition,
                    myPaint);

        horizontalPosition += 120;
        verticalPosition += 70;
    }
}
```

The previous code uses a `for` loop to loop through 360 degrees 30 degrees at a time. The value that each pass through the loop is used in the `Matrix` instance to rotate the image of Bob, and he is then drawn to the screen using the `drawBitmap` method.

Add the final two methods as shown next:

```
void drawEnlargedBitmap() {
    bobBitmap = Bitmap
                .createScaledBitmap(bobBitmap,
                            300, 400, false);
    myCanvas.drawBitmap(bobBitmap, 25,25, myPaint);


}

void drawShrunkenBitmap() {
    bobBitmap = Bitmap
                .createScaledBitmap(bobBitmap,
                            50, 75, false);
    myCanvas.drawBitmap(bobBitmap, 250,25, myPaint);
}
```

The `drawEnlargedBitmap` method uses the `createScaledBitmap` method, which is 300 by 400 pixels. The `drawBitmap` method then draws it to the screen.

`drawShrunkenBitmap` uses the exact same technique except it scales then draws a 50 by 75-pixel image.

Run the app to see Bob grow, then shrink, then spin around through 360 degrees at 30-degree intervals, as shown in this next screenshot:

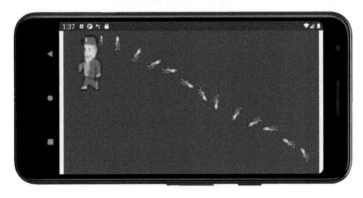

Figure 20.7 – How the app runs

The only thing missing from our drawing repertoire is the ability to watch all this activity as it happens. We will fix this gap in our knowledge in the next chapter.

Frequently asked question

1. I know how to do all this drawing but I can't see anything move. Why?

    To see things move, you need to be able to regulate when each part of the drawing occurs. You need to use animation techniques. This is not trivial but it is not beyond the grasp of a determined beginner either. We will study the required topics in the next chapter.

Summary

In this chapter, we saw how to draw custom shapes, text, and bitmaps. Now that we know how to draw and manipulate primitive shapes, text, and bitmaps, we can take things up a level.

In the next chapter, we will start our next major app, which is a kid's drawing app that actually comes to life at the press of a button.

21
Threads and Starting the Live Drawing App

In this chapter, we will get started on our next app. This app will be a kid's drawing app where the user can draw on the screen with their finger. This drawing app will be slightly different, however. The lines that the user draws will comprise particle systems that explode into thousands of pieces. We will call the project Live Drawing.

To achieve this, we will do the following:

- Get started with the Live Drawing app
- Learn about real-time interaction, sometimes called a game loop
- Learn about threads
- Code a real-time system ready to draw with in the next chapter

Let's get started.

Technical requirements

You can find the code files present in this chapter on GitHub at `https://github. com/PacktPublishing/Android-Programming-for-Beginners-Third- Edition/tree/main/chapter%2021`.

Creating the Live Drawing project

To get started, create a new project in Android Studio and call it `Live Drawing`. Use the **Empty Activity** project.

Now we will consider the name of the files and the screen real estate. In this project, we will learn something new. It is not always appropriate to use the default name for our Activity class. In this project, the Activity class isn't going to be the most significant class and `MainActivity` doesn't seem like an appropriate name. Let's rename it.

Refactoring MainActivity to LiveDrawingActivity

It is a good practice to use meaningful names for all the different parts of our code. For this project, I think `MainActivity` is a bit vague and inconclusive. We could make do with it, but let's rename it to something more meaningful. This will also let us see how we can use the **refactoring** tool of Android Studio. The reason that we use the term refactoring instead of just renaming is when we change the names we use in our code, there is often much more than just a simple name change going on behind the scenes. For example, in a moment, when we refactor the `MainActivity` filename to `LiveDrawingActivity`, Android Studio will change the name of the file as well as some code in the `AndroidManifest.xml` file and the `MainActivity.java` (soon to be `LiveDrawingActivity.java`) file.

In the project panel, right-click the `MainActivity` file and select **Refactor | Rename**. In the pop-up window, change **MainActivity** to **LiveDrawingActivity**. Leave all the other options as their defaults and left-click the **Refactor** button.

Notice the filename in the project panel has changed as expected but also multiple occurrences of `MainActivity` have been changed to `LiveDrawingActivity` in the `AndroidManifest.xml` file as well as an instance in the `LiveDrawingActivity. java` file. You can scan these files now to see this if you are interested, but we will go into more detail about both files in the upcoming sections anyway.

> **Note**
> Refactoring is an important tool and understanding that there is more going on behind the scenes is vital to avoid confusion.

Locking the game to fullscreen and landscape orientation

We want to use every pixel that the user's Android device has to offer so we will make changes to the `AndroidManifest.xml` file, which allows us to use a style for our app that hides all the default menus from the user interface.

Open the `AndroidManifest.xml` file from the `manifests` folder. In the `AndroidManifest.xml` file, locate the following line of code: `android:name=".LiveDrawingActivity">`.

Place the cursor before the closing > shown previously. Tap the *Enter* key a couple of times to move the > a couple of lines below the rest of the line shown previously.

Immediately below `".LiveDrawingActivity"` but before the newly positioned >, type or copy and paste this next line of code to make the game run without the default user interface.

Note that the line of code is shown on two lines because it is too long to fit on a printed page, but in Android Studio you should enter it as one line:

```
android:theme=
"@android:style/Theme.Holo.Light.NoActionBar.Fullscreen"
```

This is a fiddly set of steps so here I am showing you a bigger range of this file with the code we just added highlighted among it for extra context. As mentioned previously, I have had to show some lines of code over two lines:

```
...
<activity android:name=".LiveDrawingActivity"
    android:theme=
    "@android:style/
    Theme.Holo.Light.NoActionBar.Fullscreen"
    >
    <intent-filter>
        <action android:name="android.intent.action.MAIN"
        />

<category android:name= "android.intent.category.LAUNCHER" />
    </intent-filter>
</activity>

...
```

Now our app will use all the screen space the device makes available without any extra menus. We will also see some new Java code to make our app dominate every pixel of the screen.

Making some placeholder classes

This app consists of Java files only. The Java files with all the code up to the end of this chapter can all be found in the `Chapter 21` folder of the download bundle.

Next, we will create empty classes that we will code throughout the project over the next two chapters. Create a new class called `LiveDrawingView`, a new class called `ParticleSystem`, and a new class called `Particle`.

Let's look ahead a bit.

Looking ahead at the Live Drawing app

As this app is more in-depth and needs to respond in real-time, it is necessary to use a slightly more in-depth structure. At first, this seems like a complication but in the long run, it can even make our code simpler and easier to understand.

We will have four classes in the Live Drawing app:

- `LiveDrawingActivity`: The `Activity` class provided by the Android API is the class that interacts with the operating system. We have already seen how the OS interacts with `onCreate` when the user clicks the app icon to start an app. Rather than have a class called `MainActivity` that does everything, we will have an Activity-based class that just handles the startup and shutdown of our app as well as helping a bit with initialization by getting the screen resolution. It makes sense that this class will be of type `Activity`. However, as you will soon see, we will delegate interacting with touches to another class, the same class that will also handle almost every aspect of the app. This will introduce us to some interesting concepts that will be new to us.

- `LiveDrawingView`: This is the class that will be responsible for doing the drawing and creating the real-time environment, which allows the user to interact at the same time as their creations are moving and evolving.

- `ParticleSystem`: This is the class that will manage up to thousands of instances of the `Particle` class.

- `Particle`: This class will be the simplest of them all. It will have a location onscreen and a heading. It will update itself around 60 times per second when prompted to by the `LiveDrawingView` class.

Now we can start coding.

Coding the LiveDrawingActivity class

Let's get started with coding the `Activity` based class. We called this class `LiveDrawingActivity` when we refactored `MainActivity`.

Replace the contents of the `LiveDrawingActivity` class (excluding the package declaration) with the following code:

```
import android.app.Activity;
import android.graphics.Point;
import android.os.Bundle;
import android.view.Display;
import android.view.Window;


public class LiveDrawingActivity extends Activity {

    private LiveDrawingView mLiveDrawingView;

    @Override
    protected void onCreate(Bundle savedInstanceState) {
        super.onCreate(savedInstanceState);
        requestWindowFeature(Window.FEATURE_NO_TITLE);


        Display display = getWindowManager()
        .getDefaultDisplay();
        Point size = new Point();
        display.getSize(size);


        mLiveDrawingView = new LiveDrawingView(
        this, size.x, size.y);
        setContentView(mLiveDrawingView);
    }


}
```

The code shows some errors and we will talk about them shortly.

The first new line of code is this:

```
requestWindowFeature(Window.FEATURE_NO_TITLE);
```

This line of code removes the title from the user interface. The screen will be completely empty when we run this app.

The code gets the number of pixels (wide and high) for the device in the following way. Look again at the next new line of code:

```
Display display = getWindowManager().getDefaultDisplay();
```

We create an object of type `Display` called `display` and initialize it with the result of calling both `getWindowManager` then `getDefaultDisplay` methods in turn, which are part of the `Activity` class.

Then we create a new object called `size` of the `Point` type. We send `size` as an argument to the `display.getSize` method. The `Point` type has an `x` and `y` member variable, and therefore, so does the `size` object, which after the third line of code now holds the width and height (in pixels) of the display.

Now we have the screen resolution in `x` and `y` variables hidden away in the `size` object.

The next new thing is that we are declaring an instance of our `LiveDrawingView` class. Currently, this is an empty class:

```
private LiveDrawingView mLiveDrawingView;
```

Next in the `onCreate` method, we initialize `mLiveDrawingView` like this:

```
mLiveDrawingView = new LiveDrawingView(this, size.x, size.y);
```

What we are doing is passing three arguments to the `LiveDrawingView` constructor. We have obviously not coded a constructor yet and as we know the default constructor takes zero arguments. Therefore, this line will cause an error until we fix it.

The arguments passed in are interesting. First, `this`, which is a reference to the `LiveDrawingActivity` class. The `LiveDrawingView` class will need to use methods that it needs this reference for.

The second and third arguments are the horizontal and vertical screen resolution. It makes sense that our app will need these to perform tasks such as detecting the edge of the screen and scaling the drawing objects to an appropriate size. We will discuss these arguments further when we get to coding the `LiveDrawingView` constructor.

Next, take a look at the line that follows:

```
setContentView(mLiveDrawingView);
```

This is where, in the Canvas Demo app, we set the ImageView as the content for the app. Remember that the Activity class's setContentView method must take a View object and ImageView is a View. This previous line of code seems to be suggesting that we will use our LiveDrawingView class as the visible content for the app. But LiveDrawingView, despite its name, isn't a View. Not yet anyway.

We will fix the constructor and the not a View problem after we add a few more lines of code to LiveDrawingActivity.

> **Reader challenge**
> Can you guess which OOP concept the solution might be?

Add these two overridden methods and then we will talk about them. Add them below the closing curly brace of the onCreate method but before the closing curly brace of the LiveDrawingActivity class:

```
@Override
protected void onResume() {
    super.onResume();

    // More code here later in the chapter
}

@Override
protected void onPause() {
    super.onPause();

    // More code here later in the chapter
}
```

What we have done is to override two more of the methods of the Activity class. We will see why we need to do this and what we will do inside these methods. The point to note here is that by adding these overridden methods, we are giving the OS the opportunity to notify us of the user's intentions in two more situations. Much as we did when saving and loading our data in the Note to Self app.

It makes sense at this point to move on to the `LiveDrawingView` class, the main class of this app. We will come back to the `LiveDrawingActivity` class near the end of the chapter.

Coding the LiveDrawingView class

The first thing we will do is solve the problem of our `LiveDrawingView` class not being of type `View`. Update the class declaration as highlighted, like this:

```
class LiveDrawingView extends SurfaceView {
```

> **Note**
>
> You will need to import the `android.view.SurfaceView` class.

`SurfaceView` is a descendant of `View` and now `LiveDrawingView` is, by inheritance, also a type of `View`. Look again at the `import` statement that has been added. This relationship is made clear as highlighted next:

```
import android.view.SurfaceView
```

> **Note**
>
> Remember that it is because of polymorphism that we can send descendants of `View` to the `setContentView` method in the `LiveDrawingActivity` class and it is because of inheritance that the `LiveDrawingView` class is now a type of `SurfaceView`.

There are quite a few descendants of `View` that we could have extended to fix this initial problem, but we will see as we continue that the `SurfaceView` class has some very specific features that are perfect for real-time-interactive apps that made this choice the right one for us.

We still have errors in both this class and the `LiveDrawingActivity` class. Both are due to the lack of a suitable constructor method.

Here is a screenshot showing the error in the `LiveDrawingView` class since we extended `SurfaceView`:

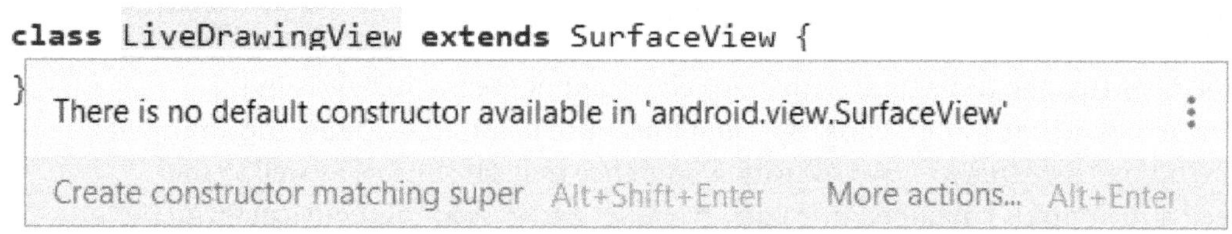

```
class LiveDrawingView extends SurfaceView {
```

Figure 21.1 – The error in the LiveDrawingView class

The error in `LiveDrawingActivity` is more obvious; we are calling a method that doesn't exist. However, the error shown in the previous screenshot is less easily understood. Let's discuss the error in the `LiveDrawingView` class declaration now.

The `LiveDrawingView` class, now it is a `SurfaceView`, must be supplied with a constructor because, as mentioned in the OOP chapters, once you have provided your own constructor the default (no parameter) one ceases to exist. As the `SurfaceView` class implements several different constructors, we must specifically implement one of these or write our own. Hence the previous error.

As none of the `SurfaceView` provided constructors are exactly what we need, we will provide our own.

> **Note**
>
> If you are wondering how on earth you know what constructors are supplied and any other details you need to find out about an Android class, just Google it. Type the class name followed by `API`. Google will almost always supply as the top result a link to the relevant page on the Android developer's website. Here is a direct link to the `SurfaceView` page: `https://developer.android.com/reference/android/view/SurfaceView.html`. Look under the **Public constructors** heading, and you will see that some constructors are optionally made available.

The `LiveDrawingActivity` also requires us to create a constructor that matches the way we try to initialize it in this line of code from the `LiveDrawingActivity` class:

```
mLiveDrawingView = new LiveDrawingView(this, size.x, size.y);
```

Let's add a constructor that matches the call from `LiveDrawingActivity` that passes in `this` and the screen resolution and solve both problems at once.

Coding the LiveDrawingView class

Remember that the `LiveDrawingView` class cannot see the variables in the `LiveDrawingActivity` class. By using the constructor, `LiveDrawingActivity` is providing `LiveDrawingView` with a reference to itself (`this`) as well as the screen size in pixels contained in `size.x` and `size.y`. Add this constructor to the `LiveDrawingView.java` file. The code must go within the opening and closing curly braces of the class. It is a convention but not required to place constructors above other methods but after member variable declarations:

```
// The LiveDrawingView constructor
// Called when this line:
// mLiveDrawingView = new LiveDrawingView(this, size.x,
size.y);
// is executed from LiveDrawingActivity
public LiveDrawingView(Context context, int x, int y) {
        // Super... calls the parent class
        // constructor of SurfaceView
        // provided by the Android API
        super(context);

}
```

> **Note**
>
> Import the `Context` class with this line of code:
>
> `import android.content.Context;`

Now we have no errors in our `LiveDrawingView` class or the `LiveDrawingActivity` class that initializes it.

At this stage, we could run the app and see that using `LiveDrawingView` as the `View` in `setContentView` has worked and we have a beautiful blank screen, ready to draw our particle systems on. Try this if you like, but we will be coding the `LiveDrawingView` class so that it does something, including adding code to the constructor, next.

We will be returning to this class constantly over the course of this project. What we will do right now is get the fundamentals set up ready to add the `ParticleSystem` instances after we have coded them in the next chapter.

To achieve this, first, we will add a bunch of member variables, then we will add some code inside the constructor to set the class up when it is instantiated/created by `LiveDrawingActivity`.

Following on, we get to code the `draw` method, which will reveal the new steps that we need to take to draw on the screen 60 times per second and we will also see some familiar code that uses our old friends `Canvas`, `Paint`, and `drawText` from the previous chapter.

At this point, we need to discuss some more theory – things such as how we will time the animations of the particles and how we lock these timings without interfering with the smooth running of Android. These last two topics, the **game loop** and **threads**, will then allow us to add the final code of the chapter and witness our particle system painting app in action – albeit with just a bit of text.

> **Note**
>
> A game loop is a concept that describes allowing virtual systems to update and draw themselves at the same time as allowing them to be altered/interacted with by the user.

Adding the member variables

Add the variables as shown below, after the `LiveDrawingView` declaration but before the constructor, then import the necessary extra classes:

```java
// Are we debugging?
private final boolean DEBUGGING = true;


// These objects are needed to do the drawing
private SurfaceHolder mOurHolder;
private Canvas mCanvas;
private Paint mPaint;


// How many frames per second did we get?
private long mFPS;
// The number of milliseconds in a second
private final int MILLIS_IN_SECOND = 1000;


// Holds the resolution of the screen
private int mScreenX;
```

```
private int mScreenY;
// How big will the text be?
private int mFontSize;
private int mFontMargin;


// The particle systems will be declared here later


// These will be used to make simple buttons
```

Add the following import code:

```
import android.graphics.Canvas;
import android.graphics.Paint;
import android.view.SurfaceHolder;
```

Be sure to study the code and then we can talk about it.

We are using the naming convention of adding m before the member variable names. As we add local variables in the methods, this will help distinguish them from each other.

Also, notice that all the variables are declared private. You could happily delete all the private access specifiers and the code would still work but as we have no need to access any of these variables from outside of this class, it is sensible to guarantee it can never happen by declaring them private.

The first member variable is DEBUGGING. We have declared this as final because we don't want to change its value during the app's execution. Note that declaring it final does not preclude us from switching its value manually when we wish to switch between debugging and not debugging.

The next three classes we declared instances of will handle the drawing on the screen. Notice the new one we have not seen before that I have highlighted:

```
// These objects are needed to do the drawing
private SurfaceHolder mOurHolder;
private Canvas mCanvas;
private Paint mPaint;
```

The SurfaceHolder class is required to enable drawing to take place. It literally is the object that *holds* the drawing surface. We will see the methods it allows us to use to draw on the screen when we code the draw method in a minute.

The next two variables give us a bit of insight into what we will need to achieve our smooth and consistent animation. Here they are again:

```
// How many frames per second did we get?
private long mFPS;
// The number of milliseconds in a second
private final int MILLIS_IN_SECOND = 1000;
```

The mFPS variable is of type long because it will be holding a huge number. Computers measure time in milliseconds since 1970 – more on that when we talk about the game loop. But for now, we need to know that monitoring and measuring the speed of each frame of animation is how we will make sure that the particles move exactly as they should.

The first mFPS will be reinitialized every frame of animation, around 60 times per second. It will be passed into each of the particle system (every frame of animation) so that it knows how much time has elapsed.

The MILLIS_IN_SECOND variable is initialized to 1000. There are indeed 1000 milliseconds in a second. We will use this variable in calculations as it will make our code clearer than if we used the literal value 1000. It is declared final because the number of milliseconds in a second will obviously never change.

The next piece of the code we just added is shown again here for convenience:

```
// Holds the resolution of the screen
private int mScreenX;
private int mScreenY;
// How big will the text be?
private int mFontSize;
private int mFontMargin;
```

The variables mScreenX and mScreenY will hold the horizontal and vertical resolution of the screen. Remember that they are being passed in from LiveDrawingActivity into the constructor.

The next two, mFontSize and mMarginSize, will be initialized based on the screen size in pixels, to hold a value in pixels to make the formatting of our text neat and more concise than constantly doing calculations for each bit of text.

Now we can begin to initialize some of these variables in the constructor.

Coding the LiveDrawingView constructor

Add the highlighted code to the constructor. Be sure to study the code as well and then we can discuss it:

```
public LiveDrawingView(Context context, int x, int y) {
    // Super... calls the parent class
    // constructor of SurfaceView
    // provided by Android
    super(context);

    // Initialize these two members/fields
    // With the values passed in as parameters
    mScreenX = x;
    mScreenY = y;

    // Font is 5% (1/20th) of screen width
    mFontSize = mScreenX / 20;
    // Margin is 1.3% (1/75th) of screen width
    mFontMargin = mScreenX / 75;

    // getHolder is a method of SurfaceView
    mOurHolder = getHolder();
    mPaint = new Paint();

    // Initialize the two buttons

    // Initialize the particles and their systems
}
```

The code we just added to the constructor begins by using the values passed in as parameters (x and y) to initialize mScreenX and mScreenY. Our entire LiveDrawingView class now has access to the screen resolution whenever it needs it. Here are the two lines again:

```
    // Initialize these two members/fields
    // With the values passed in as parameters
    mScreenX = x;
    mScreenY = y;
```

Next, we initialize mFontSize and mFontMargin as a fraction of the screen width in pixels. These values are a bit arbitrary, but they work, and we will use various multiples of these variables to align text neatly on the screen. Here are the two lines of code I am referring to:

```
// Font is 5% (1/20th) of screen width
mFontSize = mScreenX / 20;
// Margin is 1.3% (1/75th) of screen width
mFontMargin = mScreenX / 75;
```

Moving on, we initialize our Paint and SurfaceHolder objects. Paint uses the default constructor as we have done previously but mHolder uses the getHolder method, which is a method of the SurfaceView class. The getHolder method returns a reference that is initialized to mHolder so mHolder is now that reference. In short, mHolder is now ready to be used. We have access to this handy method because LiveDrawingView is a SurfaceView:

```
// getHolder is a method of SurfaceView
mOurHolder = getHolder();
mPaint = new Paint();
```

We will need to do more preparation in the draw method before we can use our Paint and Canvas classes as we have done before. We will see exactly what very soon. Notice the comments indicating where we will eventually get around to initializing the particle systems as well as two control buttons.

Let's get ready to draw.

Coding the draw method

Add the draw method shown next immediately after the constructor method. There will be a couple of errors in the code. We will deal with them, then we will go into detail about how the draw method will work in relation to the SurfaceView class because there are some completely alien-looking lines of code in there as well as some familiar ones. This is the code to add:

```
// Draw the particle systems and the HUD
private void draw() {
if (mOurHolder.getSurface().isValid()) {
// Lock the canvas (graphics memory) ready to draw
        mCanvas = mOurHolder.lockCanvas();
```

```
// Fill the screen with a solid color
mCanvas.drawColor(Color.argb(255, 0, 0, 0));

// Choose a color to paint with
mPaint.setColor(Color.argb(255, 255, 255, 255));

// Choose the font size
mPaint.setTextSize(mFontSize);

// Draw the particle systems

// Draw the buttons

// Draw the HUD
if(DEBUGGING){
        printDebuggingText();
}

    // Display the drawing on screen
    // unlockCanvasAndPost is a method of
    SurfaceHolder
    mOurHolder.unlockCanvasAndPost(mCanvas);
    }

}
```

We have two errors. One is that the Color class needs importing. You can fix this in the usual way or add the next line of code manually. Whichever method you choose, the following extra line needs to be added to the code at the top of the file:

```
import android.graphics.Color;
```

Let's deal with the other error.

Adding the printDebuggingText method

The second error is the call to `printDebuggingText`. The method doesn't exist yet. Let's add that now.

Add the code after the `draw` method:

```
private void printDebuggingText(){
    int debugSize = mFontSize / 2;
    int debugStart = 150;
    mPaint.setTextSize(debugSize);
    mCanvas.drawText("FPS: " + mFPS ,
            10, debugStart + debugSize, mPaint);

    // We will add more code here in the next chapter

}
```

The previous code uses the local variable `debugSize` to hold a value that is half that of the member variable `mFontSize`. This means that as `mFontSize` (which is used for the HUD) is initialized dynamically based on the screen resolution, `debugSize` will always be half that. The `debugSize` variable is then used to set the size of the font before we start drawing the text. The `debugStart` variable is just a guess at a good position vertically to start printing the debugging text.

These two values are then used to position a line of text on the screen that shows the current frames per second. As this method is called from `draw`, which in turn will be called from the game loop, this line of text will be constantly refreshed up to 60 times per second.

> **Note**
>
> It is possible that on very high- or very low-resolution screens, you might need to experiment with the text size to find something more appropriate for your screen.

Let's explore those new lines of code in the `draw` method and exactly how we can use `SurfaceView`, from which our `LiveDrawingView` class is derived, to handle all our drawing requirements.

Understanding the draw method and the SurfaceView class

Starting in the middle of the method and working outwards for a change, we have a few familiar things such as the calls to the drawColor, setTextSize, and drawText methods. We can also see the comment that indicates where we will eventually add code to draw the particle systems and the HUD:

- The drawColor code clears the screen with a solid color.

- The setTextSize method sets the size of the text for drawing the HUD.

- We will code drawing the HUD once we have explored particle systems a little more. We will let the player know how many particles and systems their drawing comprises.

What is totally new, however, is the code at the very start of the draw method. Here it is again:

```
if (mOurHolder.getSurface().isValid()) {
// Lock the canvas (graphics memory) ready to draw
mCanvas = mOurHolder.lockCanvas();
...
...
```

The if statement contains a call to getSurface and chains it with a call to isValid. If this line returns true, it confirms that the area of memory that we want to manipulate to represent our frame of drawing is available, and the code continues inside the if statement.

What goes on inside those methods (especially the first) is quite complex. They are necessary because all our drawing and other processing (such as moving the objects) will take place asynchronously with the code that detects the user input and listens to the operating system for messages. This wasn't an issue in the previous project because our code just drew a single frame and then sat there waiting.

Now we want to execute the code 60 times a second, we are going to need to confirm that we have access to the memory – before we access it.

This raises more questions about how this code runs asynchronously. That will be answered when we discuss threads shortly. For now, just know that the line of code checks if some other part of our code or Android itself is currently using the required portion of memory. If it is free, then the code inside the `if` statement executes.

Furthermore, the first line of code to execute inside the `if` statement calls the `lockCanvas` method so that if another app or Android tries to access the memory while our code is accessing it, it won't be able to. Then we do all our drawing.

Finally, in the `draw` method, there is this next line (plus comments) right at the end:

```
// Display the drawing on screen
// unlockCanvasAndPost is a method of SurfaceHolder
mOurHolder.unlockCanvasAndPost(mCanvas);
```

The `unlockCanvasAndPost` method sends our newly decorated `Canvas` object (`mCanvas`) for drawing to the screen and releases the lock so that other areas of code can use it again – albeit very briefly before the whole process starts again. This process happens in every single frame of animation.

We now understand the code in the `draw` method; however, we still don't have the mechanism that calls the `draw` method over and over. In fact, we don't even call the `draw` method once. We need to talk about game loops and threads.

The game loop

What is a game loop anyway? Almost every live drawing/graphics game has a game loop. Even games you might suspect do not, such as turn-based games, still need to synchronize player input with drawing and AI while following the rules of the underlying operating system.

There is a constant need to update the objects in the app, perhaps by moving them, drawing everything in its current position at the same time as responding to user input. A diagram might help:

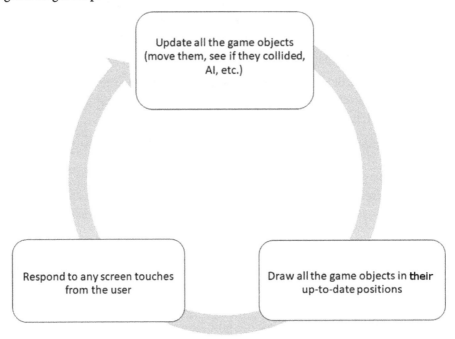

Figure 21.2 – Game loop

Our game loop comprises three main phases:

1. Update all game/drawing objects by moving them, detecting collisions, and processing AI such as the particle movements and state changes.

2. Based on the just-updated data, draw the frame of animation in its latest state.

3. Respond to screen touches from the user.

We already have a draw method for handling that part of the loop. This suggests that we will have a method to do all the updating as well. We will soon code the outline of an update method. In addition, we know that we can respond to screen touches although we will need to adapt slightly from all the previous projects because we are not working inside an Activity or using conventional UI widgets in a layout anymore.

There is a further issue in that (as I briefly mentioned) all the updating and drawing happens asynchronously to the detection of screen touches and listening to the operating system.

Note

Just to be clear, asynchronous means that it does not occur at the same time. Our game code will work by sharing execution time with Android and the user interface. The CPU will very quickly switch back and forth between our code and Android/user input.

But how exactly will these three phases be looped through? How will we code this asynchronous system within which the update and draw methods can be called and how will we make the loop run at the correct speed (frame rate)?

As we can probably guess, writing an efficient game loop is not as simple as a while loop.

Note

Our game loop will, however, also contain a while loop.

We need to consider timing, starting and stopping the loop, as well as not causing the OS to become unresponsive because we are monopolizing the entire CPU within our loop.

But when and how do we call our draw method? How do we measure and keep track of the frame rate? With these things in mind, our finished game loop can probably be better represented by this next diagram. Notice the introduction of the concept of **threads**.

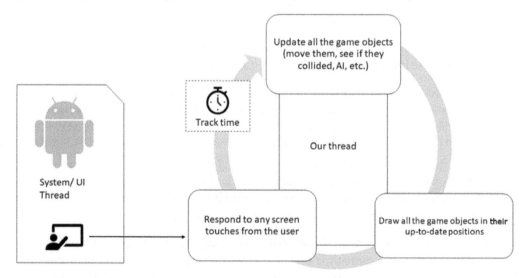

Figure 21.3 – Finished game loop

Now we know what we want to achieve, let's learn about threads.

Threads

So, what is a thread? You can think of threads in programming in the same way you do threads in a story. In one thread of a story, we might have the primary character battling the enemy on the frontline while in another thread the soldier's family is getting by, day to day. Of course, a story doesn't have to have just two threads; we could introduce a third thread. Perhaps the story also tells of the politicians and military commanders making decisions. And these decisions then subtly, or not so subtly, affect what happens in the other threads.

Programming threads are just like this. We create parts/threads in our program that control different aspects for us. In Android, threads are especially useful when we need to ensure that a task does not interfere with the main (UI) thread of the app or if we have a background task that takes a long time to complete and must not interrupt the main thread of execution. We introduce threads to represent these different aspects because of the following reasons:

- They make sense from an organizational point of view.
- They are a proven way of structuring a program that works.
- The nature of the system we are working on forces us to use them.

In Android, we use threads for all three reasons simultaneously. It makes sense, it works, and we must because the design of the Android system requires it.

Often, we use threads without knowing about it. This happens because we use classes that use threads on our behalf. All the animations we coded in *Chapter 19, Animations and Interpolations*, were all running in threads. Another such example in Android is the SoundPool class, which loads sound in a thread. We will see or rather hear SoundPool in action in *Chapter 23, Supporting Different Versions of Android, Sound Effects, and Spinner Widget*, and we saw and will see again that our code doesn't have to handle the aspects of threads we are about to learn about because it is all handled internally by the class. In this project, however, we need to get a bit more involved.

In real-time systems, think about a thread that is receiving the player's button taps for moving left and right at the same time as listening for messages from the OS such as calling onCreate (and other methods we will see soon) as one thread, and another thread that draws all the graphics and calculates all the movement.

Problems with threads

Programs with multiple threads can have problems. Like the threads of a story in which if proper synchronization does not occur, things can go wrong. What if our soldier went into battle before the battle or the war even existed? Weird.

Consider that we have a variable int x that represents a key piece of data that, say, three threads of our program use. What happens if one thread gets slightly ahead of itself and makes the data "wrong" for the other two. This problem is the problem of **correctness** caused by multiple threads racing to completion oblivious—because after all, they are just dumb code.

The problem of correctness can be solved by the close oversight of the threads and locking. **Locking** means temporarily preventing execution in one thread to be sure things are working in a synchronized manner – kind of like freezing a soldier from boarding a ship to war until the ship has docked and the gangplank has been lowered, avoiding an embarrassing splash.

The other problem with programs with multiple threads is the problem of **deadlock** where one or more threads become locked waiting for the "right" moment to access int x, but that moment never comes, and eventually, the entire program grinds to a halt.

You might have noticed that it was the solution to the first problem (correctness) that is the cause of the second problem (deadlock).

Fortunately, the problem has been solved for us. Just as we use the Activity class and override onCreate to know when we need to create our app, we can also use other classes to create and manage our threads. Just as with Activity, we only need to know how to use them – not exactly how they work.

So why did I tell you all this stuff about threads when you didn't need to know, you rightly ask. Simply because we will be writing code that looks different and is structured in an unfamiliar manner. If we can do the following, then we will have no sweat writing our Java code to create and work within our threads:

- Understand the general concept of a thread, which is just the same thing as a story thread, which happens almost simultaneously
- Learn the few rules of using a thread

There are a few different Android classes that handle threads. Different thread classes work best in different situations.

All we need to remember is that we will be writing parts of our program that run at *almost* the same time as each other.

> **Note**
>
> What do you mean almost? What is happening is that the CPU switches between threads in turn/asynchronous. However, this happens so fast that we will not be able to perceive anything but simultaneity/synchronous. Of course, in the story thread analogy, people do act entirely synchronously.

Let's take a glimpse at what our thread code will look like. Don't add any code to the project just yet. We can declare an object of type `Thread` like this:

```
Thread ourThread;
```

Initialize and start it like this:

```
ourThread = new Thread(this);
ourThread.start();
```

There is one more conundrum to this thread stuff. Look at the constructor that initializes the thread. Here is the line of code again for your convenience:

```
ourThread = new Thread(this);
```

Look at the highlighted argument that is passed to the constructor. We pass in `this`. Remember that the code is going inside the `LiveDrawingView` class, not `LiveDrawingActivity`. We can, therefore, surmise that `this` is a reference to a `LiveDrawingView` class (which extends `SurfaceView`).

It seems very unlikely that when the nerds at Android HQ wrote the `Thread` class they would have been aware that one day we would be writing our `LiveDrawingView` class. So how can this work?

The `Thread` class needs an entirely different type to be passed into its constructor. The `Thread` constructor needs an object of type `Runnable`.

> **Note**
>
> You can confirm this fact by looking at the `Thread` class on the Android developer's website here: `https://developer.android.com/reference/java/lang/Thread.html#Thread(java.lang.Runnable)`.

Do you remember we talked about interfaces in *Chapter 11, More Object-Oriented Programming*? As a reminder, we can implement an interface using the `implements` keyword and the interface name after the class declaration, like in this code:

```
class someClass extends someotherClass implements Runnable{
```

We must then implement the abstract methods of the interface. `Runnable` has just one. It is the `run` method.

> **Note**
>
> You can confirm this last fact by looking at the `Runnable` interface on the Android developer's website here: `https://developer.android.com/reference/java/lang/Runnable.html`.

We can then use the Java `@override` keyword to change what happens when the operating system allows our thread object to run its code:

```
class someClass extends someotherClass implements Runnable{
    @override
run(){
        // Anything in here executes in a thread
        // No skill needed on our part
        // It is all handled by Android, the Thread class
        // and the Runnable interface
}
}
```

Within the overridden `run` method, we will call two methods: one that we have started already, `draw`, and the other is `update`. The `update` method is where all our calculations and artificial intelligence will go. The code will look a bit like this – don't add it yet:

```
@override
public void run() {

    // Update the drawing based on
    // user input, physics,
    // collision detection and artificial intelligence
    update();
```

```
    // Draw all the particle systems in their updated
    locations
    draw();


}
```

When appropriate, we can also stop our thread like this:

```
ourThread.join();
```

Now everything that is in the run method is executing in a separate thread, leaving the default or UI thread to listen for touches and system events. We will see how the two threads communicate with each other in the drawing project shortly.

Note that exactly where all these parts of the code will go into our app has not been explained because it is so much easier to show you in the real project.

Implementing the game loop with a thread

Now we have learned about the game loop and threads, we can put it all together to implement our game loop in the Living Drawing project.

We will add the entire code for the game loop, including writing two methods in the LiveDrawingActivity class to start and stop the thread, which will control the loop.

> **Note**
>
> Can you guess how the Activity based class will start and stop the thread in the LiveDrawingView class?

Implementing Runnable and providing the run method

Update the class declaration by implementing Runnable, just like we discussed we would need to and as shown in this next highlighted code:

```
class LiveDrawingView extends SurfaceView implements Runnable{
```

Notice that we have a new error in the code. Hover the mouse pointer over the word Runnable and you will see a message informing you that we need to implement the run method, again, just as we discussed during the discussion on interfaces. Add the empty run method, including the @override label as shown in a moment.

It doesn't matter where you add it if it is within the LiveDrawingView class's curly braces and not inside another method. I added mine right after the constructor method because it is near the top and easy to get to. We will be editing this quite a bit in this chapter. Add the empty run method as shown next:

```
// When we start the thread with:
// mThread.start();
// the run method is continuously called by Android
// because we implemented the Runnable interface
// Calling mThread.join();
// will stop the thread
@Override
public void run() {
}
```

The error is gone and now we can declare and initialize a Thread object.

Coding the thread

Declare some more member variables and instances, as shown next, underneath all our other members in the LiveDrawingView class:

```
// Here is the Thread and two control variables
private Thread mThread = null;
// This volatile variable can be accessed
// from inside and outside the thread
private volatile boolean mDrawing;
private boolean mPaused = true;
```

Now we can start and stop the thread. Have a think about where we might do this. Remember that the app needs to respond to the operating system starting and stopping the app.

Starting and stopping the thread

Now we need to start and stop the thread. We have seen the code we need but when and where should we do it? Let's write two methods, one to start and one to stop, and then we can consider further when and from where to call these methods. Add these two methods inside the `LiveDrawingView` class. If their names sound familiar, it is not by chance:

```java
// This method is called by LiveDrawingActivity
// when the user quits the app
public void pause() {

    // Set mDrawing to false
    // Stopping the thread isn't
    // always instant
    mDrawing = false;
    try {
        // Stop the thread
        mThread.join();
    } catch (InterruptedException e) {
        Log.e("Error:", "joining thread");
    }

}


// This method is called by LiveDrawingActivity
// when the player starts the app
public void resume() {
    mDrawing = true;
    // Initialize the instance of Thread
    mThread = new Thread(this);

    // Start the thread
    mThread.start();
}
```

What is happening is slightly given away by the comments – did you read the comments? We now have a pause and resume method, which stop and start the Thread object using the same code we discussed previously.

Notice the new methods are public and therefore accessible from outside the class to any other class that has an instance of LiveDrawingView. Remember that LiveDrawingActivity has the fully declared and initialized instance of LiveDrawingView?

Let's use the Android Activity lifecycle to call these two new methods.

Using the Activity lifecycle to start and stop the thread

Update the overridden onResume and onPause methods in LiveDrawingActivity as shown next with the highlighted lines of code:

```java
@Override
protected void onResume() {
    super.onResume();

    // More code here later in the chapter
    mLiveDrawingView.resume();
}

@Override
protected void onPause() {
    super.onPause();

    // More code here later in the chapter
    mLiveDrawingView.pause();
}
```

Now our thread will be started and stopped when the operating system is resuming and pausing our app. Remember that onResume is called after onCreate the first time an app is created, not just after resuming from a pause. The code inside onResume and onPause uses the mLiveDrawingView object to call its resume and pause methods, which in turn has the code to start and stop the thread. This code then triggers the thread's run method to execute. It is in this run method (in LiveDrawingView) that we will code our game loop. Let's do that now.

Coding the run method

Although our thread is set up and ready to go, nothing happens because the run method is empty. Code the run method as shown next:

```
@Override
public void run() {
    // mDrawing gives us finer control
    // rather than just relying on the calls to run
    // mDrawing must be true AND
    // the thread running for the main
// loop to execute
    while (mDrawing) {

        // What time is it now at the start of the loop?
        long frameStartTime = System.currentTimeMillis();

        // Provided the app isn't paused
        // call the update method
        if(!mPaused){
            update();
            // Now the particles are in
            // their new positions

        }

        // The movement has been handled and now
        // we can draw the scene.
        draw();

        // How long did this frame/loop take?
        // Store the answer in timeThisFrame
        long timeThisFrame =
                System.currentTimeMillis() -
                frameStartTime;

        // Make sure timeThisFrame is at least 1
```

```
        // millisecond because accidentally dividing
        // by zero crashes the app
        if (timeThisFrame > 0) {
            // Store the current frame rate in mFPS
            // ready to pass to the update methods of
            // of our particles in the next frame/loop
            mFPS = MILLIS_IN_SECOND / timeThisFrame;
        }
    }
}
```

Notice there are two errors in Android Studio. This is because we have not written the update method yet. Let's quickly add an empty method (with a comment) for it. I added mine after the run method:

```
private void update() {
    // Update the particles


}
```

Now let's discuss in detail how the code in the run method achieves the aims of our game loop by looking at the whole thing a bit at a time.

This first part initiates a while loop with the condition mDrawing and it wraps the rest of the code inside run so the thread will need to be started (for run to be called) and mDrawing will need to be true for the while loop to execute:

```
@Override
public void run() {
    // mPlaying gives us finer control
    // rather than just relying on the calls to run
    // mPlaying must be true AND
    // the thread running for the main
    // loop to execute
    while (mPlaying) {
```

The first line of code inside the while loop declares and initializes a local variable frameStartTime with whatever the current time is. The static method currentTimeMillis of the System class returns this value. If later, we want to measure how long a frame has taken, then we need to know what time it started:

```
// What time is it now at the start of the loop?
long frameStartTime = System.currentTimeMillis();
```

Next, still inside the while loop, we check whether the app is paused and only if the app is not paused does this next code get executed. If the logic allows execution inside this block, then update is called:

```
// Provided the app isn't paused
// call the update method
if(!mPaused){
        update();
        // Now the particles are in
        // their new positions

    }
```

Outside of the previous if statement, the draw method is called to draw all the objects in the just-updated positions. At this point, another local variable is declared and initialized with the length of time it took to complete the entire frame (updating and drawing). This value is calculated by getting the current time, once again with currentTimeMillis, and subtracting frameStartTime from it:

```
        // The movement has been handled and collisions
        // detected now we can draw the scene.
        draw();

        // How long did this frame/loop take?
        // Store the answer in timeThisFrame
        long timeThisFrame =
                System.currentTimeMillis() -
                frameStartTime;
```

The next if statement detects whether timeThisFrame is greater than zero. It is possible for the value to be zero if the thread runs before objects are initialized. If you look at the code inside the if statement, it calculates the frame rate by dividing the elapsed time by MILLIS_IN_SECOND. If you divide by zero, the app will crash, which is why we do the check.

Once mFPS gets the value assigned to it, we can use it in the next frame to pass to the update method of all the particles, which we will code in the next chapter. They will use the value to make sure they move by precisely the correct amount based on their target speed and the length of time the frame has taken:

```
// Make sure timeThisFrame is at least 1
// millisecond because accidentally dividing
// by zero crashes the app
if (timeThisFrame > 0) {
    // Store the current frame rate in mFPS
    // ready to pass to the update methods of
    // the particles in the next frame/loop
    mFPS = MILLIS_IN_SECOND / timeThisFrame;
    }
  }
}
```

The result of the calculation that initializes mFPS in each frame is that mFPS will hold a fraction of 1. Therefore, when we use this value inside each of the particle objects, we will be able to use this calculation:

```
mSpeed / mFPS
```

In order to determine the elapsed time on any given frame, as the frame rate fluctuates, mFPS will hold a different value and supply the game objects with the appropriate number to calculate each move.

Running the app

Click the play button in Android Studio and the hard work and theory of the last two chapters will spring to life. Here are the beginnings of our app running on a tablet emulator:

Figure 21.4 – Running the app

You can see we now have a real-time system created with our game loop and a thread. If you run this on a real device, you will easily achieve 60 frames per second at this stage.

Summary

This was probably the most technical chapter so far. Threads, game loops, timing, using interfaces along with the Activity lifecycle, and so on… it's an awfully long list of topics to cram in.

If the exact interrelationships between these things are not entirely clear, it is not a problem. All you need to know is that when the user starts and stops the app, the `LiveDrawingActivity` class will handle starting and stopping the thread by calling the `LiveDrawingView` class's `pause` and `resume` methods. It achieves this via the overridden `onPause` and `onResume` methods, which are called by the OS.

Once the thread is running the code inside, the `run` method executes alongside the UI thread that is listening for user input. As we call the `update` and `draw` methods from the `run` method at the same time as keeping track of how long each frame is taking, our app is ready to rock and roll.

We just need to allow the user to add some particles to their artwork, which we can then update in each call to the `update` method and draw in each call to the `draw` method.

In the next chapter, we will be coding, updating, and drawing both the `Particle` and the `ParticleSytem` classes. In addition, we will be writing code for the user to interact (do some drawing) with the app.

22
Particle Systems and Handling Screen Touches

We already have the real-time system that we implemented in the previous chapter using a thread. In this chapter, we will create the entities that will exist and evolve in this real-time system as if they have a mind of their own; they will form the appearance of the drawings that the user can achieve.

We will also see how the user implements these entities by learning how to respond to interaction with the screen. This is different to interacting with a widget in a UI layout.

Here is what is coming up in this chapter:

- Adding custom buttons to the screen
- Coding the `Particle` class
- Coding the `ParticleSystem` class
- Handling screen touches
- The Android Studio Profiler tool

We will start by adding a custom UI to our app.

WARNING

This app produces bright flashing colors. It may cause discomfort or seizures for people with photosensitive epilepsy. Reader discretion is advised. You might like to simply read the theory for this project and not run the completed project.

Technical requirements

You can find the code files present in this chapter on GitHub at `https://github.com/PacktPublishing/Android-Programming-for-Beginners-Third-Edition/tree/main/chapter%2022`.

Adding custom buttons to the screen

We need to let the user control when to start another drawing and clear the screen of their previous work. We need the user to be able to decide if and when to bring the drawing to life. To achieve this, we will add two buttons to the screen, one for each of the tasks.

Add the members highlighted next in the `LiveDrawingView` class:

```
// These will be used to make simple buttons
private RectF mResetButton;
private RectF mTogglePauseButton;
```

We now have two `RectF` instances. These objects hold four floating-point coordinates each, one coordinate for each corner of our two proposed buttons.

Initialize the positions in the constructor of `LiveDrawingView`:

```
// Initialize the two buttons
mResetButton = new RectF(0, 0, 100, 100);
mTogglePauseButton = new RectF(0, 150, 100, 250);
```

Add the `import` for the `RectF` class:

```
import android.graphics.RectF;
```

Now we have added actual coordinates for the buttons. If you visualize the coordinates on the screen, then you will see they are in the top left-hand corner with the pause button just below the reset/clear button.

Now we can draw the buttons. Add these two lines of code in the `draw` method of the `LiveDrawingView` class:

```
// Draw the buttons
mCanvas.drawRect(mResetButton, mPaint);
mCanvas.drawRect(mTogglePauseButton, mPaint);
```

The new code uses an overridden version of the `drawRect` method, and we simply pass our two `RectF` instances straight in alongside the usual `Paint` instance. Our buttons will now be drawn to the screen.

We will see how we interact with these slightly crude buttons later in the chapter.

Implementing a particle system effect

A particle system is a system that controls particles. In our case, `ParticleSystem` is a class we will write that will spawn instances (lots of instances) of the `Particle` class (also a class we will write) that will create a simple explosion-like effect.

Here is an image of some particles controlled by a particle system:

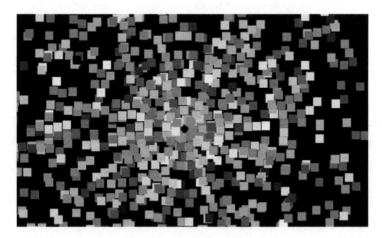

Figure 22.1 – Particle system effect

Just for clarification, each of the colored squares is an instance of the `Particle` class and all the `Particle` instances are controlled and held by the `ParticleSystem` class. In addition, the user will create multiple (hundreds) of `ParticleSystem` instances by drawing with their finger. The particles will appear as dots or blocks until the user taps the pause button, when they will come to life. We will examine the code closely enough that you will be able to set, in code, the size, color, speed, and quantity of `Particle` and `ParticleSystem` instances.

> **Note**
> It is left as an exercise for the reader to add additional buttons to the screen to allow the user to change these properties as a feature of the app.

We will start by coding the `Particle` class.

Coding the Particle class

Add the `import` statement, the member variables, and the constructor method, as shown in the following code:

```
import android.graphics.PointF;

class Particle {

    PointF mVelocity;
    PointF mPosition;

    Particle(PointF direction)
    {
        mVelocity = new PointF();
        mPosition = new PointF();

        // Determine the direction
        mVelocity.x = direction.x;
        mVelocity.y = direction.y;
    }
}
```

We have two members: one for velocity and one for position. They are both PointF objects. PointF holds two float values. The position is simple; it is just a horizontal and vertical value. The velocity is worth explaining a little more. Each of the two values in PointF will be a speed, one horizontal and the other vertical. It is the combination of these two speeds that will imply a direction.

> **Note**
>
> In the constructor, the two new PointF objects are instantiated and the x and y values of mVeleocity are initialized with the values passed in by the PointF direction parameter. Notice the way in which the values are copied from direction to mVelocity. Now, PointF mVelocity is not a reference to PointF passed in as a parameter. Each Particle instance will copy the values from direction (and they will be different for each instance), but mVelocity has no lasting connection to direction.

Next, add these three methods, and then we can then talk about them:

```
void update(float fps)
{
    // Move the particle
    mPosition.x += mVelocity.x;
    mPosition.y += mVelocity.y;
}


void setPosition(PointF position)
{
    mPosition.x = position.x;
    mPosition.y = position.y;
}


PointF getPosition()
{
    return mPosition;
}
```

Perhaps unsurprisingly, there is an update method. Each Particle instance's update method will be called each frame of the app by the ParticleSystem class' update method, which in turn will be called by the LiveDrawingView class (again in the update method), which we will code later in the chapter.

Inside the update method, the horizontal and vertical values of mPosition are updated using the corresponding values of mVelocity.

> **Note**
>
> Notice that we don't bother using the current frame rate in the update. You could amend this if you want to be certain that your particles will all fly at exactly the correct speed. But all the speeds are going to be random anyway. There is not much to gain from adding this extra calculation (for every particle). As we will soon see, however, the ParticleSystem class will need to take account of the current frames per second to measure how long it should run for.

Next, we coded the setPosition method. Notice that the method receives PointF, which is used to set the initial position. The ParticleSystem class will pass this position in when the effect is triggered.

Finally, we have the getPosition method. We need this method so that the ParticleSystem class can draw all the particles in the correct position. We could have added a draw method to the Particle class instead of the getPosition method and had the Particle class draw itself. In this implementation, there is no particular benefit to either option.

Now we can move on to the ParticleSysytem class.

Coding the ParticleSystem class

The ParticleSystem class has a few more details than the Particle class, but it is still reasonably straightforward. Remember what we need to achieve with this class: hold, spawn, update, and draw a bunch (quite a big bunch) of Particle instances.

Add the following members and import statements:

```
import android.graphics.Canvas;
import android.graphics.Color;
import android.graphics.Paint;
import android.graphics.PointF;

import java.util.ArrayList;
import java.util.Random;
```

```
class ParticleSystem {

    private float mDuration;

    private ArrayList<Particle> mParticles;
    private Random random = new Random();
    boolean mIsRunning = false;

}
```

We have four member variables: first, a float variable called mDuration that will
be initialized to the number of seconds we want the effect to run for. The ArrayList
instance called mParticles holds Particle instances and will hold all the Particle
objects we instantiate.

The Random instance called random is created as a member because we need to generate
so many random values that creating a new object each time would be sure to slow us
down a bit.

Finally, the mIsRunning Boolean will track whether the particle system is currently
being shown (updating and drawing).

Now we can code the init method. This method will be called each time we want a new
ParticleSystem. Notice that the one and only parameter is an int parameter called
numParticles.

When we call init, we can have some fun initializing crazy amounts of particles. Add the
init method and then we will look more closely at the code:

```
void init(int numParticles){

    mParticles = new ArrayList<>();
    // Create the particles

    for (int i = 0; i < numParticles; i++){
            float angle = (random.nextInt(360)) ;
            angle = angle * 3.14f / 180.f;

            // Option 1 - Slow particles
            //float speed = (random.nextFloat()/10);
```

```
        // Option 2 - Fast particles
        float speed = (random.nextInt(10)+1);


        PointF direction;

        direction = new PointF((float)Math.cos(angle) *
                    speed, (float)Math.sin(angle) *
                    speed);

        mParticles.add(new Particle(direction));
    }
}
```

The init method consists of just one for loop that does all the work. The for loop runs from zero to numParticles-1.

First, a random number between zero and 359 is generated and stored in the float variable called angle. Next, there is a little bit of math and we multiply angle by 3.14/180. This turns the angle in degrees to radian measurements, which are required by the Math class we will use in a moment.

Then we generate another random number between 1 and 10 and assign the result to a float variable called speed.

> **Note**
>
> I have added comments to suggest different options for values in this part of the code. I do this in several places in the ParticleSystem class and when we get to the end of the chapter, we will have some fun altering these values to see what effect it has on the drawing app.

Now that we have a random angle and speed, we can convert and combine them into a vector that can be used inside the update method of the Particle class to update its position each frame.

> **Note**
>
> A vector is a value that determines both direction and speed. Our vector is stored in the `direction` object until it is passed into the `Particle` constructor. Vectors can be of many dimensions. Ours is of two dimensions and therefore defines a heading between zero and 359 degrees and a speed between 1 and 10. You can read more about vectors, headings, sine, and cosine on my website here: `http://gamecodeschool.com/essentials/calculating-heading-in-2d-games-using-trigonometric-functions-part-1/`.

The single line of code that uses `Math.sin` and `Math.cos` to create a vector I have decided not to explain in full, because the magic occurs partly in the following formulas:

- Cosine of an angle * `speed`
- Sine of an angle * `speed`

It also happens partly in the hidden calculations within the cosine and sine functions provided by the `Math` class. If you want to know their full details, see the previous tip box.

Finally, a new `Particle` is created and then added to the `mParticles ArrayList` instance.

Next, we will code the `update` method. Notice that the `update` method does need the current frame rate as a parameter. Code the `update` method shown next:

```
void update(long fps){
    mDuration -= (1f/fps);

    for(Particle p : mParticles){
        p.update(fps);
    }

    if (mDuration < 0)
    {
        mIsRunning = false;
    }
}
```

The first thing that happens inside the `update` method is that the elapsed time is taken off `mDuration`. Remember that the `fps` parameter is the frames per second, so `1/fps` gives a value as a fraction of a second.

Next, there is an enhanced `for` loop that calls the `update` method for every `Particle` instance in the `mParticles` `ArrayList` instance.

Finally, the code checks to see if the particle effect has run its course with `if (mDuration < 0)`, and if it has, it sets `mIsRunning` to `false`.

Now we can code the `emitParticles` method, which will set each `Particle` instance running. This is not to be confused with `init`, which creates all the new particles and gives them their velocities. The `init` method will be called once before the user gets to interact, while the `emitParticles` method will be called each time the effect needs to be started as the user draws on the screen.

Add the `emitParticles` method:

```
void emitParticles(PointF startPosition) {
    mIsRunning = true;

    // Option 1 - System lasts for half a minute
    //mDuration = 30f;

    // Option 2 - System lasts for 2 seconds
    mDuration = 3f;

    for (Particle p : mParticles) {
        p.setPosition(startPosition);
    }

}
```

First, notice that a `PointF` reference for where all the particles will start is passed in as a parameter. All the particles will start at exactly the same position and then fan out each frame based on their individual velocities.

The `mIsRunning` Boolean is set to `true` and `mDuration` is set to `1f`, so the effect will run for one second, and the enhanced `for` loop calls `setPosition` for every particle to move them to the starting coordinates.

The final method for our `ParticleSysytem` class is the `draw` method, which will reveal the effect in all its glory. The method receives a reference to a `Canvas` instance and a `Paint` instance, so it can draw to the same canvas that the `LiveDrawingView` class has just locked in its `draw` method.

Add the `draw` method:

```
void draw(Canvas canvas, Paint paint){

        for (Particle p : mParticles) {

                // Option 1 - Coloured particles
                //paint.setARGB(255, random.nextInt(256),
                        //random.nextInt(256),
                        //random.nextInt(256));

                // Option 2 - White particles
                paint.setColor(
                Color.argb(255,255,255,255));


                // How big is each particle?
                float sizeX = 0;
                float sizeY = 0;

                // Option 1 - Big particles
                //sizeX = 25;
                //sizeY = 25;

                // Option 2 - Medium particles
                sizeX = 10;
                sizeY = 10;

                // Option 3 - Tiny particles
                //sizeX = 1;
                //sizeY = 1;

                // Draw the particle
                // Option 1 - Square particles
                //canvas.drawRect(p.getPosition().x,
                        //p.getPosition().y,
                        //p.getPosition().x + sizeX,
```

```
            //p.getPosition().y + sizeY,
            //paint);


        // Option 2 - Circle particles
        canvas.drawCircle(p.getPosition().x,
                p.getPosition().y,
                sizeX, paint);
    }
}
```

An enhanced for loop steps through each of the Particle instances in the
mParticles ArrayList instance. Each Particle, in turn, is drawn using the
drawRect method and the getPosition method. Notice the call to the paint.
setARGB method. You will see that we generate each of the color channels randomly.

Note

Notice in the comments that I have suggested different options for code
changes so we can have some fun when we have finished coding.

We can now start to put the particle system to work.

Spawning particle systems in the LiveDrawingView class

Add an ArrayList instance full of systems and some more members to keep track of
things. Add the highlighted code in the positions indicated by the existing comments:

```
// The particle systems will be declared here later
private ArrayList<ParticleSystem>
        mParticleSystems = new ArrayList<>();


private int mNextSystem = 0;
private final int MAX_SYSTEMS = 1000;
private int mParticlesPerSystem = 100;
```

Import the ArrayList class as follows:

```
import java.util.ArrayList;
```

We can now keep track of up to 1,000 particle systems with 100 particles in each. Feel free to play with these numbers.

> **Note**
>
> On a modern device, you can run particles into the millions without any trouble, but on the emulator, it will struggle with just hundreds of thousands.

Initialize the systems in the constructor by adding this highlighted code:

```
// Initialize the particles and their systems
for (int i = 0; i < MAX_SYSTEMS; i++) {
    mParticleSystems.add(new ParticleSystem());
    mParticleSystems.get(i).init(mParticlesPerSystem);
}
```

The code loops through the `ArrayList` instance, calling the constructor and then the `init` method on each of the `ParticleSystem` instances.

Update the systems for each frame of the loop by adding this highlighted code in the `update` method:

```
private void update() {
    // Update the particles
    for (int i = 0; i < mParticleSystems.size(); i++) {
        if (mParticleSystems.get(i).mIsRunning) {
            mParticleSystems.get(i).update(mFPS);
        }
    }
}
```

The previous code loops through each of the `ParticleSystem` instances, first checking if they are active and then calling the `update` method and passing in the current frames per second.

Draw the systems for each frame of the loop by adding this highlighted code to the `draw` method:

```
// Choose a color to paint with
mPaint.setColor(Color.argb(255, 255, 255, 255));
```

```
// Choose the font size
mPaint.setTextSize(mFontSize);

// Draw the particle systems
for (int i = 0; i < mNextSystem; i++) {

        mParticleSystems.get(i).draw(mCanvas, mPaint);

}

// Draw the buttons
mCanvas.drawRect(mResetButton, mPaint);
mCanvas.drawRect(mTogglePauseButton, mPaint);
```

The previous code loops through mParticleSystems, calling the draw method on each. Of course, we haven't actually spawned any instances yet. For that, we will need to learn how to respond to screen interactions.

Handling touches

To get started, add the OnTouchEvent method to the LiveDrawingView class:

```
@Override
public boolean onTouchEvent(MotionEvent motionEvent) {


    return true;
}
```

This is an overridden method and it is called by Android every time the user interacts with the screen. Look at the one and only parameter of the OnTouchEvent method.

Import the MotionEvent class with this line of code:

```
import android.view.MotionEvent;
```

It turns out that motionEvent has a whole bunch of data tucked away inside of it and this data contains the details of the touch that just occurred. The operating system sent it to us because it knows we will probably need some of it.

Notice that I said *some* of it. The `MotionEvent` class is quite extensive. It contains within it dozens of methods and variables.

> **Note**
>
> We will uncover a few details of the `MotionEvent` class in this project. You can explore the `MotionEvent` class in full here: `https://stuff. mit.edu/afs/sipb/project/android/docs/reference/ android/view/MotionEvent.html`. Note that it is not necessary to do further research to complete this project.

For now, all we need to know is the screen coordinates at the precise moment when the player's finger moves across the screen, touches the screen, or is removed from the screen.

Some of the variables and methods contained within `motionEvent` that we will use include the following.

- The `getAction` method, which unsurprisingly "gets" the action that was performed. Unfortunately, it supplies this information in a slightly encoded format, which explains the need for some of these other variables.

- The `ACTION_MASK` variable, which provides a value known as a mask, which with the help of a little bit more Java trickery can be used to filter the data from `getAction`.

- The `ACTION_UP` variable, which we can use to compare and see if the action performed is the one we want to respond to (removing a finger from the screen).

- The `ACTION_DOWN` variable, which we can use to compare and see if the action performed is the one we want to respond to.

- The `ACTION_MOVE` variable, which we can use to compare and see if the action performed is a move/drag.

- The `getX` method, which tells us a horizontal floating-point coordinate of where the event happened.

- The `getY` method, which tells us a vertical floating-point coordinate of where the event happened.

As a specific example, say we need to filter the data returned by the `getAction` method using `ACTION_MASK` and see if the result is the same as `ACTION_UP`. If it is, then we know that the user has just removed their finger from the screen, perhaps because they just tapped a button. Once we are sure the event is of the correct type, we will need to find out where it happened using the `getX` and `getY` methods.

There is one final complication. The "Java trickery" I referred to is the & bitwise operator, not to be confused with the logical && operator we have been using in conjunction with the if keyword.

The & bitwise operator checks to see if each corresponding parts in two values are true. This is the filter that is required when using ACTION_MASK with getAction.

> **Note**
>
> Sanity check. I was hesitant to go into detail about MotionEvent and bitwise operators. It is possible to complete this entire book and even a professional-quality interactive app without ever needing to fully understand them. If you know that the line of code we write in the next section determines the event type the player has just triggered, that is all you need to know. I just guessed that a discerning reader such as yourself would like to know the ins and outs. In summary, if you understand bitwise operators, great, you are good to go. If you don't, it doesn't matter, you are still good to go. If you are curious about bitwise operators (there are quite a few), you can read more about them here: https://en.wikipedia.org/wiki/Bitwise_operation.

Now we can code the onTouchEvent method and see all the MotionEvent stuff in action.

Coding the onTouchEvent method

Handle the user moving their finger on the screen by adding this highlighted code inside the onTouchEvent method to the code we already have:

```
// User moved a finger while touching screen
if ((motionEvent.getAction() &
            MotionEvent.ACTION_MASK)
        == MotionEvent.ACTION_MOVE) {

    mParticleSystems.get(mNextSystem).emitParticles(
            new PointF(motionEvent.getX(),
                    motionEvent.getY()));

    mNextSystem++;
    if (mNextSystem == MAX_SYSTEMS) {
        mNextSystem = 0;
```

```
            }
        }

        return true;
```

Add the following line of code to import the `PointF` class:

```
import android.graphics.PointF;
```

The `if` condition checks to see if the type of event was the user moving their finger. If it was, then the next particle system in `mParticleSystems` has its `emitParticles` method called. Afterward, the `mNextSystem` variable is incremented and a test is done to see if it was the last particle system. If it was, then `mNextSystem` is set to zero, ready to start reusing existing particle systems the next time one is required.

Handle the user pressing one of the buttons by adding this highlighted code right after the code we just discussed and before the `return` statement we have already coded:

```
// Did the user touch the screen
    if ((motionEvent.getAction() &
                MotionEvent.ACTION_MASK)
            == MotionEvent.ACTION_DOWN) {

        // User pressed the screen see if it was in a
        button
        if (mResetButton.contains(motionEvent.getX(),
                    motionEvent.getY())) {
                // Clear the screen of all particles
                mNextSystem = 0;
        }

        // User pressed the screen see if it was in a
        button
        if (mTogglePauseButton.contains
        (motionEvent.getX(), motionEvent.getY())) {
                mPaused = !mPaused;
```

```
            }
       }

   return true;
```

The condition of the if statement checks to see if the user has tapped the screen. If they have, then the contains method of the RectF class is used in conjunction with the getX and getY methods to see if that press was inside one of our custom buttons. If the reset button was pressed, all the particles will disappear because mNextSystem is set to zero. If the paused button is pressed, then the value of mPaused is toggled, causing the update method to stop/start being called in the thread.

Finishing the HUD

Add the highlighted code to the printDebuggingText method:

```
// We will add more code here in the next chapter
mCanvas.drawText("Systems: " + mNextSystem,
         10, mFontMargin + debugStart + debugSize * 2,
         mPaint);

mCanvas.drawText("Particles: " + mNextSystem *
mParticlesPerSystem,
         10, mFontMargin + debugStart + debugSize * 3,
         mPaint);
```

This code will print some interesting statistics to the screen to tell us how many particles and systems are currently being drawn.

> **WARNING**
>
> This app produces bright flashing colors. It may cause discomfort or seizures for people with photosensitive epilepsy. Reader discretion is advised. You might like to simply read the theory for this project and not run the completed project.

Running the app

Now we get to see the live drawing app in action and play with some of the different options we commented out in the code.

Run the app with small, round, colorful, fast particles. Just tap the screen in a few places:

Figure 22.2 – Tap the screen

Then resume drawing:

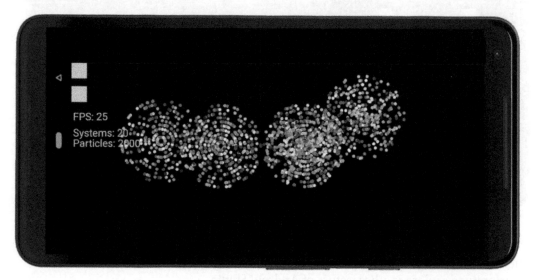

Figure 22.3 – Tap results

Do a kid's-style drawing with small, white, square, slow, long-duration particles:

Figure 22.4 – The kid's-style drawing

Then un-pause the drawing and wait for 20 seconds while the drawing comes to life and changes:

Figure 22.5 – The kid's-style drawing result

Before we move on to our next project, the Live Drawing app gives us an excellent opportunity to explore another feature of Android Studio.

The Android Studio Profiler tool

The Android Studio Profiler tool is quite complex and deep. But it is very simple to use it to do some really significant measurements with our app. We can see how much of the device's resources our app is using and therefore attempt to improve the efficiency of our app to make it run more efficiently and use less in the way of resources. By resources, I am talking about CPU and memory usage.

Code optimization is beyond the scope of the book, but a look at how we begin to monitor our app's performance is a good introduction. Select **View** from the main Android Studio menu and then select **Tool Windows | Profiler**.

You will see the following window in the lower area of Android Studio:

Figure 22.6 – Android Studio window

To get started using the Profiler tool, run the Live Drawing app. The Profiler tool should begin to display graphs and data as shown in the next figure.

Depending on the configuration of your PC firewall software, you might have to allow access for the Profiler tool to run. In addition, it is possible, but not certain, that you will have to left-click the + icon in the top left of the **Profiler** window, as highlighted in the preceding figure, and then select your AVD for the Profiler tool to connect to:

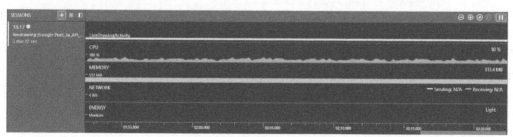

Figure 22.7 – live graph data

In the preceding figure, we can see live graph data for CPU usage, memory usage, network usage, and energy/battery usage. We will focus on CPU and memory usage.

Hover your mouse over the **CPU** row and then the **MEMORY** row to see pop-up details for each of these metrics. This next figure shows the details on my PC for these two metrics, photoshopped together:

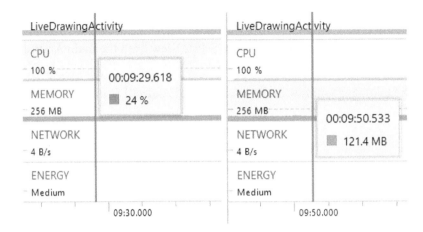

Figure 22.8 – Pop-up details for each metric

It is possible, even likely, that you will see different values to me. The previous figure shows that roughly a quarter of the CPU is in use and around 121 MB of RAM is in use.

Next, let's alter our code a little and observe the effect. In the `LiveDrawingView` class, edit the initialization of the `mParticlesPerSystem` member variable:

```
private int mParticlesPerSystem = 100;
```

Change it to this:

```
private int mParticlesPerSystem = 1000;
```

We have now increased the particle count per system by 10x. We did this to get a spike in our profiler data, as we will now use the app to draw some particle systems.

When you run the app again, draw a large number of particle systems by moving your finger/pointer across the screen. Notice that the CPU usage spikes when you draw some particle systems on the screen, though perhaps not as much as you expected. Mine spiked to just under 40% while the particles were moving and then settled back down to just over 25%. What might be more surprising if you have never played with a tool like a profiler before is that the memory usage barely changes at all.

The reason we got the results that we did is that the calculations of thousands of particles take up quite significant amounts of CPU. However, drawing particles on the screen does not require increased memory. The reason for this is that the memory for the app is all allocated near the start of the execution. Whether or not the particles are currently being shown to the user is not significant.

This short section was not intended to even scratch the surface of how we might optimize our graphics or CPU-intensive apps; it was just meant to introduce the idea that you might like to add optimization to your list of things to investigate further.

Summary

In this chapter, we saw how we can add thousands of self-contained entities to our real-time system. The entities were controlled by the `ParticleSystem` class, which in turn interacted with, and was controlled by, the game loop. As the game loop was running in a thread, we saw that the user can still interact seamlessly with the screen, and the operating system sends us the details of these interactions via the `onTouchEvent` method.

In the next chapter, our apps will finally get a bit noisier when we explore how to play sound effects; we'll also learn how to detect different versions of Android.

23
Supporting Different Versions of Android, Sound Effects, and Spinner Widget

In this chapter, we will learn how we can detect and handle different versions of Android. We will then be able to study the SoundPool class and the different ways we use it depending on the Android version of the device the app is running on. At this point, we can then put everything we have learned into producing a cool sound demo app, which will also introduce us to a new UI widget, **Spinner**.

In summary, in this chapter we will cover the following:

- Learning how to handle different versions of Android

- Learning how to use the Android SoundPool class

- Coding a sound-based app also using the SpinnerView widget

Let's get started.

Handling different versions of Android

Most of the time throughout this book, we haven't paid any attention to supporting older Android devices, the main reason being that all the up-to-date parts of the API we have been using work on such a high percentage of devices (in excess of 99%) that it has not seemed worthwhile. Unless you intend on carving out a niche in apps for ancient Android relics, this seems like a sensible approach. Regarding playing sounds, however, there have been some relatively recent modifications to the Android API.

Actually, this isn't immediately a big deal because devices newer than this can still use the old parts of the API. But it is good practice to specifically handle these differences in compatibility, because eventually, one day, the older parts might not work on newer versions of Android.

The main reason for discussing this here and now is that the slight differences in pre- and post-Android Lollipop sound handling give us a good excuse to see how we can deal with things like this in our code.

We will see how we can make our app compatible with the very latest devices and pre-Lollipop devices as well.

The class we will be using to make some noise is the `SoundPool` class. First, let's look at some simple code for detecting the current Android version.

Detecting the current Android version

We can determine the current version of Android using the static variables of the `Build.Version` class and we can determine whether it is newer than a specific version by comparing it to that version's appropriate `Build.VERSION_CODES` variable. If that explanation was a bit of a mouthful, just look at how we determine whether the current version is equal to or newer (greater) than Lollipop:

```
if (Build.VERSION.SDK_INT >= Build.VERSION_CODES.LOLLIPOP) {

    // Lollipop or newer code goes here

} else {

    // Code for devices older than lollipop here

}
```

Now let's see how to make some noise with Android devices newer, and then older, than Lollipop.

The SoundPool class

The SoundPool class allows us to hold and manipulate a collection of sound effects – literally, a pool of sounds. The class handles everything from decompressing a sound file such as a .wav or a .ogg to keeping an identifying reference to it via an integer ID, and, of course, playing the sound. When the sound is played, it is done so in a non-blocking manner (using a thread behind the scenes) that does not interfere with the smooth running of our app or our users' interaction with it.

The first thing we need to do is add the sound effects to a folder called assets in the main folder of the game project. We will do this for real shortly.

Next, in our Java code, declare an object of the SoundPool type and an int to use as an ID for each sound effect we intend to use. We also declare another int called nowPlaying, which we can use to track which sound is currently playing, and we will see how we do this shortly:

```
// create an ID
SoundPool sp;
int nowPlaying =-1;
int repeats = 2;
int idFX1 = -1;
float volume = 1;// Volumes rage from 0 through 1
```

Now we will look at the two different ways we initialize a SoundPool depending upon the version of Android the device is using. This is the perfect opportunity to use our method of writing different code for different versions of Android.

Initializing SoundPool the new way

The new way involves us using an AudioAttributes object to set the attributes of the pool of sound we want.

In the first block of code we use chaining and call four separate methods on one object that initialize our AudioAttributes object (audioAttributes):

```
// Instantiate a SoundPool dependent on Android version
if (Build.VERSION.SDK_INT >= Build.VERSION_CODES.LOLLIPOP) {

    // The new way
    // Build an AudioAttributes object
AudioAttributes audioAttributes =
        // First method call
new AudioAttributes.Builder()
// Second method call
        .setUsage
        (AudioAttributes.USAGE_ASSISTANCE_SONIFICATION)
        // Third method call
        .setContentType
        (AudioAttributes.CONTENT_TYPE_SONIFICATION)
        // Fourth method call
        .build();// Yay! A semicolon

    // Initialize the SoundPool
    sp = new SoundPool.Builder()
        .setMaxStreams(5)
        .setAudioAttributes(audioAttributes)
        .build();
}
```

In the code, we use chaining and the Builder method of this class to initialize an AudioAttributes object to let it know that it will be used for UI interaction with USAGE_ASSISTANCE_SONIFICATION.

We also use the CONTENT_TYPE_SONIFICATION value, which lets the class know it is for responsive sounds, for example, a user button click, a collision, or similar.

Now we can initialize the SoundPool (sp) itself by passing in the AudioAttributes object (audioAttributes) and the maximum number of simultaneous sounds we are likely to want to play.

The second block of code chains another four methods to initialize sp, including a call to setAudioAttributes that uses the audioAttributes object that we initialized in the earlier block of chained methods.

Now we can write an else block of code that will, of course, have the code for the old way of doing things.

Initializing SoundPool the old way

No need for an AudioAttributes object; simply initialize the SoundPool (sp) by passing in the number of simultaneous sounds. The final parameter is for sound quality and passing 0 is all we need to do. This is much simpler than the new way but also less flexible regarding the choices we can make:

```
else {
    // The old way
    sp = new SoundPool(5, AudioManager.STREAM_MUSIC, 0);
}
```

> **Note**
>
> We could use the old way and the newer versions of Android would handle it. However, we'd get a warning about using deprecated methods. That is what the official documentation says about it.
>
> Furthermore, the new way gives access to more features, as we saw. And anyway, it's a good excuse to look at some simple code to handle different versions of Android.

Now we can go ahead and load up (decompress) the sound files into our SoundPool.

Loading sound files into memory

As with our thread control, we are required to wrap our code in try-catch blocks. This makes sense because reading a file can fail for reasons beyond our control, but also we are forced to because the method that we use throws an exception and the code we write will not compile otherwise.

Inside the try block, we declare and initialize an object of the AssetManager and AssetFileDescriptor types.

The `AssetFileDescriptor` instance is initialized by using the `openFd` method of the `AssetManager` object, which actually decompresses the sound file. We then initialize our ID (`idFX1`) at the same time as we load the contents of `AssetFileDescriptor` into our `SoundPool`.

The `catch` block just outputs a message to the console to let us know if something has gone wrong. Note that this code is the same regardless of the Android version:

```
try{

    // Create objects of the 2 required classes
    AssetManager assetManager = this.getAssets();
    AssetFileDescriptor descriptor;

    // Load our fx in memory ready for use
    descriptor = assetManager.openFd("fx1.ogg");
    idFX1 = sp.load(descriptor, 0);
}catch(IOException e){

    // Print an error message to the console
    Log.d("error", "failed to load sound files");
}
```

We are ready to make some noise.

Playing a sound

At this point, there is a sound effect in our `SoundPool` instance and we have an ID by which we can refer to it.

This code is the same regardless of how we built the `SoundPool` object and this is how we play the sound. Notice in the next line of code that we initialize the `nowPlaying` variable with the return value from the same method that plays the sound.

The following code, therefore, simultaneously plays a sound and loads the value of the ID that is being played into nowPlaying:

```
nowPlaying = sp.play(idFX1, volume, volume, 0, repeats, 1);
```

> **Note**
>
> It is not necessary to store the ID in nowPlaying to play a sound, but it has its uses as we will now see.

The parameters of the play method are as follows:

- The ID of the sound effect
- The left speaker volume and the right speaker volume
- The priority over other sounds
- The number of times to repeat the sound
- The rate/speed it is played (1 is the normal rate)

Just one more thing before we make the sound demo app.

Stopping a sound

It is also very trivial to stop a sound while it is still playing with the stop method. Note that there might be more than one sound effect playing at any given time, so the stop method needs the ID of the sound effect to stop:

```
sp.stop(nowPlaying);
```

When you call play, you only need to store the ID of the currently playing sound if you want to track it so you can interact with it at a later time. As we will see soon, the code to play a sound in the Pong game will look more like this:

```
sp.play(mBeepID, 1, 1, 0, 0, 1);
```

The previous line of code would simply play the chosen sound (mBeepID) at full volume, with the lowest priority, until it ends with no repeats at the normal speed.

Now we can make the sound demo app.

Sound demo app introducing the Spinner widget

Of course, with all this talk of sound effects, we need some actual sound files. You can make your own with Bfxr (explained next) or use the ones supplied. The sound effects for this app are in the download bundle in the `assets` folder of the `Chapter 23/Sound Demo` folder. But you might like to make your own.

Making sound effects

There is an open source app called Bfxr that allows us to make our own sound effects. Here is a very fast guide to making your own sound effects using Bfxr. Grab a free copy from `www.bfxr.net`.

> **Note**
>
> Note that the sound effects for the sound demo app are supplied to you in the `Chapter 23/assets` folder. You don't have to create your own sound effects unless you want to. It is still worth getting this free software and learning how to use it.

Follow the simple instructions on the website to set it up. Try out a few of these things to make cool sound effects:

> **Note**
>
> This is a seriously condensed tutorial. You can do so much more with Bfxr. To learn more, read the tips on the website at the previous URL. If you have any trouble downloading Bfxr, you can use the website to create all your sound effects or just use the examples provided.

1.   Run Bfxr:

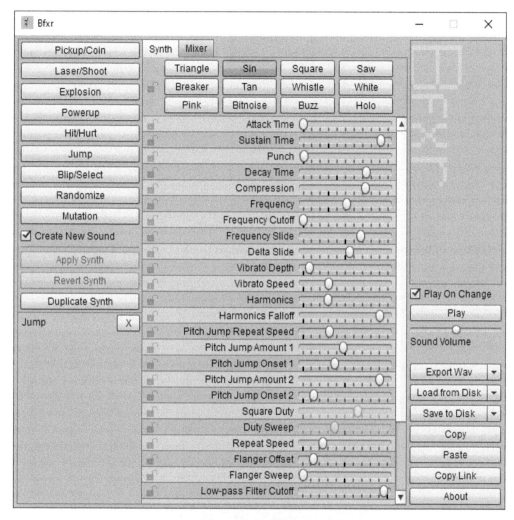

Figure 23.1 – Bfxr page

2. Try out all the preset types that generate a random sound of that type. When you have a sound that is close to what you want, move on to the next step:

Figure 23.2 – Different effects

3. Use the sliders to fine-tune the pitch, duration, and other aspects of your new sound:

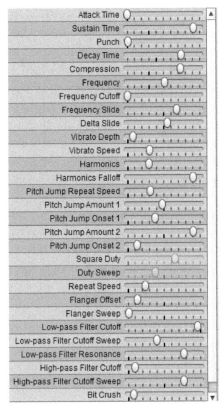

Figure 23.3 – Fine-tune your sound

4. Save your sound by clicking the **Export Wav** button. Despite the text of this button, as we will see, we can save in formats other than .wav too:

Figure 23.4 – The Export Wav button

5. Android works very well with sounds in the OGG format, so when asked to name your file, use the .ogg extension at the end of the filename.

6. Repeat *steps 2* to *5* to create three cool sound effects. Name them fx1.ogg, fx2.ogg, and fx3.ogg. We use the .ogg file format as it is more compressed than formats such as WAV.

Once you have your sound files ready, we can proceed with the app.

Laying out the sound demo

I will describe the parts of the project we are getting used to a little more concisely than in previous projects. Every time there is a new concept, however, I will be sure to explain it in full. I guess by now you will be fine with dragging a few widgets onto a ConstraintLayout and changing their text properties.

Complete the following steps. If you have any problems at all, you can copy or view the code in the Chapter 23 folder of the download bundle:

1. Create a new project, call it Sound Demo, choose the **Empty Activity** template, leave all the other settings at their defaults, and delete the **Hello world!** TextView from the activity_main.xml file.

2. Now we will build a layout in the `activity_main.xml` file, so be sure to be in design view. In this order, from top to bottom then left to right, drag a **Spinner** from the **Containers** category, a **SeekBar (discrete)** from the **Widgets** category, and four Buttons from the palette onto the layout, arranging and resizing them and setting their `text` properties as shown in the next screenshot:

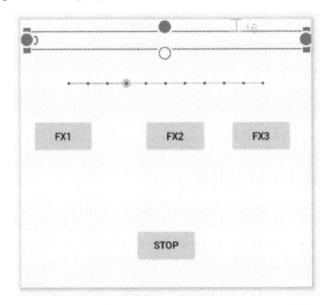

Figure 23.5 – Building a layout in the activity_main.xml file

3. Click the **Infer Constraints** button.

4. Use the following table to set their properties:

Widget	Property to change	Value to set
Spinner	id	spinner
Spinner	spinnerMode	dropdown
Spinner	entries	@array/spinner_options
SeekBar	id	seekBar
SeekBar	max	10
Button (FX 1)	id	btnFX1
Button (FX 2)	id	btnFX2
Button (FX 3)	id	btnFX3
Button (STOP)	id	btnStop

5.   Next, add the following highlighted code to the `strings.xml` file in the `values` folder. We used this array of string resources that is named `spinner_options` for the `options` property in the previous step. It will represent the options that can be chosen from our `Spinner` widget:

```
<resources>
    <string name="app_name">Sound Demo</string>
    <string name="hello_world">Hello world!</string>

    <string-array name="spinner_options">
      <item>0</item>
      <item>1</item>
      <item>3</item>
      <item>5</item>
      <item>10</item>
    </string-array>

    </resources>
```

Run the app now and you will not initially see anything that we haven't seen before. If you click on the spinner, however, you will see the options from our string array called `spinner_options`. We can use the spinner to control the number of times a sound effect repeats when played:

Figure 23.6 – spinner_options

Let's write the Java code to make this app work, including how we interact with our spinner.

Using your operating system's file browser, go to the `app\src\main` folder of the project and add a new folder called `assets`.

There are three sound files ready-made for you in the `Chapter 23/assets` folder of the download bundle. Place these three files into the assets directory you just created or use the ones you created yourself. The important thing is that their filenames are `fx1.ogg`, `fx2.ogg`, and `fx3.ogg`.

Coding the sound demo

First, we will change the class declaration so we can handle interaction with all our widgets efficiently. Edit the declaration to implement `View.OnClickListener` as highlighted next:

```
public class MainActivity extends AppCompatActivity
implements View.OnClickListener {
```

We will add the required `onClick` method shortly.

Now, we add some member variables for our `SoundPool`, sound effect IDs, `nowPlaying int` as previously discussed, and we will also add a `float` to hold a value for volume between `0` (silent) and `1` (full volume relative to the current volume of the device). We'll also add an `int` called `repeats` that unsurprisingly holds the value of the number of times we will repeat a given sound effect:

```
SoundPool sp;

int idFX1 = -1;
int idFX2 = -1;
int idFX3 = -1;
int nowPlaying = -1;

float volume = .1f;
int repeats = 2;
```

Now, in the `onCreate` method, we can get a reference and set a click listener for our buttons in the usual way. Add the following code to the project:

```
Button buttonFX1 = findViewById(R.id.btnFX1);
buttonFX1.setOnClickListener(this);


Button buttonFX2 = findViewById(R.id.btnFX2);
buttonFX2.setOnClickListener(this);


Button buttonFX3 = findViewById(R.id.btnFX3);
buttonFX3.setOnClickListener(this);


Button buttonStop = findViewById(R.id.btnStop);
buttonStop.setOnClickListener(this);
```

Still in `onCreate`, we can initialize our `SoundPool` (`sp`) based on the version of Android that the device is using. Add the following code to the project:

```
// Instantiate our SoundPool based on the version of Android
if (Build.VERSION.SDK_INT >= Build.VERSION_CODES.LOLLIPOP) {
    AudioAttributes audioAttributes =
        new AudioAttributes.Builder()
    .setUsage(AudioAttributes.
    USAGE_ASSISTANCE_SONIFICATION)

    .setContentType(
    AudioAttributes.CONTENT_TYPE_SONIFICATION)
                .build();

    sp = new SoundPool.Builder()
                .setMaxStreams(5)
                .setAudioAttributes(audioAttributes)
                .build();
} else {
    sp = new SoundPool(5, AudioManager.STREAM_MUSIC, 0);
}
```

> **Note**
>
> Add the following `import` statements for the previous code using your preferred method:
>
> import android.media.AudioAttributes;
>
> import android.media.AudioManager;
>
> import android.media.SoundPool;
>
> import android.os.Build;
>
>
> import android.view.View;
>
> import android.widget.Button;

Next, we load each of our sound effects in turn and initialize our IDs with a value that points to the related sound effect that we load into the SoundPool. The whole thing is wrapped in a try-catch block as required. Add the following code to the project:

```
try{
    // Create objects of the 2 required classes
    AssetManager assetManager = this.getAssets();
    AssetFileDescriptor descriptor;

    // Load our fx in memory ready for use
    descriptor = assetManager.openFd("fx1.ogg");
    idFX1 = sp.load(descriptor, 0);

    descriptor = assetManager.openFd("fx2.ogg");
    idFX2 = sp.load(descriptor, 0);

    descriptor = assetManager.openFd("fx3.ogg");
    idFX3 = sp.load(descriptor, 0);


}catch(IOException e){
    // Print an error message to the console
    Log.e("error", "failed to load sound files");
}
```

> **Note**
>
> Add the following `import` statements for the previous code using your preferred method:
>
> `import android.content.res.AssetFileDescriptor;`
>
> `import android.content.res.AssetManager;`
>
> `import android.util.Log;`
>
> `import java.io.IOException;`

Then we see how we are going to handle the `SeekBar` widget. As you probably have come to expect, we will use an anonymous class. We use the `OnSeekBarChangeListener` class and override the `onProgressChanged`, `onStartTrackingTouch`, and `onStopTrackingTouch` methods.

We only need to add code to the `onProgressChanged` method. Within this method, we simply change the value of our volume variable and then use the `setVolume` method on our `SoundPool` object, passing in the currently playing sound effect and the volume of the left and right channels of sound. Add the following code to the project:

```
// Now setup the seekbar
SeekBar seekBar = findViewById(R.id.seekBar);


seekBar.setOnSeekBarChangeListener(new SeekBar.
OnSeekBarChangeListener() {

    @Override
    public void onProgressChanged(SeekBar seekBar,
    int value, boolean fromUser) {

            volume = value / 10f;
            sp.setVolume(nowPlaying, volume, volume);
    }

    @Override
    public void onStartTrackingTouch(SeekBar seekBar) {
    }

    @Override
```

```
            public void onStopTrackingTouch(SeekBar seekBar) {


        }
});
```

> **Note**
>
> Add the following `import` statement for the previous code using your preferred method:
>
> `import android.widget.SeekBar;`

After the `SeekBar` code comes the `Spinner` code and another anonymous class to handle user interaction. We use `AdapterView.OnItemSelectedListener` to override the `onItemSelected` and `onNothingSelected` methods.

All our code goes in the `onItemSelected` method, which creates a temporary string named `temp` and then uses the `Integer.ValueOf` method to convert the string into an `int`, which we can use to initialize the `repeats` variable. Add the following code to the project:

```
// Now for the spinner
final Spinner spinner = (Spinner) findViewById(R.id.spinner);
spinner.setOnItemSelectedListener(
new AdapterView.OnItemSelectedListener() {

    @Override
    public void onItemSelected(AdapterView<?>
    parentView, View selectedItemView,
    int position, long id) {

            String temp = String.valueOf(
            spinner.getSelectedItem());

            repeats = Integer.valueOf(temp);
    }

    @Override
    public void onNothingSelected(AdapterView<?> parentView) {
```

```
        }


});
```

> **Note**
>
> Add the following import statements for the previous code using your preferred method:
>
> ```
> import android.widget.AdapterView;
>
> import android.widget.Spinner;
> ```

That's everything from onCreate.

Now implement the onClick method, which is required because this class implements the View.OnClickListener interface. Quite simply, there is a case statement for each button. There is a case statement to play each of our three sound effects, set the volume, and set the number of times to repeat. Notice that the return value for each call to play is stored in nowPlaying. When the user presses the **STOP** button, we simply call stop with the current value of nowPlaying, causing the most recently started sound effect to stop. Add the following code to the project:

```
@Override
public void onClick(View v) {
    switch (v.getId()){
        case R.id.btnFX1:
                sp.stop(nowPlaying);
                nowPlaying = sp.play(idFX1, volume,
                volume, 0, repeats, 1);
                break;


        case R.id.btnFX2:
                sp.stop(nowPlaying);
                nowPlaying = sp.play(idFX2,
                volume, volume, 0, repeats, 1);
                break;


        case R.id.btnFX3:
                sp.stop(nowPlaying);
                nowPlaying = sp.play(idFX3,
```

```
                        volume, volume, 0, repeats, 1);
                    break;


            case R.id.btnStop:
                    sp.stop(nowPlaying);
                    break;
        }
    }
```

We can now run the app. Make sure the volume on your device is turned up if you can't hear anything.

Click the appropriate button for the sound effect you want to play. Change the volume and the number of times it is repeated and, of course, try stopping it with the **STOP** button.

Also note you can repeatedly tap multiple play buttons when a sound effect is already playing, and the sounds will be played simultaneously up to the maximum number of streams (5) that we set.

Summary

In this chapter, we looked closely at the SoundPool class, including how we can detect which version of Android the user has and vary our code accordingly. Then, we used all this knowledge to complete the sound demo app.

In the next chapter, we will learn how to make our apps work with multiple different layouts.

24
Design Patterns, Multiple Layouts, and Fragments

We have come a long way since the start when we were just setting up Android Studio. Back then, we went through everything step by step, but as we have proceeded we have tried to show not just how to add x to y or feature a to app b, but to enable you to use what you have learned in your own ways to bring your own ideas to life.

At first glance, this chapter might seem dry and technical, but this chapter is more about your future apps than anything in the book so far. We will look at a few aspects of Java and Android that you can use as a framework or template to make evermore exciting and complex apps at the same time as keeping the code manageable. This is the key to successful modern apps. Furthermore, I will suggest areas of further study that there is simply not enough room to even scratch the surface of in this book.

In this chapter, we will learn about the following:

- Patterns and model-view-controller

- Android design guidelines

- Getting started with real-world designs and handling multiple different devices

- An introduction to Fragments

Let's get started.

Technical requirements

You can find the code files present in this chapter on GitHub at `https://github.com/PacktPublishing/Android-Programming-for-Beginners-Third-Edition/tree/main/chapter%2024`.

Introducing the model-view-controller pattern

The model-view-controller pattern involves the separation of different aspects of our app into distinct parts called layers. Android apps commonly use the model-view-controller pattern. A pattern is simply a recognized way to structure our code and other application resources such as layout files, images, databases, and so on.

Patterns are useful to us because by conforming to a pattern, we can be more confident we are doing things right and are less likely to have to undo lots of hard work because we have coded ourselves into an awkward situation.

There are many patterns in computer science but an understanding of **model-view-controller** (MVC) will be enough to create some professionally built Android apps.

We have been partly using MVC already, so let's look at each of the three layers in turn:

- **Model**: Model refers to the data that drives our app and any logic/code that specifically manages it and makes it available to the other layers. For example, in our Note to Self app, the `Note` class along with its getters, setters, and JSON code was the data and logic.

- **View**: The view of the Note to Self app was all the widgets in all the different layouts. Anything the user can see or interact with on the screen is typically part of the view. And you probably remember that the widgets came from the `View` class hierarchy of the Android API.

- **Controller**: The controller is the bit in between the view and the model. It interacts with both and keeps them separate. It contains what is known in geek speak as the application logic. If a user taps a button, the application layer decides what to do about it. When the user clicks **OK** to add a new note, the application layer listens for the interaction on the view layer. It captures the data contained in the view and passes it to the model layer.

> **Note**
>
> Design patterns are a huge topic. There are many different design patterns and if you want a beginner-friendly introduction to the topic in general, I would recommend *Head First Design Patterns*. If you want to really dive into the world of design patterns, then you can try *Design Patterns: Elements of Reusable Object-Oriented Software*, which is recognized as a kind of design pattern oracle but is much harder reading.

As the book progresses, we will also begin to utilize more of the object-oriented programming aspects we have discussed but not fully benefited from so far. We will do so step by step.

Android design guidelines

App design is a vast topic. It is a topic that could only begin to be taught in a book of its own. Also, like programming, you can only start to get good at app design with constant practice, review, and improvement.

So, what exactly do I mean by design? I am talking about where you put the widgets on the screen, which widgets, what color should they be, how big should they be, how to transition between screens, the best way to scroll a page, when and which animation interpolators to use, what screens your app should be divided into, and much more besides.

This book will hopefully leave you well qualified to be able to *implement* all your choices for the above questions. It unfortunately doesn't have the space, and the author probably doesn't have the skill, to teach you how to *make* those choices.

> **Note**
>
> You might be wondering, "What should I do?" Keep making apps and don't let a lack of design experience and knowledge stop you! Even release your apps to the app store. Keep in mind, however, that there is this whole other topic – design – that needs some attention if your apps are going to truly be world-class.

In even medium-sized development companies, the designer is rarely also the programmer, and even very small companies will often outsource the design of their app (or designers might outsource the coding).

Designing is both art and science, and Google has demonstrated that they recognize this with high-quality support for both existing designers and aspiring new designers.

> **Note**
>
> I highly recommend you visit and bookmark this web page: `https://developer.android.com/design/`. It is quite detailed and comprehensive, is totally Android focused, and has a load of resources in the form of images, color palettes, and guidelines.

Make understanding design principles a short-term goal. Make improving your actual design skills an ongoing task. Visit and read design-focused websites and try and implement the ideas that you find exciting.

Most important of all, however, don't wait until you are a design expert to make apps. Keep bringing your ideas to life and publishing them. Make a point of making each app a little better designed than the last.

We will see in the coming chapters and have seen already, that the Android API makes available to us a whole bunch of super-stylish UIs that we can take advantage of with very little code or design skill. These UIs go a long way to making your apps look like they have been designed by a professional.

Real-world apps

So far, we have built a dozen or more apps of various complexity. Most of them we designed and tested on a phone.

Of course, in the real world, our apps need to work well on any device and must be able to handle what happens when in either portrait or landscape view (on all devices).

Furthermore, it is often not enough for our apps to just work and look "OK" on different devices. Often, our apps will need to *behave* differently and appear with a significantly different UI based on whether the device is a phone or a tablet, and in landscape/portrait orientation.

Note

Android supports apps for large screen TVs, smartwatches via the Wear API, virtual reality and augmented reality, as well as "things" for the Internet of Things. We will not be covering the two latter cases in this book, but by the end of the book, it is the author's guess that you will be prepared enough to venture into these topics should you choose to.

Look at this screenshot of the BBC weather app running on an Android phone in portrait orientation. Look at the basic layout but also study the information shown as we will compare it to the tablet app in a moment:

Figure 24.1 – BBC weather app running on an Android phone in portrait orientation

For now, the purpose of the previous screenshot is not so much to show you the specific UI features but to allow you to compare it with the next screenshot. Look at the exact same app running on a tablet in landscape orientation:

Figure 24.2 – BBC weather app running on an Android phone in landscape orientation

Notice that the tablet UI has an extra panel of information compared to the phone app. This extra panel is highlighted in the preceding screenshot.

The point of this screenshot again is not so much the specific UI or even how we might implement one like it, but more that the UIs are so different they could easily be considered totally different apps. Yet if you download this app, it is the same download for tablet and phone.

Android allows us to design real-world apps like this where not only is the layout different for varying device types/orientations/sizes but also (and this is important) the behavior is different. The Android secret weapon that makes this possible is Fragments.

Google says:

"A Fragment represents a behavior or a portion of user interface in an Activity. You can combine multiple fragments in a single activity to build a multi-pane UI and reuse a fragment in multiple activities.

You can think of a fragment as a modular section of an activity, which has its own lifecycle, receives its own input events, and which you can add or remove while the activity is running (sort of like a "sub activity" that you can reuse in different activities).

A fragment must always be embedded in an activity and the fragment's lifecycle is directly affected by the host activity's lifecycle."

We can design multiple different layouts in different XML files and we will do so soon. We can also detect things such as device orientation and screen resolution in our Java code, so we can then make decisions about layout, dynamically.

Let's try this out using device detection and then we will have our first look at Fragments.

Device detection mini-app

The best way to learn about detecting and responding to devices and their varying attributes (screens, orientations, and so on) is to make a simple app:

1. Create a new **Empty Activity** project and call it `Device Detection`. Leave all the other settings as their defaults.

2. Open the `activity_main.xml` file in the design tab and delete the default **Hello world!** `TextView`.

3. Drag a **Button** onto the top of the screen and set its **onClick** property to `detectDevice`. We will code this method in a minute.

4. Drag two **TextView** widgets onto the layout, one below the other, and set their **id** properties to `txtOrientation` and `txtResolution`.

5. Check you have a layout that looks something like this next screenshot:

> **Note**
> I have stretched my widgets (mainly horizontally) and increased the
> `textSize` attributes to `24sp` to make them clearer on the screen, but this is
> not required for the app to work correctly.

Figure 24.3– Layout check

6. Click the **Infer Constraints** button to secure the positions of the UI elements.

Now we will do something new. We will build a layout specifically for landscape
orientation.

In Android Studio, make sure the `activity_main.xml` file is selected in the editor and
locate the **Orientation for preview** button as shown next:

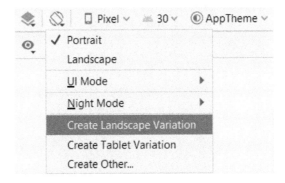

Figure 24.4 – Create Landscape Variation

Click it and then select **Create Landscape Variation**.

You now have a new layout XML file with the same name but orientated in landscape mode. The layout appears blank in the editor, but as we will see, this is not the case. Look at the `layout` folder in the Project Explorer and notice that there are indeed two files named `activity_main`, and one of them (the new one we just created) is postfixed with **land**. This is shown in the next screenshot:

Figure 24.5 – activity_main folder

Select this new file (the one postfixed with **land**) and now look at the component tree. It is pictured in the next screenshot:

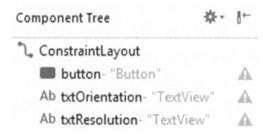

Figure 24.6 – Component tree

It would appear that the layout already contains all our widgets – we just cannot see them in the design view. The reason for this anomaly is that when we created the landscape layout, Android Studio copied the portrait layout, including all the constraints. The portrait constraints rarely match the landscape constraints.

To solve the problem, click the **Remove all constraints** button; it's the button to the left of the **Infer constraints** button. The UI is now unconstrained. All the UI widgets will appear jumbled up in the top-left corner. One at a time, rearrange them to look like this next screenshot. I had to add the constraints manually to make this design work so I have shown the constraints in the following screenshot:

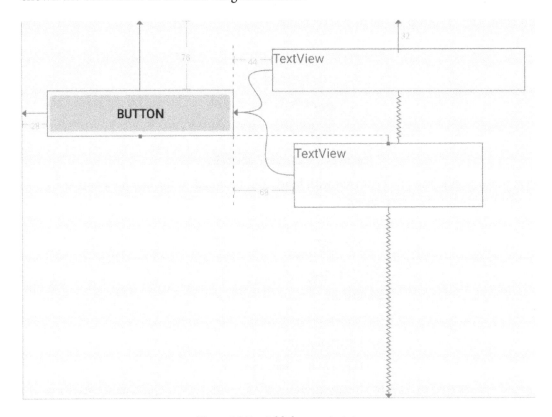

Figure 24.7 – Add the constraints

Click the **Infer constraints** button or set them manually, whichever works best for you. If you have any trouble recreating this layout, then you can grab the code from the download bundle in the `Chapter 24/Device Detection/layout-land` folder.

> **Note**
>
> The appearance doesn't really matter as long as you can see the contents of both `TextView` widgets and click the button.

Now we have a basic layout for two different orientations, we can turn our attention to coding the Java.

Coding the MainActivity class

Add the following member variables just after the `MainActivity` class declaration, to hold references to our two `TextView` widgets:

```
private TextView txtOrientation;
private TextView txtResolution;
```

> **Note**
>
> Import the `TextView` class at this point:
>
> `import android.widget.TextView;`

Now, in the `onCreate` method of the `MainActivity` class, just after the call to `setContentView`, add this code:

```
// Get a reference to our TextView widgets
txtOrientation = findViewById(R.id.txtOrientation);
txtResolution = findViewById(R.id.txtResolution);
```

After `onCreate`, add the method that handles our button click and runs our detection code:

```
public void detectDevice(View v){

    // What is the orientation?
    Display display =
    getWindowManager().getDefaultDisplay();
    txtOrientation.setText("" + display.getRotation());

    // What is the resolution?
    Point xy = new Point();
    display.getSize(xy);
    txtResolution.setText("x = " + xy.x + " y = " + xy.y);

}
```

> **Note**
>
> Import the following three classes:
>
> ```
> import android.graphics.Point;
>
> import android.view.Display;
>
> import android.view.View;
> ```

This code works by declaring and initializing an object of type `Display` called `display`. This object (`display`) now holds a whole bunch of data about the specific display properties of the device.

The result of the `getRotation` method is output into the top `TextView` widget.

The code then initializes an object of type `Point` called `xy`. The `getSize` method then loads up the screen resolution into `xy`. The `setText` method is then used to output the horizontal (`xy.x`) and vertical (`xy.y`) resolution into the `TextView` widget.

> **Note**
>
> You might remember we used the `Display` and `Point` classes in the Kids drawing app.

Each time the button is clicked, the two `TextView` widgets will be updated.

Unlocking the screen orientation

Before we run the app, we want to make sure the device isn't locked in portrait mode (most new phones are by default). From the app drawer of the emulator (or the device you will be using), tap the **Settings** app and choose **Display** and use the switch to set **Auto-rotate screen** to on. I have shown this setting in the next screenshot:

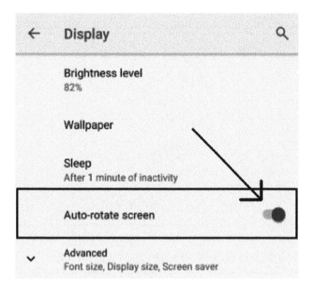

Figure 24.8 – Auto-rotate screen

Running the app

Now you can run the app and click the button:

Figure 24.9 – Click the button

Rotate the device, using one of the rotate buttons on the emulator control panel, to landscape:

Figure 24.10 – Rotate the device

> **Note**
> You can also use *Ctrl + F11* on a PC or *Ctrl + FN + F11* on Mac.

Now click the button again and you will see the landscape layout in action:

Figure 24.11 – Landscape layout

The first thing you will probably notice is that when you rotate the screen, it briefly goes blank. This is the Activity restarting and calling the onCreate method again – just what we need. It calls the setContentView method on the landscape version of the layout and the code in MainActivity refers to widgets with the same ID so the exact same code works.

> **Note**
>
> Don't spend too long pondering this because we will discuss it later in the chapter.

If the 0 and 1 results are less than obvious regarding device orientation, they refer to `public static final` variables of the `Surface` class – `Surface.ROTATION_0` equals 0 and `Surface.ROTATION_180` equals 1.

> **Note**
>
> Note that if you rotated the screen to the left, then your value will be 1 – the same as mine, but if you rotated it to the right, you would have seen the value 3. If you rotate the device to portrait mode upside down, you will get the value 4.

And we could code a `switch` block based on the results of these detection tests and load up different layouts.

But as we have just seen, Android makes this simpler than this for us by allowing us to add specific layouts into folders with configuration qualifiers, such as **land**, short for Landscape.

Configuration qualifiers

We have already met configuration qualifiers such as `layout-large` and `layout-xhdpi` in *Chapter 3, Exploring Android Studio and the Project Structure*. Here, we will refresh and expand our understanding of them.

We can begin to remove reliance on the controller layer to influence app layout by using configuration qualifiers. There are configuration qualifiers for size, orientation, and pixel density. To take advantage of a configuration qualifier, we simply design a layout in the usual way, optimized for our preferred configuration, and then place that layout in a folder with a name that Android recognizes as being for that particular configuration.

For example, in the previous app, putting a layout in the `land` folder tells Android to use the layout when the device is in the landscape orientation.

It is likely that the above statement will seem slightly ambiguous. This is because the Android Studio **Project Explorer** window shows us a file and folder structure that doesn't exactly correspond to reality – it is trying to simplify things and "help" us. If you select the **Project Files** option from the drop-down list at the top of the **Project Explorer** window and then examine the project contents, you will indeed see that there is a `layout` and `layout-land` folder as shown next:

Figure 24.12 – layout and layout-land folder

Switch back to the **Android** view or leave it on the **Project Files** view – whichever you prefer.

So, if we want to have a different layout for landscape and portrait, we would create a folder called `layout-land` in the `res` folder (or use the shortcut we used in the previous app) and place our specially designed layout within it.

When the device is in portrait position, the regular layout from the `layout` folder will be used and when it is in landscape position, the layout from the `layout-land` folder would be used.

If we are designing for different sizes of screen, we place layouts into folders with the following names:

- `layout-small`
- `layout-normal`
- `layout-large`
- `layout-xlarge`

If we are designing for screens with different pixel densities, we can place XML layouts into folders with names like these:

- `layout-ldpi` for low-DPI devices

- `layout-mdpi` for medium-DPI devices

- `layout-hdpi` for high-DPI devices

- `layout-xhdpi` for extra-high DPI devices

- `layout-xxhdpi` for extra-extra-high DPI devices

- `layout-xxxhdpi` for extra-extra-extra-high DPI devices

- `layout-nodpi` for devices with a DPI you have not otherwise catered for

- `layout-tvdpi` for TVs

What exactly qualifies as low, high, or extra-high DPI and so on can be researched at the link in the next info box. The point here is the principal.

It is worth pointing out that what we have just discussed is a long way from being the whole story regarding configuration qualifiers and, as with design, it is worth putting this on your list of things to study further.

> **Note**
>
> Often, the Android developer site has lots of detailed information on handling layouts for different devices. Try this link for more information: `https://developer.android.com/guide/practices/screens_support`.

The limitation of configuration qualifiers

What the previous app and our discussion on configuration qualifiers have shown us is certainly very useful in a number of situations. Unfortunately, however, configuration qualifiers and detecting attributes in code only solves the problem in the view layer of our MVC pattern.

As discussed, our apps sometimes need to have different *behavior* as well as layout. This perhaps implies multiple branches of our Java code in the controller layer (`MainActivity` in most of our previous apps) and perhaps summons nightmarish visions of having huge great `if` or `switch` blocks with different code for each different scenario.

Fortunately, this is not how it's done. For such situations, in fact for most apps, Android has fragments.

Fragments

Fragments will likely become a staple of almost every app you make. They are so useful, there are so many reasons to use them, and once you get used to them, they are so simple, there is almost no reason not to use them.

Fragments are reusable elements of an app just like any class, but as mentioned previously, they have special features, such as the ability to load their own view/layout as well as their very own lifecycle methods, which make them perfect for achieving the goals we discussed in the *Real-world apps* section and having different layouts and code for different devices (like the weather app we looked at).

Let's dig a bit deeper into fragments, one feature at a time.

Fragments have a lifecycle too

We can set up and control fragments very much like we do Activities, by overriding the appropriate lifecycle methods:

- onCreate: In the onCreate method, we can initialize variables and do almost all the things we would typically have done in the Activity onCreate method. The big exception to this is initializing our UI.

- onCreateView: In this method, we will, as the name suggests, get a reference to any of our UI widgets, set up anonymous classes to listen for clicks, and more besides, as we will soon see.

- onAttach and onDetach: These methods are called just before Fragment is put into use/taken out of use.

- onResume, onStart, onPause, and onStop: In these methods, we can take certain actions, such as creating or deleting objects or saving data, just like we have done with their Activity based counterparts.

> **Note**
>
> If you want to study the details of the Fragment lifecycle, you can do so on the Android developer website at this link: https://developer.android.com/guide/components/fragments.

This is all fine, but we need a way to create our fragments in the first place and to be able to call these methods at the right time.

Managing Fragments with FragmentManager

The `FragmentManager` class is part of the `Activity`. We use it to initialize a `Fragment`, add Fragments to the Activities layout, and to end a `Fragment`. We briefly saw `FragmentManager` before when we initialized our `FragmentDialog`.

> **Note**
>
> It is very hard to learn much about Android without bumping into the `Fragment` class, just as it is tough to learn much about Java without constantly bumping into OOP/classes, and so on.

The following highlighted code shows how we used `FragmentManager` (which is already a part of `Activity`) being passed in as an argument to create the pop-up dialog:

```
button.setOnClickListener(new View.OnClickListener() {
    @Override
    public void onClick(View v) {


        // Create a new DialogShowNote called dialog
        DialogShowNote dialog = new DialogShowNote();

        // Send the note via the sendNoteSelected method
        dialog.sendNoteSelected(mTempNote);

        // Create the dialog
        dialog.show(getFragmentManager(), "123");
    }
});
```

At the time, I asked you not to concern yourself with the arguments of the method call. The second argument of the method call is an ID for `Fragment`. We will see how we use `FragmentManager` more extensively, as well as how to use the `Fragment` ID.

`FragmentManager` does exactly what its name suggests. What is important here is that `Activity` only has one `FragmentManager`, but it can take care of many fragments. This is just what we need to have multiple behaviors and layouts within a single app.

`FragmentManager` also calls the various lifecycle methods of the fragments it is responsible for. This is distinct from the `Activity` lifecycle methods that are called by Android, yet closely related because `FragmentManager` calls many of the `Fragment` lifecycle methods *in response to* the `Activity` lifecycle methods being called. As usual, we don't need to worry too much about when and how if we respond appropriately in each situation.

> **Note**
>
> Fragments are going to be a fundamental part of many, if not all our future apps. As we did with naming conventions, string resources, and encapsulation, however, we will not use fragments for simple learning purposes or very small apps when they would be overkill. The exception to this will of course be when we are learning about fragments.

Our first Fragment app

Let's build `Fragment` in its simplest possible form so we can understand what is going on before, in later chapters, we start producing Fragments all over the place that are of genuine usefulness.

> **Note**
>
> I urge all readers to go through and build this project. There is a lot of jumping around from file to file and just reading alone can make it seem more complex than it really is. Certainly, you can copy and paste the code from the download bundle but please also follow the steps and create your own projects and classes. Fragments are not too tough but their implementation, as their name suggests, is a little fragmented.

Create a new project called `Simple Fragment` using the Empty Activity template and leaving the rest of the settings at their defaults.

Switch to activity_main.xml and delete the default **Hello world!** TextView widget.

Now make sure the root ConstraintLayout is selected by left-clicking it in the **Component tree** window, then change its **id** property to fragmentHolder. We will now be able to get a reference to this layout in our Java code and as the id property implies, we will be adding a Fragment to it.

Now we will create a layout that will define our fragment's appearance. Right-click the **layout** folder and choose **New | Layout resource file**. In the **File name** field, type fragment_layout, in the **RootElement** field, type LinearLayout, and left-click **OK**. We have just created a new layout of type LinearLayout.

Add a single **Button** widget anywhere on the new layout and make its **id** property button.

Now we have a simple layout for our Fragment to use, let's write some Java code to make the actual fragment.

> **Note**
>
> Note that you can create a Fragment by simply dragging and dropping one from the palette, but doing things this way is much less flexible and controllable and flexibility and control are the big benefits to fragments, as we will see throughout the next chapter. By creating a class that extends Fragment, we can make as many fragments from it as we like.

In the Project Explorer, right-click the folder that contains the MainActivity file. From the context menu, choose **New | Java class** and call it SimpleFragment.

> **Note**
>
> Note that there are options to create Fragment classes in various pre-coded states to implement a Fragment more quickly, but now they would slightly cloud the learning objectives of this app.

In our new `SimpleFragment` class, change the code to extend `Fragment`. As you type the code, you will be asked to choose the specific `Fragment` class to import, as shown in the next screenshot:

Figure 24.13 – Choose the specific Fragment class

Choose the top option, which is `androidx.fragment.app`.

Note

We will need all of the following `import` statements in this class. The preceding step has already added the `androidx.fragment.app.Fragment` class:

```
import androidx.fragment.app.Fragment;

import android.os.Bundle;

import android.view.LayoutInflater;

import android.view.View;

import android.view.ViewGroup;

import android.widget.Button;

import android.widget.Toast;
```

Now add a single `String` variable called `myString` and a `Button` variable called `myButton` as members.

Now override the onCreate method. Inside the onCreate method, initialize myString to Hello from SimpleFragment. Our code so far (excluding the package declaration and import statements) will look exactly like this next code:

```
public class SimpleFragment extends Fragment {

    // member variables accessible from anywhere in this
    fragment
    String myString;
    Button myButton;

    @Override
    public void onCreate(Bundle savedInstanceState){
        super.onCreate(savedInstanceState);

        myString = "Hello from SimpleFragment";
    }
}
```

In the previous code, we created a member variable called myString, then in the onCreate method, we initialized it. This is very much like what we did for our previous apps when only using Activity.

The difference, however, is that we did not set the view or attempt to get a reference to our Button member variable, myButton.

When using Fragment, we need to do this in the onCreateView method. Let's override that now and see how we set the view and get a reference to our Button widget.

Add this code to the SimpleFragment class after the onCreate method:

```
@Override
public View onCreateView(LayoutInflater inflater, ViewGroup
container, Bundle savedInstanceState) {

    View view = inflater.inflate(R.layout.fragment_layout,
    container, false);

    myButton = view.findViewById(R.id.button);
```

```
    return view;
}
```

To understand the previous block of code, we must first look at the `onCreateView` method signature. First, notice the start of the method states that it must return an object of type `View`:

```
public View onCreateView...
```

Next, we have three arguments. Let's look at the first two:

```
(LayoutInflater inflater, ViewGroup container,...
```

We need a `LayoutInflater` reference as we cannot call the `setContentView` method because the `Fragment` class provides no such method. In the body of `onCreateView`, we use the `inflate` method of `inflater` to inflate our layout contained in `fragment_layout.xml` and initialize `view` (an object of type `View`) with the result.

We use `container`, which was passed into `onCreateView` as an argument, in the `inflate` method also. The `container` variable is a reference to the layout in `activity_main.xml`.

It might seem obvious that `activity_main.xml` is the containing layout, but as we will see later in the chapter, the `ViewGroup container` argument allows *any* `Activity` with *any* layout to be the container for our fragment. This is exceptionally flexible and makes our `Fragment` code reusable to a significant extent.

The third argument we pass in to `inflate` is `false`, which means that we don't want our layout immediately added to the containing layout. We will do this ourselves soon from another part of the code.

The third argument of `onCreateView` is `Bundle savedInstanceState`, which is there to help us maintain the data that our fragments hold.

Now we have an inflated layout contained in `view`, we can use this to get a reference to our `Button` widget like this:

```
myButton = view.findViewById(R.id.button);
```

And use the `view` instance as the return value to the calling code, as required:

```
return view;
```

Now we can add an anonymous class to listen for clicks on our button in the usual manner. In the `onClick` method, we display a pop-up `Toast` message to demonstrate that everything is working as expected.

Add this code just before the `return` statement in the `onCreateView` method as highlighted in this next code:

```
@Override
public View onCreateView(LayoutInflater inflater,
ViewGroup container,
Bundle savedInstanceState) {

View view = inflater.inflate(R.layout.fragment_layout,
container, false);

myButton = view.findViewById(R.id.button);

myButton.setOnClickListener(
   new View.OnClickListener() {

      @Override
      public void onClick(View v) {

              Toast.makeText(getActivity(),
              myString ,
              Toast.LENGTH_SHORT).
              show();
               }
          });

return view;
}
```

> **Note**
>
> As a reminder, the `getActivity()` method call used as an argument
> in `makeText` gets a reference to the `Activity` that contains the
> `Fragment`. This is required to display a `Toast` message. We also used the
> `getActivity` method in our `FragmentDialog` based classes in the
> Note to Self app.

We can't run our app just yet; it will not work because there is one more step required.
We need to create an instance of our `SimpleFragment` class and initialize it
appropriately. This is where the `FragmentManager` class will get introduced.

This next code creates a new `FragmentManager` by calling
`getSupportFragmentManager`. The code then creates a new `Fragment`, based
on our `SimpleFragment` class using the `FragmentManager` and passing in the
ID of the layout (within the `Activity`) that will hold it.

Add this code in the `onCreate` method of `MainActivity.java`, just after the
call to the `setContentView` method:

```
// Get a fragment manager
FragmentManager fManager = getSupportFragmentManager();


// Create a new fragment using the manager
// Passing in the id of the layout to hold it
Fragment frag = fManager.findFragmentById(R.id.fragmentHolder);


// Check the fragment has not already been initialized
if(frag == null){


    // Initialize the fragment based on our SimpleFragment
    frag  = new SimpleFragment();
    fManager.beginTransaction()
            .add(R.id.fragmentHolder, frag)
            .commit();


}
```

> **Note**
>
> You will need to add the following import statements to the
> MainActivity class:
>
> import androidx.fragment.app.Fragment;
>
> import androidx.fragment.app.FragmentManager;
>
> import android.os.Bundle;

Now run the app and gaze in wonder at our clickable button that displays a message with
the Toast class and took two layouts and two whole classes to create:

Figure 24.14 – Displaying a message with the Toast class

If you remember achieving more than this way back in *Chapter 2, First Contact: Java, XML,
and the UI Designer*, and with far less code, then it is clear that we need a fragment reality
check to fully understand the answer to the question of why we are doing it like this!

Fragment reality check

So, what does this Fragment stuff really do for us? Our first Fragment mini-app
would have the same appearance and functionality had we not bothered with the
Fragment at all.

In fact, using the Fragment class has made the whole thing more complicated! Why
would we want to do this?

We know that a Fragment instance or fragments can be added to the layout of
an Activity.

We know that a Fragment not only contains its own layout (view) but also its very own code (controller), which, although hosted by an Activity, the Fragment instance is virtually independent.

Our quick app only showed one Fragment instance in action, but we could have an Activity that hosts two or more fragments. We then effectively have two almost independent controllers displayed on a single screen.

What is most useful about this, however, is that when the Activity starts, we can detect attributes of the device our app is running on – perhaps phone or tablet; portrait or landscape. We can then use this information to decide to display either just one or two of our fragments simultaneously.

This not only helps us achieve the kind of functionality discussed in the section *Real-world apps* at the start of the chapter but it also allows us to do so using the exact same Fragment code for both possible scenarios!

This really is the essence of fragments. We create a whole app by pairing up both functionality (controller) and appearance (view) into a bunch of fragments that we can reuse in different ways, almost without a care.

It is, of course, possible to foresee a few stumbling blocks so take a look at this FAQ.

Frequently asked question

1. The missing link is that if all these fragments are fully functioning independent controllers, then we need to learn a bit more about how we would implement our model layer. If we simply have, say, an ArrayList, like with the Note to Self app, where will the ArrayList instance go? How would we share it between fragments (assuming both/all fragments need access to the same data)?

    There is an entirely more elegant solution we can use to create a model layer (both the data itself and the code to maintain the data). We will see this when we explore the NavigationView layout in *Chapter 26, Advanced UI with Navigation Drawer and Fragment*, and Android databases in *Chapter 27, Android Databases*.

Summary

Now we have a broad understanding of what Fragments are for and how we can begin to use them, we can start to go deeper into how they are used. In the next chapter, we will complete a couple of apps that use multiple Fragments in different ways.

25
Building a Simple Image Gallery App

Paging is the act of moving from page to page, and on Android, we do this by swiping a finger across the screen. When we do this, the current page transitions in a direction and speed to match the finger movement. This is a useful and practical way to navigate around an app but perhaps even more than this, it creates an extremely satisfying visual effect for the user. Also, as with the `RecyclerView` widget, we can selectively load just the data required for the current page and perhaps the data for the previous and next pages.

The Android API, as you will have come to expect, has some solutions for achieving paging in quite a simple manner.

In this chapter, we will learn how to do the following:

- Achieve paging and swiping with images as you might find in a photo gallery app.

First, let's look at a swiping example.

Technical requirements

You can find the code files present in this chapter on GitHub at `https://github.com/PacktPublishing/Android-Programming-for-Beginners-Third-Edition/tree/main/chapter%2025`.

Angry Birds classic swipe menu

Here we can see the famous Angry Birds level selection menu showing swiping/paging in action:

Figure 25.1 – Angry Birds level selection menu

Let's build a paging app.

Building an image gallery/slider app

Create a new project in Android Studio called Image Pager. Use the **Empty Activity** template and leave all the rest of the settings at their defaults.

The images are in the download bundle in the Chapter 25/Image Pager/ drawable folder. This next screenshot shows them in Windows File Explorer:

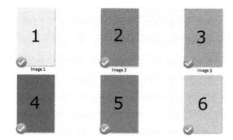

Figure 25.2 – Add images

Add the images to the `drawable` folder in the Project Explorer in Android Studio or you could add more interesting images, perhaps some photos you have taken.

Implementing the layout

For a simple image paging app, we use the `PagerAdapter` class. We can think of this as being like `RecyclerAdapter` but for images as it will handle the display of an array of images in a `ViewPager` widget. This is much like how `RecyclerAdapter` handles the display of the contents of an `ArrayList` in a `ListView`. All we need to do is override the appropriate methods.

To implement an image gallery with `PagerAdapter`, we first need a `ViewPager` widget in our main layout. So you can see precisely what is required, here is the actual XML code for `activity_main.xml`. Edit `activity_main.xml` to look exactly like this:

```
<RelativeLayout xmlns:android=
    "http://schemas.android.com/apk/res/android"
    android:layout_width="fill_parent"
    android:layout_height="fill_parent" >

    <androidx.viewpager.widget.ViewPager
        android:id="@+id/pager"
        android:layout_width="wrap_content"
        android:layout_height="wrap_content" />

</RelativeLayout>
```

The class named `androidx.ViewPager.widget.ViewPager` is the class that makes this functionality available in Android versions that were released before `ViewPager`.

Next, a bit like how we needed a layout to represent a list item, we need a layout to represent an item, in this case, an image, in `ViewPager`. Create a new layout file in the usual way and call it `pager_item.xml`. Add a single `ImageView` with an ID of `imageView`.

Use the visual designer to achieve this or copy the following XML into `pager_item.xml`:

```xml
<?xml version="1.0" encoding="utf-8"?>
<RelativeLayout
    xmlns:android="http://schemas.android.com/apk/res/android"
    android:layout_width="fill_parent"
    android:layout_height="fill_parent" >

    <ImageView
        android:id="@+id/imageView"
        android:layout_width="match_parent"
        android:layout_height="match_parent" />

</RelativeLayout>
```

Now we can make a start on our `PagerAdapter` class.

Coding the PagerAdapter class

Next, we need to extend `PagerAdapter` to handle images. Create a new class called `ImagePagerAdapter` and make it extend `PagerAdapter`.

Add the following imports to the top of the `ImagePagerAdapter` class. We often rely on using the *Alt + Enter* shortcut to add imports. We are doing things slightly differently this time because there are some very similarly named classes that will not suit our objectives.

Add the following imports to the `ImagePagerAdapter` class:

```java
import android.content.Context;
import android.view.LayoutInflater;
import android.view.View;
import android.view.ViewGroup;
```

```
import android.widget.ImageView;
import android.widget.RelativeLayout;


import androidx.viewpager.widget.PagerAdapter;
import androidx.viewpager.widget.ViewPager;
```

Here is the class declaration with the extends... code added as well as a couple of member variables. These variables are a Context object that we will use shortly and an int array called images. The reason for having an int array for images is that we will store int identifiers for each of the images. We'll see how this works in a few code blocks time. The last member variable is a LayoutInflater instance, which you can probably guess will be used to inflate each of the instances of pager_item.xml.

Extend the PagerAdapter class and add the member variables we have just discussed:

```
public class ImagePagerAdapter extends PagerAdapter {


    Context context;


    int[] images;
    LayoutInflater inflater;
}
```

Now we need a constructor that sets up ImagerPagerAdapter by receiving the Context from the MainActivity class as well as the int array for the images and initializing the member variables with them.

Add the constructor method to the ImagePagerAdapter class:

```
public ImagePagerAdapter(
    Context context,  int[] images) {


    this.context = context;
    this.images = images;
}
```

Now we must override the required methods of `PagerAdapter`. Immediately after the previous code, add the overridden `getCount` method, which simply returns the number of image IDs in the array. This method is used internally by the class:

```
@Override
public int getCount() {

    return images.length;
}
```

Now we must override the `isViewFromObject` method, which returns a Boolean depending upon whether the current `View` instance is the same or associated with the current `Object` as passed in as a parameter. Again, this is a method that is used internally by the class. Immediately after the previous code, add this `Override` method:

```
@Override
public boolean isViewFromObject(View view, Object object) {
    return view == object;
}
```

Now we must override the `instantiateItem` method; this is where we get most of the work that concerns us done. First, we declare a new `ImageView` object, and then we initialize our `LayoutInflater` member. Next, we use the `LayoutInflater` instance to declare and initialize a new `View` instance from our `pager_item.xml` layout file.

After this, we get a reference to the `ImageView` widget inside the `pager_item. xml` layout. We can now add the appropriate image as the content of the `ImageView` widget based on the `position` parameter of the `instantiateItem` method and the appropriate ID integer from the `images` array.

Finally, we add the layout to the `PagerAdapter` instance with the `addView` method and return from the method.

Add the method we have just discussed:

```
@Override
public Object instantiateItem(
    ViewGroup container, int position) {

    ImageView image;

    inflater = (LayoutInflater)
```

```
            context.getSystemService(
            Context.LAYOUT_INFLATER_SERVICE);


    View itemView = inflater.inflate(
            R.layout.pager_item, container, false);


        // get reference to imageView in pager_item layout
        image =
            itemView.findViewById(R.id.imageView);


        // Set an image to the ImageView
        image.setImageResource(images[position]);


        // Add pager_item layout as the current page to the
        ViewPager
        ((ViewPager) container).addView(itemView);


        return itemView;
    }
```

The last method we must override is the destroyItem method, which the class can call when it needs to remove an appropriate item based on the value of the position parameter.

Add the destroyItem method after the previous code and before the closing curly brace of the ImagePagerAdapter class:

```
@Override
public void destroyItem(ViewGroup container,
    int position,
    Object object) {


    // Remove pager_item layout from ViewPager
    container.removeView((RelativeLayout) object);
}
```

As we saw when coding the `ImagePagerAdapter` class, there is very little to it. It is just a case of properly implementing the overridden methods that the `ImagePagerAdapter` class uses to help make things work smoothly behind the scenes.

Now we can code the `MainActivity` class, which will use our `ImagePagerAdapter` implementation.

Coding the MainActivity class

Finally, we can code our `MainActivity` class. As with the `ImagePagerAdapter` class, for clarity, add the following `import` statements manually to the `MainActivity.java` class before the class declaration as shown next:

```
import androidx.appcompat.app.AppCompatActivity;
import androidx.viewpager.widget.PagerAdapter;
import androidx.viewpager.widget.ViewPager;
```

We need a few member variables. Unsurprisingly, we need a `ViewPager` instance, which will be used to hold a reference to the `ViewPager` in our layout. Also, we need an `ImagePagerAdapter` reference for the class we have just coded. We also need an `int` array to hold an array of image IDs.

Adapt the `MainActivity` class to be as follows:

```
public class MainActivity extends AppCompatActivity {

    ViewPager viewPager;
    PagerAdapter adapter;

    int[] images;

    @Override
    public void onCreate(Bundle savedInstanceState) {
        super.onCreate(savedInstanceState);
        ...
```

All the rest of the code goes in the `onCreate` method. We initialize our `int` array with each of the images that we added to the `drawable-xhdpi` folder.

We initialize the ViewPager in the usual way with the findViewById method. We also initialize our ImagePagerAdapter instance by passing in a reference of the MainActivity class and the images array, as required by the constructor that we coded previously. Finally, we bind the adapter to the pager with the setAdapter method.

Code the onCreate method to look just like this next code:

```java
@Override
public void onCreate(Bundle savedInstanceState) {
    super.onCreate(savedInstanceState);

    setContentView(R.layout.activity_main);

    // Grab all the images and stuff them in our array
    images = new int[] { R.drawable.image1,
                R.drawable.image2,
                R.drawable.image3,
                R.drawable.image4,
                R.drawable.image5,
                R.drawable.image6 };

    // get a reference to the ViewPager in the layout
    viewPager = findViewById(R.id.pager);

    // Initialize our adapter
    adapter = new
            ImagePagerAdapter(MainActivity.this, images);

    // Binds the Adapter to the ViewPager
    viewPager.setAdapter(adapter);

}
```

Now we are ready to run the app.

Running the gallery app

Here we can see the first image from our `int` array:

Figure 25.3 – First image

Swipe a little right and left to see the smooth, pleasing way the images transition:

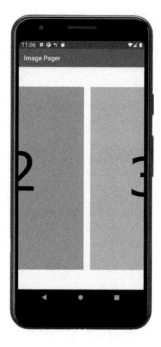

Figure 25.4 – Swipe to view images

That's it for this chapter. Let's review what we have done.

Summary

In this chapter, we saw how we can use pagers for simple image galleries with just a few lines of code and some very simple layouts. We achieved this so easily because of the `ImagePagerAdapter` class.

In the next chapter, we will look at another really cool UI element that is used in many of the latest Android apps, probably because it looks great and is a real pleasure, as well as extremely practical, to use. The `NavigationView` layout will enable us to design and implement different layouts with entirely different behavior (code). Let's take a look at the `NavigationView` layout.

26
Advanced UI with Navigation Drawer and Fragment

In this chapter, we will see what is (arguably) the most advanced UI. The `NavigationView` widget or navigation drawer, because of the way it slides out its contents, can be created simply by choosing it as a template when you create a new project. We will do just that and then we will examine the autogenerated code and learn how to interact with it. Then we will use all we know about `Fragment` to populate each of the "drawers" with different behavior and views. Then in the next chapter, we will learn about databases to add some new functionality to each `Fragment`.

And here is what we will be doing in this chapter:

- Introducing `NavigationView`
- Getting started with the simple database app
- Implementing a `NavigationView` project based on the autogenerated Android Studio template
- Adding multiple Fragments and layouts to `NavigationView`

Let's take a look at this extremely cool UI pattern.

Technical requirements

You can find the code files present in this chapter on GitHub at `https://github.com/PacktPublishing/Android-Programming-for-Beginners-Third-Edition/tree/main/chapter%2026`.

Introducing NavigationView

What's so great about `NavigationView`? Well, the first thing that might catch your eye is that it can be made to look extremely stylish. Take a look at this next screenshot, which shows off a `NavigationView` in action in the Google Play app:

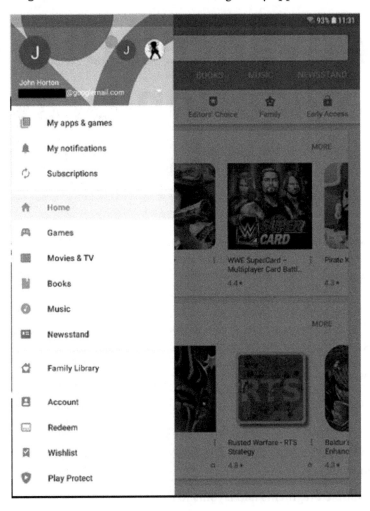

Figure 26.1 – NavigationView in action

To be honest, right from the start, ours is not going to be as fancy as the one in the Google Play app. But the same functionality will be present in our app.

What else is neat about this UI is the way that it slides to hide/reveal itself when required. It is because of this behavior that it can be a significant size, making it extremely flexible with regard to the options that can be put on it, and when the user is finished with it, it completely disappears, like a drawer.

I suggest trying the Google Play app now and seeing how it works if you haven't already.

You can slide your thumb/finger from the left-hand edge of the screen and the drawer will slowly slide out. You can of course slide it away again in the opposite direction.

While the navigation drawer is open, the rest of the screen is slightly dimmed (as seen in the previous screenshot), helping the user to focus on the navigation options offered.

You can also tap anywhere off the Navigation Drawer while it is open, and it will slide itself away, leaving the entire screen clear for the rest of the app.

The drawer is also opened by tapping on the menu icon in the top-left corner.

We can also tweak and refine the behavior of the navigation drawer, as we will see towards the end of the chapter.

Examining the Simple Database app

In this chapter, we will focus on creating the NavigationView and populating it with four Fragment class instances and their respective layouts. In the next chapter, we will learn about and implement the database functionality.

The screens of the database app are as follows. Here is what our `NavigationView` layout looks like in all its glory. Note that many of the options and most of the appearance and decoration are provided by default when using the `NavigationView` Activity template.

Figure 26.2 – NavigationView layout

The four main options are what we will add to the UI. They are **Insert**, **Delete**, **Search**, and **Results**. The layouts are shown, and their purposes are described as follows.

Insert

The first screen allows the user to insert a person's name and their associated age into the database:

Figure 26.3 – Insert

This simple layout has two EditText widgets and a button. The user will enter a name and an age and then click the **INSERT** button to add them to the database.

Delete

This screen is even simpler. The user will enter a name in the EditText widget and click the button:

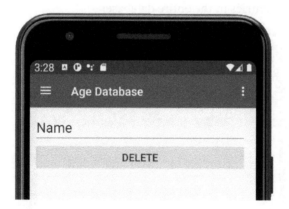

Figure 26.4 – Delete

If the name entered is present in the database, then the entry (name and age) will be deleted.

Search

This layout is much the same as the previous layout but has a different purpose:

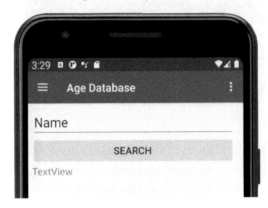

Figure 26.5 – Search

The user will enter a name into the EditText widget and then click the **SEARCH** button. If the name is present in the database, then it will be displayed along with the matching age.

Results

This screen shows all the entries in the entire database:

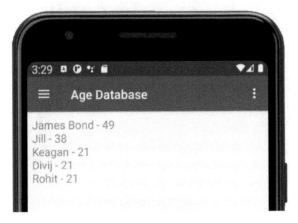

Figure 26.6 – Results

Let's get started with the Navigation Drawer.

Starting the Simple Database project

Create a new project in Android Studio. Call it Age Database, use the **Navigation Drawer Activity** template. Before we do anything else, it is well worth running the app on an emulator to see how much has been autogenerated as part of this template:

Figure 26.7 – Home page

At first glance, it is just a plain old layout with a `TextView` widget. But swipe from the left edge of the screen or press the menu button and the Navigation Drawer layout reveals itself:

Figure 26.8 – Navigation page

Now we can modify the options and insert a `Fragment` (with a layout) for each option. To understand how it works, let's examine some of the autogenerated code.

Exploring the autogenerated code and assets

Open the `res/menu` folder. Notice there is an extra file titled `activity_main_drawer.xml`. This next code is an excerpt from this file, so we can discuss its contents:

```
<group android:checkableBehavior="single">
    <item
```

```
                    android:id="@+id/nav_home"
                    android:icon="@drawable/ic_menu_camera"
                    android:title="@string/menu_home" />
            <item
                    android:id="@+id/nav_gallery"
                    android:icon="@drawable/ic_menu_gallery"
                    android:title="@string/menu_gallery" />
            <item
                    android:id="@+id/nav_slideshow"
                    android:icon="@drawable/ic_menu_slideshow"
                    android:title="@string/menu_slideshow" />
    </group>
```

Notice there are four item tags within a group tag. Now notice the title tags from top to bottom exactly correspond to the three text options in the menu of the autogenerated navigation drawer. Also notice that within each item tag, there is an id tag, so we can refer to them in our Java code as well as an icon tag, which corresponds to one of the icons in the drawable folder and is the icon displayed next to the option in the navigation drawer.

There are also some files that we will not be using that have been autogenerated.

Let's code the Fragment based classes and their layouts.

Coding the Fragment classes and their layouts

We will create the four classes including the code that loads the layout as well as the actual layouts as well, but we won't put any of the database functionality into Java until we have learned about Android databases in the next chapter.

After we have our four classes and their layouts, we will see how to load them from the Navigation Drawer menu. By the end of the chapter, we will have a fully working Navigation Drawer that lets the user swap between fragments but the fragments won't actually have any functionality until the next chapter.

Creating the empty files for the classes and layouts

Create four layout files with vertical `LinearLayout` as their parent view by right-clicking on the `layout` folder and selecting **New | Layout resource file**. Name the first file `content_insert`, the second `content_delete`, the third `content_search`, and the fourth `content_results`. All the options apart from the `LinearLayout` option and the filename can be left as their defaults.

You should now have four new layout files containing `LinearLayout` parents.

Let's code the related Java classes.

Coding the classes

Create four new classes by right-clicking the folder that contains the `MainActivity.java` file and selecting **New | Java class**. Name them `InsertFragment`, `DeleteFragment`, `SearchFragment`, and `ResultsFragment`. It should be plain from the names which fragments will show which layouts.

Just to make it clear, let's add some code to each class to make the classes extend `Fragment` and load their associated layout.

Open `InsertFragment.java` and edit it to contain the following code:

```java
import android.os.Bundle;
import android.view.LayoutInflater;
import android.view.View;
import android.view.ViewGroup;

import androidx.fragment.app.Fragment;

public class InsertFragment extends Fragment {

    @Override
    public View onCreateView(
            LayoutInflater inflater,
            ViewGroup container,
            Bundle savedInstanceState) {

        View v = inflater.inflate(
                R.layout.content_insert,
```

```
                  container, false);

        // Database and UI code goes here in next chapter

        return v;
    }
}
```

Open DeleteFragment.java and edit it to contain the following code:

```
import android.os.Bundle;
import android.view.LayoutInflater;
import android.view.View;
import android.view.ViewGroup;

import androidx.fragment.app.Fragment;

public class DeleteFragment extends Fragment {

    @Override
    public View onCreateView(
                LayoutInflater inflater,
                ViewGroup container,
                Bundle savedInstanceState) {

        View v = inflater.inflate(
                R.layout.content_delete,
                container, false);

        // Database and UI code goes here in next chapter

        return v;
    }
}
```

Open `SearchFragment.java` and edit it to contain the following code:

```java
import android.os.Bundle;
import android.view.LayoutInflater;
import android.view.View;
import android.view.ViewGroup;


import androidx.fragment.app.Fragment;


public class SearchFragment extends Fragment{

    @Override
    public View onCreateView(
                LayoutInflater inflater,
                ViewGroup container,
                Bundle savedInstanceState) {

            View v = inflater.inflate(
                    R.layout.content_search,
                    container, false);

            // Database and UI code goes here in next
            chapter

        return v;
    }
}
```

Open `ResultsFragment.java` and edit it to contain the following code:

```java
import android.os.Bundle;
import android.view.LayoutInflater;
import android.view.View;
import android.view.ViewGroup;


import androidx.fragment.app.Fragment;
```

```java
public class ResultsFragment extends Fragment {

    @Override
    public View onCreateView(
                LayoutInflater inflater,
                ViewGroup container,
                Bundle savedInstanceState) {

        View v = inflater.inflate(
                    R.layout.content_results,
                    container, false);

        // Database and UI code goes here in next chapter

        return v;
    }
}
```

Each class is completely empty of functionality except that in the `onCreateView` method, the appropriate layout is loaded from the associated layout file.

Let's add the UI to the layout files we created earlier.

Designing the layouts

As we saw at the start of the chapter, all the layouts are simple. Getting your layouts identical to mine is not essential but as always, the ID values must be the same or the Java code we write in the next chapter won't work.

Designing content_insert.xml

Drag two `Plain Text` widgets from the `Text` category of the palette onto the layout. Remember that `Plain Text` widgets are `EditText` instances. Now drag a `Button` widget onto the layout after the two `Plain Text` widgets.

Configure the widgets according to this table:

Widget	Attribute and value
Top edit text	id = editName
Top edit text	text = Name
Second edit text	id = editAge
Second edit text	text = Age
Button	id = btnInsert
Button	text = Insert

This is what your layout should look like in the design view in Android Studio:

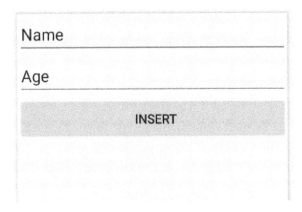

Figure 26.9 – Insert layout

Designing content_delete.xml

Drag a `Plain Text` onto the layout with a `Button` widget below it. Configure the widgets according to this table:

Widget	Attribute value
EditText	id = editDelete
EditText	text = Name
Button	id = btnDelete
Button	text = Delete

This is what your layout should look like in the design view in Android Studio:

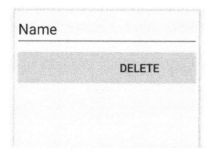

Figure 26.10 – Delete layout

Designing content_search.xml

Drag a `Plain Text` followed by a button and then a regular `TextView` onto the layout and then configure the widgets according to this table:

Widget	Attribute value
EditText	id = `editSearch`
EditText	text = `Name`
Button	id = `btnSearch`
Button	text = `Search`
TextView	id = `textResult`

This is what your layout should look like in the design view in Android Studio:

Figure 26.11 – Search layout

Designing content_results.xml

Drag a single `TextView` widget (not `Plain Text/EditText` this time) onto the layout. We will see in the next chapter how to add an entire list into this single `TextView` widget.

Configure the widget according to this table:

Widget	Attribute value
TextView	id = textResults

This is what your layout should look like in the design view in Android Studio:

Figure 26.12 – Results layout

Now we can use the `Fragment` based classes and their layouts.

Using the Fragment classes and their layouts

This stage has three steps. First, we need to edit the menu of the Navigation Drawer layout to reflect the options the user has. Next, we need a `View` instance in the layout to hold whatever the active `Fragment` instance is, and finally, we need to add code to `MainActivity.java` to switch between the different `Fragment` instances when the user taps on the menu.

Editing the Navigation Drawer menu

Open the `activity_main_drawer.xml` file in the `res/menu` folder of the project explorer. Edit the code within the `group` tags that we saw earlier to reflect our menu options of **Insert**, **Delete**, **Search**, and **Results**:

```
<group android:checkableBehavior="single">
    <item
        android:id="@+id/nav_insert"
        android:icon="@drawable/ic_menu_camera"
```

```
            android:title="Insert" />
    <item
            android:id="@+id/nav_delete"
            android:icon="@drawable/ic_menu_gallery"
            android:title="Delete" />
    <item
            android:id="@+id/nav_search"
            android:icon="@drawable/ic_menu_slideshow"
            android:title="Search" />
    <item
            android:id="@+id/nav_results"
            android:icon="@drawable/ic_menu_camera"
            android:title="Results" />
</group>
```

Note that the results item reuses the camera icon. It is left as a challenge for you if you wish to add a unique icon of your own.

Now we can add a layout within the main layout to hold whatever the current active fragment is.

Adding a holder to the main layout

Open the content_main.xml file in the layout folder. Locate the following existing code, which is the current fragment holder that is not right for our uses:

```
<fragment
        android:id="@+id/nav_host_fragment"
        android:name="androidx.navigation
            .fragment.NavHostFragment"
        android:layout_width="match_parent"
        android:layout_height="match_parent"
        app:defaultNavHost="true"
        app:layout_constraintLeft_toLeftOf="parent"
        app:layout_constraintRight_toRightOf="parent"
        app:layout_constraintTop_toTopOf="parent"
        app:navGraph="@navigation/mobile_navigation" />
```

Delete the preceding code and replace it with this XML code just before the closing tag of `ConstraintLayout`:

```xml
<FrameLayout
    android:id="@+id/fragmentHolder"
    android:layout_width="368dp"
    android:layout_height="495dp"
    tools:layout_editor_absoluteX="8dp"
    tools:layout_editor_absoluteY="8dp">
</FrameLayout>
```

Switch to design view and click the **Infer constraints** button to fix the new layout in place.

Now we have a `FrameLayout` widget with an `id` attribute of `fragmentHolder`, which we can get a reference to and load all our `Fragment` instance layouts into.

Coding the MainActivity.java class

Replace all the existing `import` directives with the following:

```java
import android.os.Bundle;
import com.google.android.material.
        floatingactionbutton.FloatingActionButton;

import com.google.android.material.snackbar.Snackbar;
import android.view.View;
import com.google.android.material.navigation.
        NavigationView;

import androidx.core.view.GravityCompat;
import androidx.drawerlayout.widget.DrawerLayout;
import androidx.appcompat.app.ActionBarDrawerToggle;
import androidx.appcompat.app.AppCompatActivity;
import androidx.appcompat.widget.Toolbar;
import androidx.fragment.app.FragmentTransaction;
import android.view.MenuItem;
```

Open the `MainActivity.java` file and edit the entire code to match the following.

> **Note**
>
> It might be quickest to delete everything except the `import` directives we have just added.

We will discuss the code next, so study the variable names and the various classes and their related methods:

```java
public class MainActivity extends AppCompatActivity
        implements NavigationView.
OnNavigationItemSelectedListener {

    @Override
    protected void onCreate(Bundle savedInstanceState) {
        super.onCreate(savedInstanceState);
        setContentView(R.layout.activity_main);
        Toolbar toolbar = findViewById(R.id.toolbar);
        setSupportActionBar(toolbar);

        FloatingActionButton fab = findViewById(R.id.fab);
        fab.setOnClickListener(new View.OnClickListener() {
            @Override
            public void onClick(View view) {
                Snackbar.make(view, "
                Replace with your own action",
                Snackbar.LENGTH_LONG)
                        .setAction("Action", null).show();
            }
        });

        DrawerLayout drawer =
        findViewById(R.id.drawer_layout);
        ActionBarDrawerToggle toggle = new
        ActionBarDrawerToggle(
                this, drawer, toolbar,
                    R.string.navigation_drawer_open,
```

```
                          R.string.navigation_drawer_close);

        drawer.addDrawerListener(toggle);
        toggle.syncState();

        NavigationView navigationView
            = findViewById(R.id.nav_view);

        navigationView
            .setNavigationItemSelectedListener(this);
    }
}
```

In the preceding code, the onCreate method handles aspects of our UI. The code gets a reference to a DrawerLayout widget that corresponds to the layout we have just seen. The code also creates a new instance of ActionBarDrawerToggle, which allows the controlling/toggling of the drawers. Next, a reference is captured to the layout file of the navigation drawer itself (nav_view) and the final line of code sets a listener on NavigationView.

Now add the onBackPressed method as follows:

```
@Override
public void onBackPressed() {
    DrawerLayout drawer =
    findViewById(R.id.drawer_layout);
    if (drawer.isDrawerOpen(GravityCompat.START)) {
        drawer.closeDrawer(GravityCompat.START);
    } else {
        super.onBackPressed();
    }
}
```

The onBackPressed method is an overridden method of Activity and it handles what happens when the user presses the back button on their device. The code closes the drawer if it is open and if it is not, simply calls super.onBackPressed. This means that the back button will close the drawer if it is open or have the default behavior if it was already closed.

Add the onCreateOptionsMenu and onOptionsItemSelected methods, which aren't really used in this app but will add the default functionality to the options button:

```
@Override
public boolean onCreateOptionsMenu(Menu menu) {
    // Inflate the menu; this adds items to the action bar
    if it is present.
    getMenuInflater().inflate(R.menu.main, menu);
    return true;
}


@Override
public boolean onOptionsItemSelected(MenuItem item) {
    // Handle action bar item clicks here. The action bar
    will
    // automatically handle clicks on the Home/Up button,
    so long
    // as you specify a parent activity in
    AndroidManifest.xml.
    int id = item.getItemId();

    //noinspection SimplifiableIfStatement
    if (id == R.id.action_settings) {
        return true;
    }


    return super.onOptionsItemSelected(item);
}
```

Now add the onNavigatioItemSelected method shown next:

```
@Override
public boolean onNavigationItemSelected(MenuItem item) {
    // Handle navigation view item clicks here.

    // Create a transaction
    FragmentTransaction transaction =
```

```
          getSupportFragmentManager().beginTransaction();

    int id = item.getItemId();

    if (id == R.id.nav_insert) {
        // Create a new fragment of the appropriate type
        InsertFragment fragment = new InsertFragment();
        // What to do and where to do it
        transaction.replace(R.id.fragmentHolder,
        fragment);

    } else if (id == R.id.nav_search) {
        SearchFragment fragment = new SearchFragment();
        transaction.replace(R.id.fragmentHolder,
        fragment);

    } else if (id == R.id.nav_delete) {
        DeleteFragment fragment = new DeleteFragment();
        transaction.replace(R.id.fragmentHolder,
        fragment);

    } else if (id == R.id.nav_results) {
        ResultsFragment fragment = new ResultsFragment();
        transaction.replace(R.id.fragmentHolder,
        fragment);

    }

    // Ask Android to remember which
    // menu options the user has chosen
    transaction.addToBackStack(null);

    // Implement the change
    transaction.commit();

    DrawerLayout drawer =
```

```
        findViewById(R.id.drawer_layout);
        drawer.closeDrawer(GravityCompat.START);
        return true;
    }
```

Let's go through the code in the onNavigationItemSelected method. Most of the code should look familiar. For each of our menu options, we create a new Fragment of the appropriate type and insert it into our RelativeLayout with an id property value of fragmentHolder.

Finally, for the MainActivity.java file, the transaction.addToBackStack method means that the chosen Fragment instance will be remembered in order with any others. The result of this is that if the user chooses the insert fragment, then the results fragment then taps the back button, then the app will return the user to the insert fragment.

You can now run the app and use the Navigation Drawer menu to flip between all our different Fragment instances. They will look just as they did in the screenshots at the start of this chapter, but they don't have any functionality yet.

Summary

In this chapter, we saw how straightforward it is to have an attractive and pleasing UI and although our Fragment instances don't have any functionality yet, they are set up ready to go once we have learned about databases.

In the next chapter, we will learn about databases in general, the specific database that Android apps can use, and we will then add the functionality to our Fragment classes.

27
Android Databases

If we are going to make apps that offer our users significant features, then we are almost certainly going to need a way to manage, store, and filter significant amounts of data.

It is possible to store very large amounts of data efficiently with JSON, but when we need to use that data selectively rather than simply restricting ourselves to the options of "save everything" and "load everything," we need to think about what other options are available.

A good computer science course would probably teach you about the algorithms necessary to handle sorting and filtering our data, but the effort involved would be quite extensive, and what are the chances of us coming up with a solution that is as good as something made by the people who gave us the Android API?

As is so often the case, it makes the most sense to use the solutions provided in the Android API. As we have seen, the JSON and SharedPreferences classes have their place, but at some point, we need to move on to using real databases for real-world solutions. Android uses the SQLite database management system, and as you would expect, there is an API to make it as easy as possible.

In this chapter, we will do the following:

- Find out exactly what a database is
- Learn what SQL and SQLite are
- Learn the basics of the SQL language
- Take a look at the Android SQLite API
- Code the Age Database app that we started in the previous chapter

Technical requirements

You can find the code files present in this chapter on GitHub at `https://github.com/PacktPublishing/Android-Programming-for-Beginners-Third-Edition/tree/main/chapter%2027`.

Databases 101

Let's answer a whole bunch of database-related questions and then we can get started making apps that use SQLite.

What is a database?

A **database** is both a place of storage and a means to retrieve, store, and manipulate data. It helps to be able to visualize a database before learning how to use it. The actual structure of the internals of a database varies greatly depending upon the database in question. SQLite actually stores all its data in a single file.

It aids our comprehension greatly, however, if we visualize our data as if it were in a spreadsheet, or sometimes multiple spreadsheets. Our database, like a spreadsheet, will be divided into multiple columns, which represent different types of data, and rows, which represent entries of the database.

Think about a database with names and exam scores. Take a look at this visual representation of such data and imagine what it would look like in a database:

_ID	name	score
1	Bart	23
2	Lisa	100
3	Jim	66

Figure 27.1 – Database example

Notice, however, that there is an extra column of data: an **_ID** column. We will talk more about this as we proceed. This single spreadsheet-like structure is called a **table**. As mentioned before, there might be, and often are, multiple tables in a database. Each column of the table will have a name that can be referred to when speaking to the database.

What is SQL?

SQL stands for **Structured Query Language**. It is the syntax that is used to get things done with a database.

What is SQLite?

SQLite is the name of the database system that is favored by Android, and it has its own version of SQL. The reason the SQLite version of SQL needs to be slightly different to some other versions is that the database has different features.

The SQL syntax primer that follows will be focused on SQLite.

SQL syntax primer

Before we can learn how to use SQLite with Android, we need to first learn the basics of how to use SQLite in general, in a platform-neutral context.

Let's look at some example SQL code that could be used on a SQLite database directly, without any Java or Android classes; then we can more easily understand what our Java code is doing later on.

SQLite example code

SQL has keywords, much like Java, that cause things to happen. Here is a flavor of some of the SQL keywords we will soon be using:

- INSERT: Allows us to add data to the database
- DELETE: Allows us to remove data from the database
- SELECT: Allows us to read data from the database
- WHERE: Allows us to specify parts of the database, matching specific criteria, that we want to use INSERT, DELETE, or SELECT on
- FROM: Used to specify a table or column name in a database

> **Note**
> There are many more SQLite keywords than this; for a full list of types, take a look at this link: `https://sqlite.org/lang_keywords.html`.

In addition to keywords, SQL has **types**. Some examples of SQL types are as follows:

- **integer**: Just what we need for storing whole numbers

- **text**: Perfect for storing a simple name or address

- **real**: For large floating-point numbers

> **Note**
> There are many more SQLite types than this; for a full list of types, take a look at this link: `https://www.sqlite.org/datatype3.html`.

Let's look at how we can combine those types with keywords to create tables and add, remove, modify, and read data using full SQLite statements.

Creating a table

It would be a perfectly decent question to ask why we don't first create a new database. The reason for this is that every Android app has access to a SQLite database by default. The database is private to that app. Here is the statement we would use to create a table within that database. I have highlighted a few parts to make the statement clearer:

```
create table StudentsAndGrades
    _ID integer primary key autoincrement not null,
    name text not null,
    score int;
```

The previous code creates a table called `StudentsAndGrades` with an integer row ID that will be automatically increased (incremented) each time a row of data is added.

The table will also have a `name` column that will be of type `text` and cannot be blank (`not null`).

It will also have a `score` column that will be of type `int`. Also, notice that the statement is completed by a semicolon.

Inserting data into the database

Here is how we might insert a new row of data into that database:

```
INSERT INTO StudentsAndGrades
    (name, score)
    VALUES
    ("Bart", 23);
```

The previous code added a row to the database. After the preceding statement, the database will have one entry with the values (1, Bart, 23) for the columns (_ID, name, score).

Here is how we might insert another new row of data into that database:

```
INSERT INTO StudentsAndGrades
    (name, score)
    VALUES
    ("Lisa", 100);
```

The previous code added a new row of data with the values (2, Lisa, 100) for the columns (_ID, name, score).

Our spreadsheet-like structure would now look as follows:

_ID	name	score
1	Bart	23
2	Lisa	100

Figure 27.2 – Updated spreadsheet

Retrieving data from the database

Here is how we would access all the rows and columns from our database:

```
SELECT * FROM StudentsAndGrades;
```

The previous code asks for every row and column. The * symbol can be read as "all."

We can also be a little more selective, as this code demonstrates:

```
SELECT score FROM StudentsAndGrades
    where name = "Lisa";
```

The previous code would only return 100, which of course is the score associated with the name Lisa.

Updating the database structure

We can even add new columns after the table has been created and the data added. This is simple, as far as the SQL is concerned, but can cause some issues with regard to users' data on already-published apps. The next statement adds a new column called `age` that is of type `int`:

```
ALTER TABLE StudentsAndGrades
    ADD
    age int;
```

There are many more data types, keywords, and ways to use them than we have seen so far. Next, let's look at the Android SQLite API; we will begin to see how we can use our new SQLite skills.

Android SQLite API

There are a number of different ways that the Android API makes it fairly easy to use our app's database. The first class we need to get familiar with is `SQLiteOpenHelper`.

SQLiteOpenHelper and SQLiteDatabase

The `SQLiteDatabase` class is the class that represents the actual database. The `SQLiteOpenHelper` class, however, is where most of the action takes place. This class will enable us to get access to a database and initialize an instance of `SQLiteDatabase`.

In addition, `SQLiteOpenHelper`, which we will extend in our Age Database app, has two methods to override. First, it has an `onCreate` method, which is called the first time a database is used; therefore, it makes sense that we would put our SQL to create our table structure in.

The other method we must override is `onUpgrade`, which, as you can probably guess, is called when we upgrade our database (use `ALTER` to change its structure).

Building and executing queries

As our database structures get more complex and as our SQL knowledge grows, our SQL statements will get quite long and awkward. The potential for errors is high.

The way we will help overcome the problem of complexity is to build our queries from parts into a string. We can then pass that string to the method that will execute the query for us.

Furthermore, we will use `final` strings to represent things such as table and column names so we don't get in a muddle with them.

For example, we could declare the following members, which would represent the table name and column names from the fictitious example from earlier. Note that we will also give the database itself a name and have a string for that too:

```
private static final String DB_NAME = "MyCollegeDB";
private static final String TABLE_S_AND_G = "
StudentsAndGrades";


public static final String TABLE_ROW_ID = "_id";
public static final String TABLE_ROW_NAME = "name";
public static final String TABLE_ROW_SCORE = "score";
```

Notice in the preceding code how we will benefit from accessing the strings outside the class, as we declare them `public`. You might be thinking that this breaks the rules of encapsulation. It does, but when the intention of the class is to be used as widely as possible, that is OK. And remember, all the variables are final. An external class using these string variables cannot change them or mess things up. They can only refer to and use the values that they hold.

We could then build a query like in this next example. The example adds a new entry to our hypothetical database and incorporates Java variables into the SQL statement:

```
String name = "Onkar";
int score = 95;


// Add all the details to the table
String query = "INSERT INTO " + TABLE_S_AND_G + " (" +
        TABLE_ROW_NAME + ", " +
        TABLE_ROW_SCORE +
        ") " +
        "VALUES (" +
        "'" + name + "'" + ", " +
        score +
        ");";
```

Notice in the previous code that the regular name and score Java variables are highlighted. The previous string called query is now the SQL statement, exactly equivalent to this:

```
INSERT INTO StudentsAndGrades (
    name, score)
    VALUES ('Onkar',95);
```

> **Note**
>
> It is not essential to completely grasp the previous two blocks of code in order to proceed with learning Android programming. But if you want to build your own apps and construct SQL statements that do exactly what you need, it *will* help to do so. Why not study the previous two blocks of code in order to discern the difference between the pairs of double-quote marks, ", which are the parts of the string joined together with +; the pairs of single quote marks, ', which are part of the SQL syntax; the regular Java variables; and the distinct semicolons in the SQL statement in the string and Java.

Throughout the typing of the query, Android Studio prompts us as to the names of our variables, making the chances of an error much lower, even though it is more verbose than simply typing the query.

Now we can use the classes we introduced previously to execute the query:

```
// This is the actual database
private SQLiteDatabase db;

// Create an instance of our internal CustomSQLiteOpenHelper
class
CustomSQLiteOpenHelper helper = new
    CustomSQLiteOpenHelper(context);

// Get a writable database
db = helper.getWritableDatabase();

// Run the query
db.execSQL(query);
```

When adding data to the database, we will use execSQL as in the previous code; when getting data from the database, we will use the rawQuery method as shown next:

```
Cursor c = db.rawQuery(query, null);
```

Notice that the rawQuery method returns an object of type Cursor.

> **Note**
>
> There are several different ways we can interact with SQLite, and they each have their advantages and disadvantages. We have chosen to use raw SQL statements as it makes what we are doing entirely transparent, as well as reinforcing our knowledge of the SQL language. See the next tip if you want to know more.

Database cursors

Besides the classes that give us access to the database and the methods that allow us to execute our queries, there is the issue of exactly how the results we get back from our queries are formatted.

Fortunately, there is the Cursor class. All our database queries will return objects of type Cursor. We can use the methods of the Cursor class to selectively access the data returned from the queries, as here:

```
Log.i(c.getString(1), c.getString(2));
```

The previous code would output to logcat the two values stored in the first two columns of the result that the query returned. It is the Cursor object itself that determines which row of our returned data we are currently reading.

We can access a number of methods of the `Cursor` object, including the `moveToNext` method, which unsurprisingly would move `Cursor` to the next row, ready for reading:

```
c.moveToNext();

/*
    This same code now outputs the data in the
    first and second column of the returned
    data but from the SECOND row.
*/

Log.i(c.getString(1), c.getString(2));
```

On some occasions, we will be able to bind `Cursor` to a part of our UI (such as `RecyclerView`), as we did with an `ArrayList` instance in the Note to Self app, and just leave everything to the Android API.

There are many more useful methods of the `Cursor` class, some of which we will see soon.

> **Note**
>
> This introduction to the Android SQLite API really only scratches the surface of its capabilities. We will bump into a few more methods and classes as we proceed further. It is, however, worth studying further if your app idea requires complex data management.

Now we can see how all this theory comes together and how we will structure our database code in the Age Database app.

Coding the database class

Here we will put into practice everything we have learned so far and finish coding the Age Database app. Before our `Fragment` classes from the previous section can interact with a shared database, we need a class to handle interaction with, and the creation of, the database.

We will create a class that manages our database by using the SQLiteOpenHelper class. It will also define some final strings to represent the names of the table and its columns. Furthermore, it will supply a bunch of helper methods we can call to perform all the necessary queries. Where necessary, these helper methods will return a Cursor object that we can use to show the data we have retrieved. It would be trivial, then, to add new helper methods, should our app need to evolve.

Create a new class called DataManager and add the following member variables:

```java
import android.database.sqlite.SQLiteDatabase;
public class DataManager {

    // This is the actual database
    private SQLiteDatabase db;

    /*
        Next we have a public static final string for
        each row/table that we need to refer to both
        inside and outside this class
    */

    public static final String TABLE_ROW_ID = "_id";
    public static final String TABLE_ROW_NAME = "name";
    public static final String TABLE_ROW_AGE = "age";

    /*
        Next we have a private static final strings for
        each row/table that we need to refer to just
        inside this class
    */

    private static final String DB_NAME = "name_age_db";
    private static final int DB_VERSION = 1;
    private static final String TABLE_N_AND_A =
                                "name_and_age";

}
```

Next, we add the constructor that will create an instance of our custom version of
`SQLiteOpenHelper`. We will actually implement this class as an inner class soon. The
constructor also initializes the `db` member, which is our `SQLiteDatabase` reference.

Add the following constructor that we have just discussed to the `DataManager` class:

```
public DataManager(Context context) {
    // Create an instance of our internal
    CustomSQLiteOpenHelper

    CustomSQLiteOpenHelper helper = new
        CustomSQLiteOpenHelper(context);

    // Get a writable database
    db = helper.getWritableDatabase();
}
```

Now we can add the helper methods we will access from our Fragment classes. Start with
the `insert` method, which executes an `INSERT` SQL query based on the `name` and `age`
parameters passed into the method.

Add the `insert` method to the `DataManager` class:

```
// Here are all our helper methods

// Insert a record
public void insert(String name, String age){

    // Add all the details to the table
    String query = "INSERT INTO " + TABLE_N_AND_A + " (" +
                    TABLE_ROW_NAME + ", " +
                    TABLE_ROW_AGE +
                    ") " +
                    "VALUES (" +
                    "'" + name + "'" + ", " +
                    "'" + age + "'" +
                    ");";
```

```
    Log.i("insert() = ", query);

    db.execSQL(query);

}
```

This next method called `delete` will delete a record from the database if it has a value in the name column that matches the passed-in `name` parameter. It achieves this using the SQL `DELETE` keyword.

Add the `delete` method to the `DataManager` class:

```
// Delete a record
public void delete(String name){

    // Delete the details from the table if already exists
    String query = "DELETE FROM " + TABLE_N_AND_A +
                    " WHERE " + TABLE_ROW_NAME +
                    " = '" + name + "';";

    Log.i("delete() = ", query);

    db.execSQL(query);

}
```

Next, we have the `selectAll` method, which also does as the name suggests. It achieves this with a `SELECT` query using the `*` parameter, which is equivalent to specifying all the columns individually. Also, note that the method returns a `Cursor` instance, which we will use in some of the `Fragment` classes.

Add the `selectAll` method to the `DataManager` class:

```
// Get all the records
public Cursor selectAll() {
    Cursor c = db.rawQuery("SELECT *" +" from " +
                TABLE_N_AND_A, null);

    return c;
}
```

Now we add a searchName method that has a String parameter for the name the user wants to search for. It also returns a Cursor instance that will contain all the entries that were found. Notice that the SQL statement uses SELECT, FROM, and WHERE to achieve this:

```
// Find a specific record
public Cursor searchName(String name) {
    String query = "SELECT " +
                    TABLE_ROW_ID + ", " +
                    TABLE_ROW_NAME +
                    ", " + TABLE_ROW_AGE +
                    " from " +
                    TABLE_N_AND_A + " WHERE " +
                    TABLE_ROW_NAME + " = '" + name + "';";

    Log.i("searchName() = ", query);

    Cursor c = db.rawQuery(query, null);


    return c;
}
```

Finally, for the DataManager class, we create an inner class that will be our implementation of SQLiteOpenHelper. It is a barebones implementation.

We have a constructor that receives a Context object, the database name, and the database version.

We also override the onCreate method that has the SQL statement, which creates our database table with _ID, name, and age columns.

The onUpgrade method is left intentionally blank for this app.

Add the inner CustomSQLiteOpenHelper class to the DataManager class:

```
// This class is created when our DataManager is initialized
private class CustomSQLiteOpenHelper extends SQLiteOpenHelper {
    public CustomSQLiteOpenHelper(Context context) {
```

```
            super(context, DB_NAME, null, DB_VERSION);
    }


    // This runs the first time the database is created
    @Override
    public void onCreate(SQLiteDatabase db) {

            // Create a table for photos and all their details
            String newTableQueryString = "create table "
                            + TABLE_N_AND_A + " ("
                            + TABLE_ROW_ID
                            + " integer primary key
                            autoincrement not null,"
                            + TABLE_ROW_NAME
                            + " text not null,"
                            + TABLE_ROW_AGE
                            + " text not null);";


            db.execSQL(newTableQueryString);

    }


    // This method only runs when we increment DB_VERSION
    @Override
    public void onUpgrade(SQLiteDatabase db,
int oldVersion, int newVersion) {
// Not needed in this app
// but we must still override it

    }

}
```

Now we can add code to our Fragment classes to use our new DataManager class.

Coding the Fragment classes to use the DataManager class

Add this highlighted code to the InsertFragment class to update the onCreateView method:

```
View v = inflater.inflate(R.layout.content_insert,
    container, false);

final DataManager dm =
    new DataManager(getActivity());

Button btnInsert =
    v.findViewById(R.id.btnInsert);

final EditText editName =
    v.findViewById(R.id.editName);

final EditText editAge =
    v.findViewById(R.id.editAge);

btnInsert.setOnClickListener(new View.OnClickListener() {
    @Override
    public void onClick(View v) {
            dm.insert(editName.getText().toString(),
                        editAge.getText().toString());
    }
});

return v;
```

In the code, we get an instance of our DataManager class and a reference to each of our UI widgets. Then, in the onClick method, we use the insert method to add a new name and age to the database. The values to insert are taken from the two EditText widgets.

Add this highlighted code to the DeleteFragment class to update the onCreateView method:

```
View v = inflater.inflate(R.layout.content_delete,
    container, false);

final DataManager dm =
    new DataManager(getActivity());

Button btnDelete =
    v.findViewById(R.id.btnDelete);

final EditText editDelete =
    v.findViewById(R.id.editDelete);

btnDelete.setOnClickListener(new View.OnClickListener() {
    @Override
    public void onClick(View v) {
            dm.delete(editDelete.getText().toString());
    }
});

return v;
```

In the DeleteFragment class, we create an instance of our DataManager class and then get a reference to the EditText and Button widgets from our layout. When the button is clicked, the delete method is called, passing in the value of any text from the EditText widget that the user has entered. The delete method searches our database for a match, and if one is found, it deletes it.

Add this highlighted code to the SearchFragment class to update the onCreateView method:

```
View v = inflater.inflate(R.layout.content_search,
    container,false);

Button btnSearch =
    v.findViewById(R.id.btnSearch);
```

```java
final EditText editSearch =
    v.findViewById(R.id.editSearch);

final TextView textResult =
    v.findViewById(R.id.textResult);

// This is our DataManager instance
final DataManager dm =
    new DataManager(getActivity());

btnSearch.setOnClickListener(new View.OnClickListener() {
    @Override
    public void onClick(View v) {

        Cursor c = dm.searchName(
                editSearch.getText().toString());

        // Make sure a result was found before using the
        Cursor
        if(c.getCount() > 0) {
            c.moveToNext();
            textResult.setText("Result = " +
                c.getString(1) + " - " +
                c.getString(2));
        }

    }
});

return v;
```

As we do for all our different `Fragment` classes, we create an instance of the `DataManager` class and get a reference to all the different UI widgets in the layout. In the `onClick` method, the `searchName` method is used, passing in the value from the `EditText` widget. If the database returns a result in the `Cursor` instance, then the `TextView` widget uses its `setText` method to output the results.

Add this highlighted code to the ResultsFragment class to update the onCreateView method:

```
View v = inflater.inflate(R.layout.content_results,
    container, false);

// Create an instance of our DataManager
DataManager dm =
    new DataManager(getActivity());

// Get a reference to the TextView to show the results
TextView textResults =
    v.findViewById(R.id.textResults);

// Create and initialize a Cursor with all the results
Cursor c = dm.selectAll();

// A String to hold all the text
String list = "";

// Loop through the results in the Cursor
while (c.moveToNext()){
    // Add the results to the String
    // with a little formatting
    list+=(c.getString(1) + " - " + c.getString(2) + "\n");
}

// Display the String in the TextView
textResults.setText(list);


return v;
```

In this class, the Cursor instance is loaded up with data using the selectAll method before any interactions take place. The contents of Cursor are then output into the TextView widget by concatenating the results. \n in the concatenation is what creates a new line between each result in the Cursor instance.

Running the Age Database app

Let's run through some of the functions of our app to make sure it is working as expected.

First, I added a new name to the database using the **Insert** menu option:

Figure 27.3 – Insert menu

Then I confirmed it was there by viewing the **Results** option:

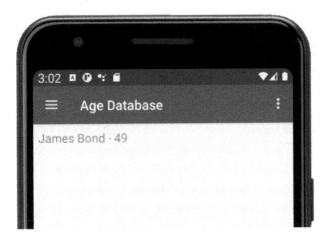

Figure 27.4 – Results option

After that, I added a few more names and ages just to fill the database up a little bit:

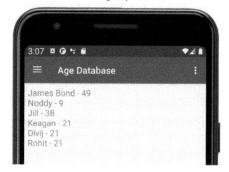

Figure 27.5 – Filling the database

Then I used the **Delete** menu option and looked at the **Results** option again to check that my chosen name was in fact removed:

Figure 27.6 – Delete menu

I then searched for a name that I knew existed to test the **Search** menu option:

Figure 27.7 – Search menu

Let's review what we have done in this chapter.

Summary

We have covered a lot in this chapter. We have learned about databases and in particular the database used by Android apps, SQLite. We have practiced the basics of communicating with a database using the SQL language.

We have seen how the Android API helps us use a SQLite database and have implemented our first working app with a database.

You have come a long way and have reached the end of the book. Let's talk about what might come next.

28
A Quick Chat before You Go

We are just about done with our journey. This chapter gives just a few ideas and pointers that you might like to look at before rushing off and making your own apps:

- Publishing
- Making your first app
- Keep learning
- Thanks

Publishing

You easily know enough to design your own app. You could even just make some modifications to one of the apps from this book.

I decided not to include a step-by-step guide to publishing on Google's Play Store because the steps are not complicated. They are, however, quite in-depth and a little laborious. Most of the steps involve entering personal information about you and your app as well as images. Such a tutorial would read something like this:

1. Fill this text box.

2. Now fill that text box.

3. Upload this image.

4. And so on.

Not much fun, and not very useful.

To get started, you just need to visit `https://play.google.com/apps/publish` and pay a modest one-off fee (around $25, depending on your region's currency). This allows you to publish games for life.

> **Note**
>
> If you want a checklist for publishing, take a look at this link, `https://developer.android.com/distribute/best-practices/launch/launch-checklist.html`, but you will find the process intuitive (if very drawn out).

Make an app!

You could ignore everything else in this chapter if you just put this one thing into practice:

Don't wait until you are an expert before you start making apps!

Start building your dream app, the one with all the features, that's going to take Google Play by storm. A simple piece of advice, however, is this: do some planning first! But not too much; then get started.

Have some smaller and more easily achievable projects on the sidelines: projects you will be able to show to friends and family and that explore areas of Android that are new to you. If you are confident in these apps, you could upload them on Google Play. If you are worried about how they might be received by reviewers, then make them free and put a note in the description about it being "just a prototype" or something similar.

If your experience is anything like mine, you will find that as you read, study, and build apps, you will discover that your dream app can be improved in many ways and you will probably be inspired to redesign it or even start again.

If you do this, I can guarantee that the next time you build the app you will do it in half the time and twice as good, at least!

Keep learning

If you feel like you have come a long way, you are right. There is always more to learn, however.

Keep reading

You will find that as you make your first app, you suddenly realize that there is a gap in your knowledge that needs to be filled to make some feature come to life. This is normal and guaranteed, so don't let it put you off. Think of how to describe the problem and search for the solution on Google.

You might also find that specific classes in a project will grow beyond the practical and maintainable. This is a sign that there is a better way to structure things and there is probably a ready-made design pattern out there somewhere that will make your life easier.

To pre-empt this almost inevitability, why not study some patterns right away? One great source is *Head First: Java Design Patterns*, available from all good book stores.

GitHub

GitHub allows you to search and browse code that other people have written and see how they have solved problems. This is useful because seeing the file structure of classes and then dipping into them often shows how to plan your apps from the start and prevents you from starting off on the wrong path. You can even get a GitHub app that allows you to do this from the comfort of your phone or tablet. Or, you can configure Android Studio to save and share your projects to GitHub. For example, search for `Android fragment` on the home page, `www.github.com`, and you will see more than 1,000 related projects that you can snoop through:

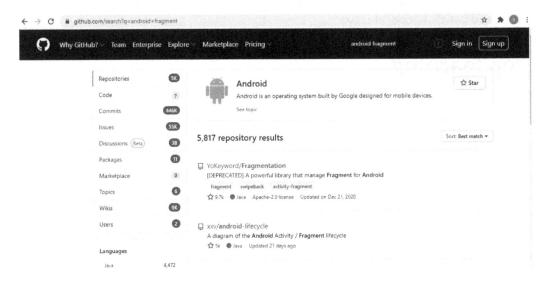

Figure 28.1 – Android fragment result

Stack Overflow

If you get stuck, have a weird error, or get an unexplained crash, often the best place to turn is Google. Do this and you will be surprised at how often Stack Overflow seems to be prominent in the search results, and for good reason.

Stack Overflow allows users to post a description of their problem along with sample code so the community can respond with answers. In my experience, however, it is rarely necessary to post a question because there is almost always somebody who has had the exact same problem.

Stack Overflow is especially good for bleeding-edge issues. If a new Android Studio version has a bug or a new version of the Android API seems to not be doing what it should, then you can be almost certain that a few thousand other developers around the world are having the same problem as you. Then, some smart coder, often from the Android development team itself, will be there with an answer.

Stack Overflow is also good for a bit of light reading. Go to the home page, www.stackoverflow.com, type Android in the search box, and you will see a list of all the latest problems that the Stack Overflow community is having:

Figure 28.2 – Android list

I am not suggesting that you dive in and start trying to answer them all just yet but reading the problems and the suggestions will teach you a lot and you will probably find that more often than you expect, you have the solution or at least an idea of the solution.

Android user forums

Also, it is well worth signing up to some Android forums and visiting them occasionally to find out what the hot topics and trends are from a user's perspective. I won't list any here because a quick web search is all that is required.

If you're serious about the topic, then you can attend some Android conferences where you can rub shoulders with thousands of other developers and attend lectures. If this interests you, do a web search for droidcon, Android Developer Days, and GDG DevFest.

Higher-level study

You can now read a wider selection of other Android books. I mentioned at the start of this book that there are very few books, arguably even none, that teach Android programming to readers with no Java experience. That was the reason I wrote this book.

Now that you have a good understanding of OOP and Java, as well as a brief introduction to app design and the Android API, you are well placed to read the Android "beginner" books for people who already know how to program in Java, like you now do.

These books are packed full of good examples that you can build or just read about to reinforce what you have learned in this book, use your knowledge in different ways, and, of course, learn some completely new stuff too.

It might also be worth reading further some pure Java books. It might be hard to believe, having just waded through around 750 pages, but there is a whole lot more to Java than there was time to cover here.

I could name some titles but the books with the largest number of positive reviews on Amazon tend to be the ones worth exploring.

My other channels

Please keep in touch!

- `gamecodeschool.com`
- `facebook.com/gamecodeschool`
- `twitter.com/gamecodeschool`
- `youtube.com/c/Gamecodeschool/videos`
- `linkedin.com/in/gamecodeschool`

Goodbye and thank you

I had a lot of fun writing this book. I know that's a cliché but it's also true. Most importantly, though, I hope you managed to take something from it and use it as a stepping stone for your future in programming.

You are perhaps reading this for a bit of fun or the kudos of releasing an app, a stepping stone to a programming job, or maybe you actually will build an app that takes Google Play by storm.

Whatever the case, a big thank you from me for buying this book and I wish you all the best in your future endeavors.

I think that everybody has an app inside of them and all you need is to do enough work to get it out of you.

Packt.com

Subscribe to our online digital library for full access to over 7,000 books and videos, as well as industry leading tools to help you plan your personal development and advance your career. For more information, please visit our website.

Why subscribe?

- Spend less time learning and more time coding with practical eBooks and Videos from over 4,000 industry professionals

- Improve your learning with Skill Plans built especially for you

- Get a free eBook or video every month

- Fully searchable for easy access to vital information

- Copy and paste, print, and bookmark content

Did you know that Packt offers eBook versions of every book published, with PDF and ePub files available? You can upgrade to the eBook version at packt.com and as a print book customer, you are entitled to a discount on the eBook copy. Get in touch with us at customercare@packtpub.com for more details.

At www.packt.com, you can also read a collection of free technical articles, sign up for a range of free newsletters, and receive exclusive discounts and offers on Packt books and eBooks.

Other Books You May Enjoy

If you enjoyed this book, you may be interested in these other books by Packt:

Android Programming with Kotlin for Beginners

John Horton

ISBN: 978-1-78961-540-1

- Understand how Kotlin and Android work together
- Build a graphical drawing app using object-oriented programming(OOP) principles
- Add user interaction, data captures, sound, and animation to your apps
- Implement dialog boxes to capture input from the user
- Build a simple database app that sorts and stores the user's data

Flutter Projects

Simone Alessandria

ISBN: 978-1-83864-777-3

- Design reusable mobile architectures that can be applied to apps at any scale
- Get up to speed with error handling and debugging for mobile application development
- Apply the principle of composition over inheritance' to break down complex problems into many simple problems
- Update your code and see the results immediately using Flutter's hot reload
- Identify and prevent bugs from reappearing with Flutter's developer tools
- Manage an app's state with Streams and the BLoC pattern

Packt is searching for authors like you

If you're interested in becoming an author for Packt, please visit `authors.packtpub.com` and apply today. We have worked with thousands of developers and tech professionals, just like you, to help them share their insight with the global tech community. You can make a general application, apply for a specific hot topic that we are recruiting an author for, or submit your own idea.

Leave a review - let other readers know what you think

Please share your thoughts on this book with others by leaving a review on the site that you bought it from. If you purchased the book from Amazon, please leave us an honest review on this book's Amazon page. This is vital so that other potential readers can see and use your unbiased opinion to make purchasing decisions, we can understand what our customers think about our products, and our authors can see your feedback on the title that they have worked with Packt to create. It will only take a few minutes of your time, but is valuable to other potential customers, our authors, and Packt. Thank you!

Index